Crochet Flowers

Step-by-Step

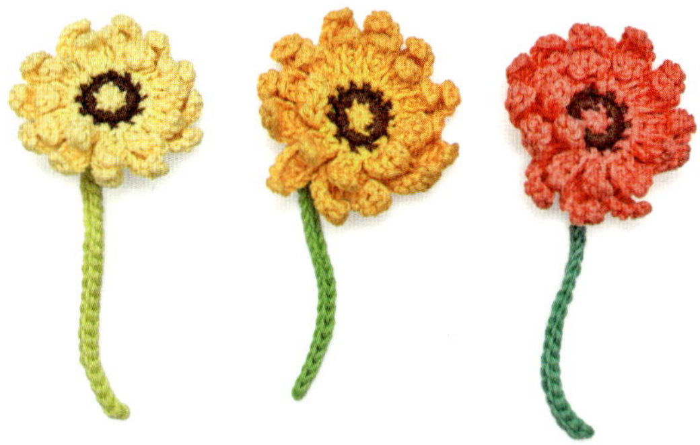

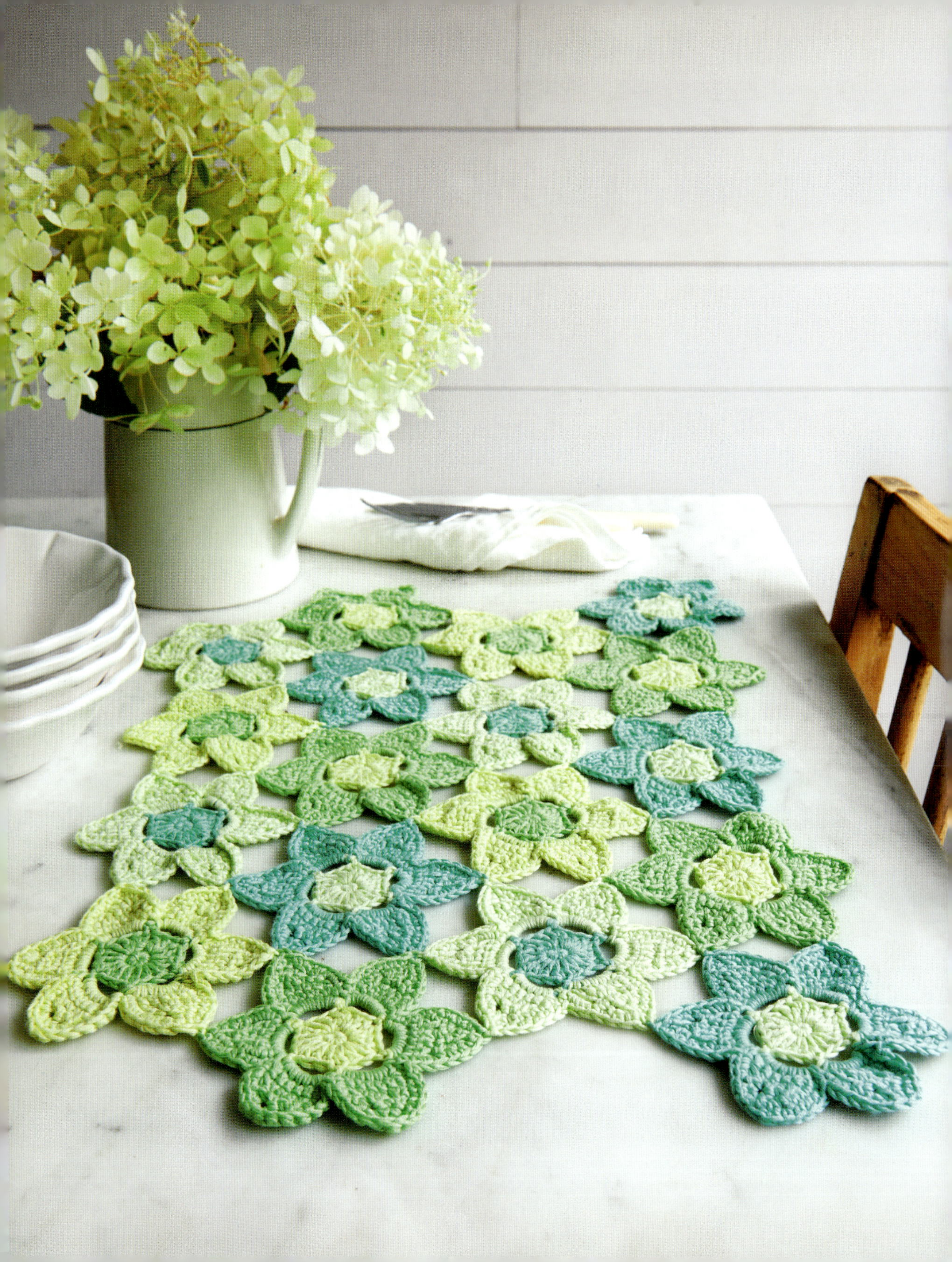

Crochet Flowers

Step-by-Step

35 delightful blooms for beginners

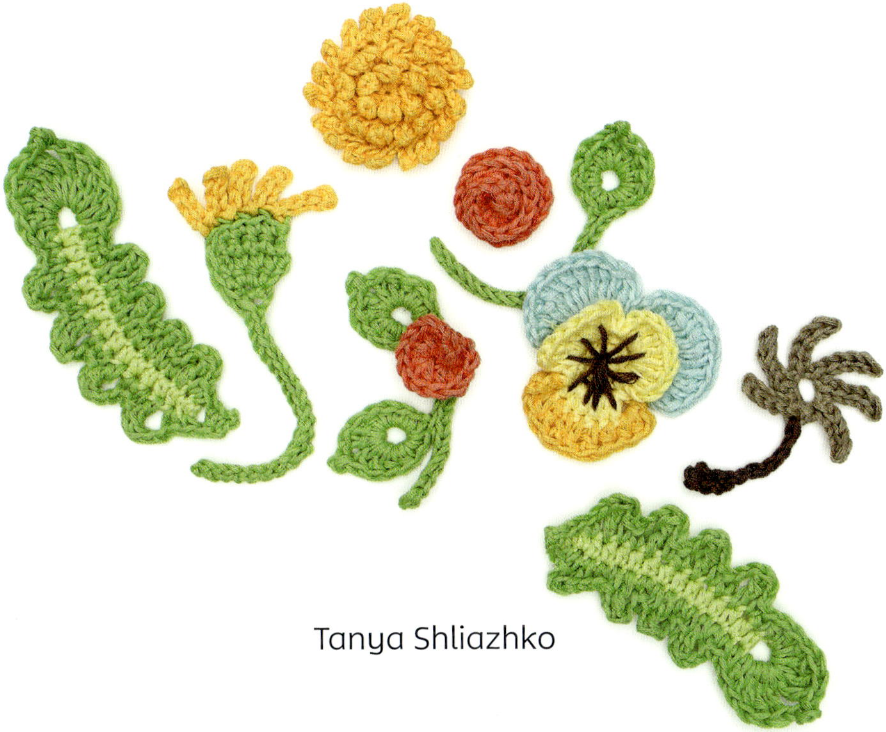

Tanya Shliazhko

Search Press

A QUARTO BOOK

First published in 2016 by
Search Press Ltd
Wellwood
North Farm Road
Kent TN2 3DR

ISBN 978-1-78221-381-9

Conceived, designed and produced by
Quarto Publishing plc
The Old Brewery
6 Blundell Street
London N7 9BH

QUAR.CFLS

Senior Editor: Lily de Gatacre
Art Editor: Jackie Palmer
Pattern Checker: Therese Chynoweth
Photographer: Nicki Dowey (location)
Phil Wilkins (studio), Simon Pask (model)
Designer: Grand Union Design
Illustrator: Kuo Kang Chen
Proofreader: Caroline West
Indexer: Helen Snaith
Art Director: Caroline Guest

Creative Director: Moira Clinch
Publisher: Paul Carslake

Colour separation in Singapore by Pica Digital Pte Limited
Printed in China by Toppan Leefung Printing Limited

10 9 8 7 6 5 4 3 2 1

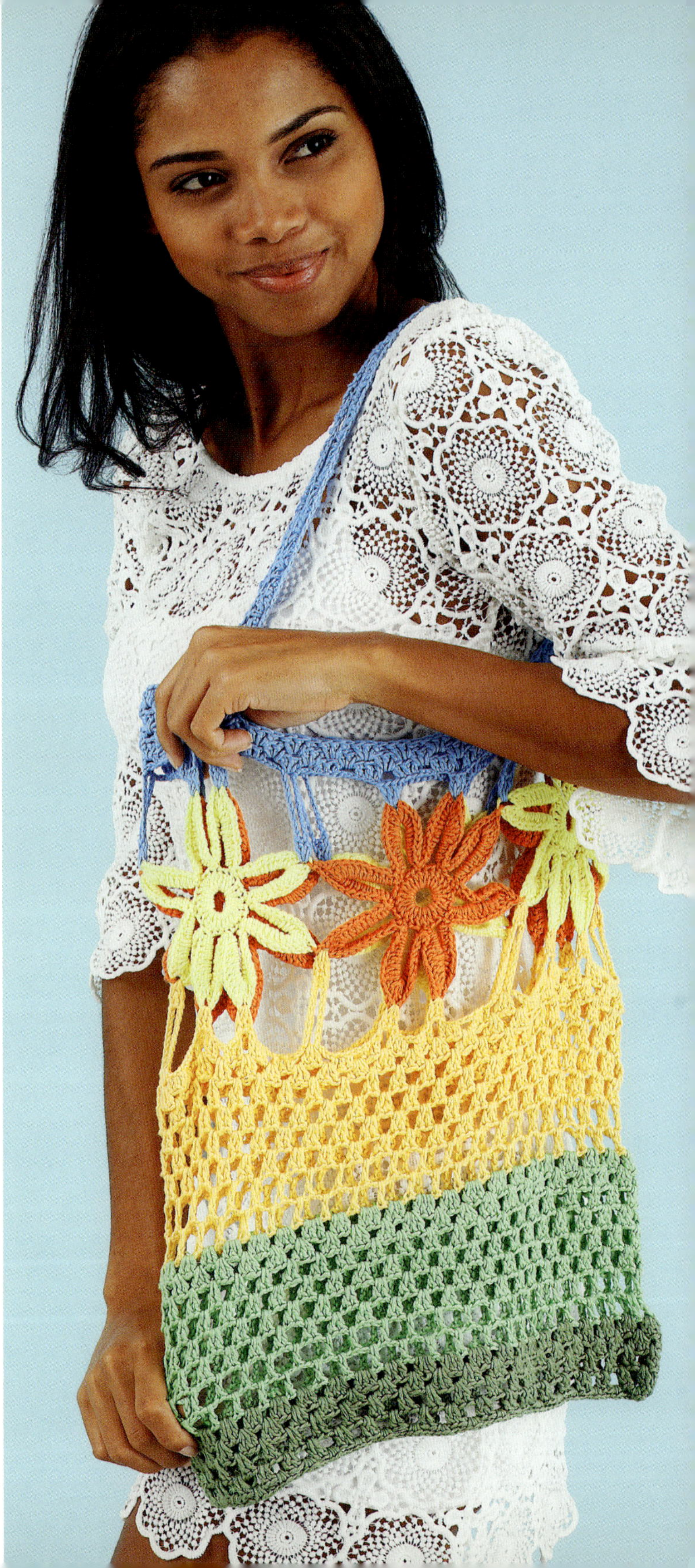

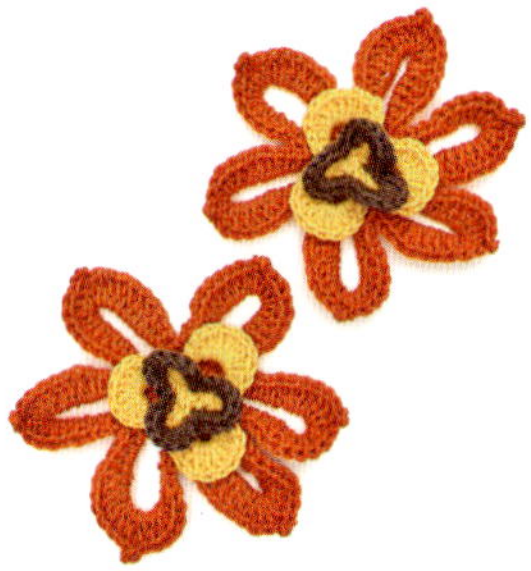

Contents

Choose a Flower

There are 35 beautiful flowers for you to create in the pages of this book. Pick one that catches your eye, start crocheting and soon you'll have a whole crochet bouquet.

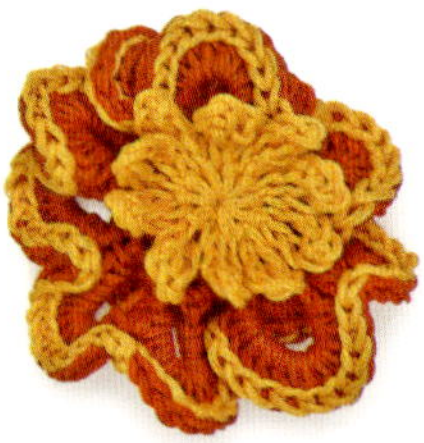
Marigold 28

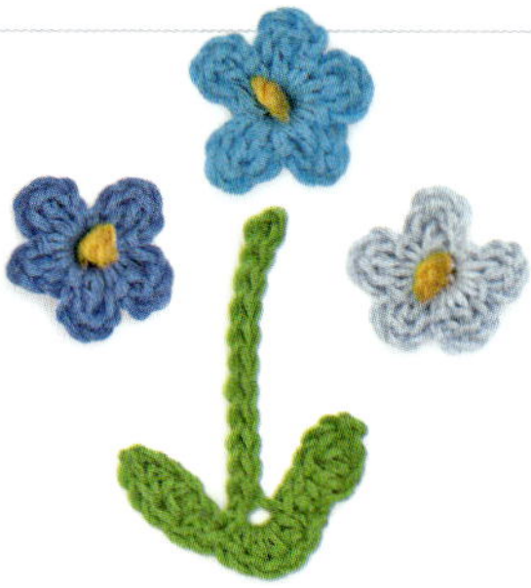
Forget-Me-Not 30

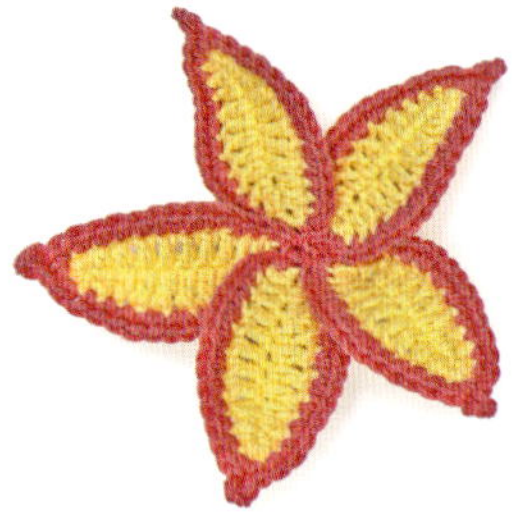
Hawaiian Plumeria 32

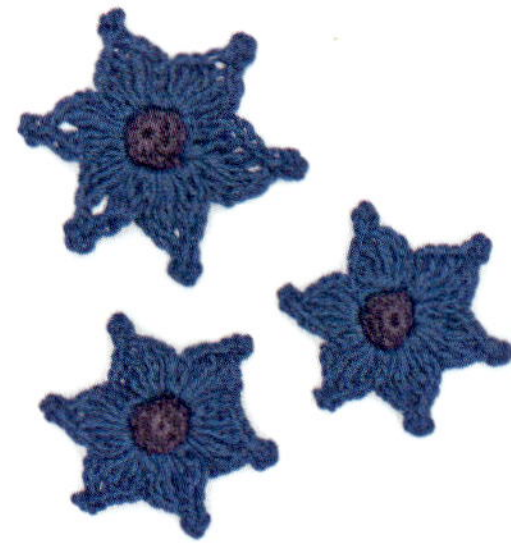
Clematis 34

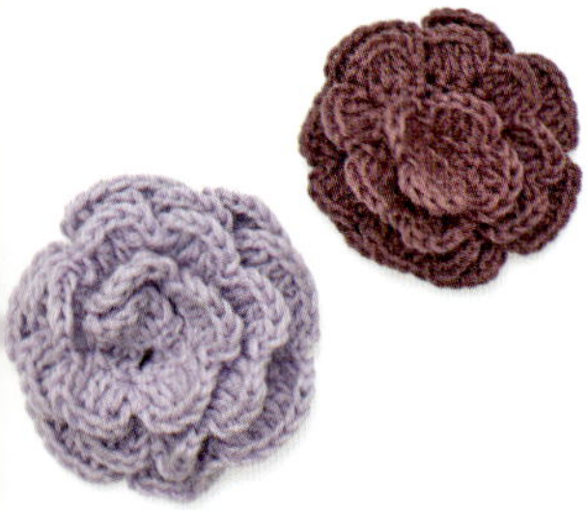
Purple Rose 44

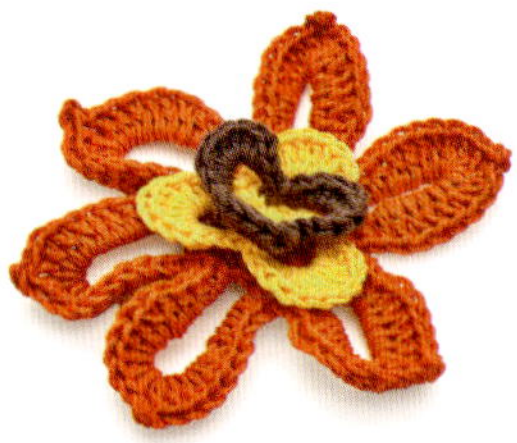
Harlequin 46

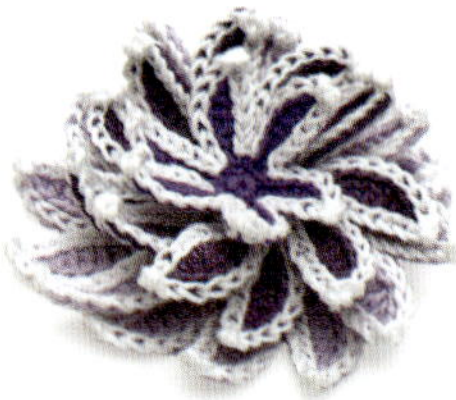
Purple Dahlia 48

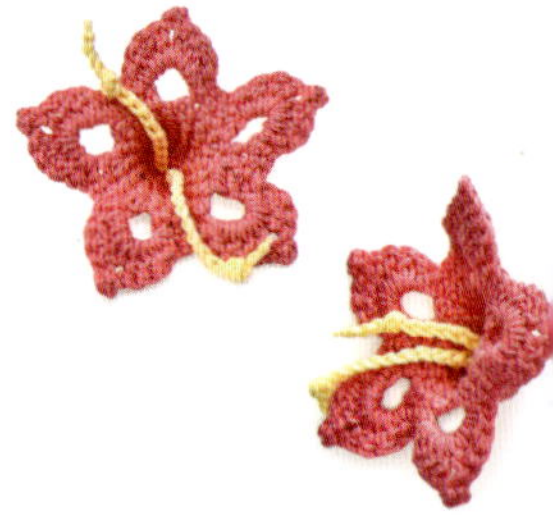
Rain Lily 50

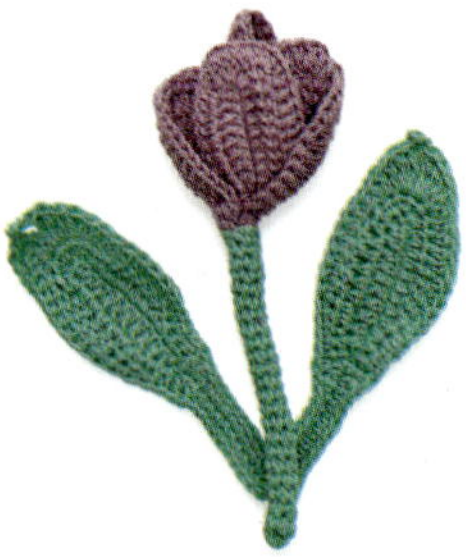
Tulip 60

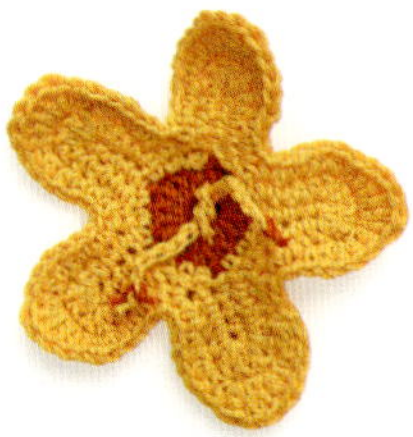
Hibiscus 64

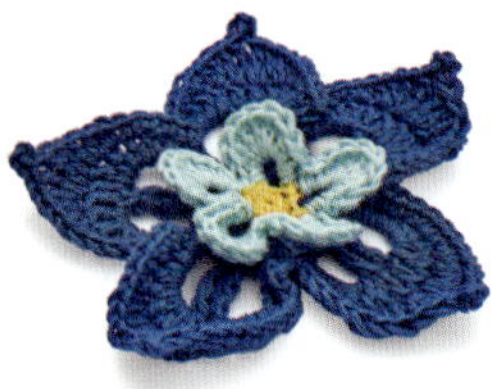
Blue Columbine 66

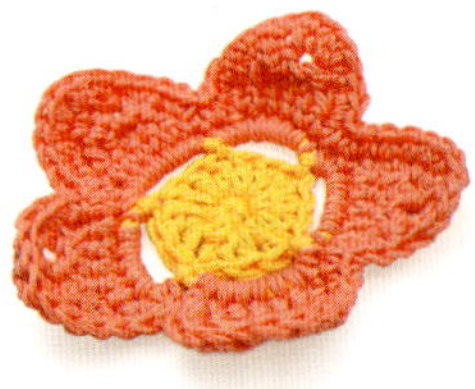
Chaenomeles Japonica 68

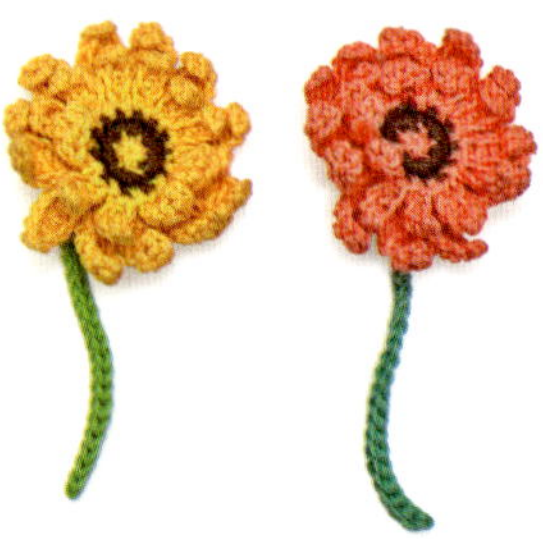
African Daisy 78

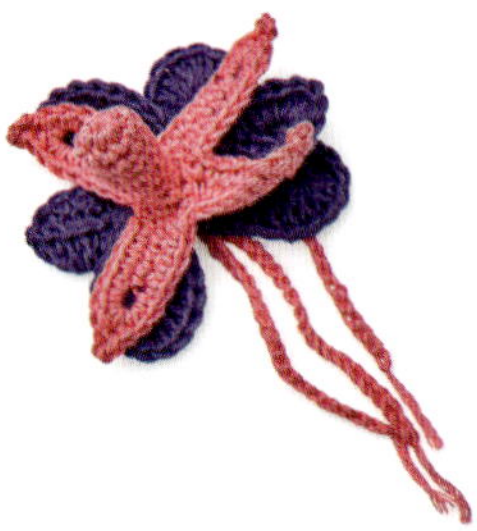
Fuchsia 80

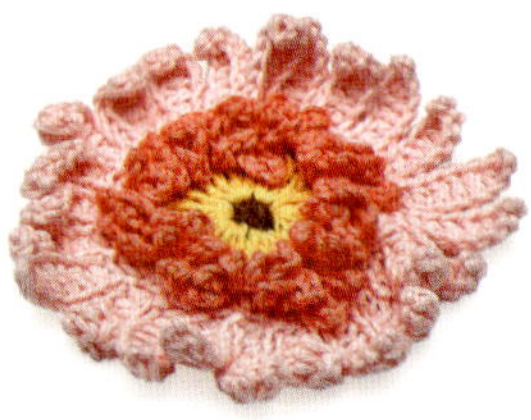
Gerbera 82

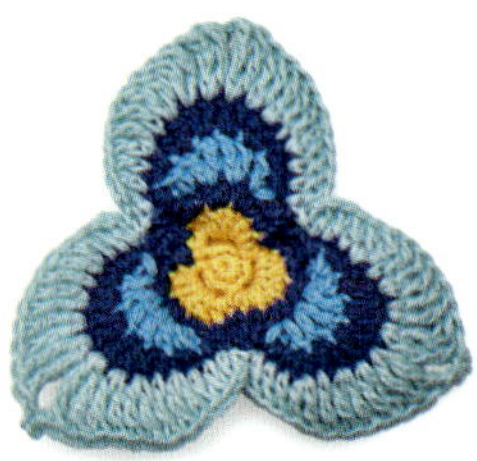
Peacock Flower 84

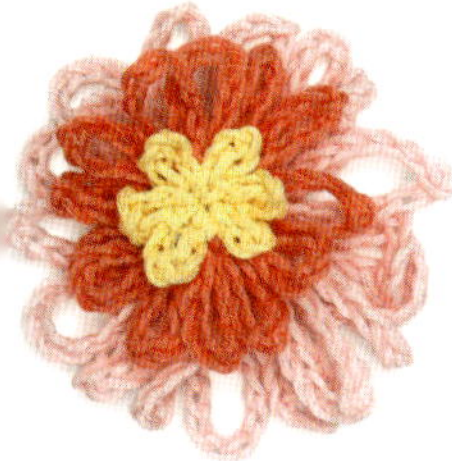
Chrysanthemum 20

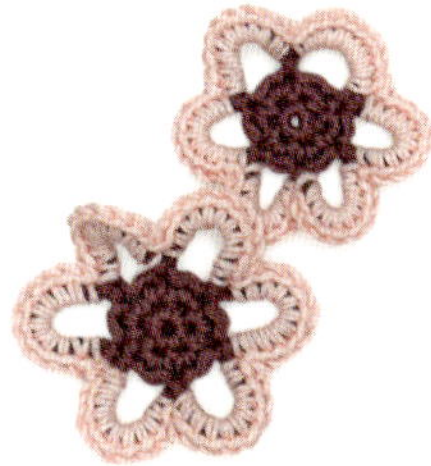
Anemone 22

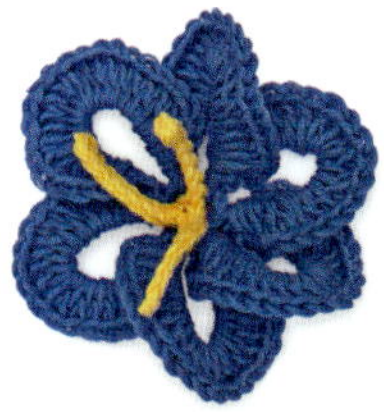
Crocus 24

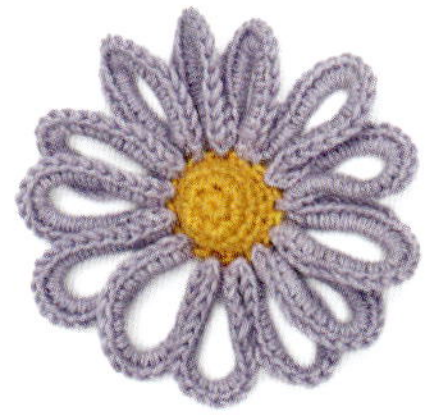
Hawkesbury River Daisy 26

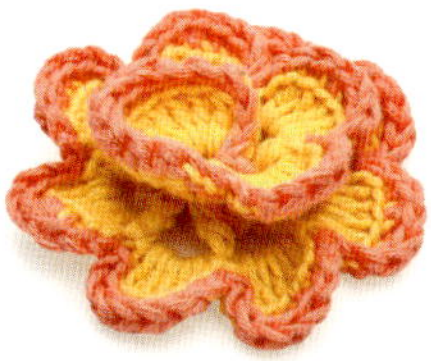
Begonia 36

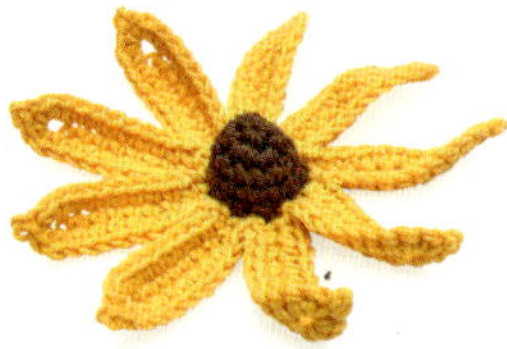
Black-Eyed Susan 38

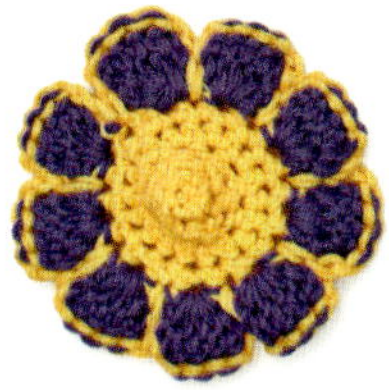
Bumblebee Primrose 40

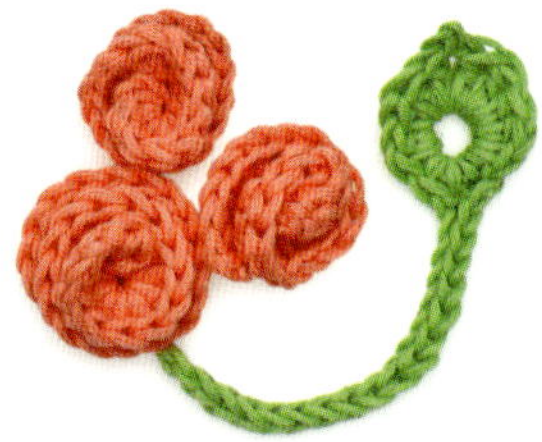
Mini Rose 42

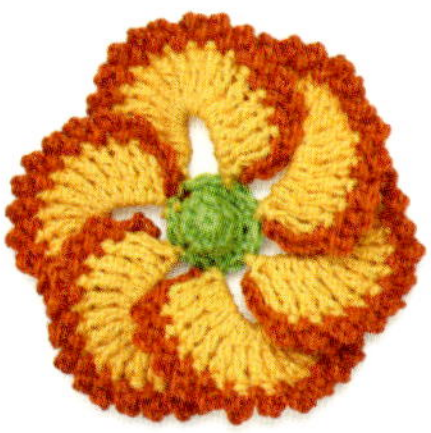
Yellow Poppy 52

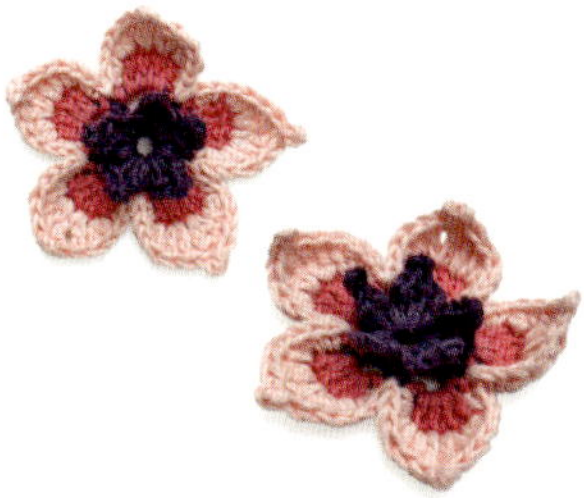
Cherry Blossom 54

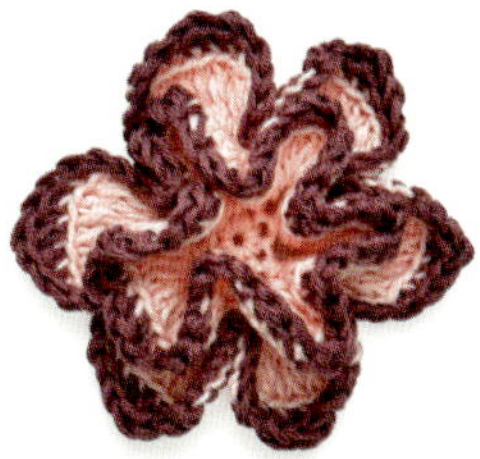
Lacy Carnation 56

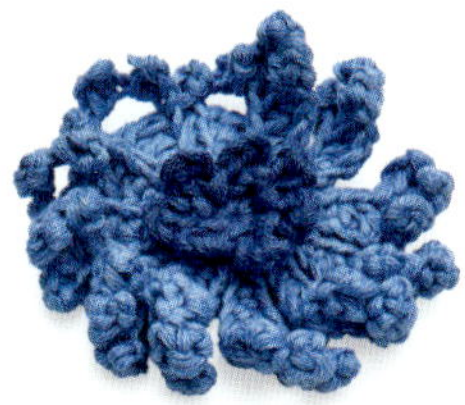
Cornflower 58

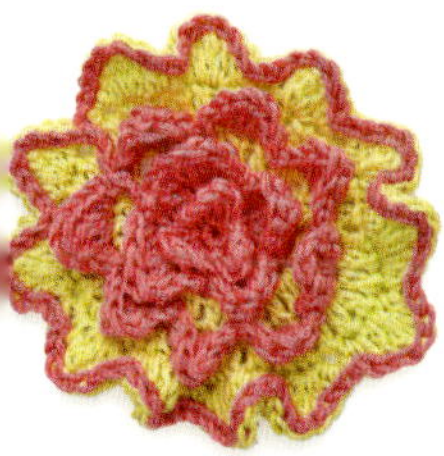
Esperanse Rose 70

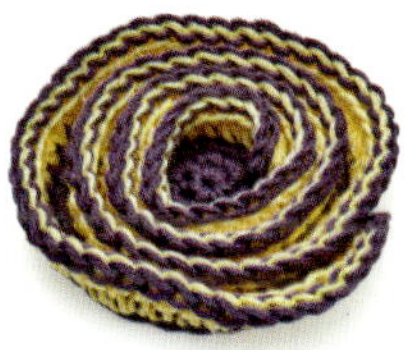
Ranunculus 72

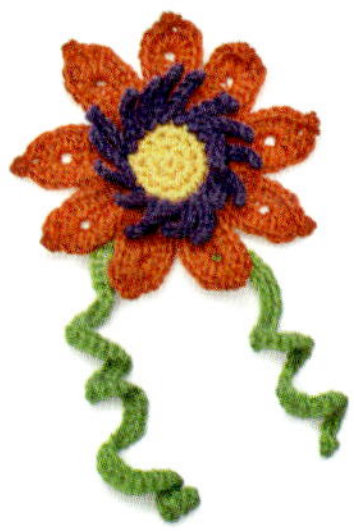
Passion Flower 74

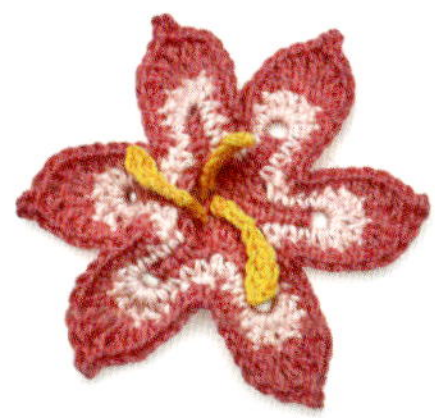
Tiger Lily 76

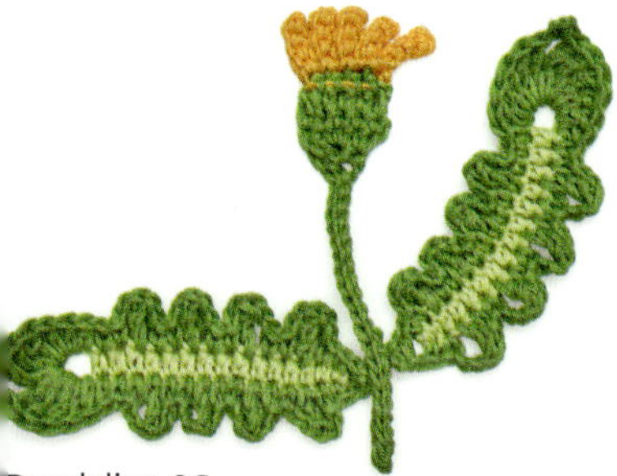
Dandelion 86

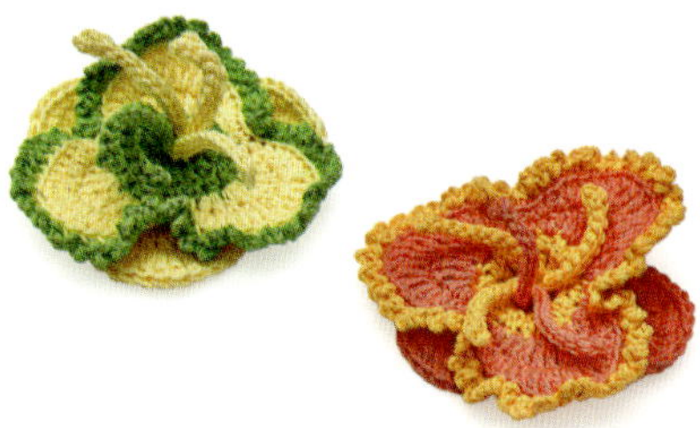
Day Lily 90

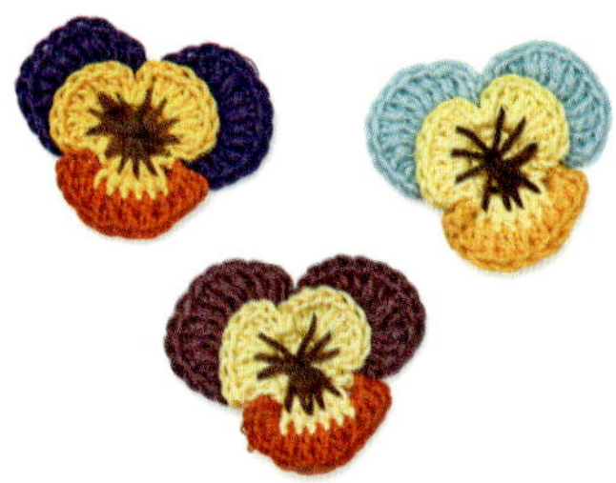
Pansy 94

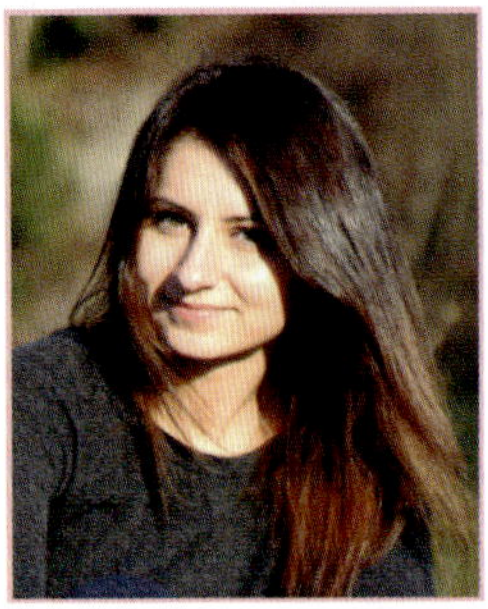

Welcome to Tanya's World

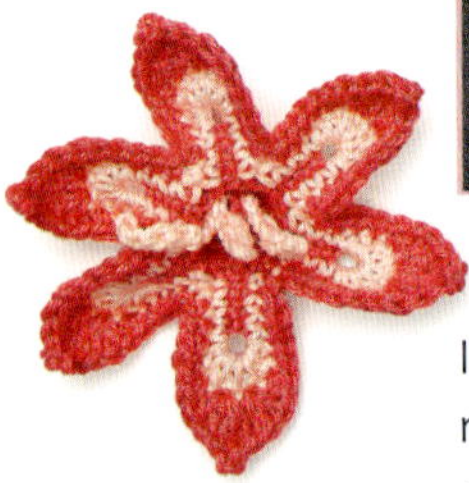

I live a very simple life in Vancouver, Canada, where I work as a nurse. Crochet has been my creative outlet for a number of years; I used it as an activity to help me de-stress during nursing school, and now it helps me to unwind after long shifts at the hospital.

I enjoy the outdoors – I love picnics and sitting outside cafés. I do not have a craft room, or an area in my house dedicated to my crafting; instead I carry it with me. I take it along to picnics with friends, work on projects while watching films or crochet while listening to an audio book.

My late grandma was always an inspiration to me: whilst bringing up seven children on a farm, she managed to beautifully decorate her home with intricate and colourful floral embroidery.

I love sharing my patterns and making the flowers for this book has been such a wonderful journey. I drew inspiration from nature and the world around me – every flower I saw, I thought about the ways I could crochet it, and how I could show you new techniques through these flowers. I hope you enjoy them.

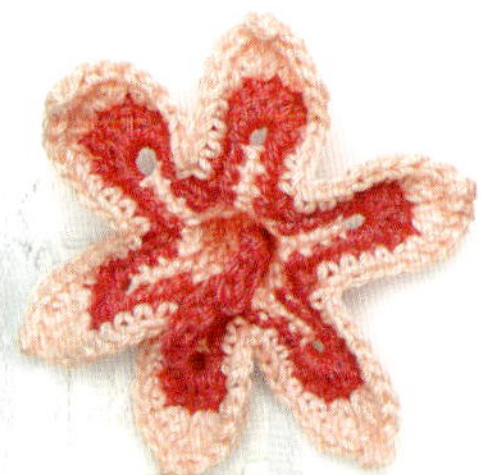

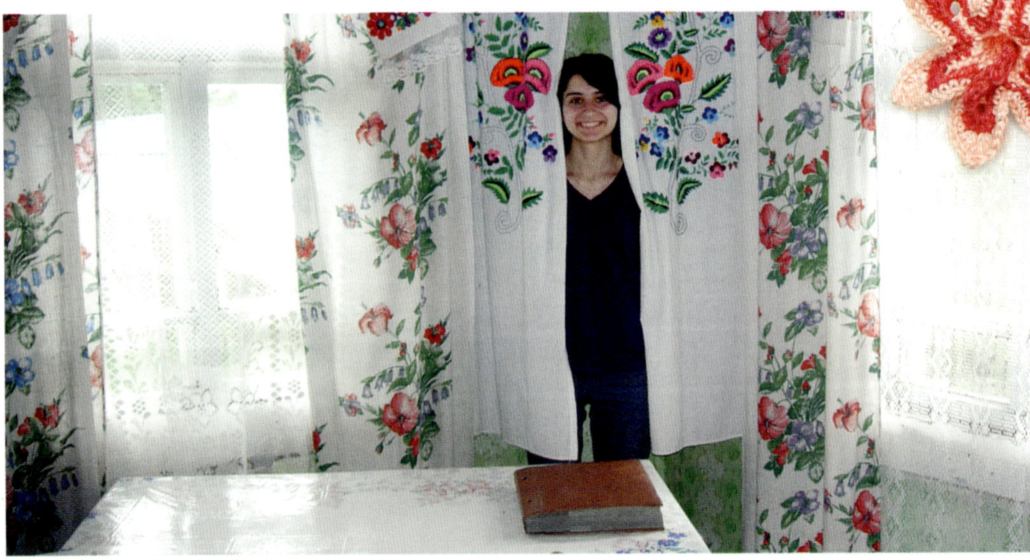

In my late grandma Kate's home. I'm sixteen years old, here.

About this Book

The Basics (pages 10–17)

First learn about the essential equipment you'll need and then delve into the world of crochet. The most basic crochet skills are explained with step-by-step sequences here so, whether you're an absolute beginner or just need a refresher, you'll be armed with all the know-how you need to start creating crochet flowers.

Crochet Flowers (pages 18–97)

Organised by complexity so you can build your skills, in this section you will find instructions for creating each of the 35 crochet flowers. Each flower features a chart, a photograph of the finished flower and a written pattern. You'll find step-by-step instructions and photographs that will guide you through the trickiest parts of the pattern, give you extra information and introduce you to new stitches and techniques. Once you're confident in your crochet skills, check out 'Choose a Flower' on pages 6-7 to see all the flowers side by side and pick the ones that appeal to you.

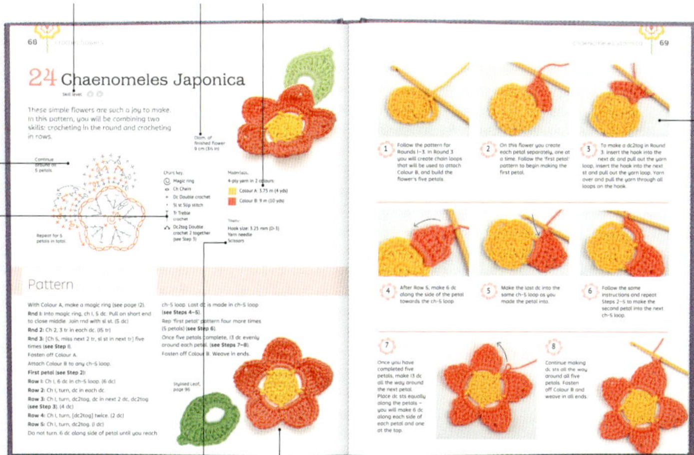

Projects (pages 98–109)

You can use your finished flowers as embellishments, but you can also make them into unique projects, and here you will learn how. Five varied projects for garments and home accessories are presented here with full patterns, charts and construction diagrams.

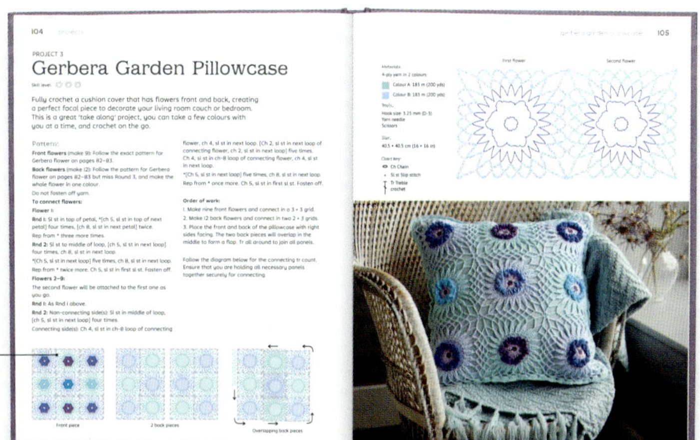

Tools and Materials

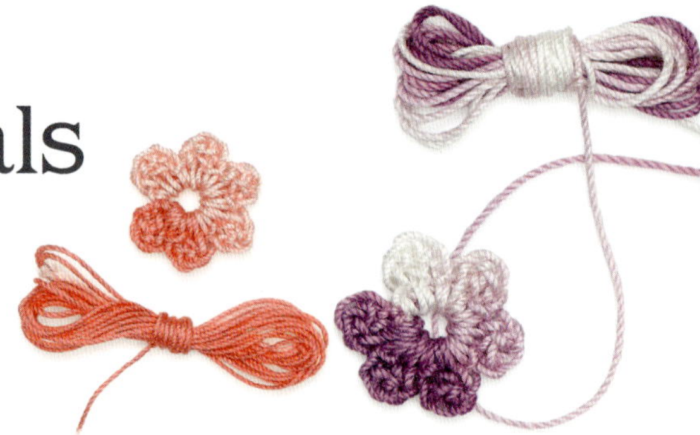

The right tools are an important part of any project, and crochet is no exception. Luckily, all you need to get started is a crochet hook, some yarn and just a few additional tools.

Yarns

Yarns differ in composition and weight (how thick the yarn is). Cotton yarn and threads are usually the most smooth and will give the most definition to crochet flowers. For each flower in this book I have listed a recommended yarn weight and hook size, but you can experiment with different yarns and combine them with different hook sizes to get various results, as shown here.

Yarn: Cotton thread # 30
Hook size: 1.3 mm (10)

Yarn: Cotton thread # 10
Hook size: 1.9 mm (5)

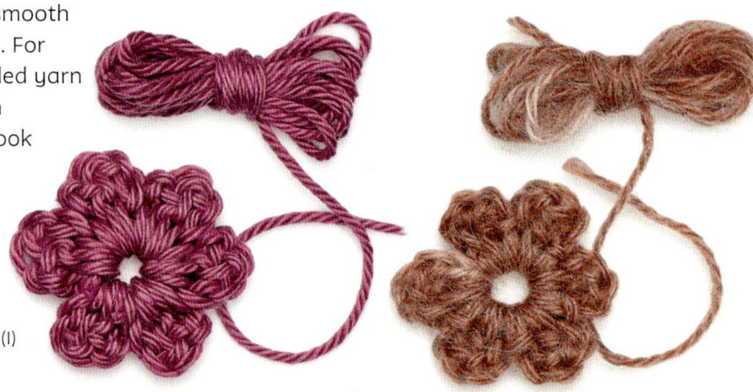

Yarn: Cotton 5-ply
Hook size: 2.5 mm (I)

Yarn: Acrylic/wool/mohair 2-ply
Hook size: 2.5 mm (I)

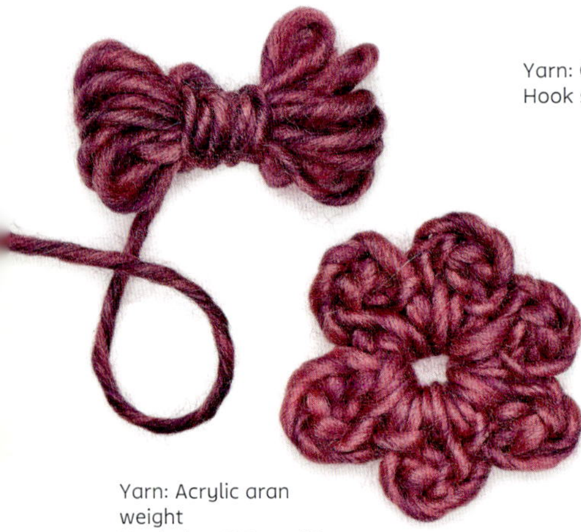

Yarn: Acrylic aran weight
Hook size: 3.5 mm (E)

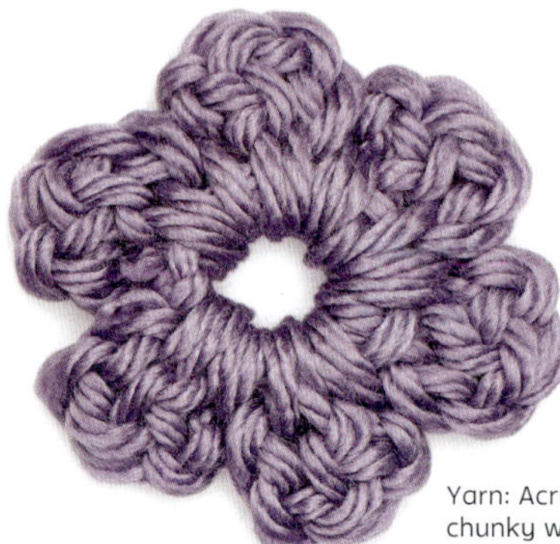

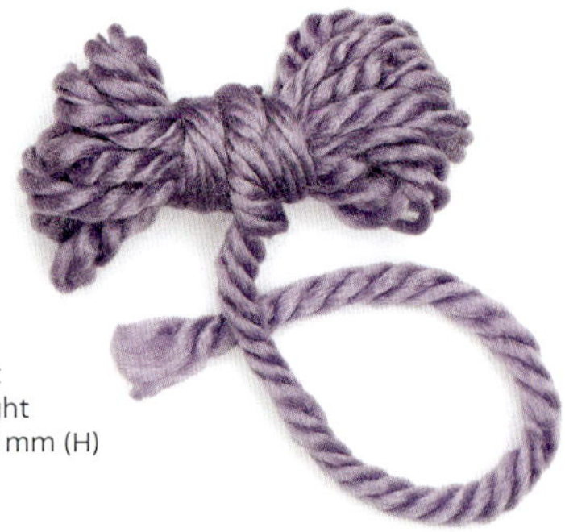

Yarn: Acrylic chunky weight
Hook size: 5 mm (H)

Other Useful Tools

Scissors

Any sharp scissors will do the job. Consider getting a small pair of very sharp scissors with a cover or holder to use exclusively for your crochet projects.

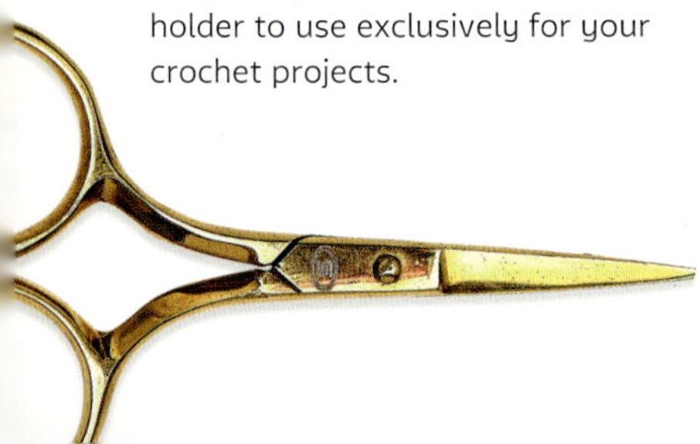

Stitch markers

For crochet you need a stitch marker that has a fastening on it so it will stay in place. You don't need to go out and purchase stitch markers, though; you can always use a scrap piece of yarn in a contrasting colour to mark your rounds (see page 59).

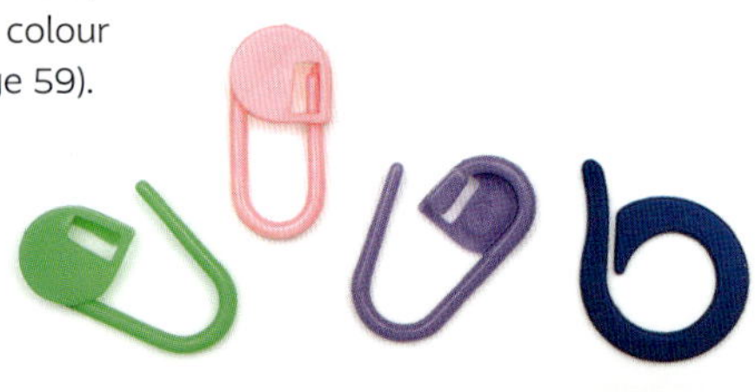

Yarn needle

For weaving in ends you need a special yarn needle with a big eye and blunt point.

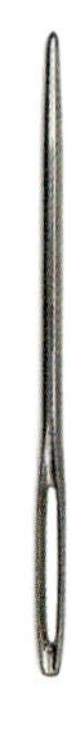

Approximate equivalent hook sizes

For guidance only, sizes given do not necessarily correspond exactly.

International standard range (ISR)	Imperial steel hooks	Imperial aluminium or plastic hooks	US steel hooks	US aluminium or plastic hooks
0.6 mm	6		14	
0.75 mm	5		13	
1 mm	4		12	
	3½		11	
1.25 mm	3		10	
			9	
1.5 mm	2½		8	
			7	
1.75 mm	2		6	
	1½		5	
2 mm	1	14	4	
			3	
2.25 mm	1/0 or 0	13	2	B
2.5 mm	2/0 or 00	12	1	C
3 mm	3/0 or 000	11	0	D
		10		
3.5 mm		9	00	E
				F
4 mm		8		
				G
4.5 mm		7		
5 mm		6		H
5.5 mm		5		I
6 mm		4		J
6.5 mm		3		K
7 mm		2		L
8 mm		1		M
9 mm		0		N
10 mm				
12 mm				
15 mm				

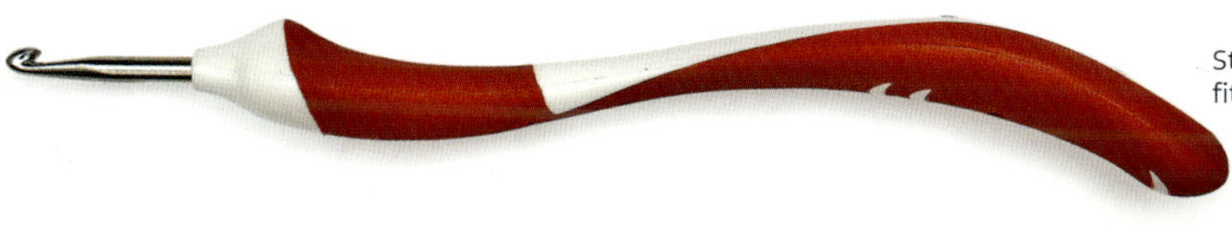

Steel hook with rubber handle, intended to fit the hand and reduce strain on the wrist

Crochet Hooks

Crochet hooks can be made of various materials: steel, aluminium, plastic and bamboo. Picking a hook material is often a matter of preference and availability, so try out different options.

Crochet hook sizes are chosen according to the yarn you are using. Look at the yarn label to pick out the correct hook. You can also take your yarn when you are shopping for hooks, and make sure that the yarn strand fits nicely in. Remember that using different sizes of hooks with the same yarn size will yield different sizes of flower.

Crochet hooks are sized in different ways in different countries, and can vary from manufacturer to manufacturer. The chart on the left will help you to make sure you have the right size crochet hook for any project.

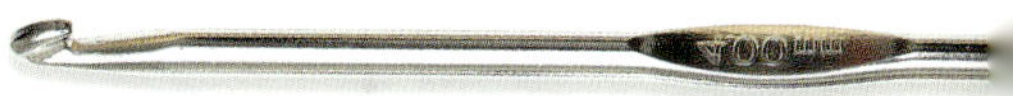

Steel hook

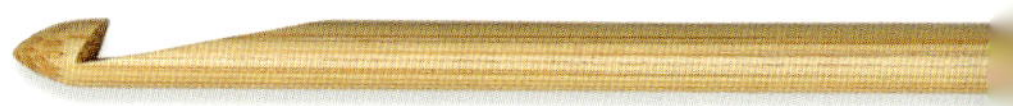

Lightweight bamboo hook

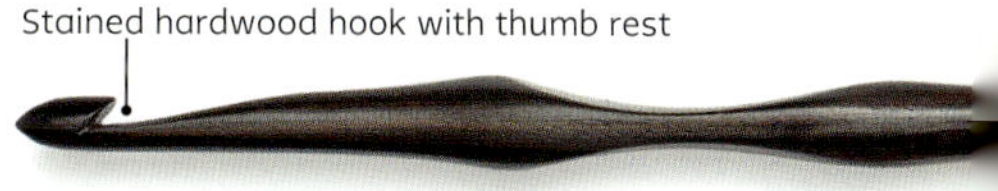

Stained hardwood hook with thumb rest

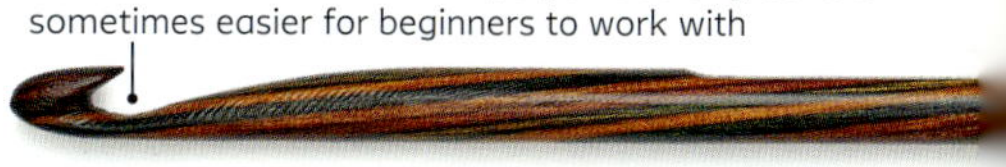

Stained bamboo hook. A deeper, smoother groove is sometimes easier for beginners to work with

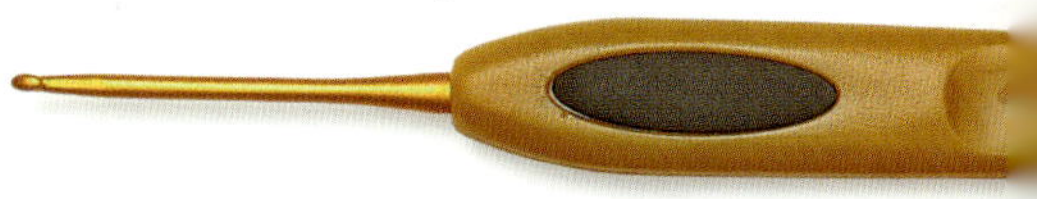

Aluminium hook with ergonomic handle

Get Started Crocheting

This section will walk you through the essentials of crocheting. Learn how to begin a project, basic stitches, useful techniques and how to read a crochet chart. Before you know it you'll be ready to start your first crochet flower project.

Getting Started

Start all crochet work with either a slip knot or a magic ring.

Slip knot

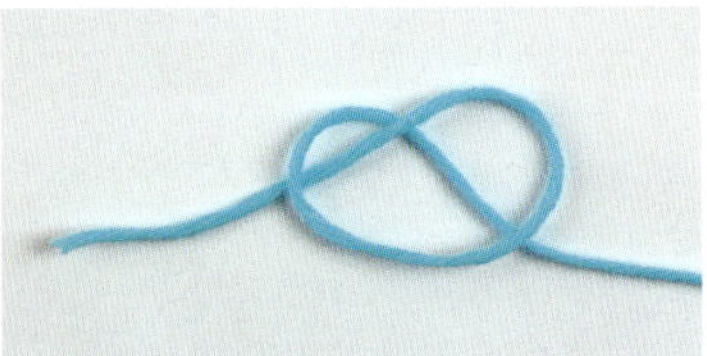

1. Make a yarn loop, as pictured.

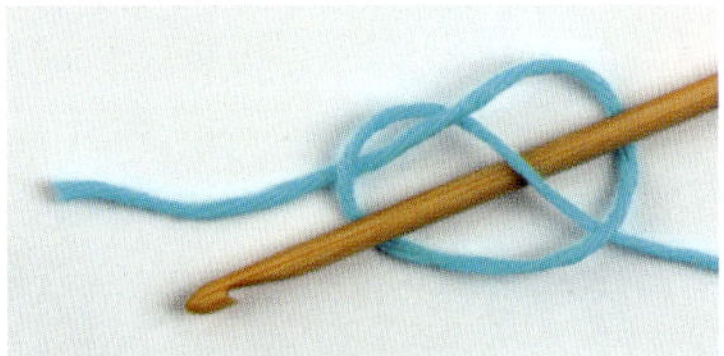

2. Insert your crochet hook, as shown.

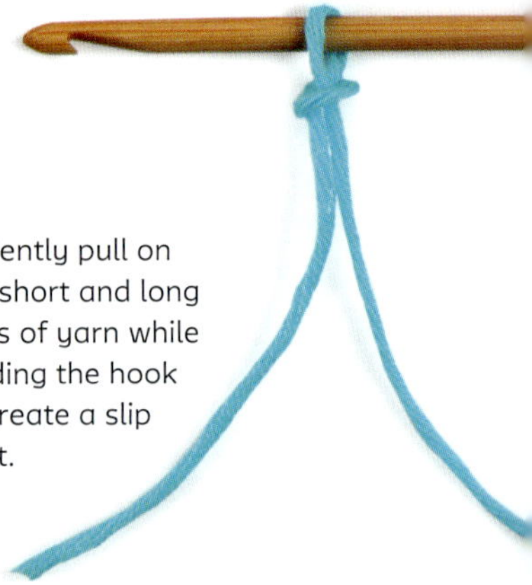

3. Gently pull on the short and long ends of yarn while holding the hook to create a slip knot.

Magic ring

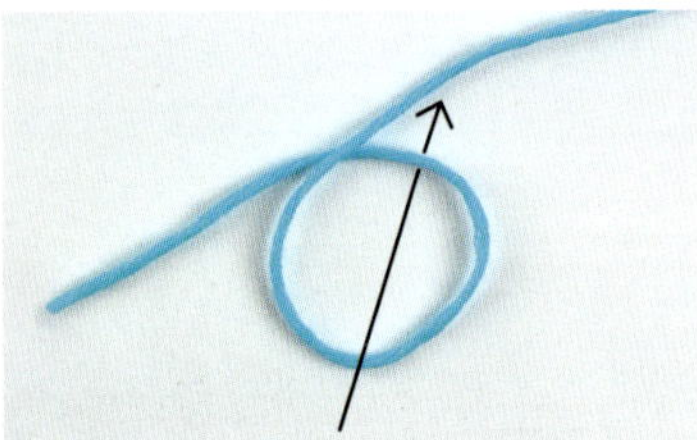

1. Start by making a loop in your yarn, as pictured. Insert the hook into the loop from the top, following the direction of the arrow.

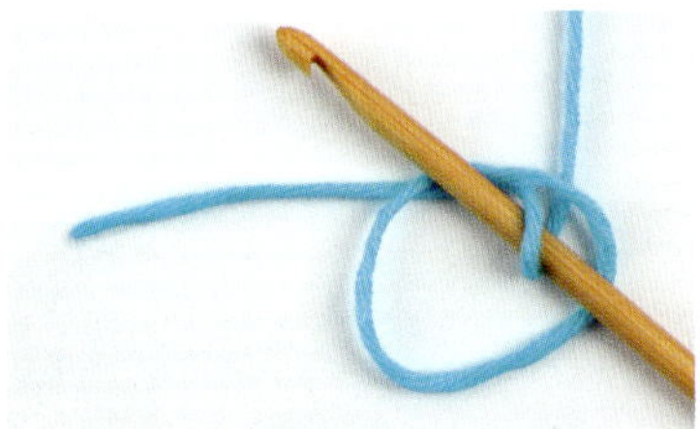

2. Hook the working yarn and pull through the loop, as pictured.

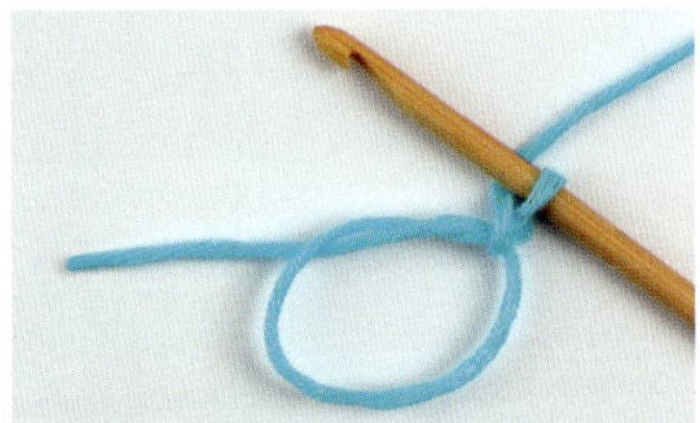

3. Make one chain stitch (or more, if directed by the pattern).

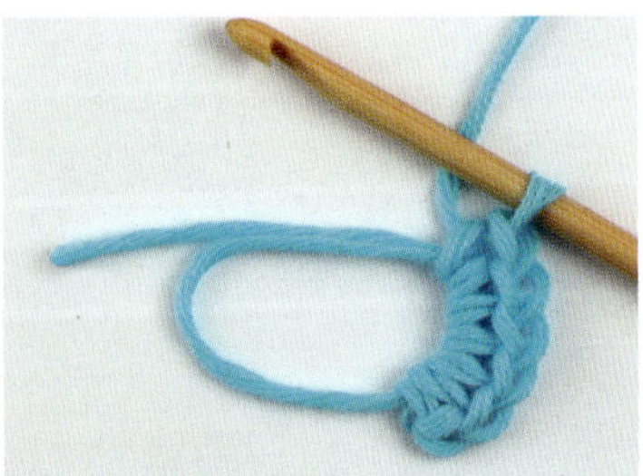

4. Crochet the desired number of stitches into the centre of the loop.

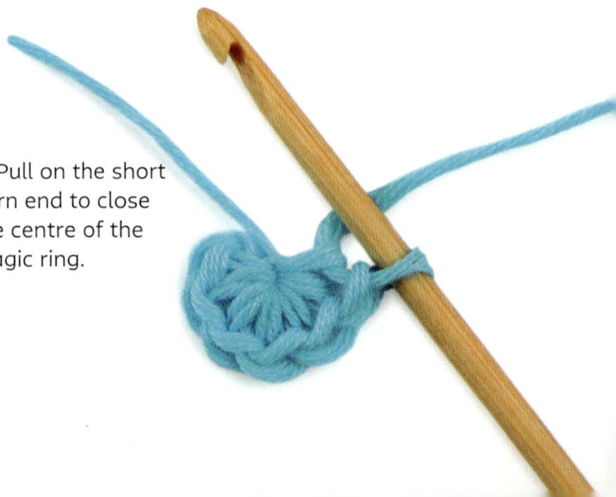

5. Pull on the short yarn end to close the centre of the magic ring.

Essential Stitches

If you're new to crocheting, take some time to practise these essential stitches as they will form the basis of the flower patterns.

Chain (ch)

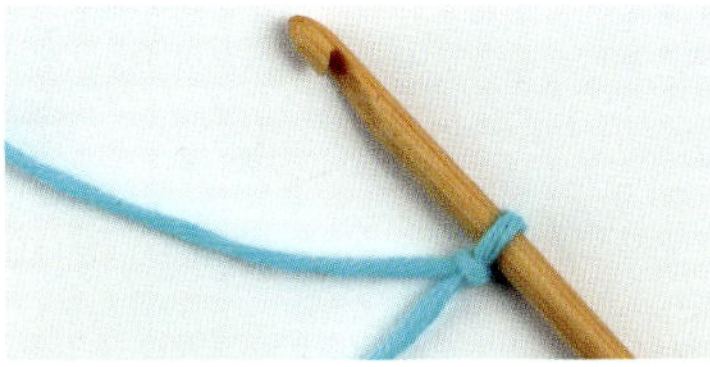

1. Start by making a slip knot (see page 12).

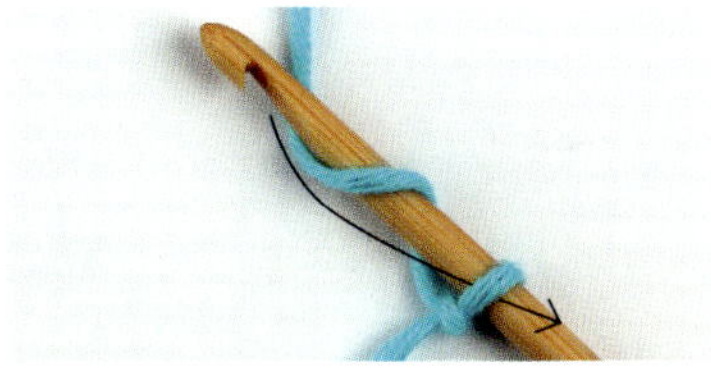

2. Wrap the working yarn around the hook, as pictured. Pull on the end of hook while holding the short yarn, and pull the yarn through the loop that is on the hook.

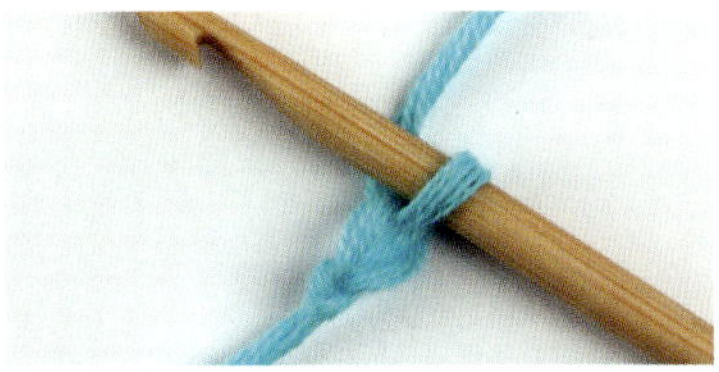

3. You have now made one chain stitch (the slip knot does not count as a stitch).

4. Repeat Steps 1–3 until you have the desired number of chain stitches.

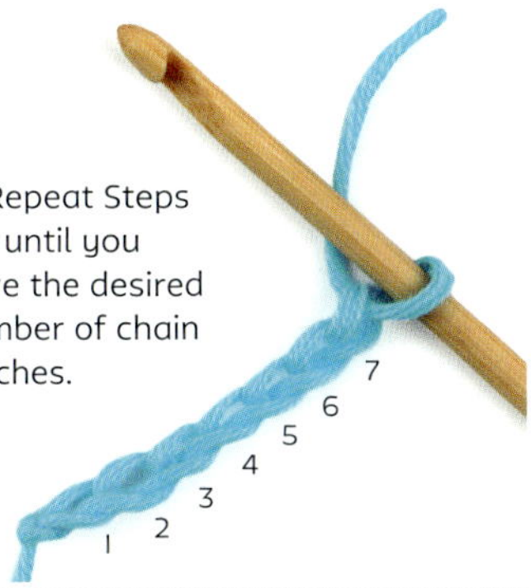

Slip stitch (sl st)

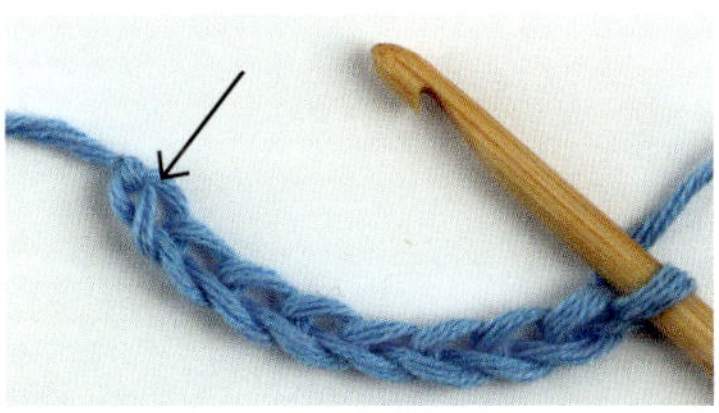

1. Locate the stitch in which you need to make a slip stitch. For example, if you need to join a round after making chain stitches, you will make a slip stitch into the first chain, shown here with an arrow.

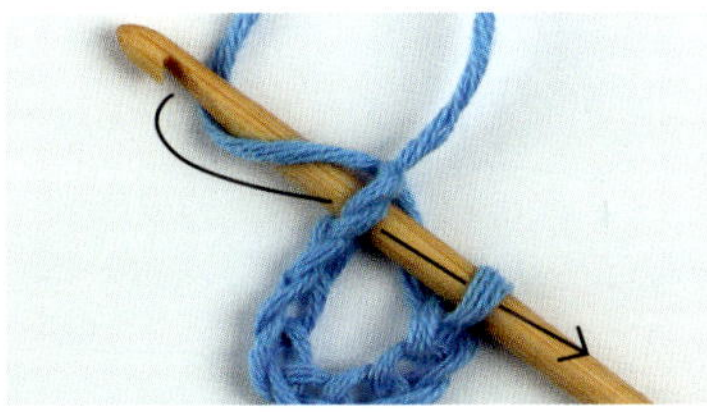

2. Insert the hook into the stitch. Wrap the working yarn around the hook (this is also called a yarn over, or yo). Draw the yarn through both loops on the hook.

3. One slip stitch made.

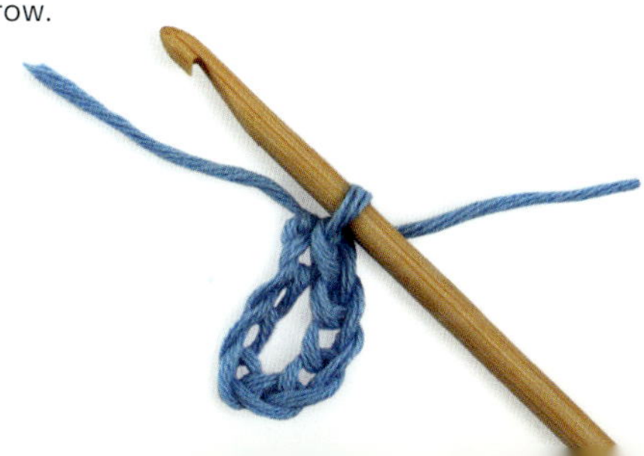

Double crochet (dc)

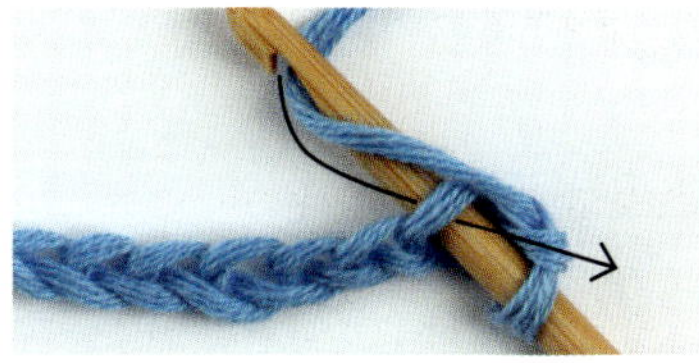

1. Insert the hook into the loop where the stitch will be made. Yarn over. Pull the yarn through the first loop on the hook only (indicated with an arrow).

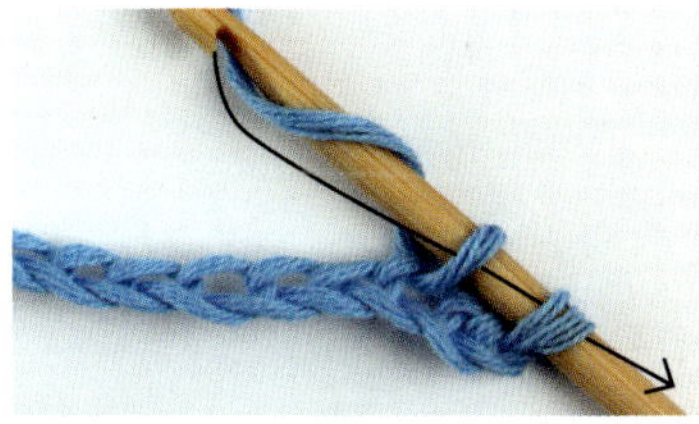

2. Now you have two loops on the hook. Yarn over again. Pull the yarn through both loops on the hook (follow the arrow).

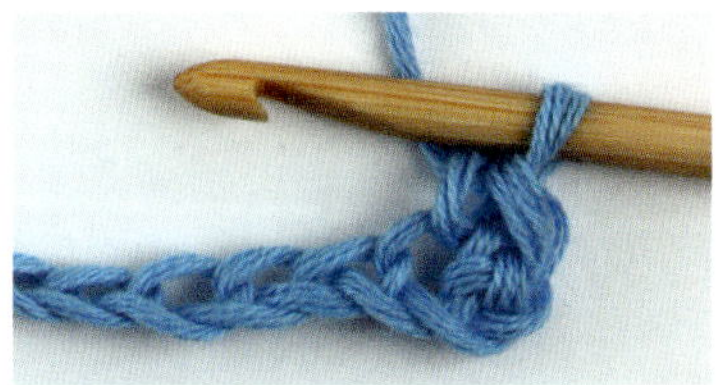

3. You have one loop left on the hook. One double crochet stitch has been made.

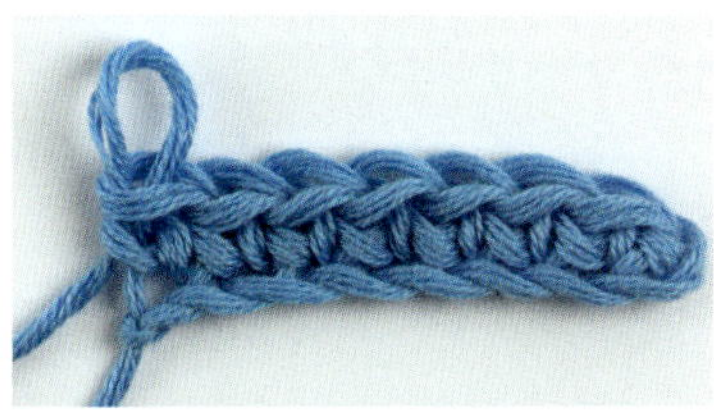

4. Repeat Steps 1–3 until you have the desired number of double crochet stitches.

Half treble crochet (htr)

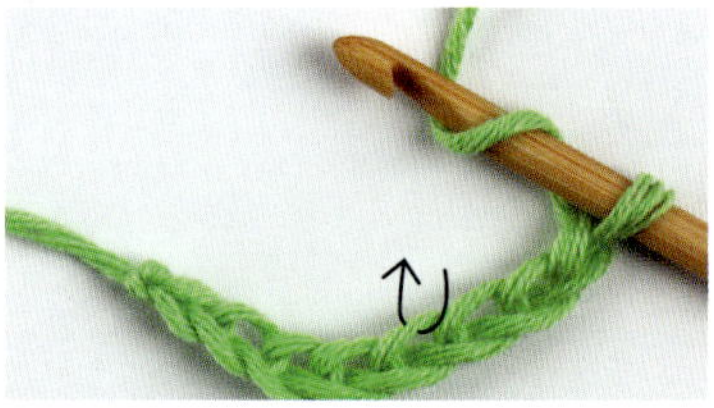

1. Yarn over. Find the loop where an htr will be made and insert the hook into the loop from front to back.

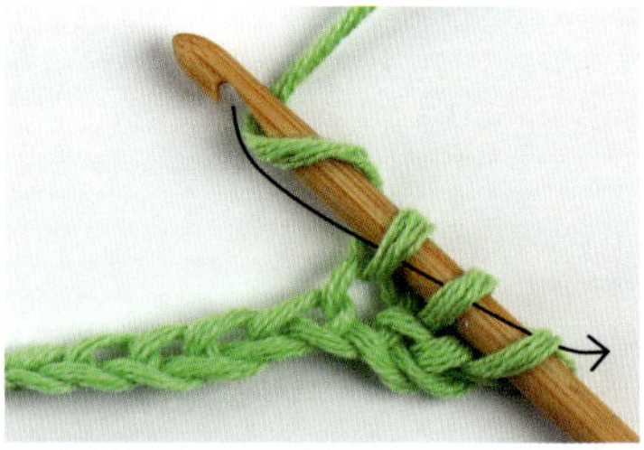

2. Pull a loop through this chain. You will have three loops on the hook. Yarn over again. Pull the yarn through all three loops on the hook.

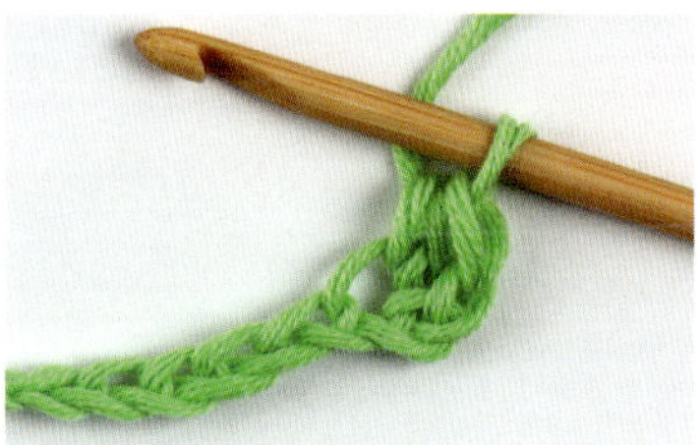

3. One half treble crochet (htr) stitch made.

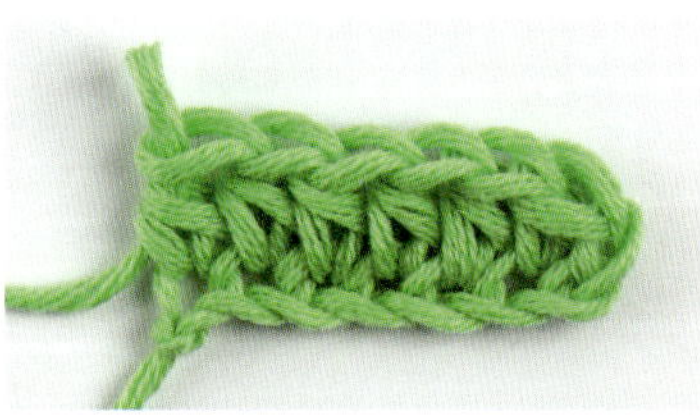

4. Repeat Steps 1–3 until you have the desired number of half treble crochet stitches.

Treble crochet (tr)

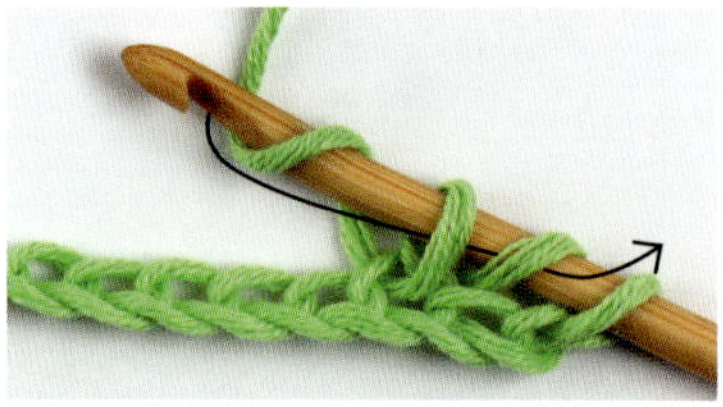

1. Start making a treble crochet exactly the same way as you did with the htr. Yarn over, insert hook into the loop. Pull a loop through the chain. Yarn over, and pull the yarn through the first two loops on the hook only (follow the arrow).

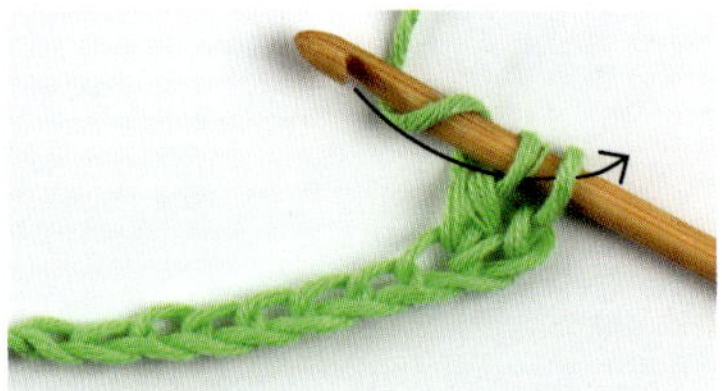

2. Yarn over again and pull the yarn through the remaining two loops on the hook.

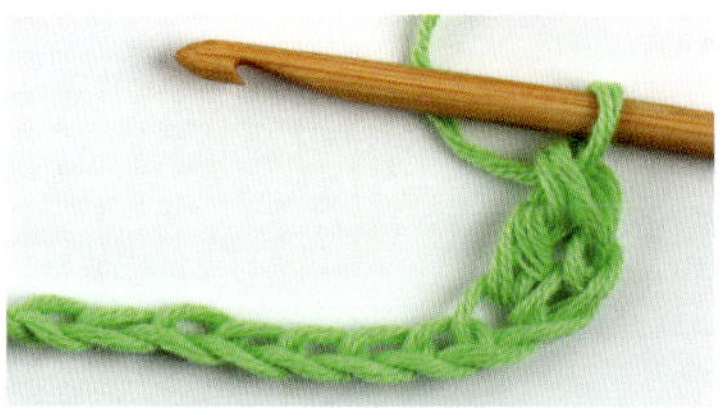

3. You have completed one treble crochet (tr) stitch.

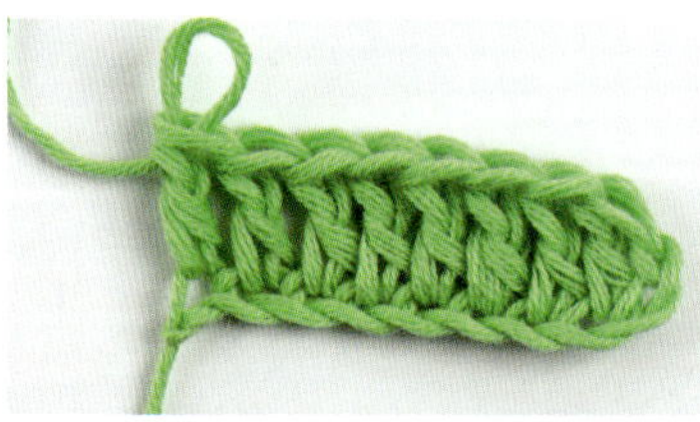

4. Repeat Steps 1–3 until you have the desired number of treble crochet stitches.

Double treble crochet (dtr)

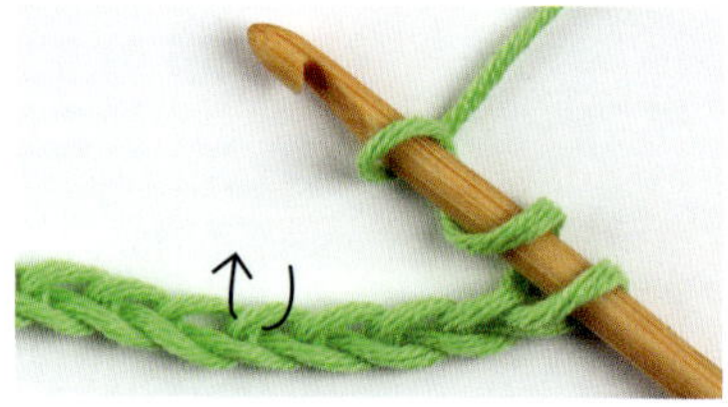

1. A double treble crochet is made in a similar way to a treble crochet. Start with making a yarn over twice, as pictured. Insert the hook into the loop where you want to make the stitch. Pull a loop through the chain.

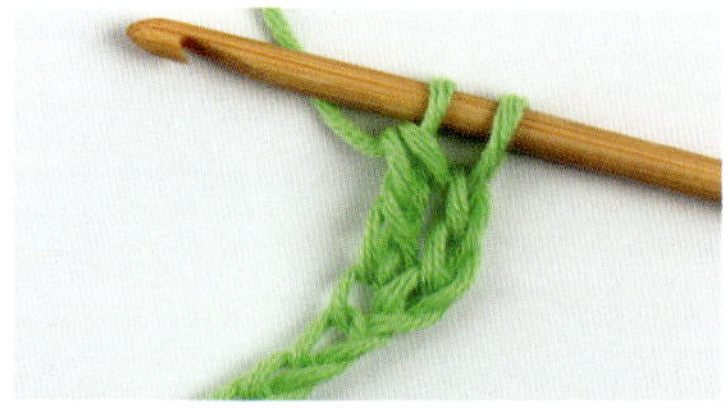

2. Yarn over, and pull the yarn through the first two loops on the hook. Do this three times.

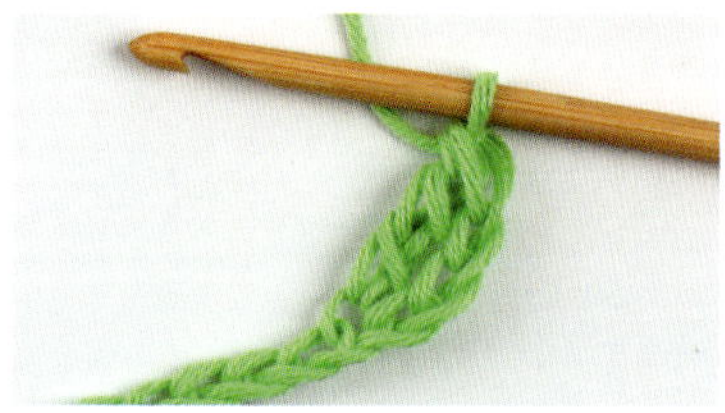

3. In the end only one loop will remain on the hook. You have completed one double treble (dtr) stitch.

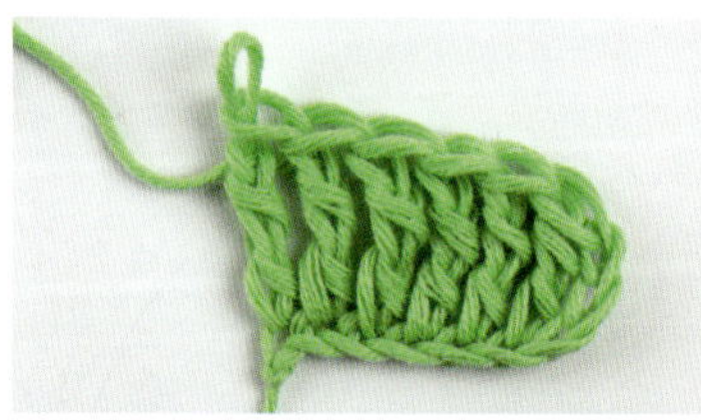

4. Repeat Steps 1–3 until you have the desired number of double treble crochet stitches.

Crochet Crash Course

You can crochet in rows or in rounds, depending on the pattern.

Working in rows

To crochet in rows, you generally start by making a long chain, and then make stitches across that chain.

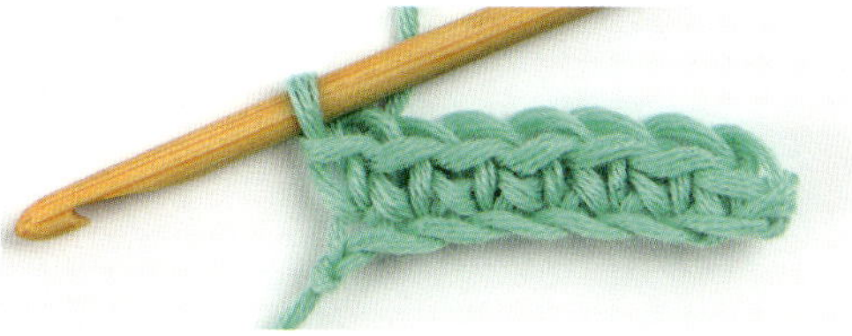

If you are right-handed, you will crochet from right to left.

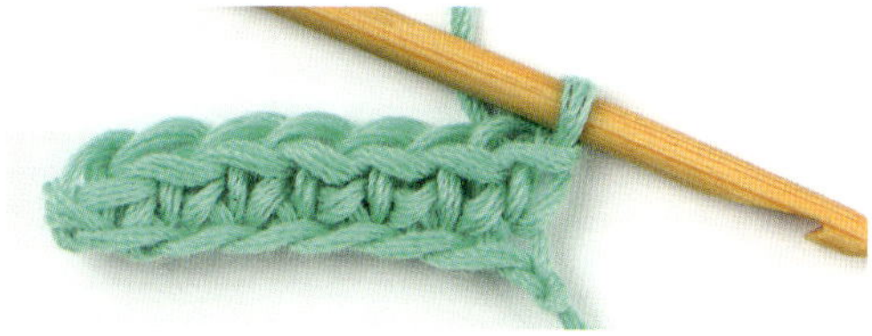

If you are left-handed, you will crochet from left to right.

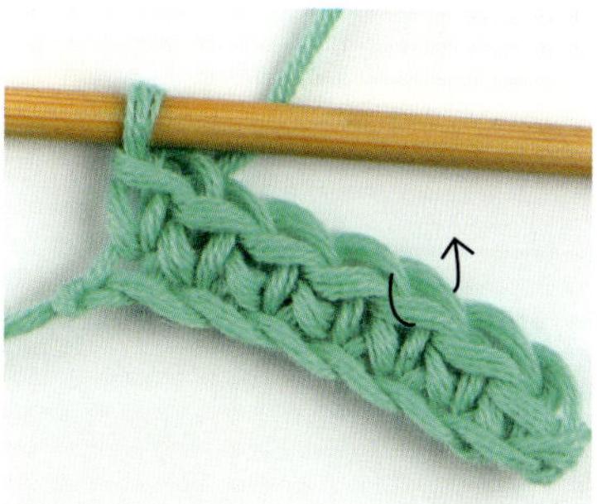

As you finish a row, and instructions tell you to turn work, turn your crocheted piece and start working on top of the stitches you have made in the first row. You can turn clockwise or anticlockwise but you will get a neater edge if you are consistent.

After you finish crocheting in the row, it is a good idea to count your stitches to make sure you are on the right track. Looking at the stitches from the top, you will notice V-shaped stitches – each V-shape is one stitch. The row pictured here has seven stitches. In the next round, insert the hook into the V-shape as shown to make a new stitch. Insert the hook so that it catches both sides of the V-shape, unless the pattern states otherwise.

Working in rounds

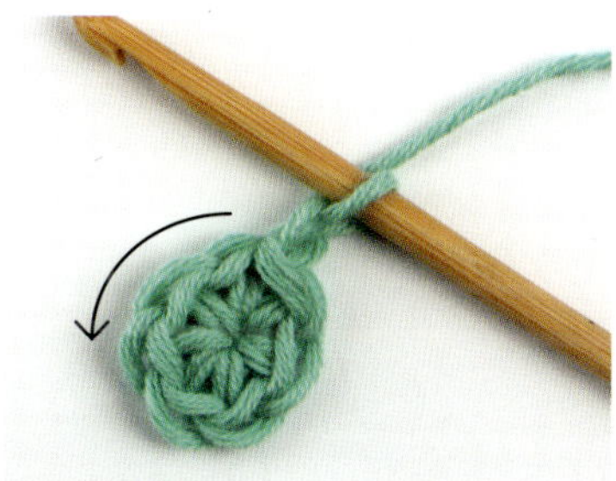

1. Working in rounds is similar to working in rows. You will be crocheting anticlockwise if you are right-handed, or clockwise, if you are left-handed.

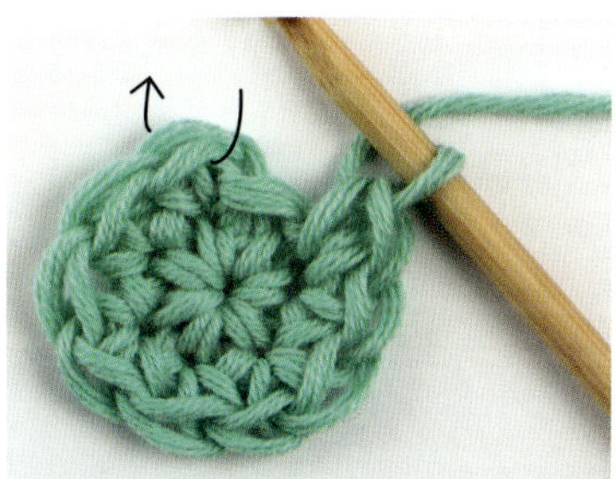

2. As you finish the round, often you will need to 'join round with slip stitch'. To do that, make a slip stitch into the very first stitch of the round, as shown by the arrow. It is a good idea to use a stitch marker to mark the first stitch in each round so that you will always know where your first stitch is and when you have reached the end of the round.

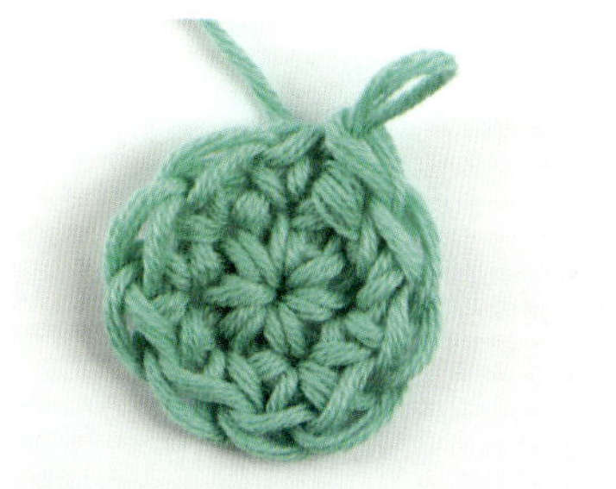

3. After you finish the round, you can count the stitches as you did with the row. A joining slip stitch doesn't usually count as an extra stitch, so you will have one extra V-shape.

Increasing stitches

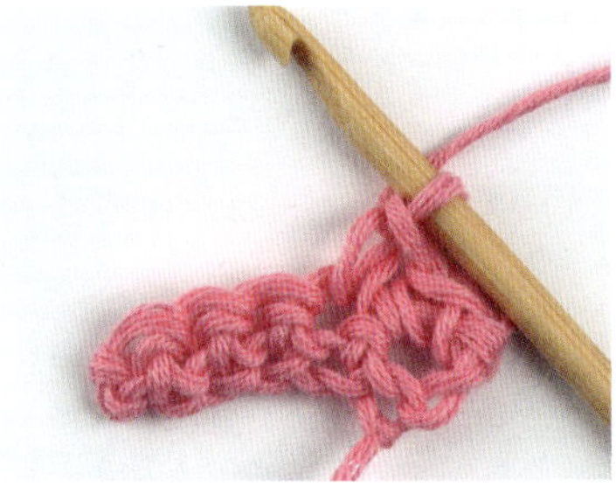

1. To increase the number of stitches you have in a row or a round, you will need to make a few new stitches into one stitch of a previous row.

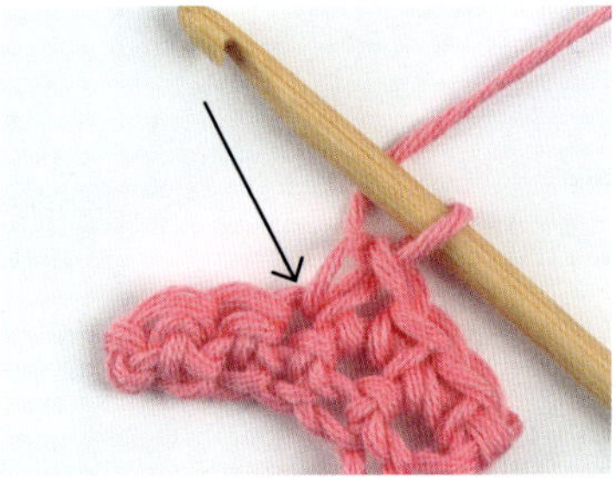

2. Start by making the first stitch, and then insert the hook back into the same stitch that you just crocheted into.

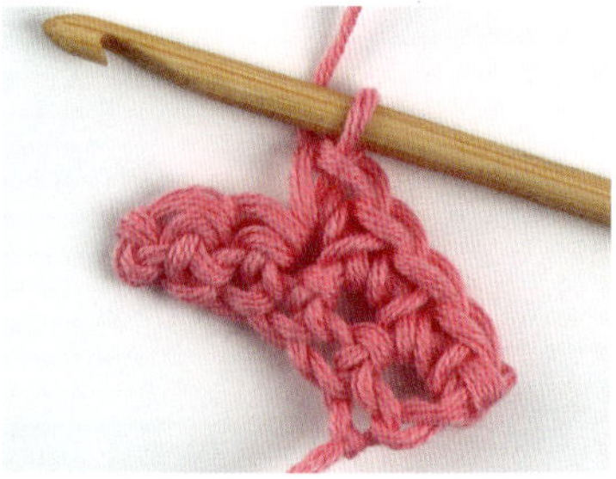

3. Make the second stitch into that same stitch also.

Decreasing stitches

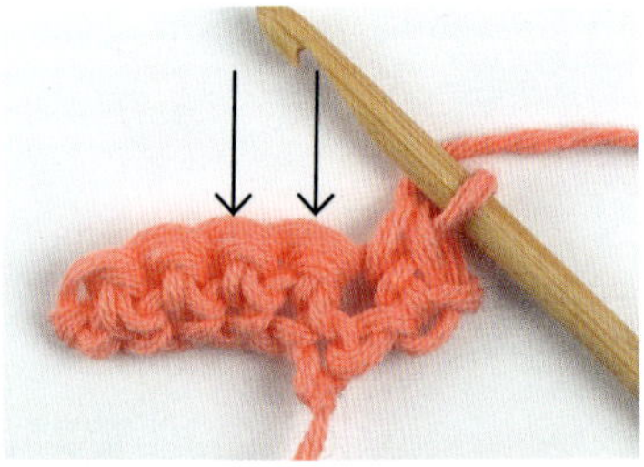

1. To decrease the number of stitches in a row or a round, in this book you will notice this abbreviation: dc2tog (which means 2 double crochet stitches together). Start by locating the next two stitches.

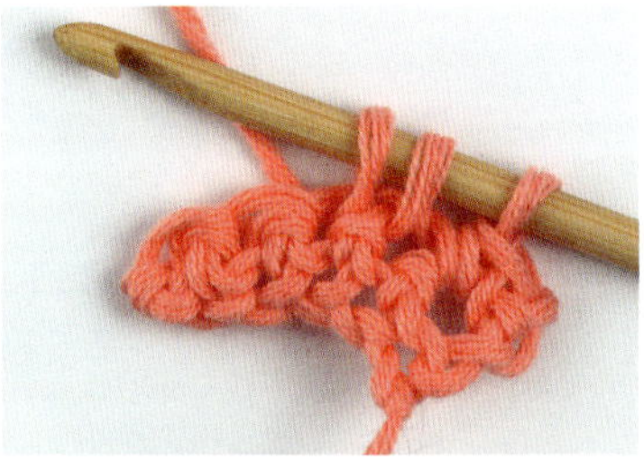

2. Insert the hook into the next stitch, yarn over, pull the yarn through the first loop on the hook. Insert the hook into the next stitch, yarn over, pull the yarn through the first loop on the hook. You will have three loops on the hook now.

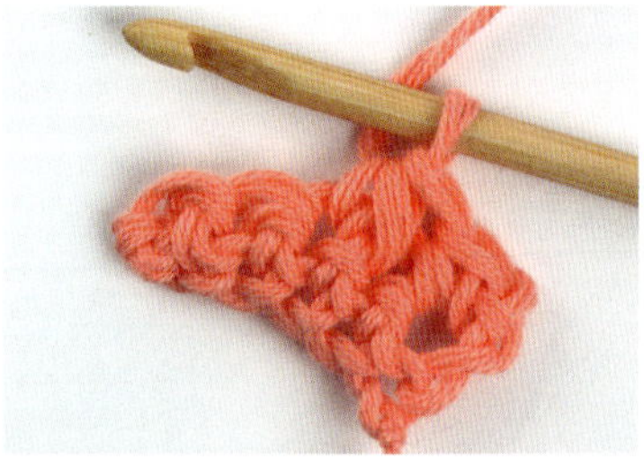

3. Yarn over and pull the yarn through all three loops on the hook. One dc2tog stitch is complete.

Fastening off and weaving in ends

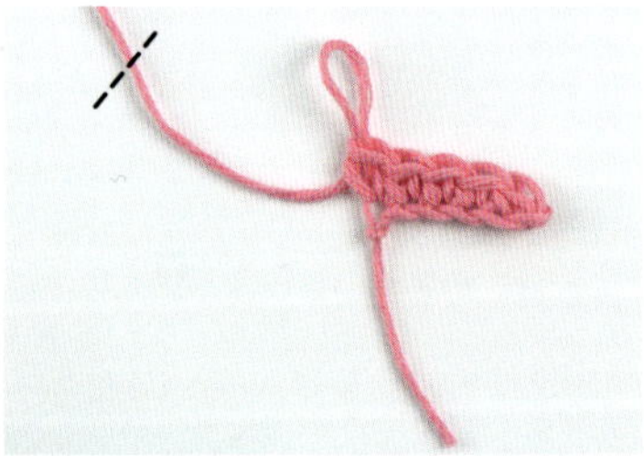

1. To fasten off, cut off the long yarn end 7.5–10 cm (3–4 inches) away from the hook.

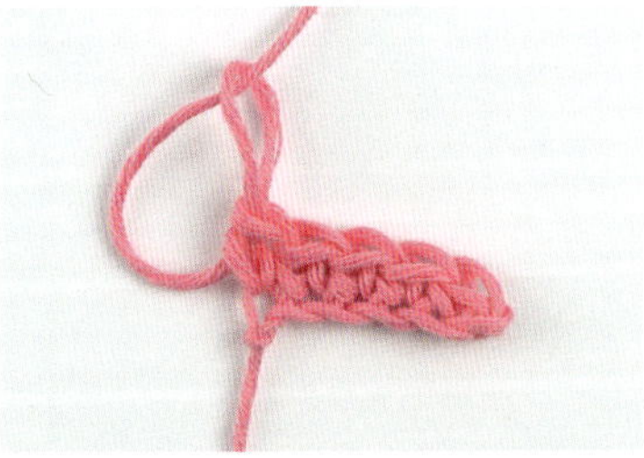

2. Insert the yarn end into the last loop and pull on the yarn to tighten the last loop.

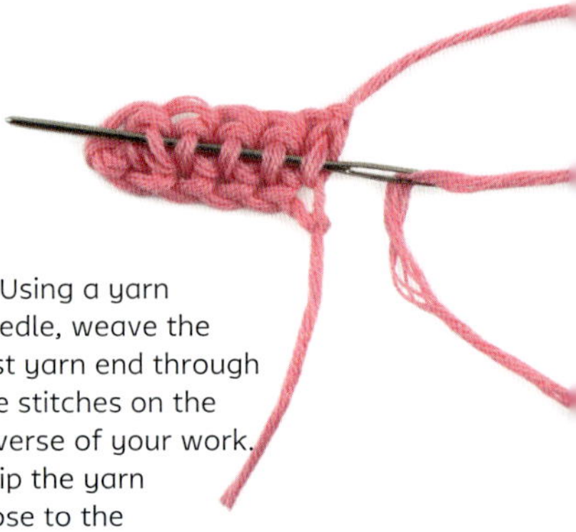

3. Using a yarn needle, weave the last yarn end through the stitches on the reverse of your work. Snip the yarn close to the fabric to hide the yarn end.

Reading Charts

Working in rounds

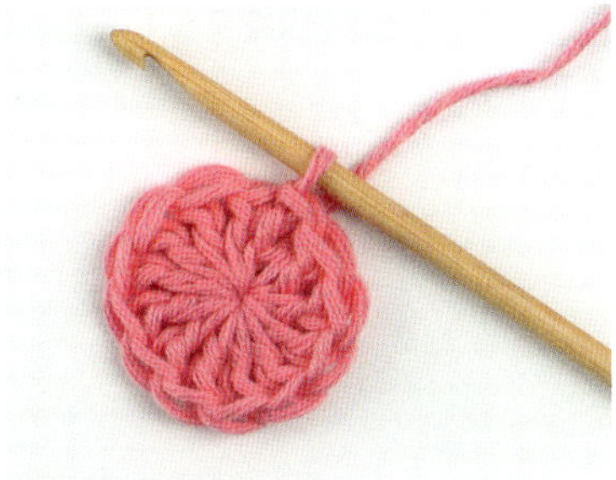

Rnd 1: Into magic ring: Ch 2, 12 tr. Pull on short end to close middle. Join rnd with sl st.

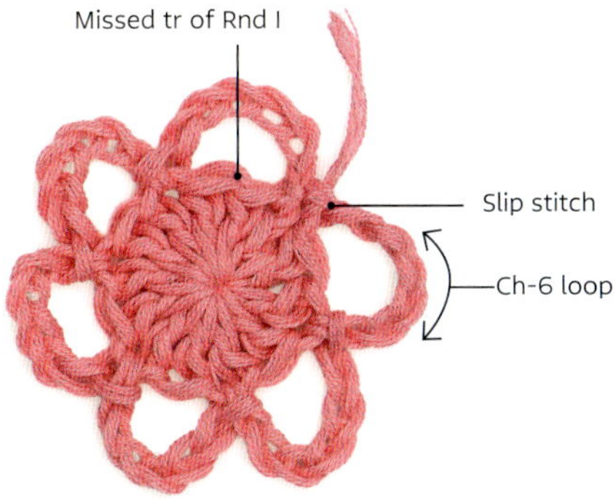

Rnd 2: [Ch 6, miss next tr, sl st in next tr] six times.

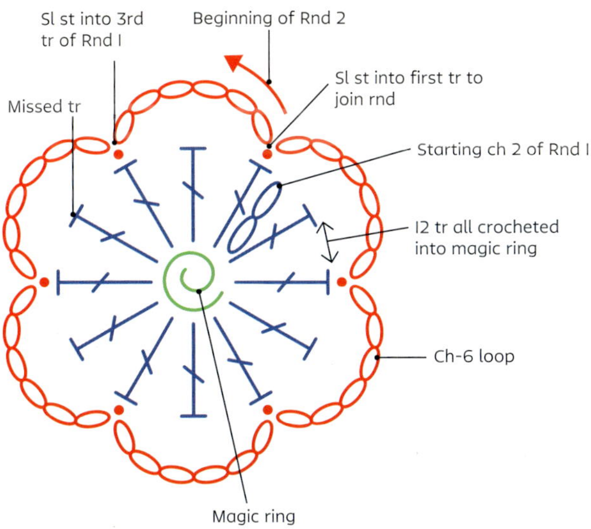

Working in rows

Ch 12.
Row 1: Starting with 2nd ch from hook, sl st in 2 ch, dc in next 2 ch, htr in next 2 ch, tr in next 2 ch, dtr in next 3 ch.

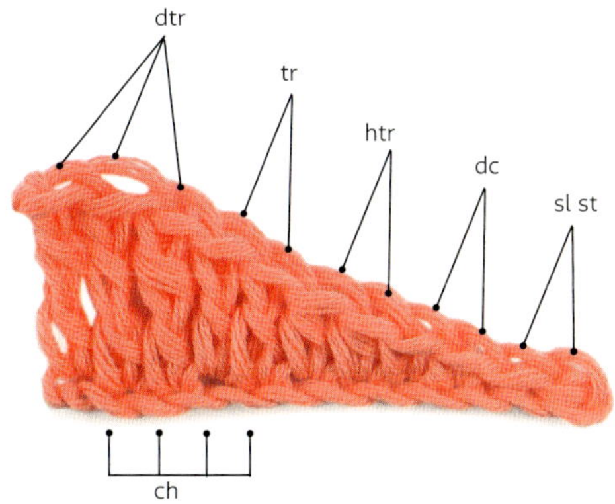

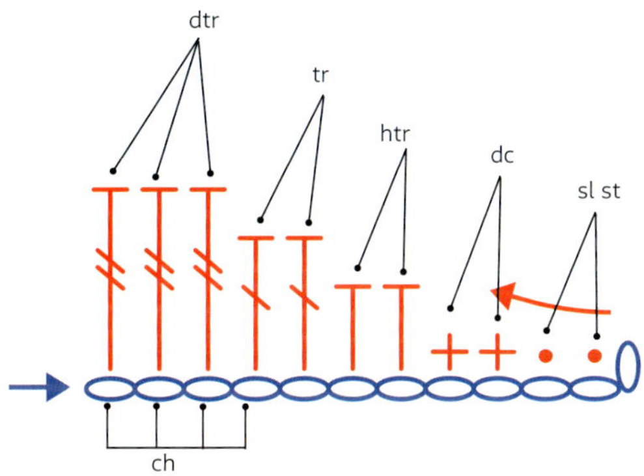

For a complete list of the stitches, symbols and abbreviations used in this book, turn to page 110.

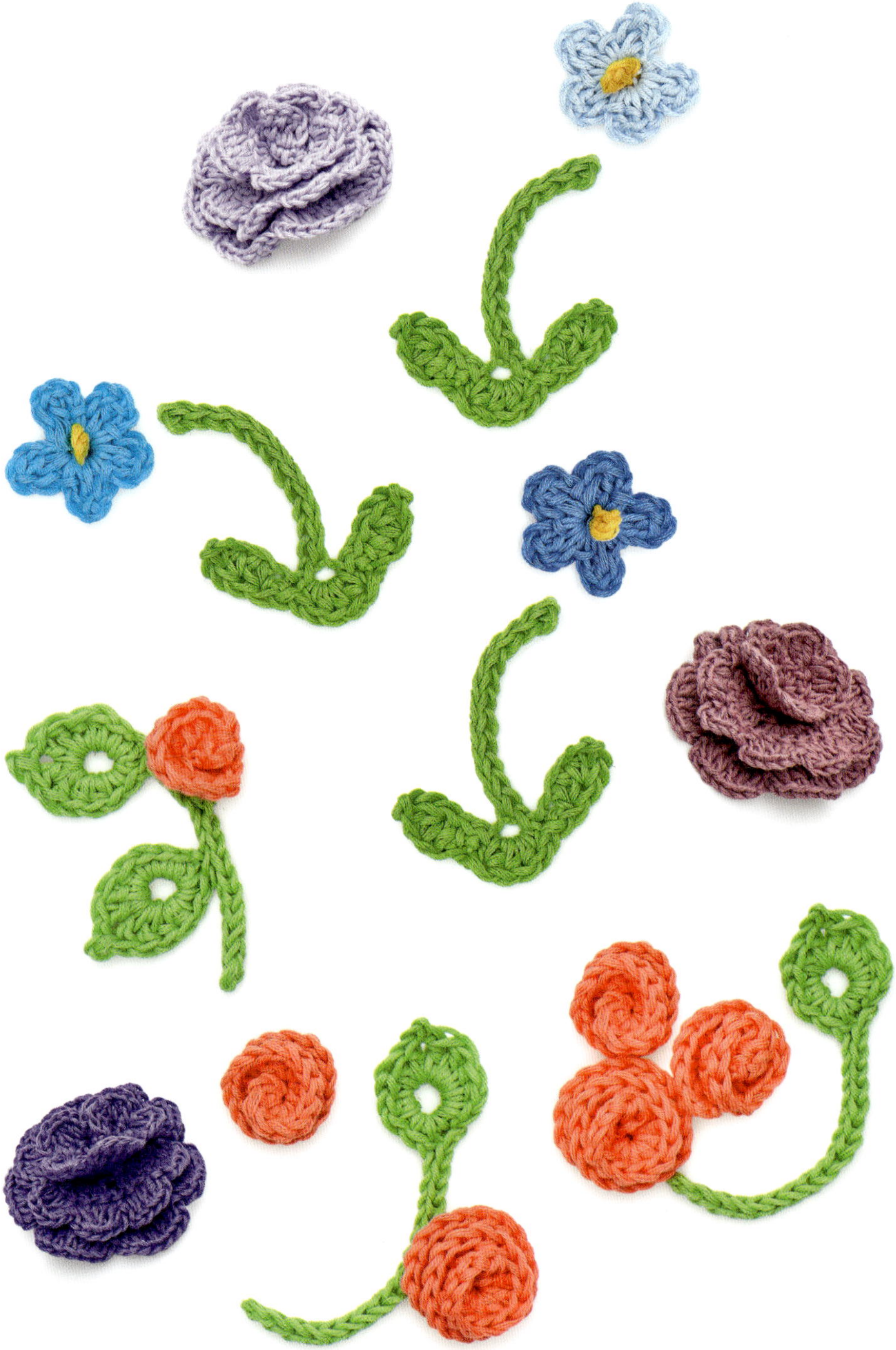

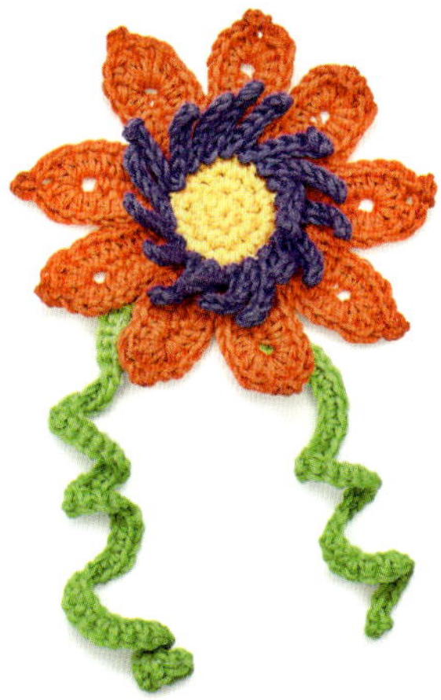

Crochet Flowers

This section of the book presents a selection of 35 flower designs for you to crochet, complete with written patterns, charts and helpful step-by-step instructions to guide you along the way. Start at the beginning to gradually build your crochet skills or turn to pages 6–7 for a colourful visual guide to help you choose your favourite flower.

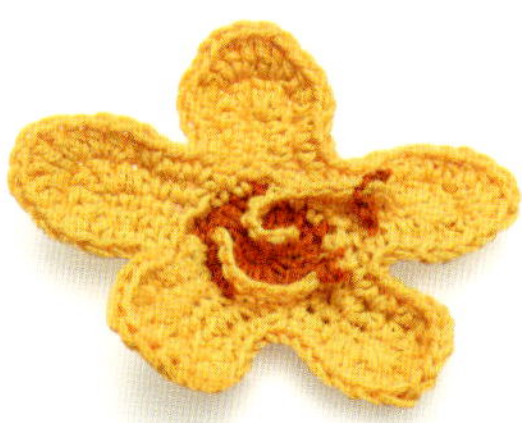 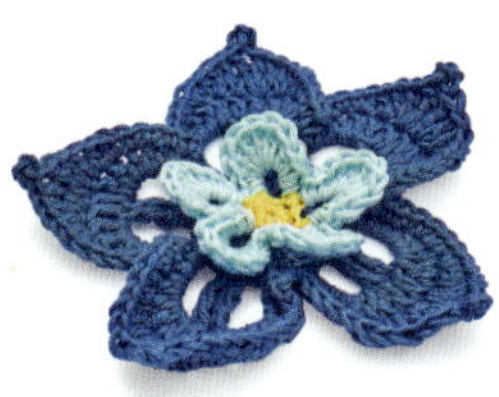 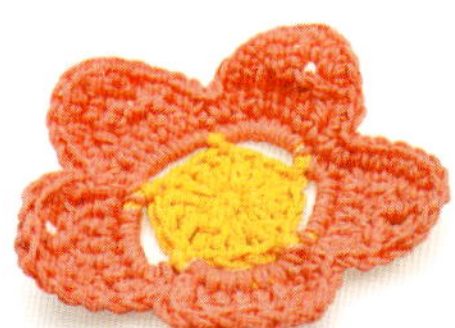

1 Chrysanthemum

Skill level:

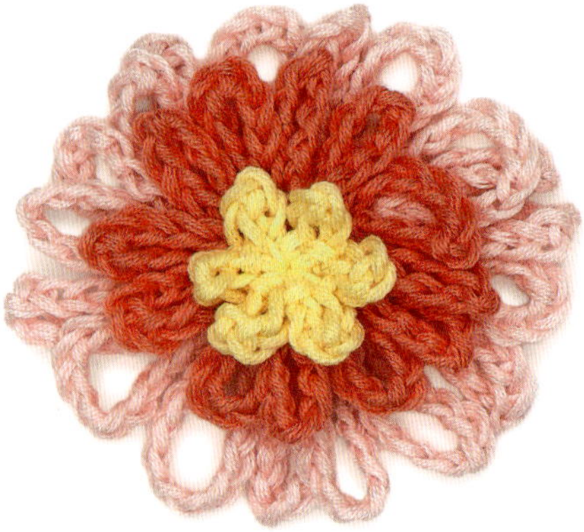

This is a perfect first project as you learn to crochet! This beautiful, layered flower can be made using only two basic stitches: chain and slip stitch. Try adding even more layers to make a three-dimensional flower.

Materials:

4-ply yarn in 3 colours:

- Colour A: 1 m (1 yd)
- Colour B: 2.75 m (3 yds)
- Colour C: 6.5 m (7 yds)

Diam. of finished flower: 7.5 cm (3 in)

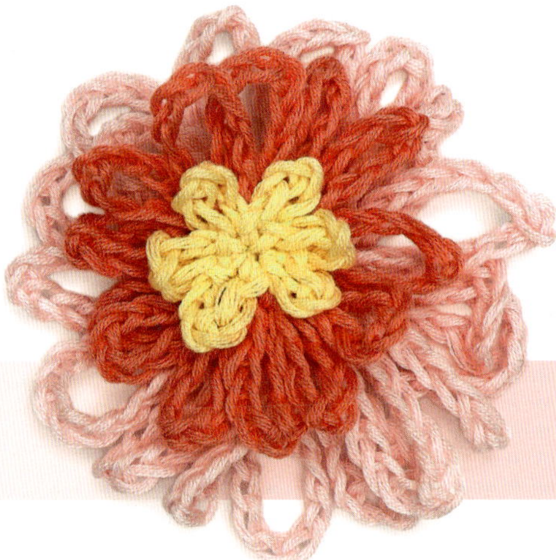

Tools:

Hook size: 3.25 mm (D-3)
Yarn needle
Scissors

Chart key:

- Magic ring
- Ch Chain
- Sl st Slip stitch

Pattern

Small petals:

With Colour A, make a magic ring (**see Steps 1–3**).

[Ch 5, sl st into magic ring] six times.

Medium petals: With Colour B, make a magic ring.

[Ch 10, sl st into magic ring] 12 times (**see Steps 4–6**).

Large petals:

With Colour C, make a magic ring.

[Ch 15, sl st into magic ring] 18 times.

Fasten off (**see Step 7**).

Connect all flowers (**see Step 8**).

Small petals

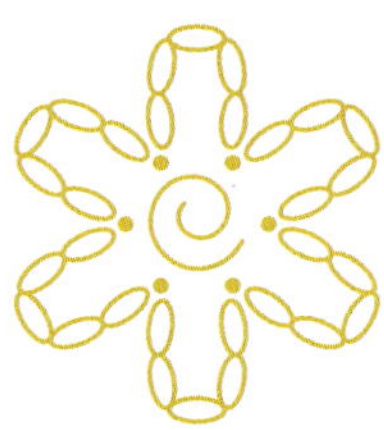

Medium petals

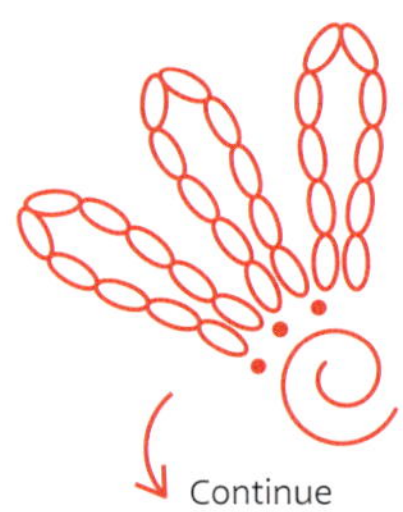

Large petals

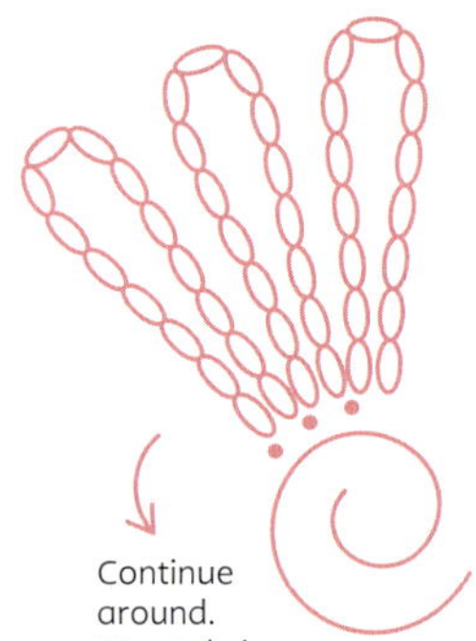

Tip: After you have practised following this pattern, you can adjust the number of chain stitches you make for each petal, and the number of petals, to create any size flower you like!

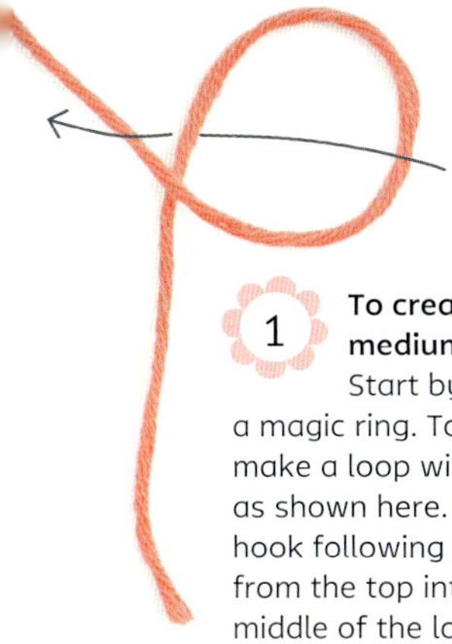

1 **To create the medium petals:** Start by making a magic ring. To do that, make a loop with the yarn as shown here. Insert the hook following the arrow: from the top into the middle of the loop, and under one side of the loop.

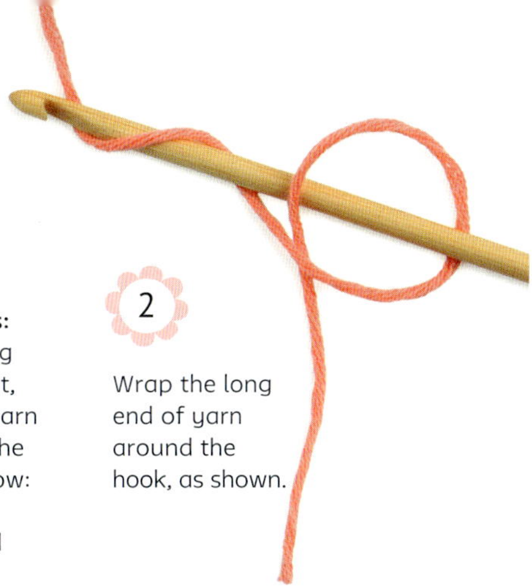

2 Wrap the long end of yarn around the hook, as shown.

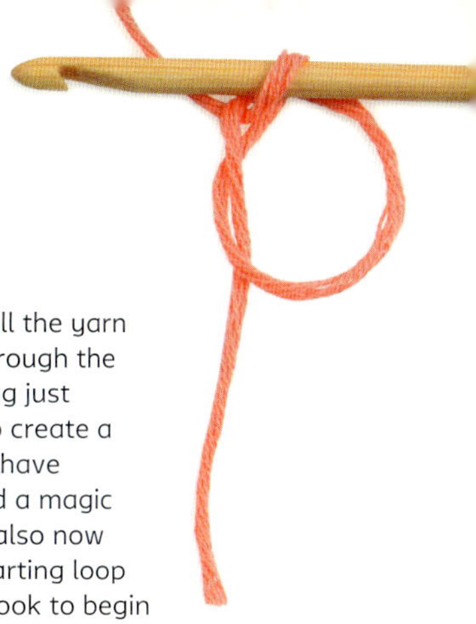

3 Pull the yarn through the ring just enough to create a loop. You have completed a magic ring. You also now have a starting loop on your hook to begin crocheting.

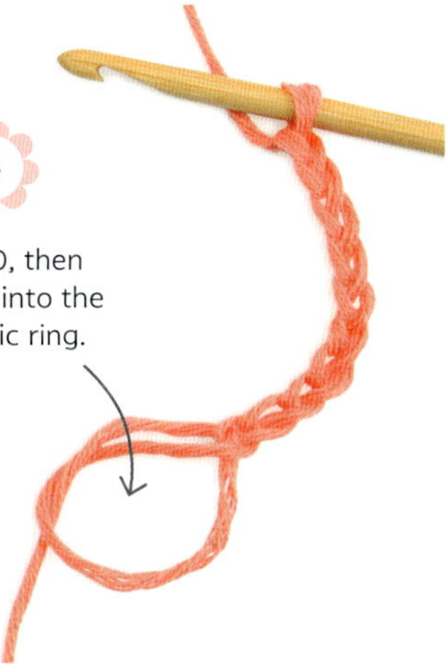

4 Ch 10, then sl st into the magic ring.

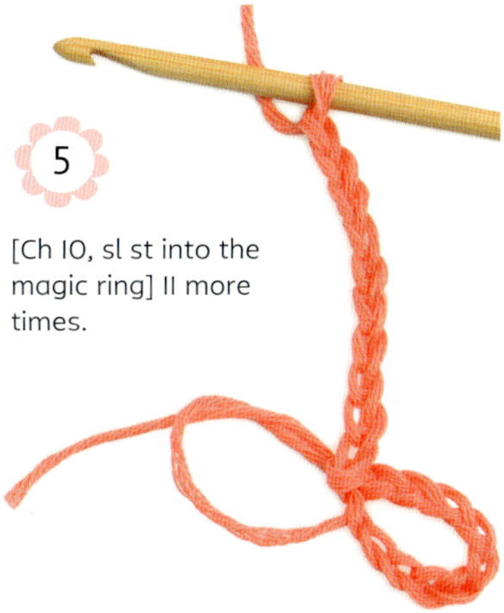

5 [Ch 10, sl st into the magic ring] 11 more times.

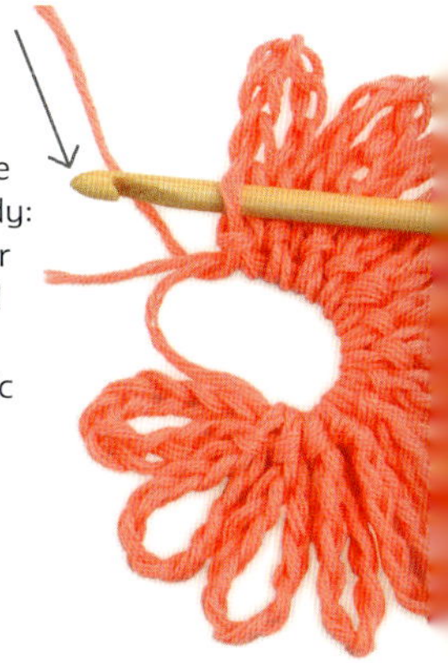

6 Now you have all the petals ready: 12 petals altogether on a medium-sized layer. To close the middle of the magic ring, pull the short yarn tail tightly.

7 Fasten off and weave in all ends, except for the long end on the smallest petal.

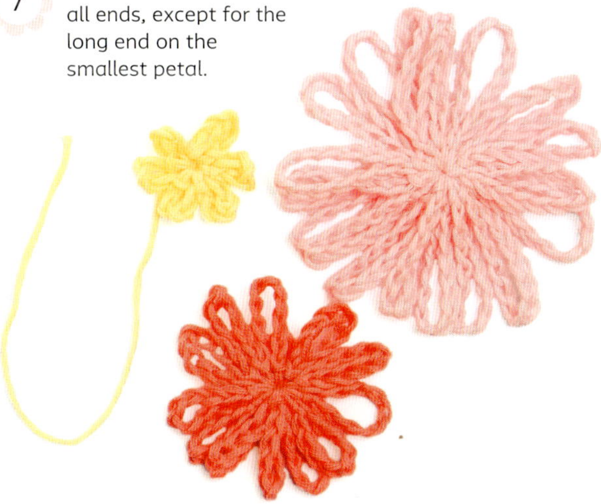

8 Follow the three patterns on the left to create different sizes of petals, leaving a long yarn end on the smallest petals. Use the long yarn end to sew the petals together into a flower.

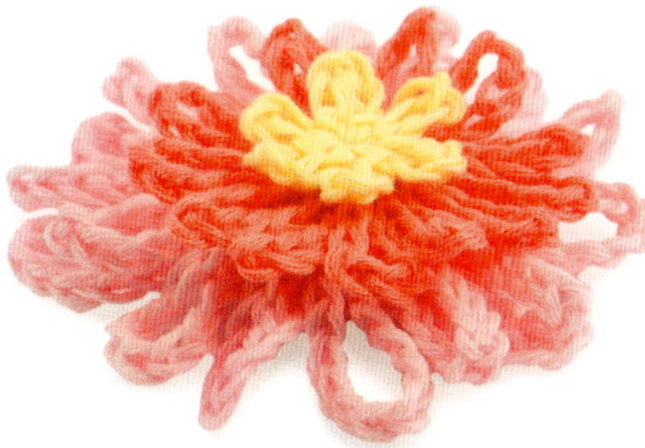

2 Anemone

Skill level:

This flower is quick and easy to make, using only chains, double crochets and slip stitches. It is simple enough to be the very first crochet project for a beginner, and is an excellent project for practising your stitches.

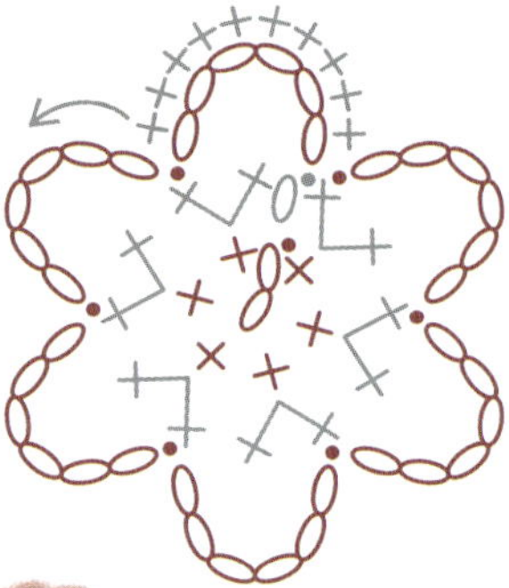

Materials:

4-ply yarn in 2 colours:

- Colour A: 3.75 m (4 yds)
- Colour B: 3.75 m (4 yds)

Tools:

Hook size: 3.25 mm (D-3)
Yarn needle
Scissors

Chart key:

- ⬭ Ch Chain
- • Sl st Slip stitch
- + Dc Double crochet

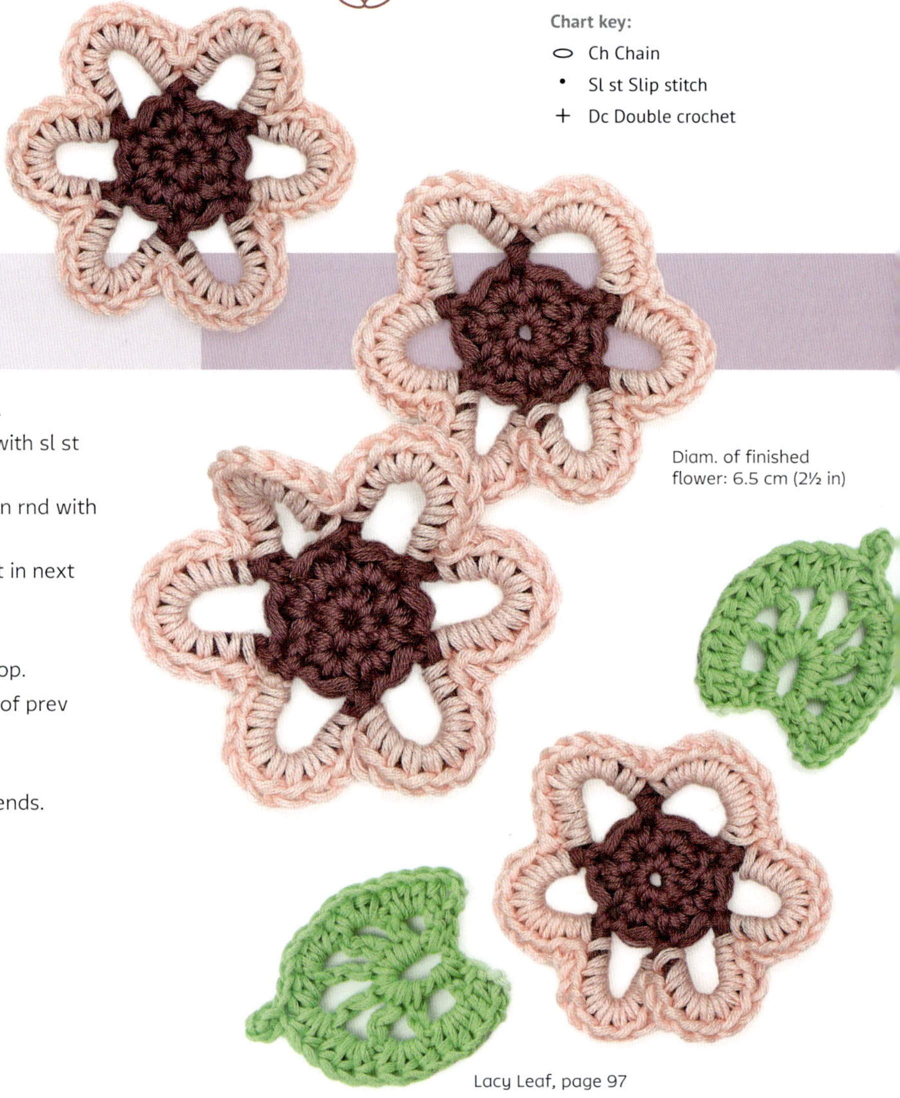

Diam. of finished flower: 6.5 cm (2½ in)

Lacy Leaf, page 97

Pattern

With Colour A, ch 2 (**see Step 1**).

Rnd 1: 6 dc in 2nd ch. Join rnd with sl st (**see Steps 1–2**). (6 dc)

Rnd 2: Ch 1, 2 dc in each dc. Join rnd with sl st (**see Steps 3–4**). (12 dc)

Rnd 3: [Ch 6, miss next dc, sl st in next dc] six times (**see Steps 5–6**).

Fasten off Colour A.

Attach Colour B to any ch-6 loop.

Rnd 4: [10 dc in first ch-6 loop of prev rnd] six times (**see Steps 7–8**).

Join rnd with sl st in first dc.

Fasten off Colour B. Weave in ends.

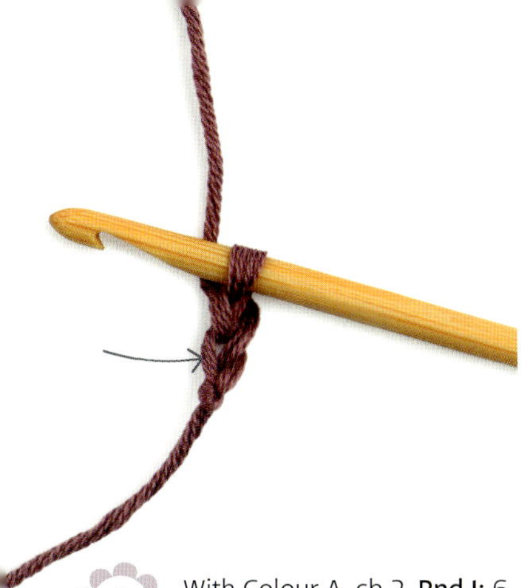

1 With Colour A, ch 2. **Rnd 1:** 6 dc into the 2nd ch from the hook (as marked by the arrow).

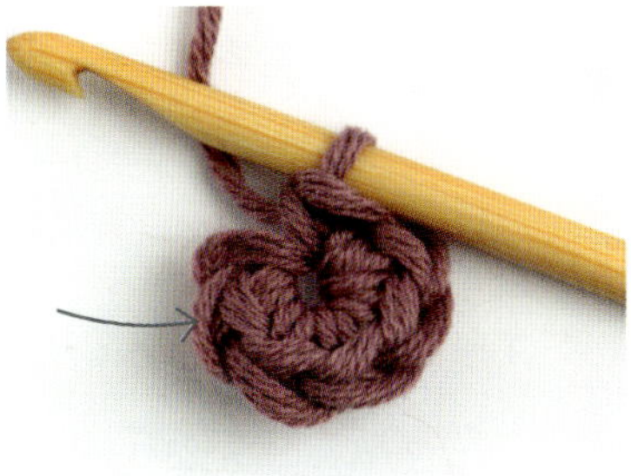

2 Join the round with a sl st into the first dc of the round as marked by the arrow.

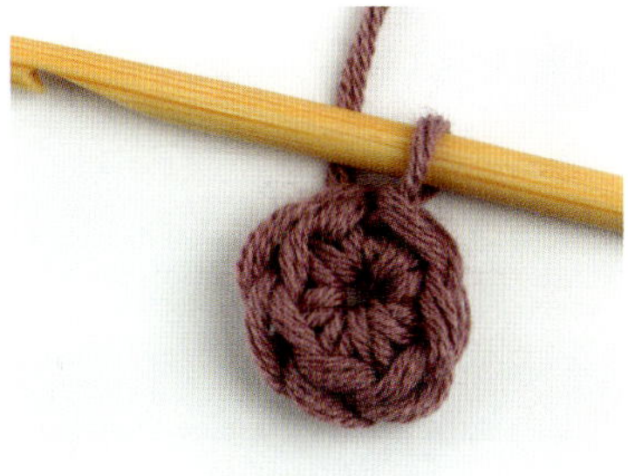

3 **Rnd 2:** Ch 1, 2 dc in the first st, 2 dc into each of the next 5 dc. Join the round with a sl st. (12 dc in the round).

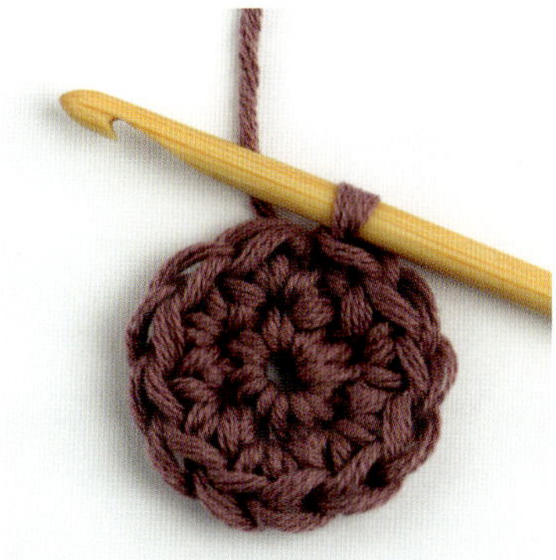

4 When both rounds are completed, your flower will look like this.

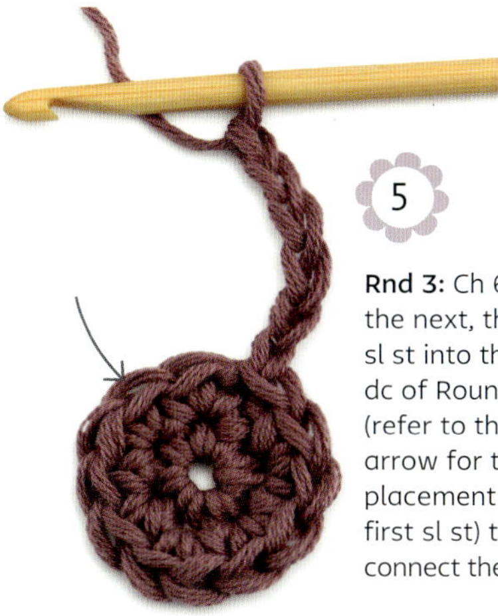

5 **Rnd 3:** Ch 6, miss the next, then sl st into the next dc of Round 2 (refer to the arrow for the placement of the first sl st) to connect the petal.

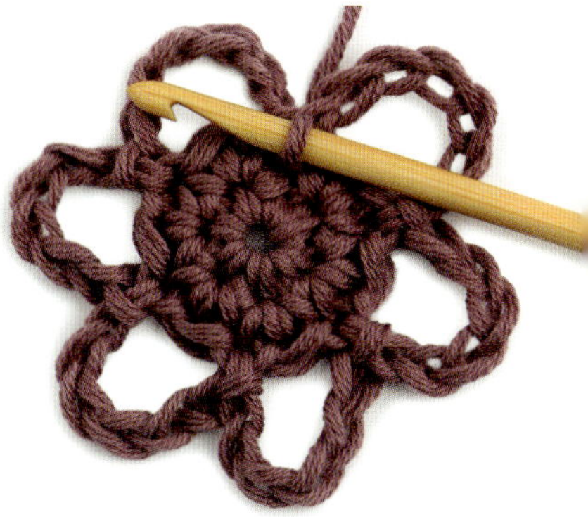

6 Repeat Step 5 five more times to create six petals in total.

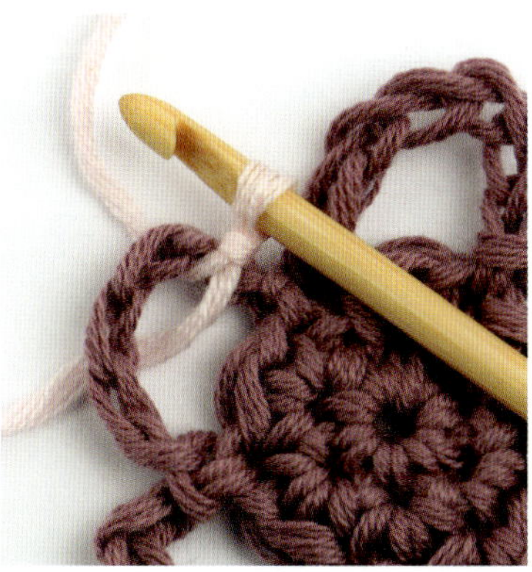

7 Attach Colour B to the first loop of any of the ch-6 loops in Round 3. Ch 1. **Rnd 4:** Work 10 dc evenly along the first ch-6 loop.

8 Continue crocheting 10 dc into each ch-6 loop. Finish the round with a sl st into the first dc of the round. Fasten off Colour B.

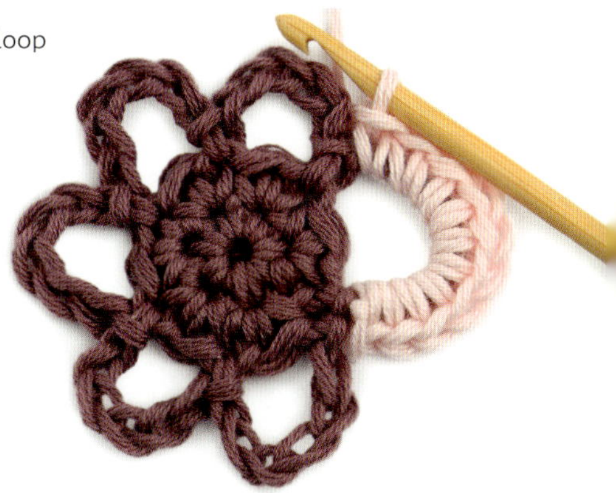

3 Crocus

Skill level:

Using just two simple techniques, you can make a three-dimensional crocus flower. Use contrasting colours for the two parts of the flower and vary them to make different flowers for all your decoration needs.

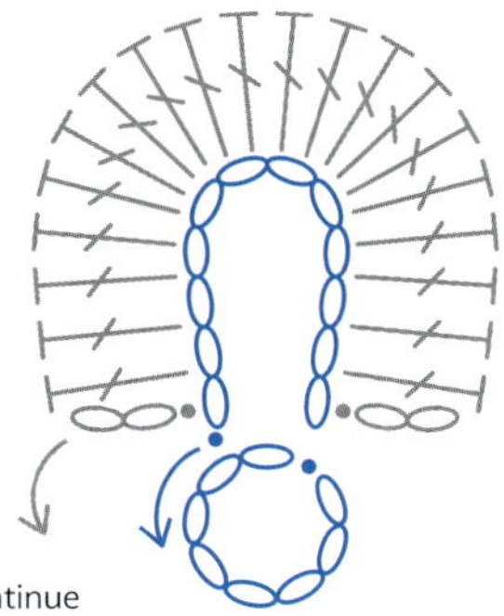

Materials:

5-ply yarn in 2 colours:

- Colour A: 9 m (10 yds)
- Colour B: 1 m (1 yd)

Tools:

Hook size: 3.25 mm (D-3)
Yarn needle
Scissors

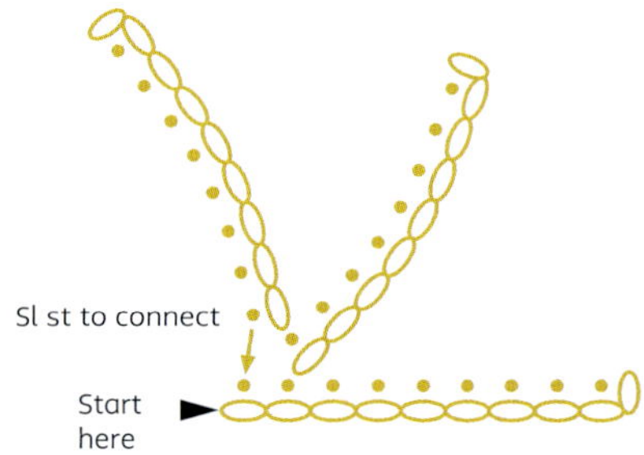

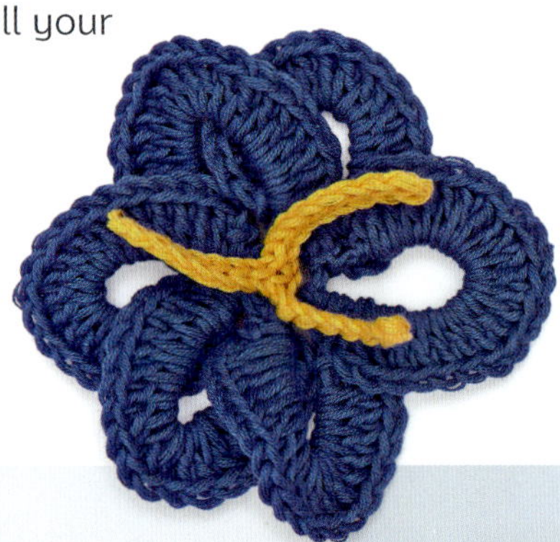

Pattern

Petals:
With Colour A, ch 8, sl st in first ch to make ring (**see Step 1**).

Rnd 1: [Ch 12, sl st in ring] six times (**see Step 2–3**).

Rnd 2: *[Sl st, ch 2, 20 tr, ch 2, sl st] in ch-12 loop].

Rep from * five more times (**see Steps 4–6**).

Fasten off Colour A. Weave in ends.

Stamens:
With Colour B, ch 10, starting from 2nd ch from hook, sl st in next 8 ch (**see Step 7**).

[Ch 9, starting from 2nd ch from hook, sl st in next 8 ch] twice (**see Step 8**).

Finish with sl st in first ch of stamen. Leave long end to sew flower together. Sew stamens to centre of petals. Weave in short end.

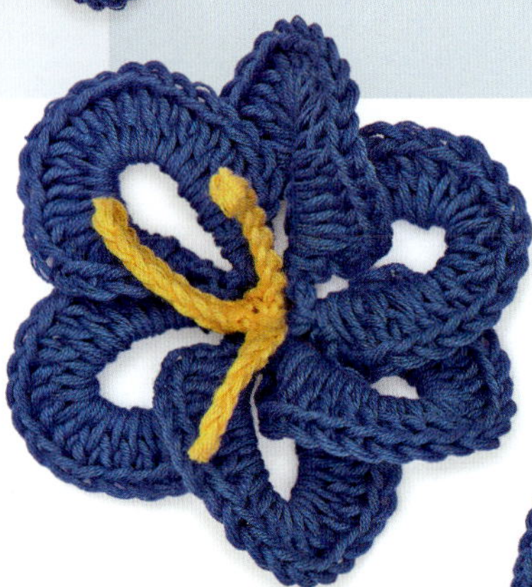

Chart key:

- Ch Chain
- Sl st Slip stitch
- Tr Treble

Diam. of finished flower: 10 cm (4 in)

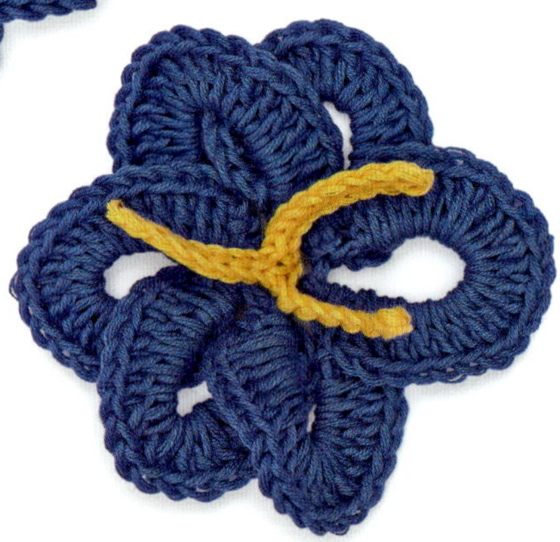

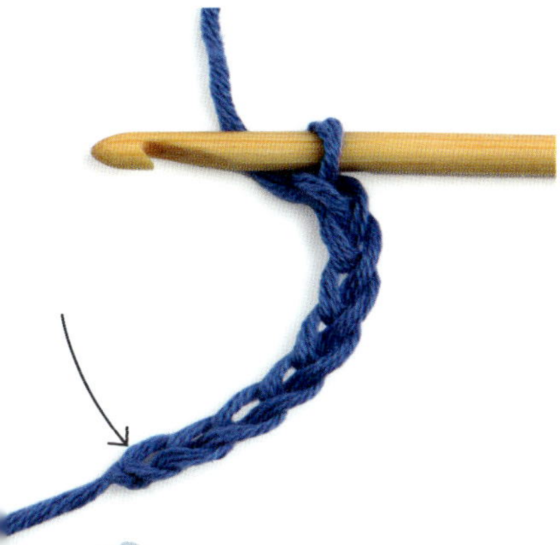

1 With Colour A, ch 8, then sl st into the first ch (follow the arrow) to make a ring.

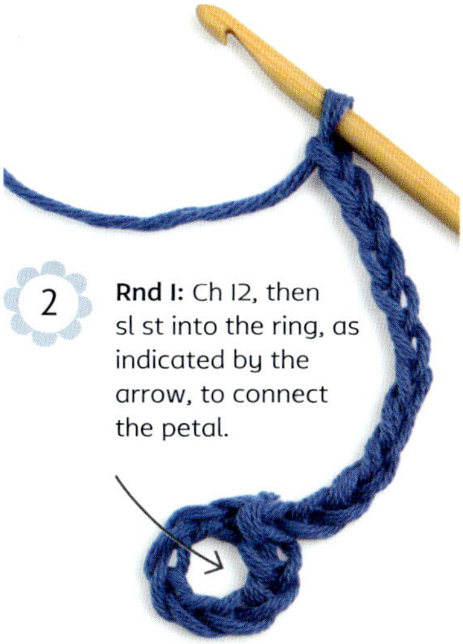

2 **Rnd 1:** Ch 12, then sl st into the ring, as indicated by the arrow, to connect the petal.

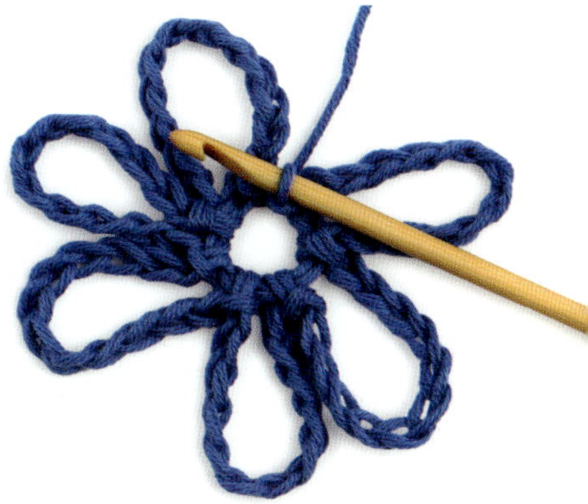

3 [Ch 12, sl st into the ring] five more times. You will now have six petals altogether.

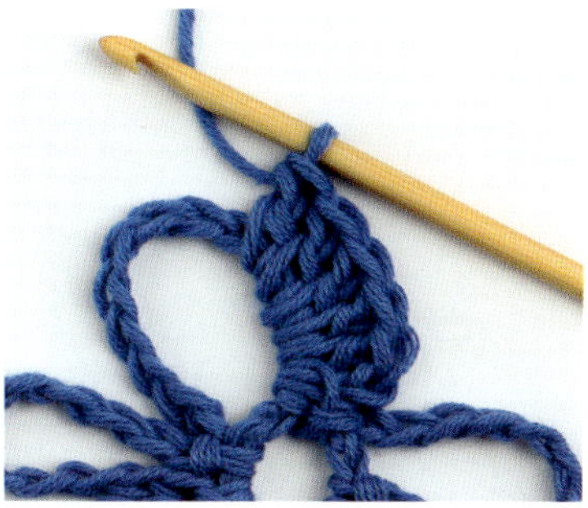

4 **Rnd 2:** Work a sl st into the beginning of any ch-12 loop petal. Ch 2, 20 tr into the loop.

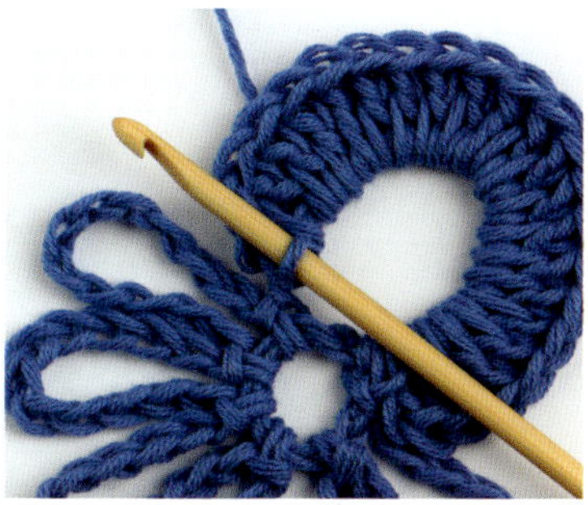

5 Make sure your stitches are equally distributed around the loop. Ch 2, then sl st into the same loop.

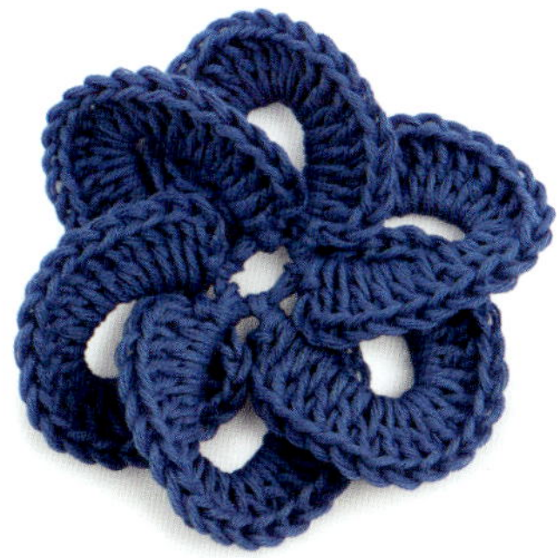

6 Into the next ch-12 loop, sl st, ch 2, 20 tr, ch 2, sl st. Repeat this for each petal. Fasten off Colour A and weave in the ends.

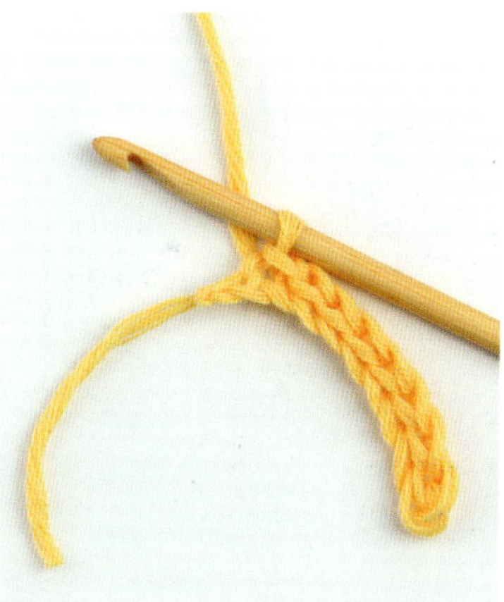

7 With Colour B, ch 10, then, starting from the 2nd ch from the hook, sl st into the next 8 ch.

8 [Ch 9, starting from the 2nd ch from the hook, sl st into the next 8 ch] twice more. Finish by making a sl st into the first ch of the stamens (indicated by the arrow). Leave a long end and use this to sew the stamens to the petals. Weave in the short end.

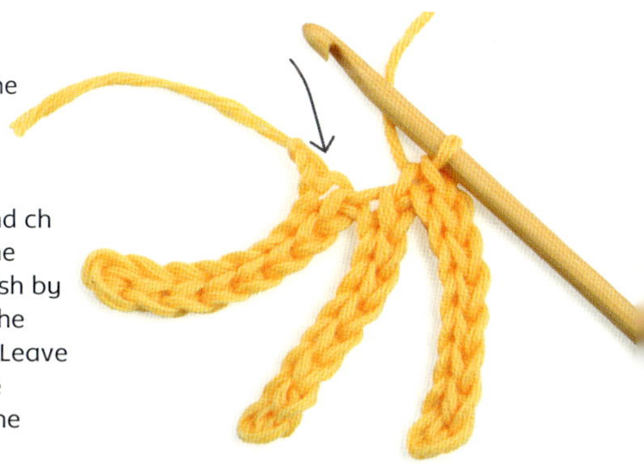

4 Hawkesbury River Daisy

Skill level:

Using only double crochet and chain stitches, you will be able to create this beautiful daisy flower with loopy petals. Practising this flower is a great way to learn a simple technique for attaching a second colour to your work.

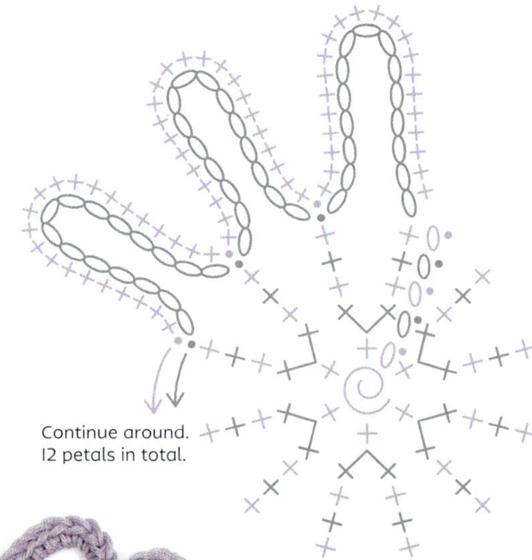

Materials:

5-ply yarn in 2 colours:

Colour A: 2.75 m (3 yds)

Colour B: 16.5 m (18 yds)

Tools:

Hook size: 3.25 mm (D-3)
Yarn needle
Scissors

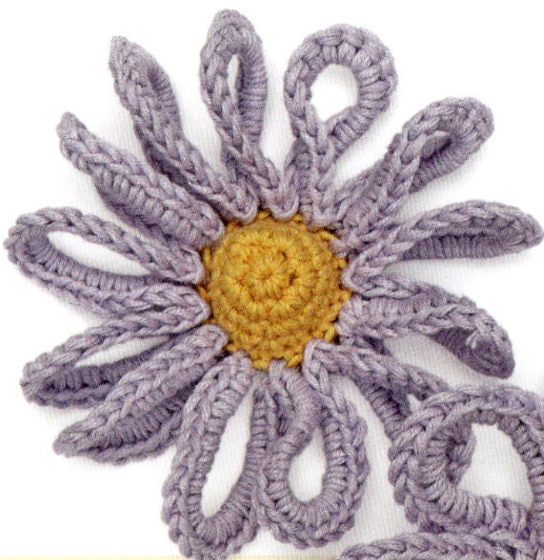

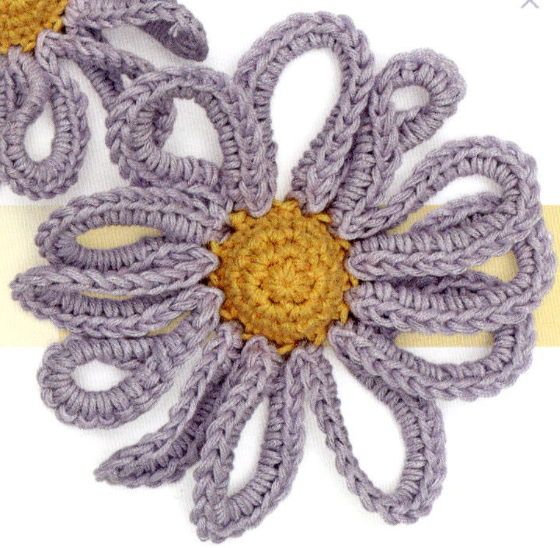

Pattern

With Colour A, make a magic ring (see page 12).

Rnd 1: Into magic ring, ch 1, 6 dc. Pull on short end to close middle. Join rnd with sl st. (6 dc) (**see Step 1**).

Rnd 2: Ch 1, 2 dc in each dc. Join rnd with sl st. (12 dc) (**see Step 2**).

Rnds 3–5: Ch 1, dc in each dc. Join rnd with sl st. (**see Step 3**).

Fasten off Colour A.
Attach Colour B (**see Steps 4–5**).

Rnd 6: [Ch 15, sl st in next dc of Rnd 5] 12 times (**see Steps 6–7**).

Rnd 7: [22 dc in ch-15 loop, sl st in sl st between petals] 12 times (**see Step 8**).

Fasten off Colour B. Weave in ends.

Chart key:

- Magic ring
- Ch Chain
- \+ Dc Double crochet
- • Sl st Slip stitch

Diam. of finished flower: 11.5 cm (4½ in)

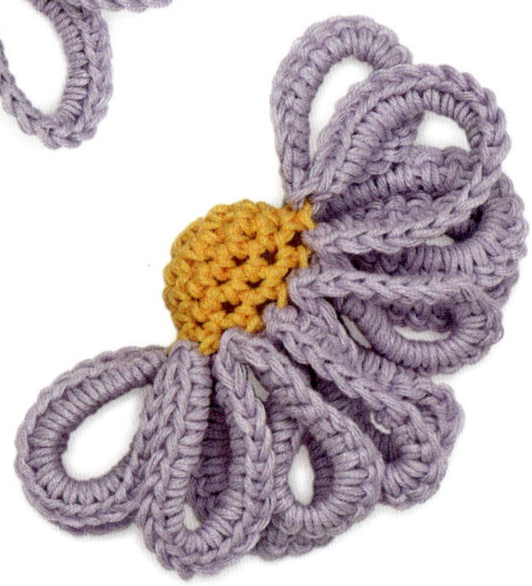

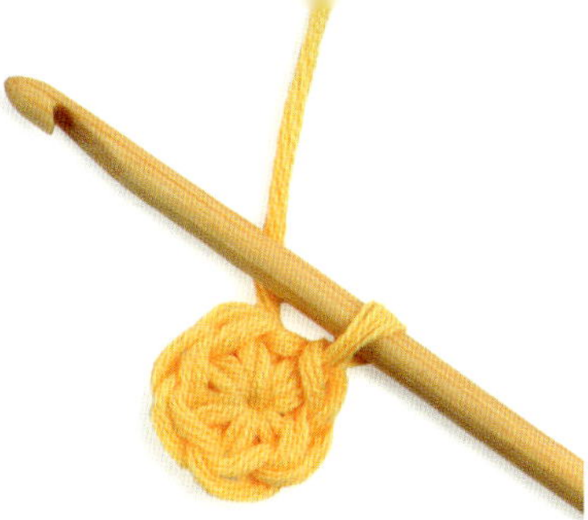

1 With Colour A: **Rnd 1:** Into a magic ring (see page 12), ch 1, then work 6 dc. Pull on the short end to close the middle. Join the round with a sl st into the first ch.

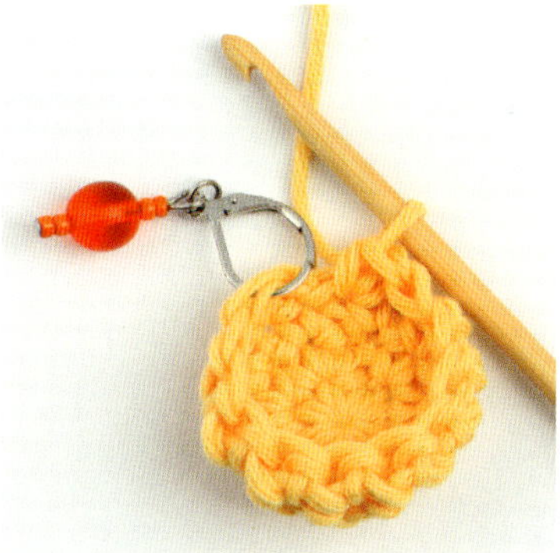

2 **Rnd 2:** Ch 1, work 2 dc into each dc. Join the round with a sl st. You may find it useful to use a stitch marker to indicate the beginning of each round. Just attach a marker to the first stitch of the round, and move it outwards to the beginning of the next round each time you reach it.

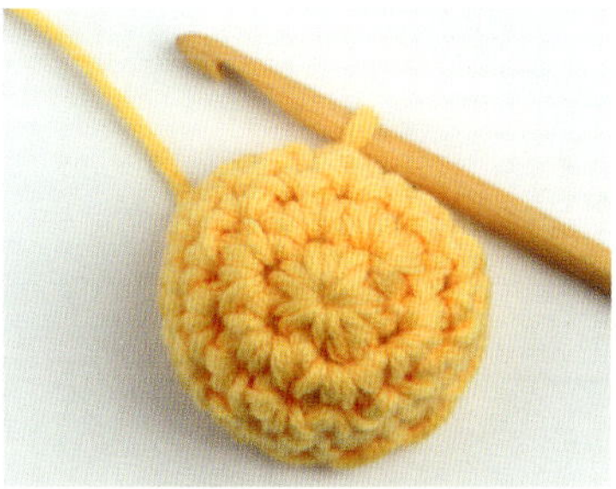

3 **Rnds 3–5:** Ch 1, dc into each dc. Join the round with a sl st. At the end of Round 5, fasten off Colour A.

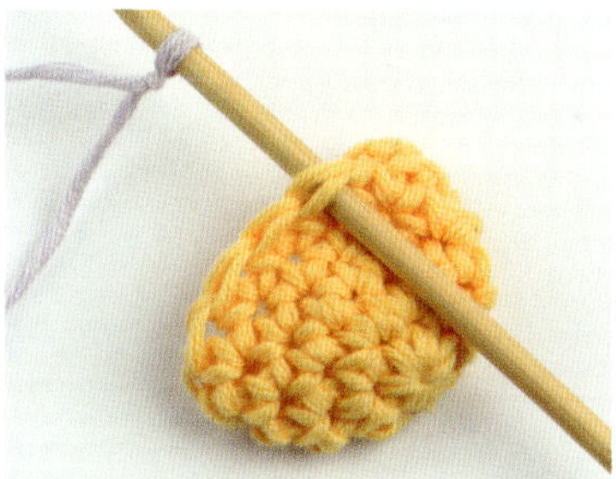

4 Attach Colour B, following these steps: insert your hook into the loops of a stitch on the previous round. Make a slip knot on the hook with the Colour B yarn.

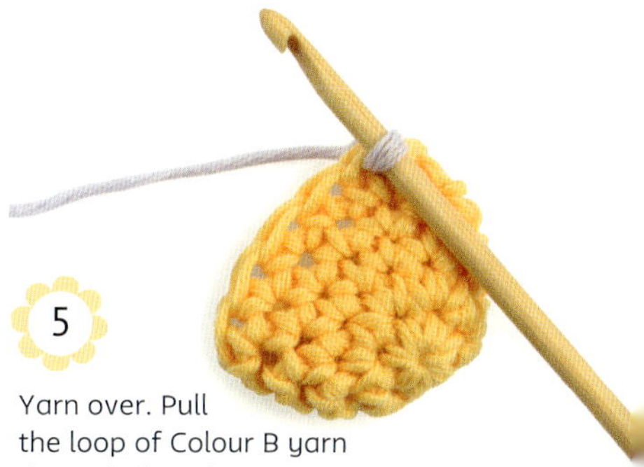

5 Yarn over. Pull the loop of Colour B yarn through the other two loops on the hook. Colour B is now attached and you can continue as normal.

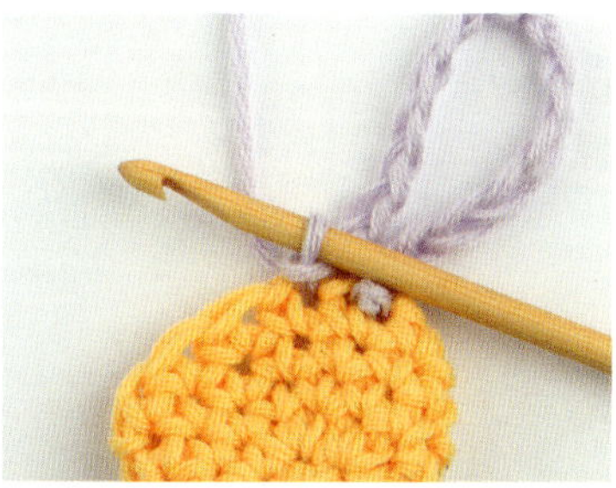

6 **Rnd 6:** Ch 15, sl st into the next dc of Round 5 to connect the petal.

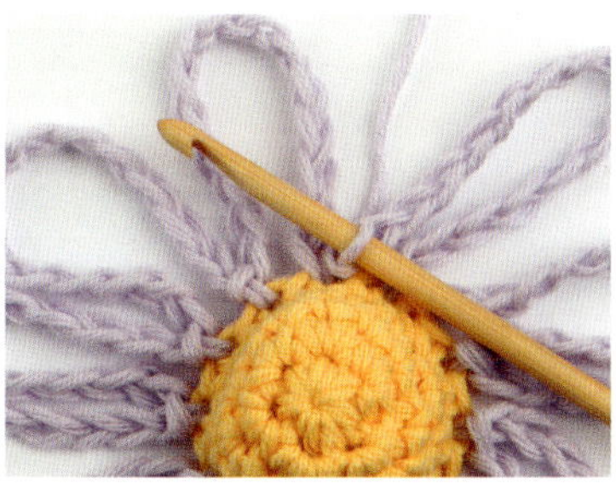

7 Repeat Step 6 11 more times to create 12 petals.

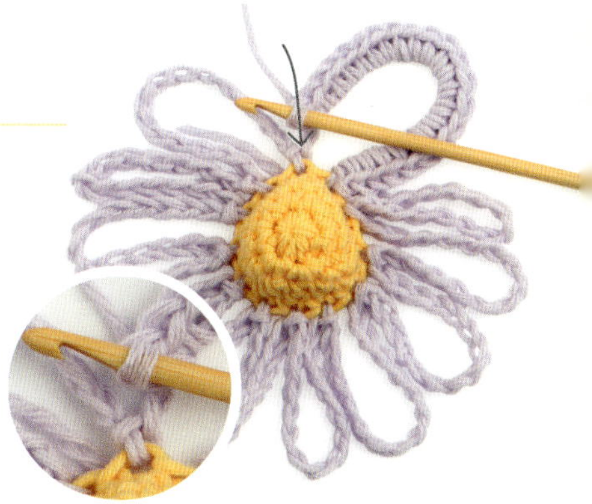

8 **Rnd 7:** [Work 22 dc evenly into the ch-15 loop, sl st into the sl st between the petals – marked here with an arrow] 12 times. Fasten off Colour B and weave in ends to finish.

5 Marigold

Skill level:

This flower pattern combines a few of the techniques that you have already learnt to create a beautiful layered marigold flower. You will also learn how to create a lovely contrasting border.

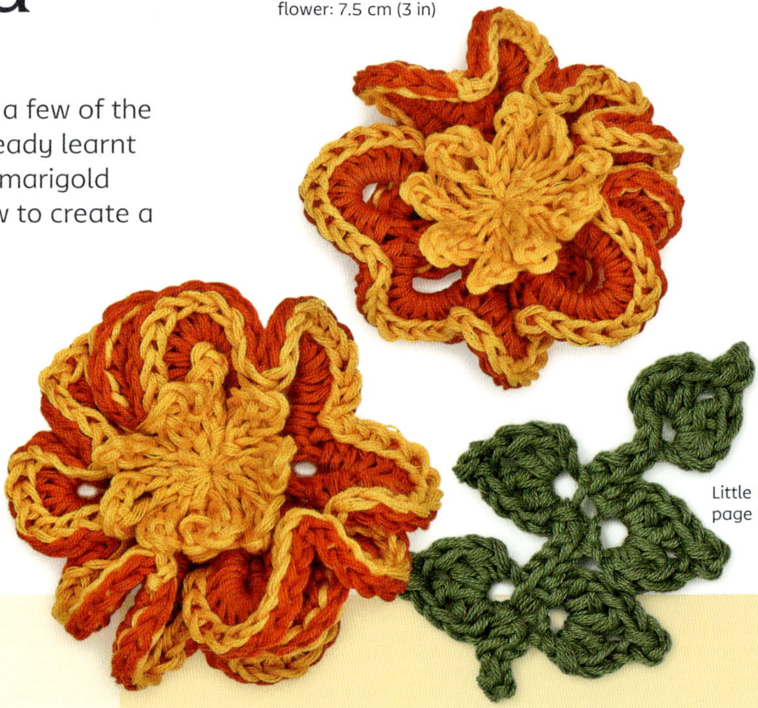

Diam. of finished flower: 7.5 cm (3 in)

Little Leaves, page 97

Tools:

Hook size: 3.25 mm (D-3)
Yarn needle
Scissors

Materials:

5-ply yarn in 2 colours:

Colour A: 3.75 m (4 yds)

Colour B: 9 m (10 yds)

Pattern

Small petals:

With Colour A, make a magic ring (see page 12).

[Ch 8, sl st in magic ring] 10 times (**see Step 1**).

Fasten off Colour A.

Large petals:

With Colour B, make a magic ring.

Rnd 1: Into magic ring, ch 1, 6 dc. Pull on short end to close middle. Join rnd with sl st. (6 dc)

Rnd 2: Ch 1, 2 dc in each dc. Join rnd with sl st (**see Step 2**). (12 dc)

Rnd 3: [Ch 6, sl st in next dc] 12 times (**see Step 3**).

Rnd 4: [11 htr in ch-6 loop] 12 times. Join rnd with sl st in first htr (**see Step 4**).

Fasten off Colour B (**see Step 5**).

Attach Colour A (**see Step 6**).

Sl st in each htr (**see Step 7**).

Fasten off Colour A. Sew flower together and weave in ends (**see Step 8**).

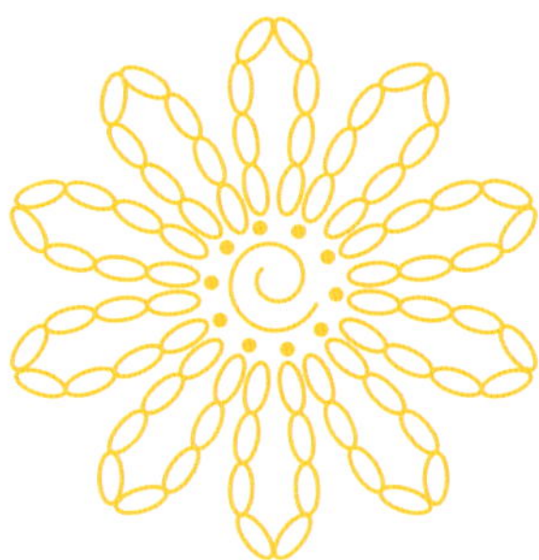

Small petals

Chart key:

- Magic ring
- Ch Chain
- Sl st Slip stitch
- DC Double crochet
- Htr Half treble crochet

Large petals

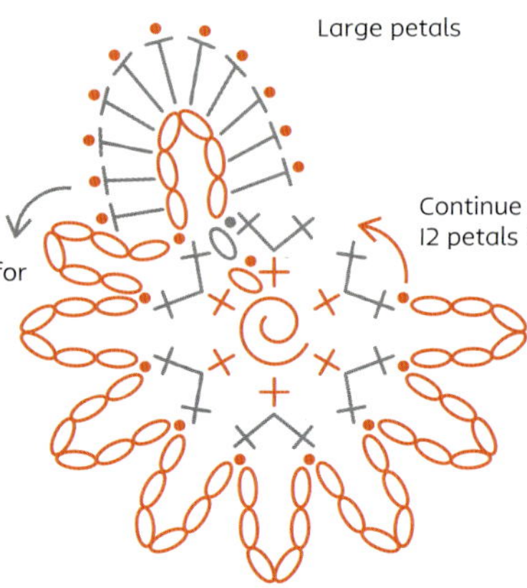

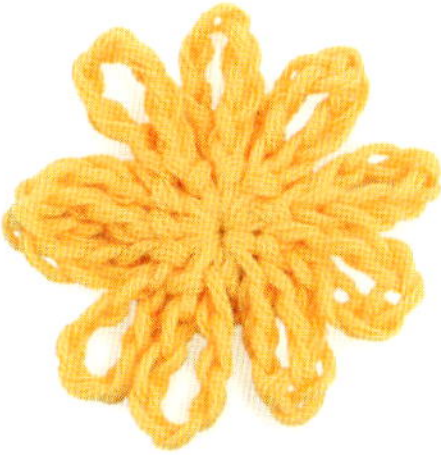

1 **Small petals:** With Colour A, [ch 8, sl st into a magic ring] 10 times. Tighten the magic ring by pulling on the short end, and fasten off Colour A, leaving a long end for sewing the flower together.

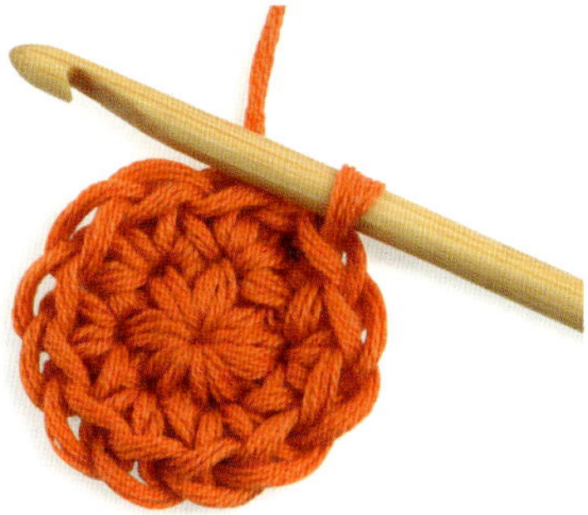

2 **Large petals:** With Colour B, make a magic ring (see page 12). Follow the pattern for Rounds 1 and 2. At the end of Round 2, your flower will look like this.

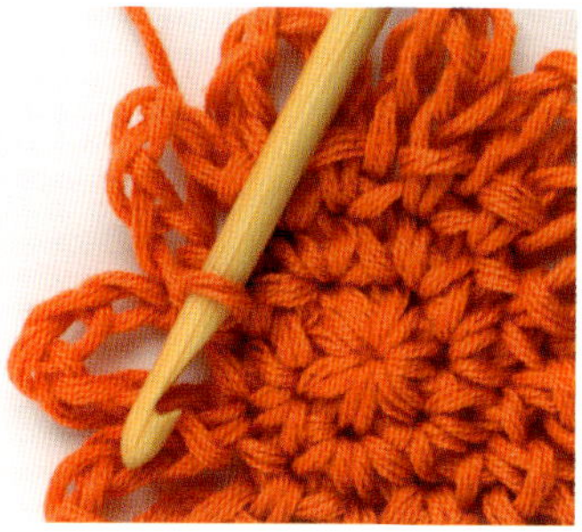

3 **Rnd 3:** [Ch 6, sl st into the next dc] 12 times to create 12 petals.

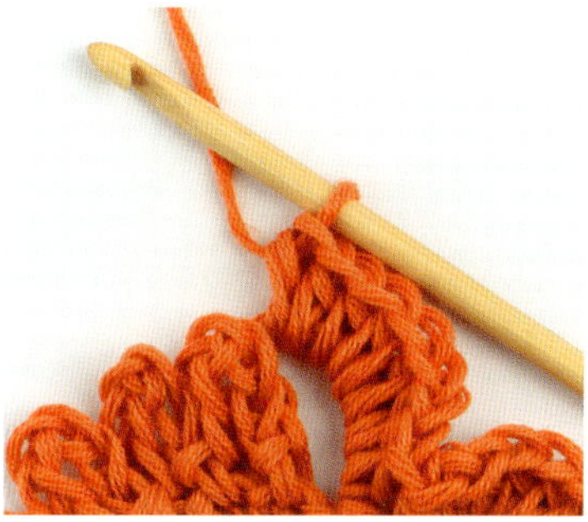

4 **Rnd 4:** [11 htr into the ch-6 loop] 12 times. Join the round with a sl st into the first htr of the round.

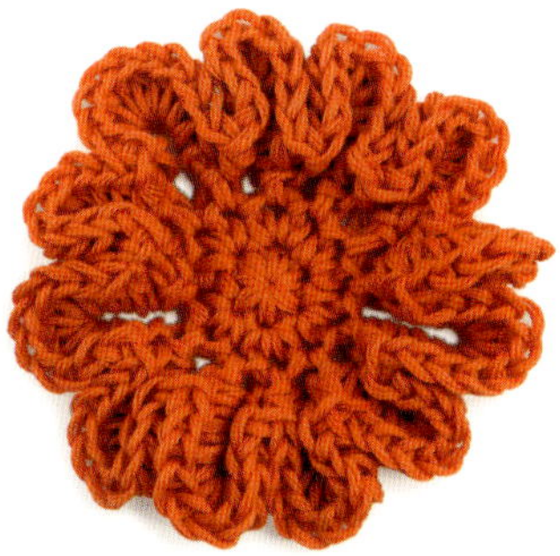

5 Fasten off Colour B. Your large petals will now look like this.

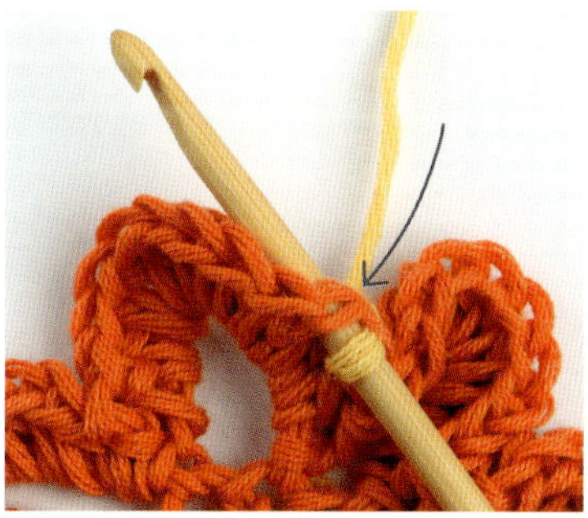

6 Attach Colour A to the last round of stitches (see page 27, Steps 4–5).

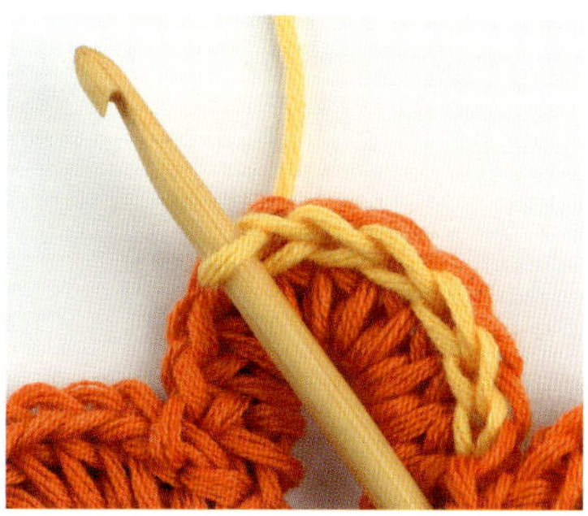

7 Make a sl st in every htr all the way around the previous round. Fasten off Colour A.

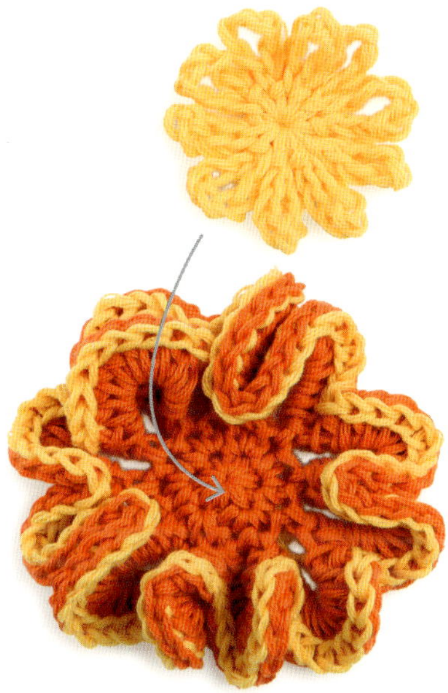

8 Using the long thread you left in Step 1, connect both parts of the flower together with a yarn needle, as shown. Weave in all ends.

6 Forget-Me-Not

Skill level:

These delicate crochet flowers are perfect to decorate girls' dresses and accessories. You may find making a stem intimidating at first, but just follow the step-by-step instructions and you will see the shape unfold perfectly.

Materials:

5-ply yarn in 3 colours:

- Colour A: 1 m (1 yd) per flower
- Colour B: 3.75 m (4 yds)
- Colour C: 23 cm (¼ yd) per flower

Tools:

Hook size: 3.25 mm (D-3)
Yarn needle
Scissors

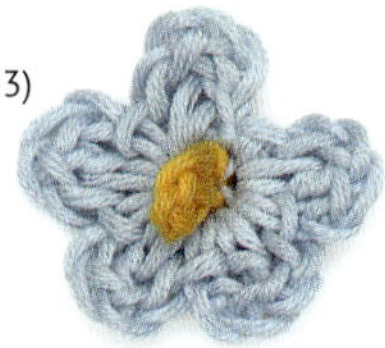

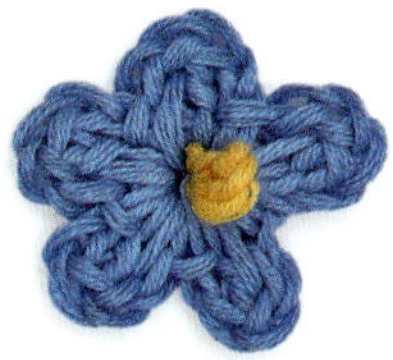

Diam. of finished flower: 2.5 cm (1 in)

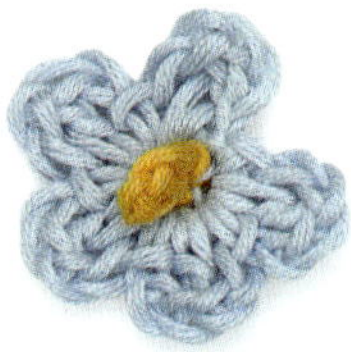

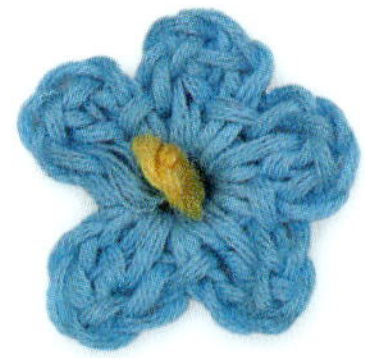

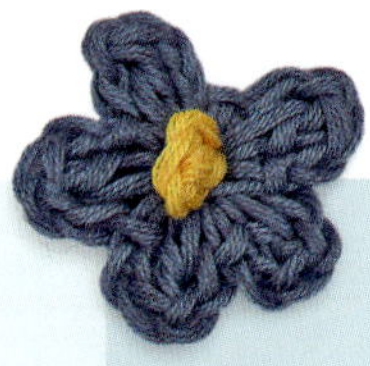

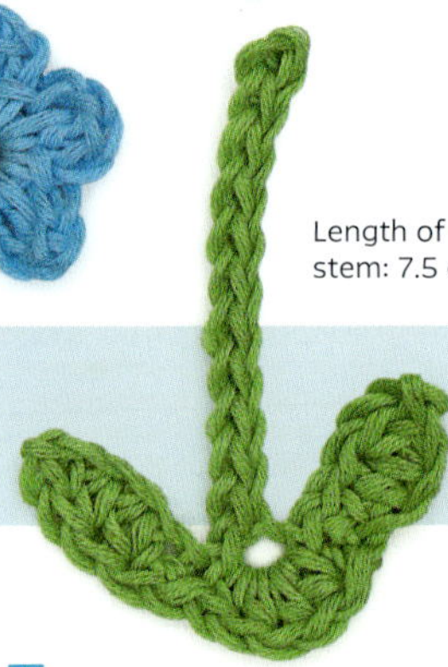

Length of finished stem: 7.5 cm (3 in)

Pattern

Stem:

With Colour B, ch 6, dc in 2nd ch from hook, htr in next 2 ch, dc in next ch, sl st in next ch (**see Step 1**).

Ch 13, starting from 2nd ch from hook, sl st in next 12 ch (**see Steps 2–3**).

Ch 6, dc in 2nd ch from hook, htr in next 2 ch, dc in next ch, sl st in next ch (**see Step 4**).

4 htr in stem between two leaves.

Sl st in first ch of pattern (**see Step 5**).

Fasten off. Weave in ends.

Flower (**see Step 7**):

With Colour A, ch 5, sl st in first ch to make ring.

Rnd 1: [Ch 2, tr in ring, ch 2, sl st in ring] five times.

Fasten off, weave in ends.

Pollen:

With Colour C, ch 4. Join rnd with sl st. Fasten off, leaving long ends (**see Step 8**).

Sew pollen, flower and stem together.

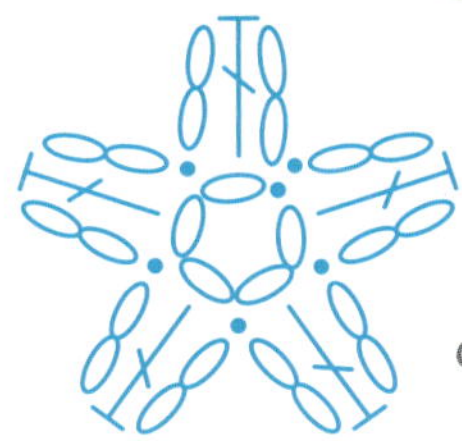

Chart key:

- + Ch Chain
- + DC Double crochet
- Htr Half treble crochet
- • Sl st Slip stitch
- Tr Treble crochet

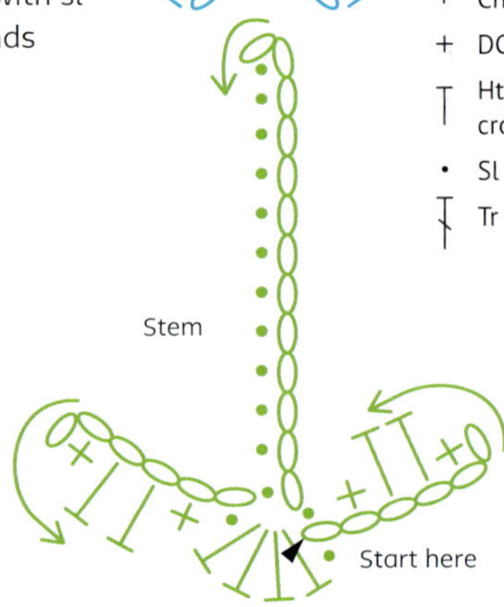

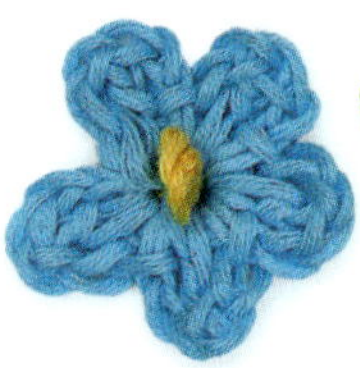

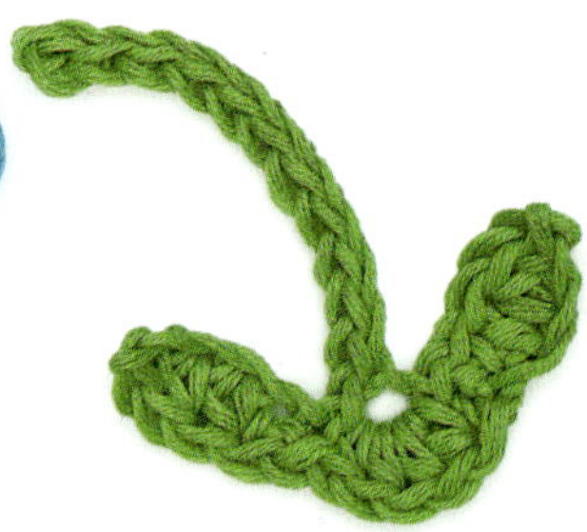

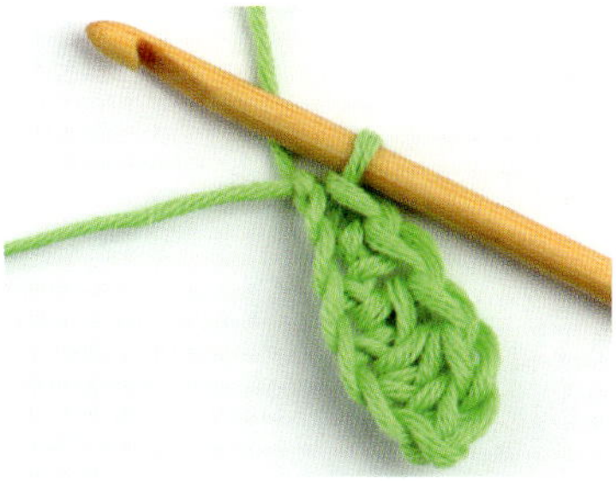

1 **To make the stem:** To form the first leaf, ch 6 and then, starting from the 2nd ch from the hook, dc into the next ch, htr into the next 2 ch, dc into the next ch, sl st into the next ch.

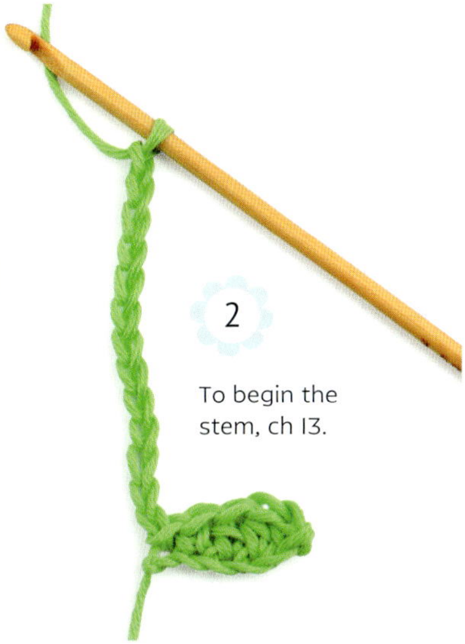

2 To begin the stem, ch 13.

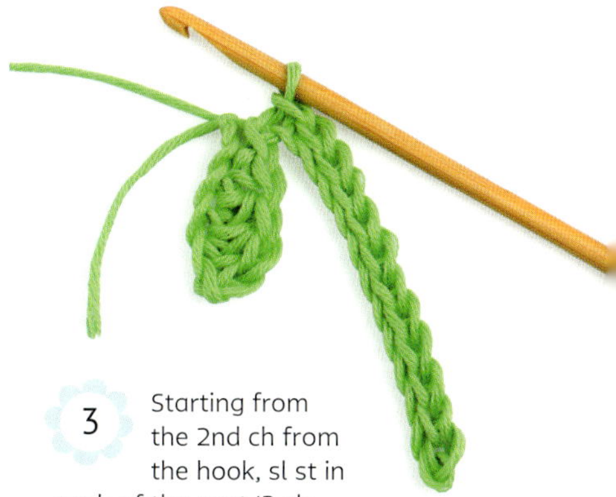

3 Starting from the 2nd ch from the hook, sl st in each of the next 12 ch.

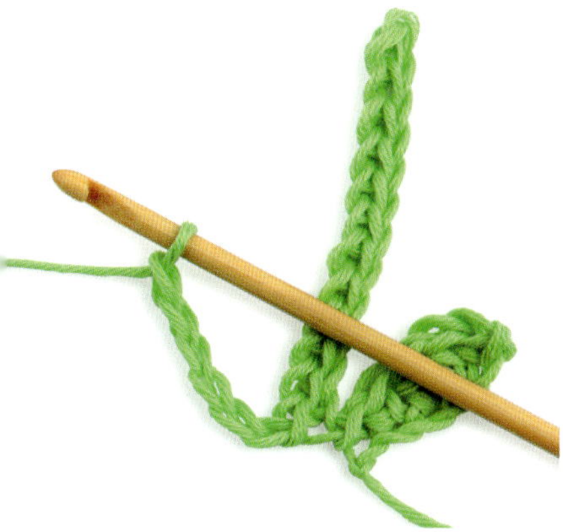

4 Ch 6 and then, starting from the 2nd ch from the hook, dc, htr into the next 2 ch, dc into the next ch, sl st into the next ch.

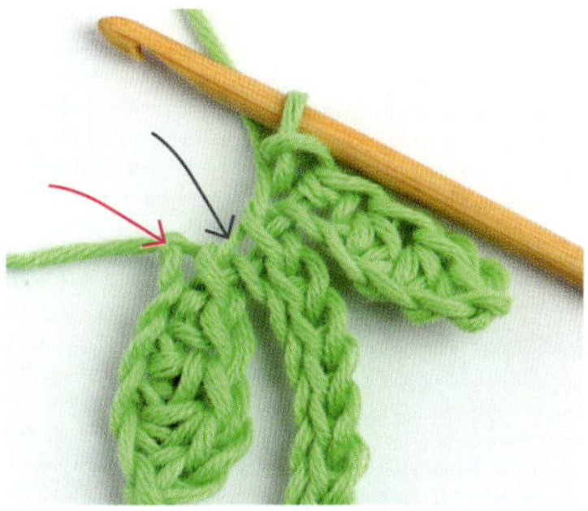

5 Work 4 htr into the stem between the two leaves (see the black arrow above). Sl st into the first ch of the pattern (indicated by the red arrow).

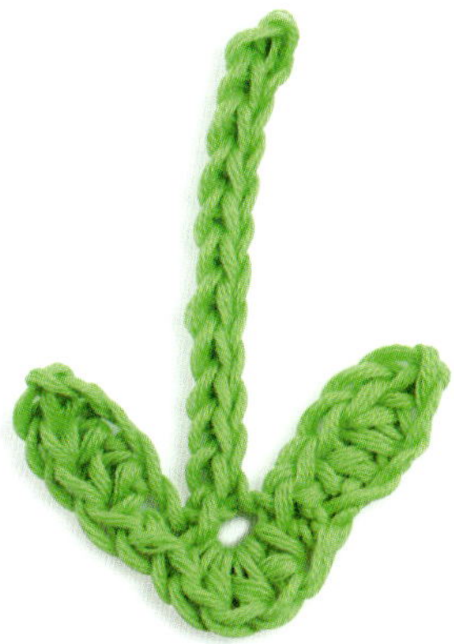

6 The stem and leaves are now complete. Fasten off and weave in ends.

7 **To make the flower:** Ch 5 and join into a ring with a sl st.
Rnd 1: [Ch 2, tr into the ring, ch 2, sl st into the ring] five times. You will have created five petals. Fasten off and weave in ends.

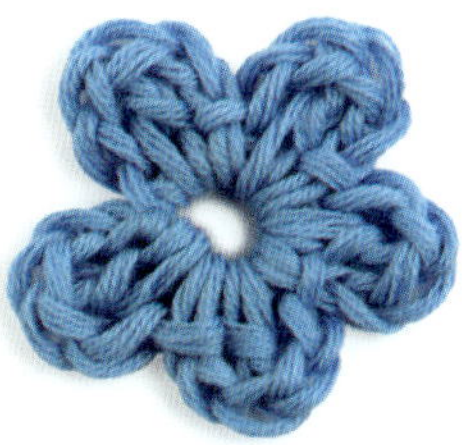

8 **To make the pollen:** Ch 4 and join into a round with a sl st. Fasten off, leaving long ends of yarn. Using a yarn needle and the long ends you left, sew the pollen part to the flower and the stem. You could also make simple flower heads without the stems.

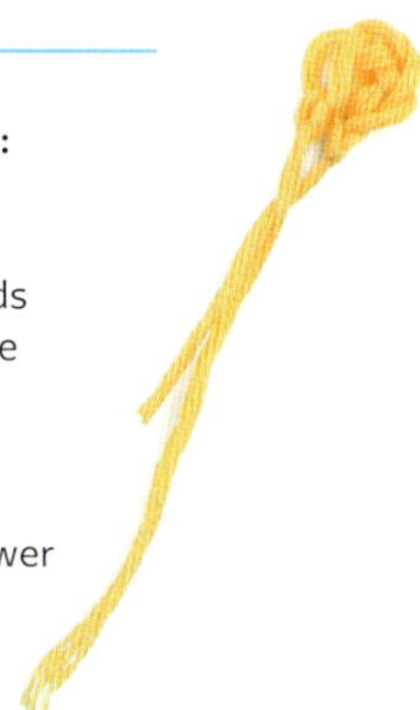

7 Hawaiian Plumeria

Skill level:

This is the perfect pattern to teach you how to create various shapes by crocheting around a long chain. In this case, the result is a beautiful Hawaiian flower which will inspire the feeling of an exotic holiday.

Tools:

Hook size: 3.25 mm (D-3)
Yarn needle
Scissors

Materials:

5-ply yarn in 2 colours:

Colour A: 9 m (10 yds)

Colour B: 7.75 m (8½ yds)

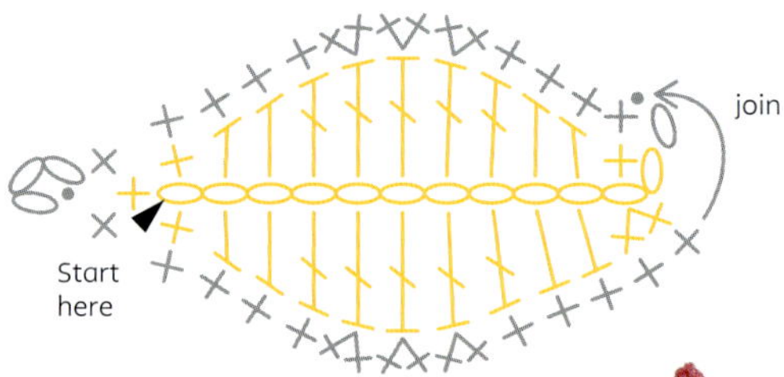

Chart key:

- Ch Chain
- Dc Double crochet
- Htr Half treble crochet
- Tr Treble crochet
- Sl st Slip stitch
- 3 ch picot (ch 3, sl st in 3rd ch from hook)

Pattern

With Colour A:

Rnd 1: Ch 12, dc in 2nd ch from hook, htr in next 2 ch, tr in next 5 ch, htr in next 2 ch, 3 dc in next ch (corner) (**see Steps 1–2**).

Continue on the other side of chain:

Htr in next 2 ch, tr in next 5 ch, htr in next 2 ch, 2 dc in next ch.
Fasten off Colour A (**see Step 3**).

Attach Colour B to first dc of Colour A (**see Step 4**).

Rnd 2: Ch 1, dc in same dc, dc in next 3 sts, 2 dc in next 3 tr, dc in next 5 sts, 3 ch picot, dc in same dc as last dc, dc in next 4 sts, 2 dc in next 3 tr, dc in next 5 sts. Join to first dc of Rnd 2 with sl st. Fasten off (**see Steps 5–6**). One petal made.

Make five petals. Weave in all ends, leaving long yarn tail on one petal for sewing. Sew all parts together at base of petals, making sure the picot is on the outside (**see Steps 7–8**).

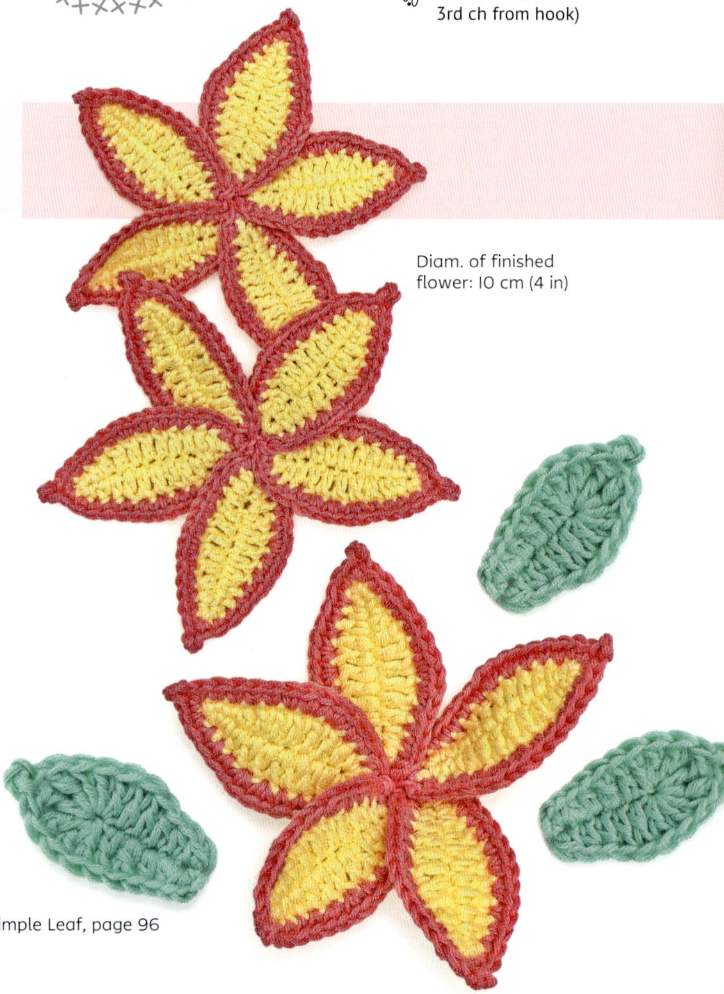

Diam. of finished flower: 10 cm (4 in)

Simple Leaf, page 96

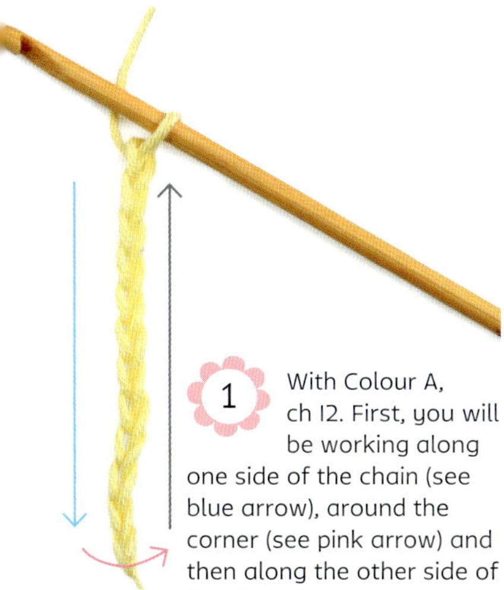

1 With Colour A, ch 12. First, you will be working along one side of the chain (see blue arrow), around the corner (see pink arrow) and then along the other side of the chain (see grey arrow).

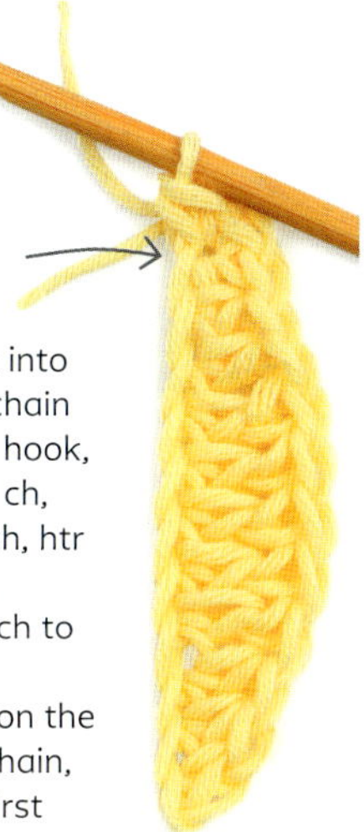

2 **Rnd 1:** Dc into the 2nd chain from the hook, htr into the next 2 ch, tr into the next 5 ch, htr into the next 2 ch, 3 dc into the next ch to form the corner. Continue working on the other side of the chain, starting with the first chain, marked by an arrow.

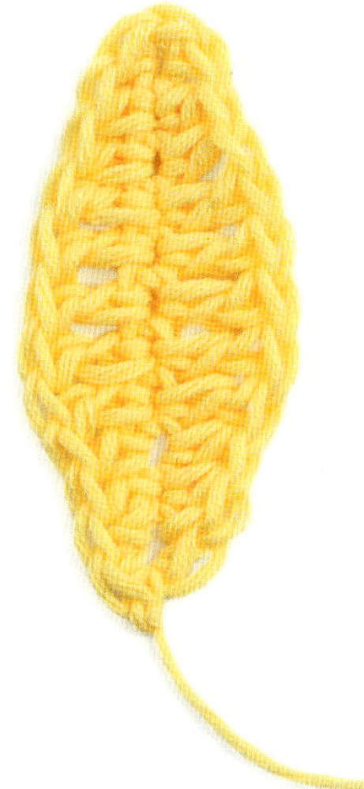

3 Htr into the next 2 ch, tr into the next 5 ch, htr into the next 2 ch, 2 dc into the next ch. Fasten off Colour A.

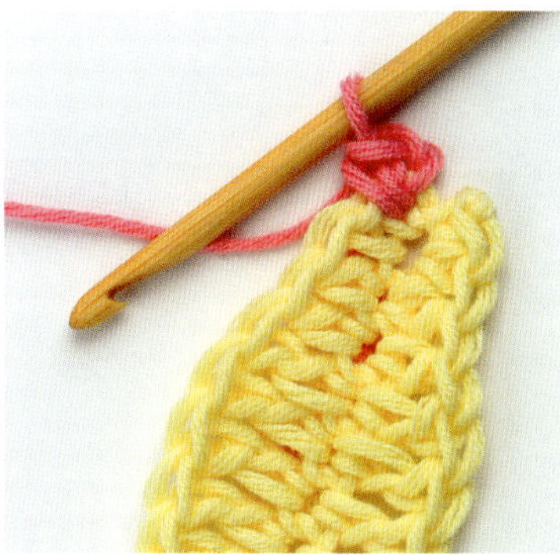

4 Attach Colour B to the first dc of Round 1 (see page 27, Steps 4–5). **Rnd 2:** Ch 1 then dc into the same dc.

5 Dc into the next 3 sts, 2 dc into the next 3 tr, dc into the next 5 sts, make a 3 ch picot as follows: ch 3, sl st into the 3rd ch from the hook (as marked by the arrow).

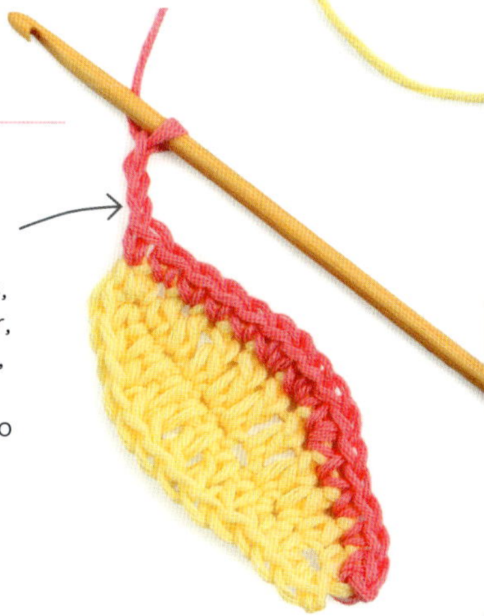

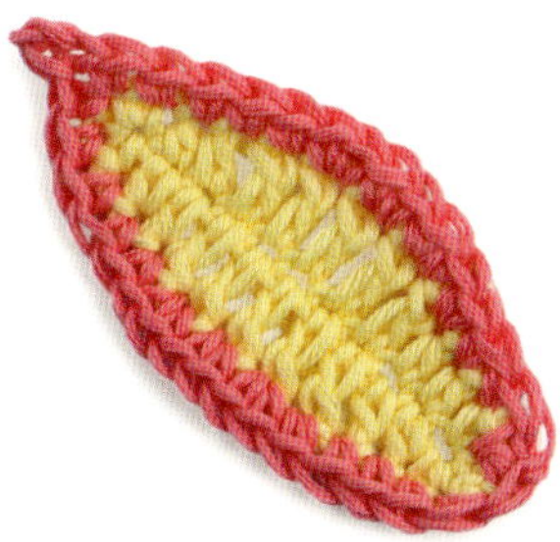

6 Dc into the same dc as the last dc, dc in the next 4 sts, 2 dc into the next 3 tr, dc into the next 5 sts. Join to the first dc worked in Colour A with a sl st. Fasten off Colour B.

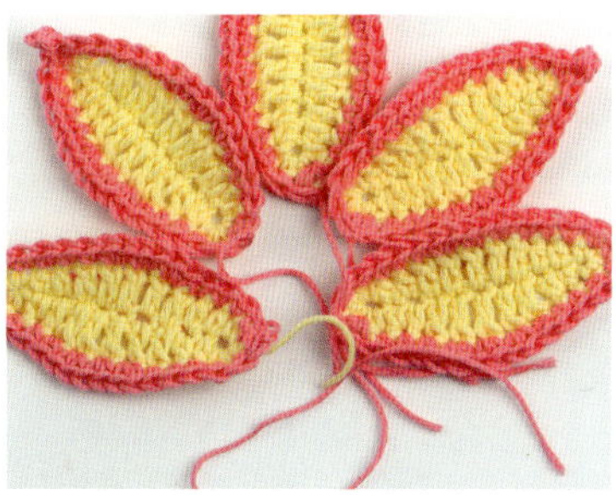

7 Make five petals by following the pattern on the left. Weave in the ends but leave a long yarn tail on one of the petals for joining the petals.

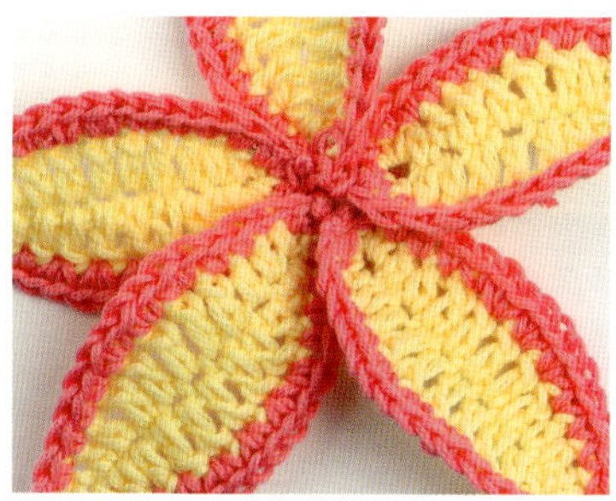

8 Gather the bases of the five petals together and sew them together using the long yarn tail and the yarn needle. Make sure that the picot corners of the petals are facing outwards for the best look.

8 Clematis

Skill level:

This is a gorgeous little flower, and simple to make, so why not make a bouquet? You will learn a new stitch in this pattern: the double treble crochet, and will use a different variation of the picot that you learnt in the Hawaiian Plumeria pattern on pages 32–33.

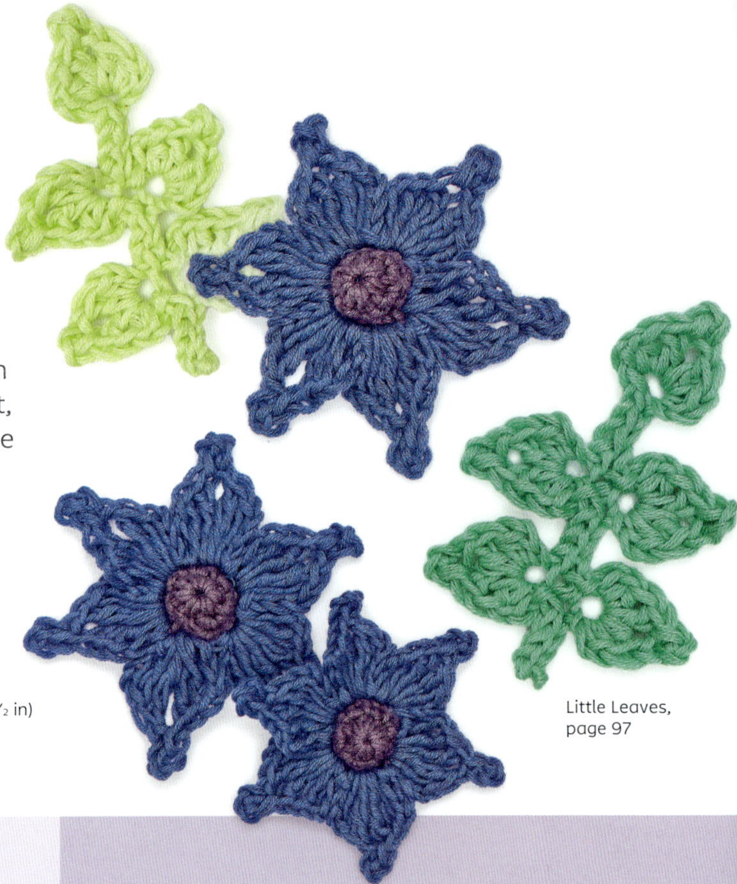

Diam. of finished flower: 6.5 cm (2½ in)

Little Leaves, page 97

Pattern

With Colour A, make a magic ring (see page 12).

Rnd 1: Into magic ring, ch 1, 6 dc. Pull on short end to close middle. Join rnd with sl st. (6 dc)

Rnds 2–3: Ch 1, dc in each dc. Join rnd with sl st.

Fasten off Colour A.

Attach Colour B.

Rnd 4: *[Sl st, ch 3, tr, dtr, 4 ch picot, dtr, tr, ch 3, sl st] in first dc (**see Steps 2–4** for instructions on the double treble crochet, and **Steps 5–6** to learn the 4 ch picot).

Rep from * five more times (**see Step 7**).

Fasten off. Weave in ends.

Continue around. 6 petals in total.

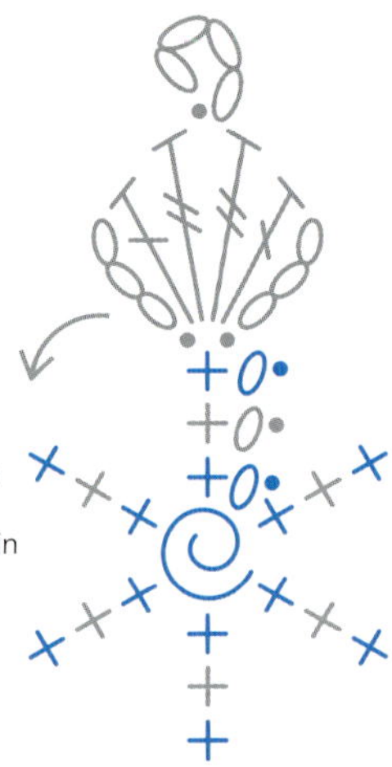

Materials:

5-ply yarn in 2 colours:

Colour A: 1.4 m (1.5 yds)

Colour B: 4.5 m (5 yds)

Tools:

Hook size: 3.5 mm (E-4)
Yarn needle
Scissors

Chart key:

Magic ring
Ch Chain
Dc Double crochet
Sl st Slip stitch
Tr Treble crochet
Dtr Double treble crochet
4 ch picot (ch 4, sl st in 4th ch from hook)

1 After completing the centre of the flower, fasten off Colour A and attach Colour B (see page 27, Steps 4–5). Sl st, ch 3, tr into the first dc.

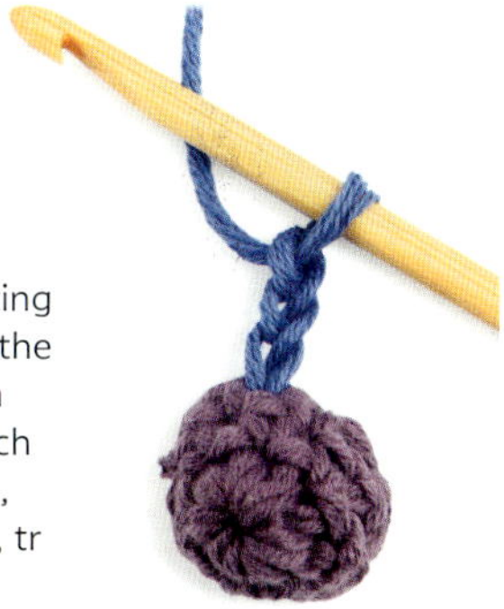

2 Making a double treble crochet stitch is similar to making a treble crochet stitch. First, wrap the yarn around the hook twice.

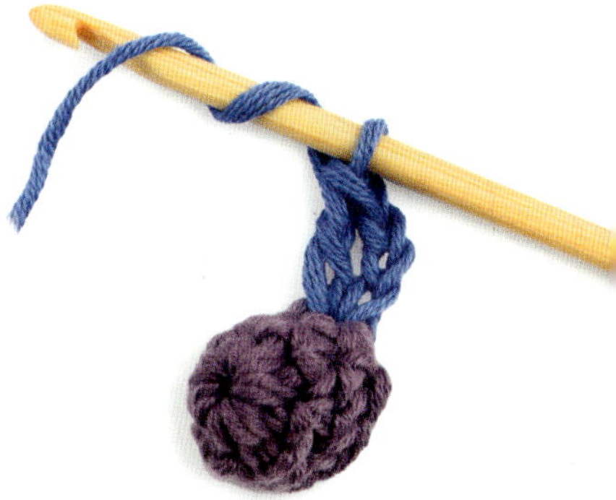

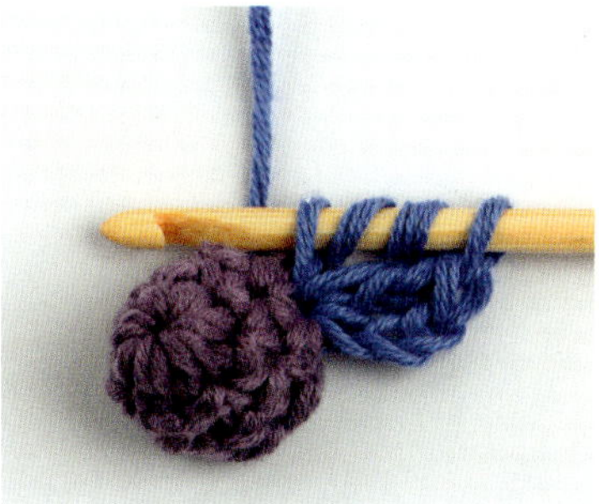

3 Insert the hook into the foundation stitch and pull out a loop. Now you have four loops on the hook. Now work: [yarn over, pull loop through two loops on hook] three times.

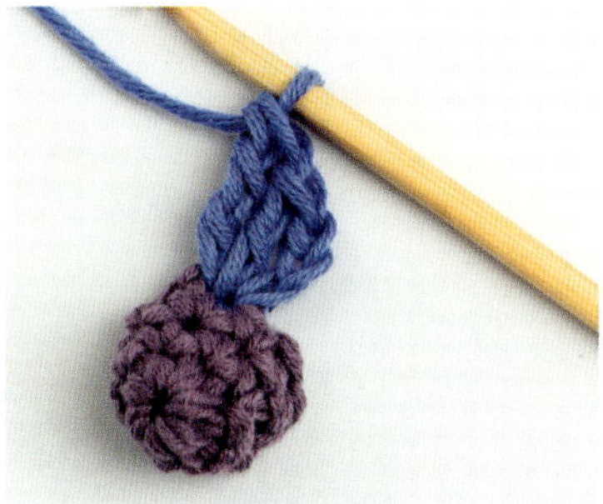

4 One double treble crochet stitch is completed.

5 To make a 4 ch picot: ch 4, then sl st into the 4th ch from the hook, as marked by the arrow.

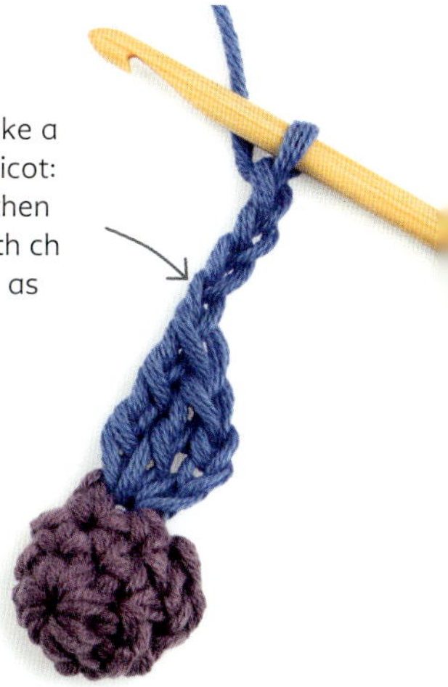

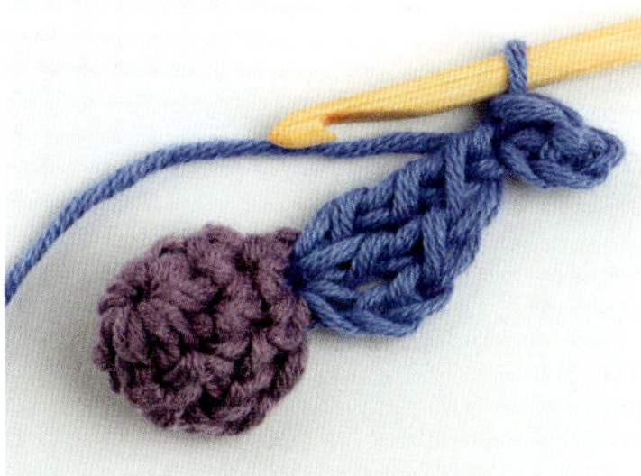

6 The 4 ch picot stitch is complete.

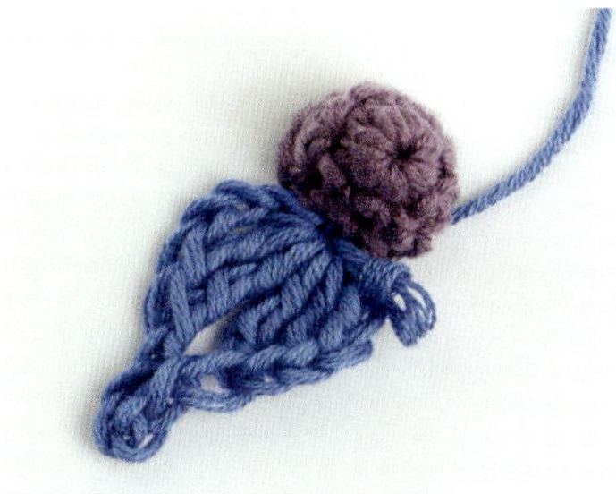

7 [Dtr, tr, ch, sl st] into the same dc to complete the petal. Each petal is made into one dc of Round 3.

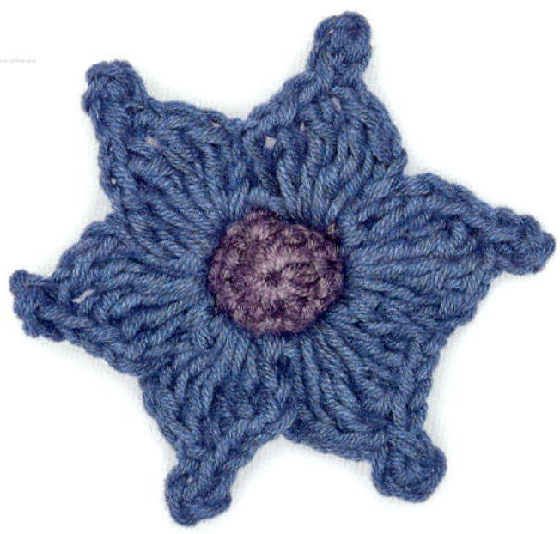

8 When you have a finished flower with six petals, fasten off Colour B and weave in all ends. Make sure that the middle of the flower is pointing outwards.

9 Begonia

Skill level:

Here you'll learn another way to create a flower – by crocheting in rows. Using contrasting yarns, you will recreate the beautiful, delicate edging of a begonia.

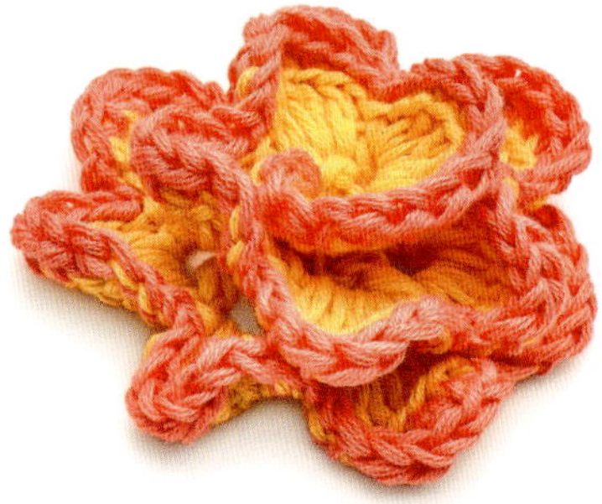

Materials:

4-ply weight yarn in 2 colours:

Colour A: 7.3 m (8 yds)

Colour B: 2.75 m (3 yds)

Tools:

Hook size: 3.25 mm (D-3)
Yarn needle
Scissors

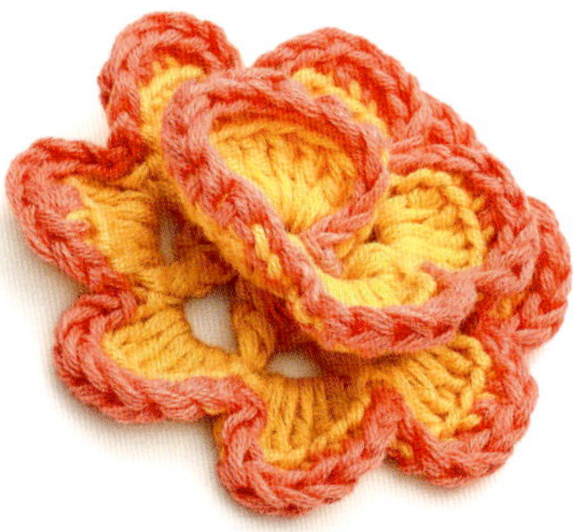

Diam. of finished flower: 6.5 cm (2½ in)

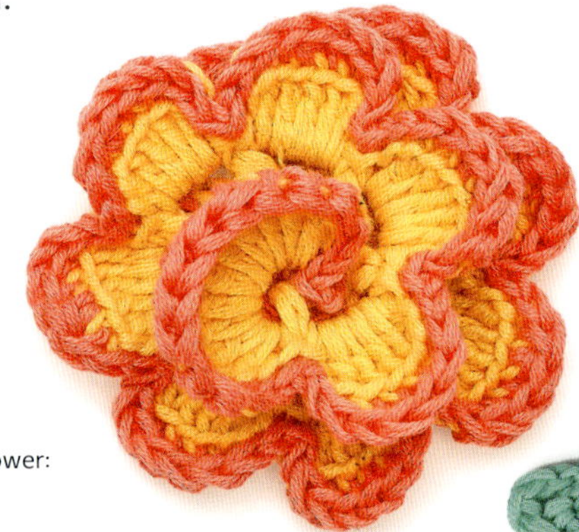

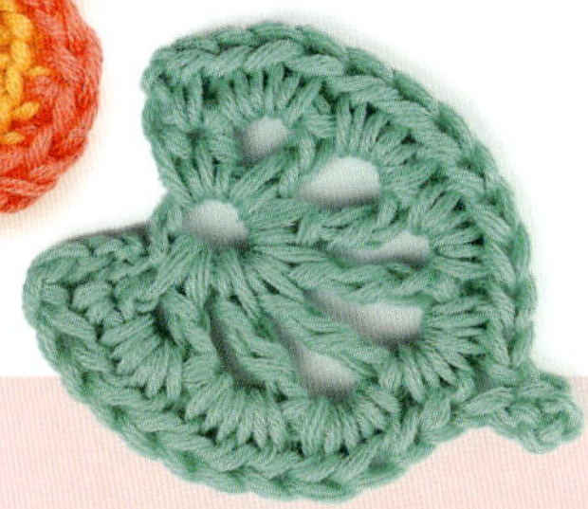

Lacy Leaf, page 97

Pattern

With Colour A, ch 40.

Row 1: Tr in 4th ch from hook, [ch 2, miss 2 ch, tr in next ch] 12 times to end of beg ch (**see Steps 1–2**).

Row 2: Ch 2, 10 tr in first ch loop, ch 2, sl st in same loop, [ch 2, 5 tr in next ch-2 loop, ch 2, sl st in same loop] in each of remaining ch-2 loops (**see Steps 3–4**).

Fasten off Colour A, leaving a 30.5-cm (12-in) tail for sewing.

Attach Colour B to beginning of Row 2 (**see Step 5**).

Row 3: Work into back loops only.

Ch 2, dc in next 3 tr, htr in next 4 tr, dc in next 3 tr, ch 2, sl st in sl st between petals (**see Step 6**).

*Ch 2, dc in next tr, htr in next 3 tr, dc in next tr, ch 2, sl st in sl st between petals (**see Step 7**).

Rep from * for each remaining petal. Last sl st will be in last sl st of Row 2.

Fold into flower shape with the large petal in the middle (**see Step 8**). Use long yarn end to sew flower together.

Fasten off and weave in ends.

Chart key:

- Ch Chain
- Tr Treble crochet
- Sl st Slip stitch
- Dc Double crochet
- Back loop
- Htr Half treble crochet

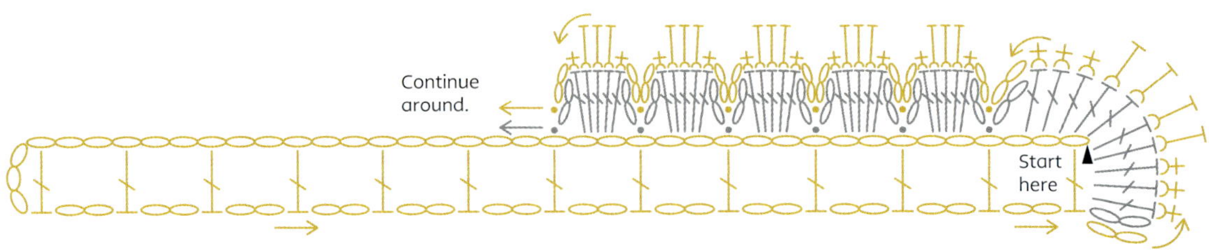

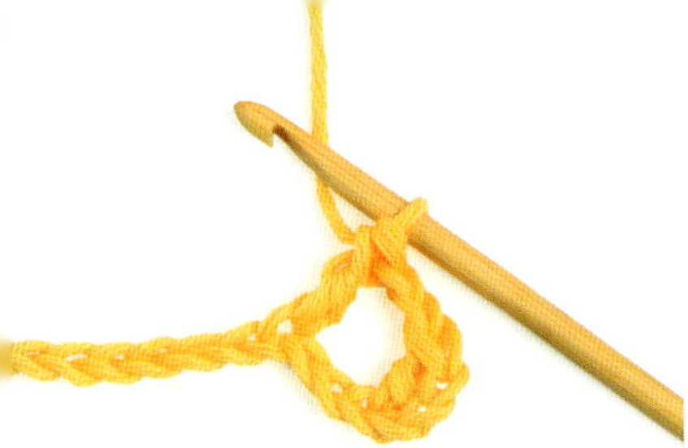

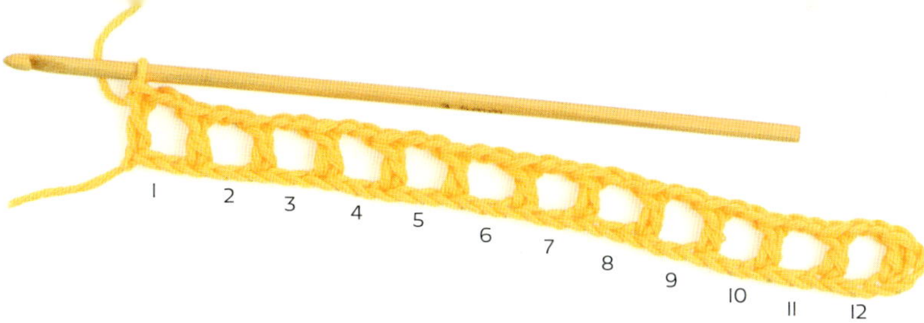

1 With Colour A, ch 40.
Row 1: Tr into the 4th ch from the hook.

2 [Ch 2, miss next 2 ch, tr into the next ch] 12 times until you reach the end of the beginning chain.

3 You will be crocheting into each of the spaces as marked above. Use this picture as a guide.

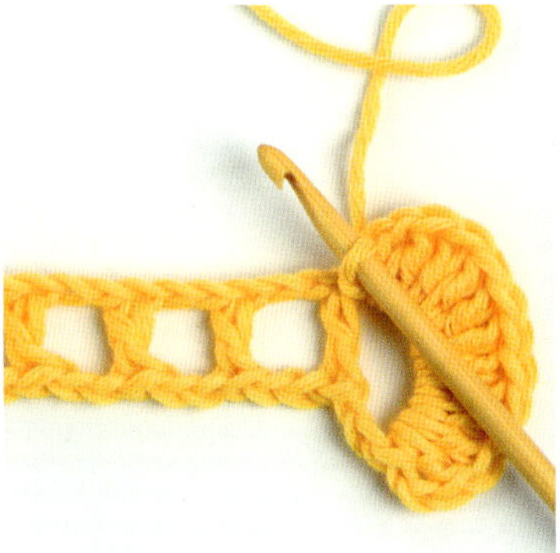

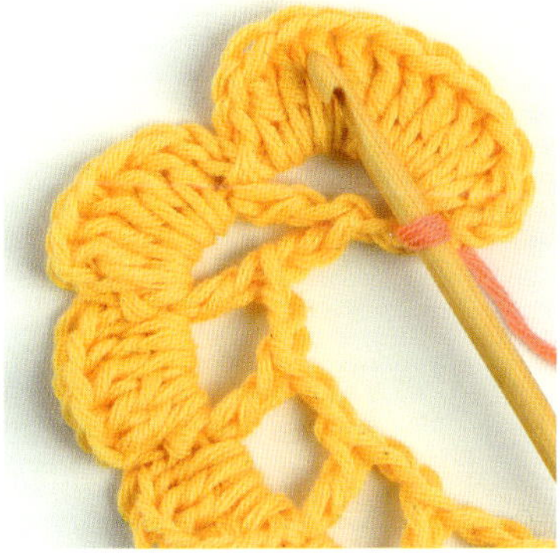

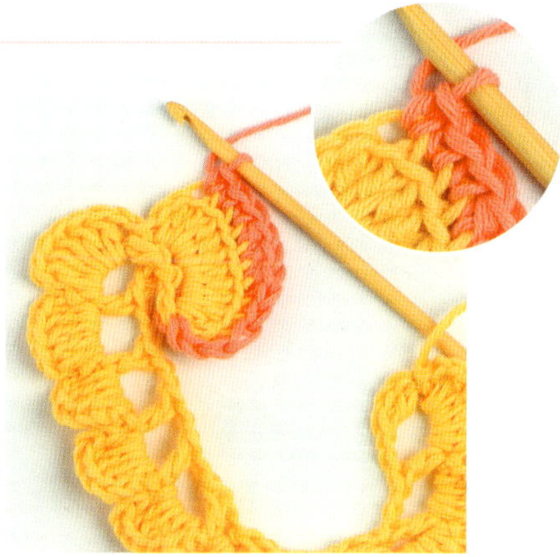

4 **Row 2:** Ch 2, 10 tr into the first ch loop, then ch 2, sl st into the same loop. Then work the rest of the row as follows: [ch 2, 5 tr into the next ch-2 loop, ch 2, sl st into the same loop] into each of the remaining ch-2 loops.

5 Fasten off Colour A, leaving a long tail of 30.5 cm (12 in) to sew the flower together. Attach Colour B to the beginning of Row 2.

6 **Row 3:** Working into the back loops only, ch 2, dc into the next 3 tr, htr into the next 4 tr, dc into the next 3 tr, ch 2, sl st into the sl st between the petals.

7 *Ch 2, dc into the next tr, htr into the next 3 tr, dc into the next tr, ch 2, sl st into the sl st between the petals. Repeat from * for each petal. The last sl st will be made into the last sl st of Row 2.

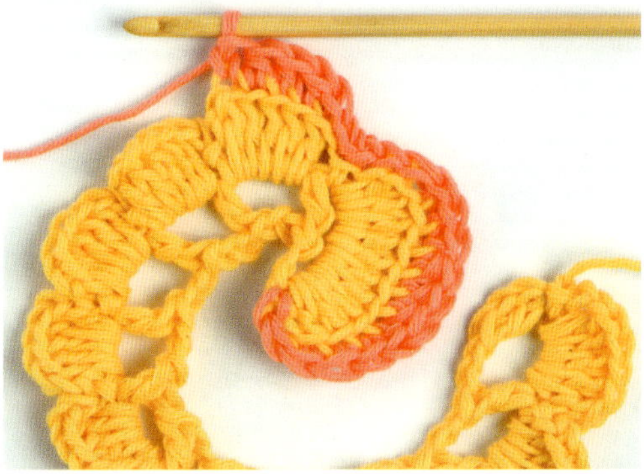

8 Fold into a flower shape as below, with the large petal in the centre. Use the long yarn end you left in Step 5 to sew the flower together. Fasten off and weave in all the ends.

10 Black-Eyed Susan

Skill level:

These flowers are made using techniques you will already be familiar with, adding just a few small new tricks. You can use this pattern to make simple daisies too; just change the colours to yellow and white.

Materials:

4-ply weight yarn in 2 colours:

Colour A: 1.8 m (2 yds)

Colour B: 9 m (10 yds)

Tools:

Hook size: 3.25 mm (D-3)
Yarn needle
Scissors

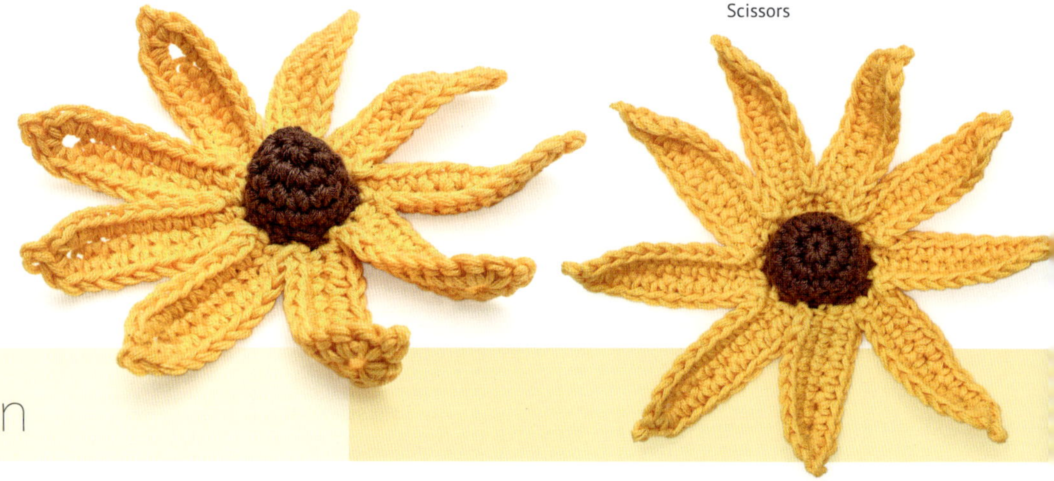

Pattern

With Colour A, make a magic ring (see page 12).

Rnd 1: Into magic ring, ch 1, 6 dc. Pull on short end to close middle. Join rnd with sl st. (6 dc)

Rnd 2: Ch 1, 2 dc in each dc. Join rnd with sl st. (12 dc)

Rnds 3–4: Ch 1, dc in each dc. Join rnd with sl st.

Rnd 5: Ch 1, [dc in next dc, dc2tog, dc in next dc] three times (**see Steps 1–4** to learn dc2tog). Join rnd with sl st. (9 sts)

Fasten off Colour A.

Attach Colour B.

Rnd 6: *Ch 12, starting from 5th ch from hook, dc in next 8 ch, sl st in next dc. Rep from * eight more times (**see Step 5**).

Rnd 7: *Dc in 8 ch, [2 dc, 3 ch picot, 2 dc] in ch-4 loop, dc in next 8 dc, sl st in sl st.

Rep from * eight more times, crocheting around each petal. Fasten off Colour B. Weave in ends (**see Steps 6–8**).

Diam. of finished flower: 12.5 cm (5 in)

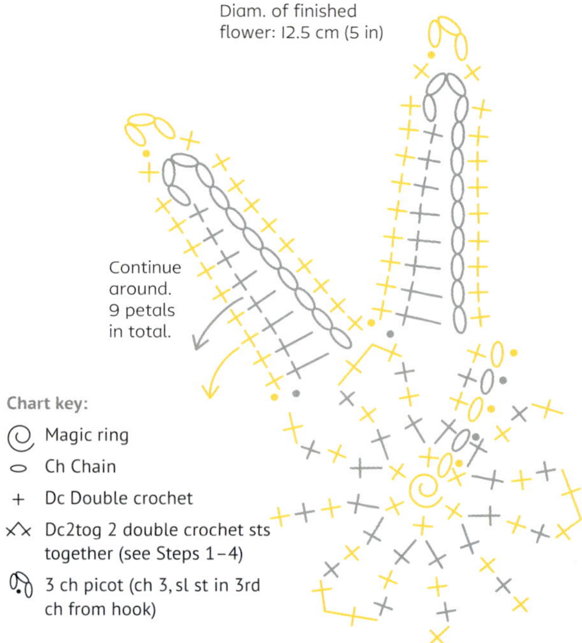

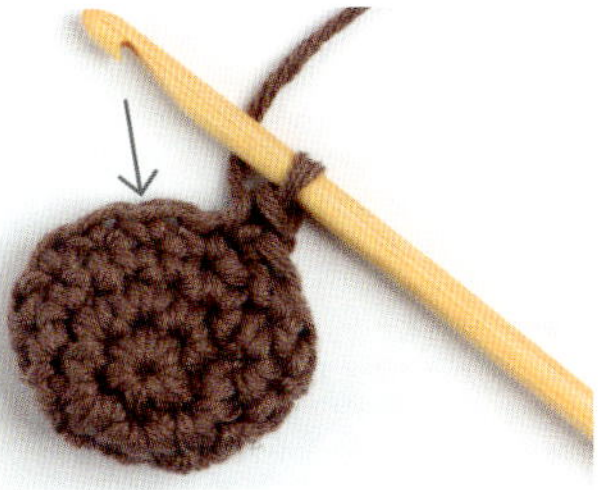

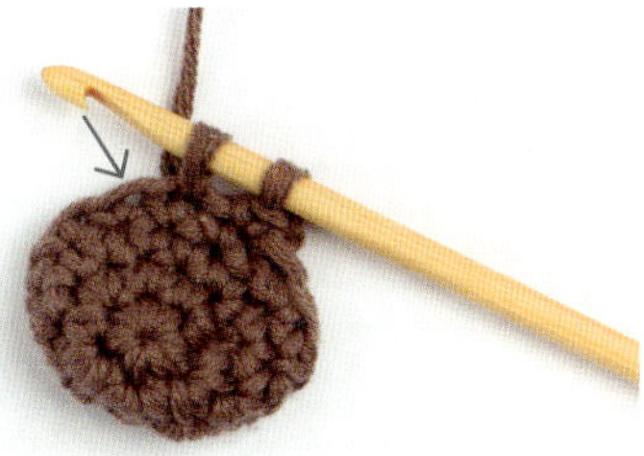

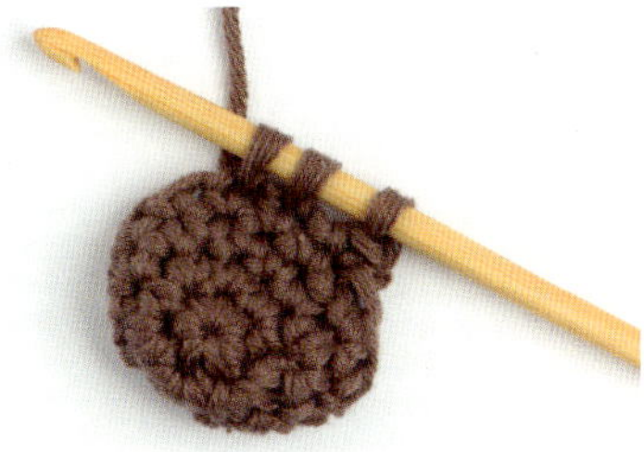

1 Follow the pattern for Rounds 1–5. To make a dc2tog: insert the hook into the next st (marked here with an arrow), yarn over and pull the yarn through.

2 With two loops on the hook, insert the hook into the next st (marked here with an arrow), yarn over and pull the yarn through again.

3 You will now have three loops on the hook.

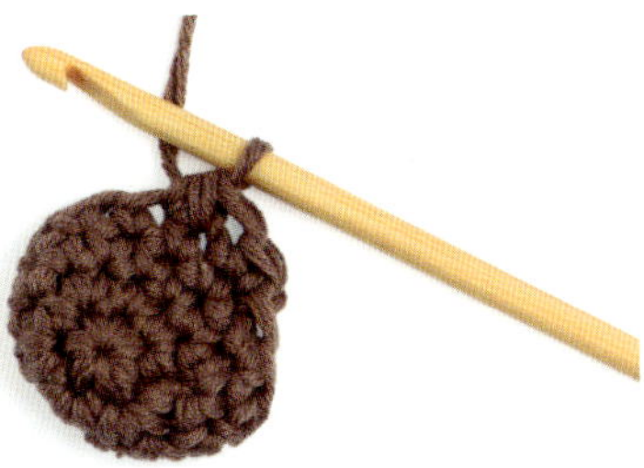

4 Yarn over and pull the yarn through all three loops on the hook. The dc2tog is now complete. Continue following the pattern for Round 5.

5 Attach Colour B.
Rnd 6: *Ch 12, starting from the 5th ch from the hook, dc into the next 8 ch. Sl st into the next st. Repeat from * eight more times to create nine petals in total.

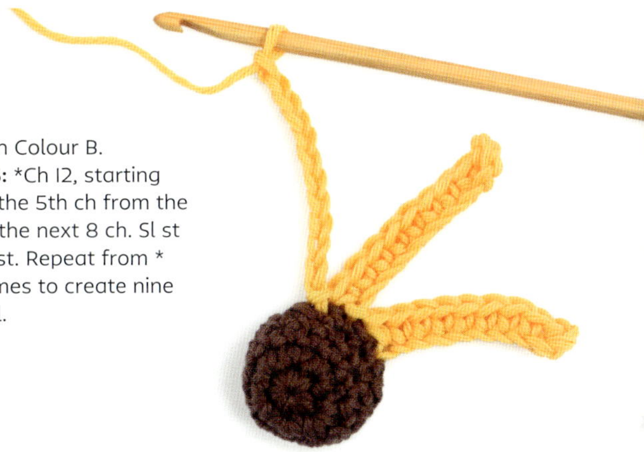

6 You will crochet Round 7 around the existing petals.

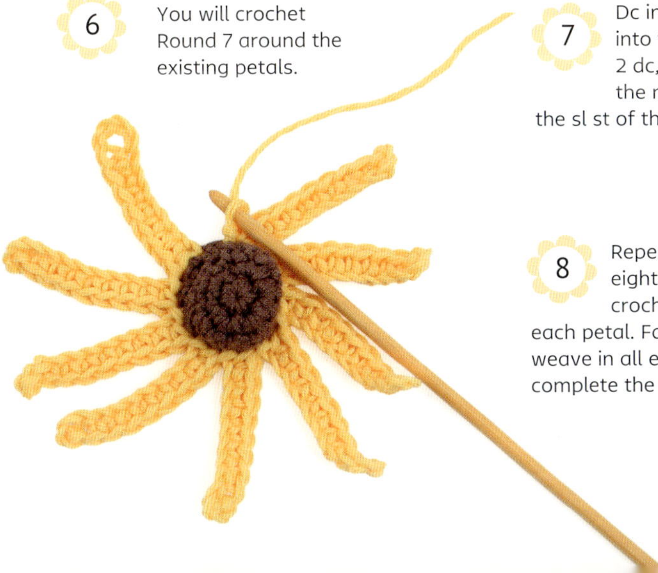

7 Dc into the next 8 ch. Then, into the ch-4 loop, work: 2 dc, 3 ch picot, 2 dc. Dc into the next 8 dc, then sl st into the sl st of the previous round.

8 Repeat Step 7 eight more times, crocheting around each petal. Fasten off and weave in all ends to complete the flower.

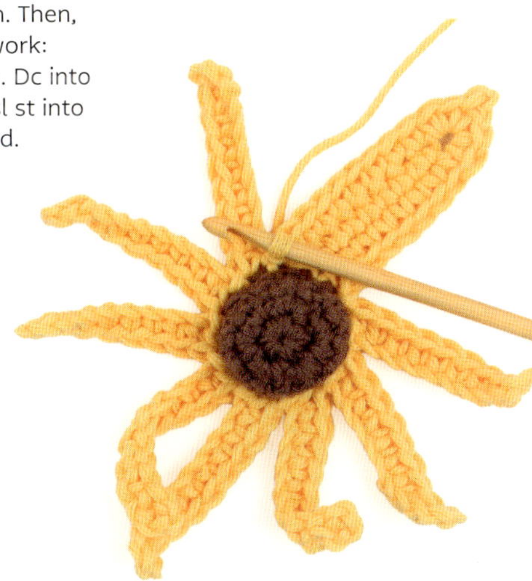

11 Bumblebee Primrose

Skill level: ✿✿

Using contrasting colours of yarn creates the most beautiful effect. I was inspired by the bumblebee primrose, which has a lovely combination of a yellow centre and dark plum petals.

Materials:

4-ply yarn in 2 colours:

- Colour A: 5.5 m (6 yds)
- Colour B: 3.75 m (4 yds)

Tools:

Hook size: 3.25 mm (D-3)
Stitch marker
Yarn needle
Scissors

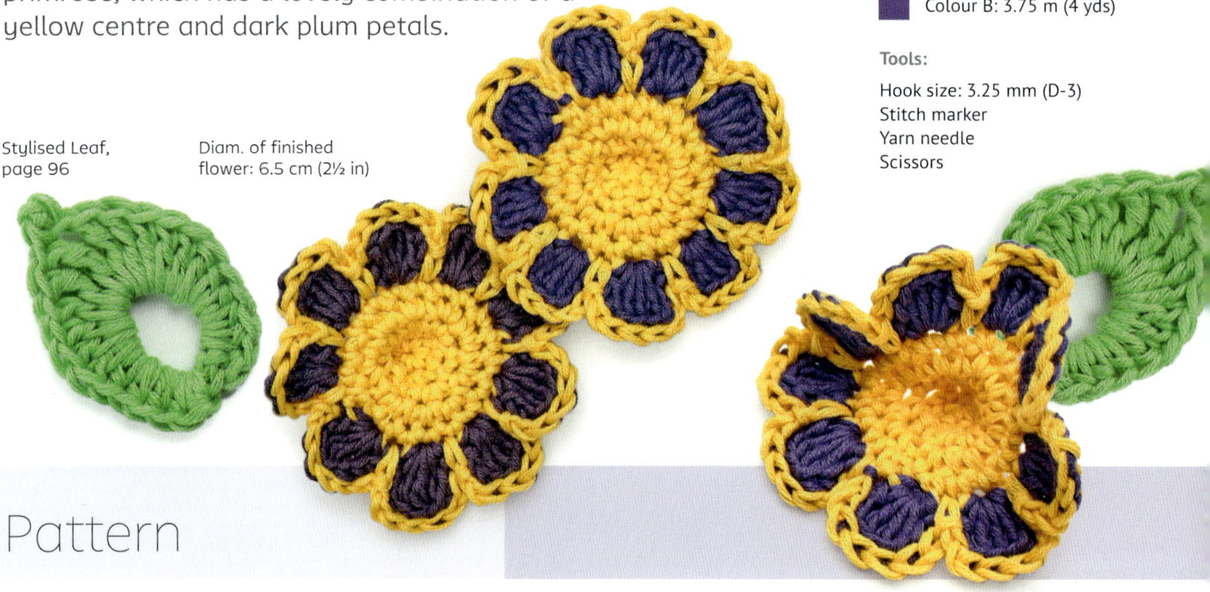

Stylised Leaf, page 96

Diam. of finished flower: 6.5 cm (2½ in)

Pattern

With Colour A, make a magic ring (see page 12).

Rnd 1: Into magic ring, ch 1, 6 dc. Pull on short end to close middle. Join rnd with sl st. (6 dc)

Use st marker to mark the beginning of each rnd.

Rnd 2: Ch 1, dc in each dc. Join rnd with sl st (**see Step 1**).

Rnd 3: Ch 1, [dc in next dc, 2 dc in next dc] three times. Join rnd with sl st. (9 dc)

Rnd 4: Ch 1, 2 dc in each dc. Join rnd with sl st. (18 dc)

Rnd 5: Ch 1, dc in each dc. Do not join rnd with sl st (**see Step 2**).

Change to Colour B. Do not fasten off Colour A (**see Steps 3–4** for instructions).

Rnd 6: Ch 1, *[dc, ch 2, tr, dtr, tr, ch 2, dc] in next dc, sl st in next dc. Rep from * eight more times (**see Step 5**).

Fasten off Colour B.

Change to Colour A (**see Step 6**).

Rnd 7: *Ch 2, sl st in next 3 sts, ch 2, dc in sl st. Rep from * eight more times (**see Step 7**).

Fasten off Colour A. Weave in ends (**see Step 8**).

Chart key:

- Magic ring
- Ch Chain
- Dc Double crochet
- Sl st Slip stitch
- Tr Treble crochet
- Dtr Double treble crochet

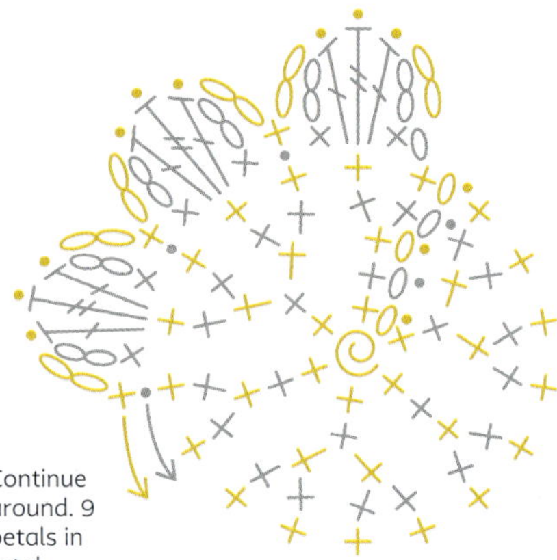

Continue around. 9 petals in total.

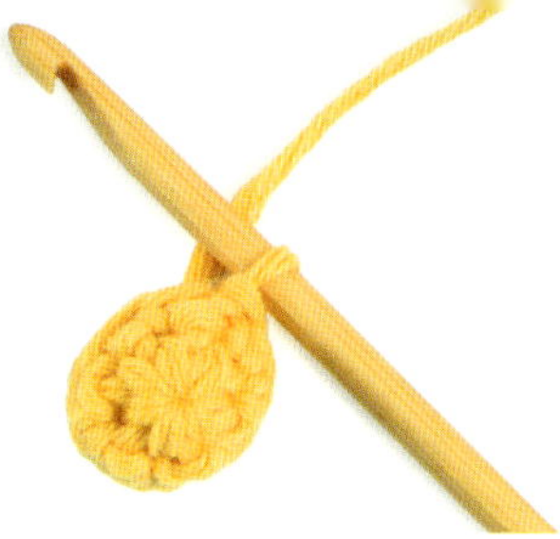

1 With Colour A: **Rnd I:** Into a magic ring (see page I2), ch I, 6 dc into the ring. Pull on the short end to close the middle. Join the round with a sl st.
Rnd 2: Ch I, dc into each dc. Join the round with a sl st.

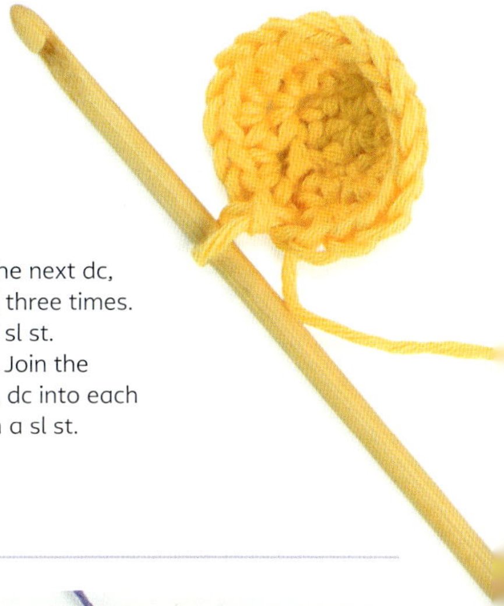

2 **Rnd 3:** Ch I, [dc into the next dc, 2 dc into the next dc] three times. Join the round with a sl st.
Rnd 4: Ch I, 2 dc into each dc. Join the round with a sl st. **Rnd 5:** Ch I, dc into each dc. Do not join this round with a sl st.

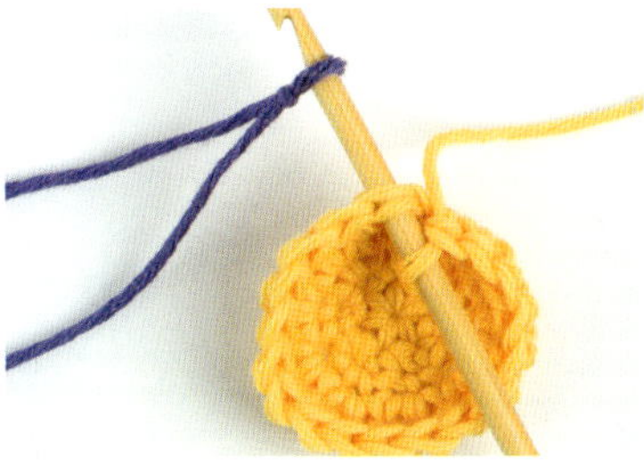

3 Change to Colour B but do not fasten off Colour A. To change colours invisibly, insert the hook into the first dc of the round. Attach the yarn loop in Colour B to the hook, as shown here.

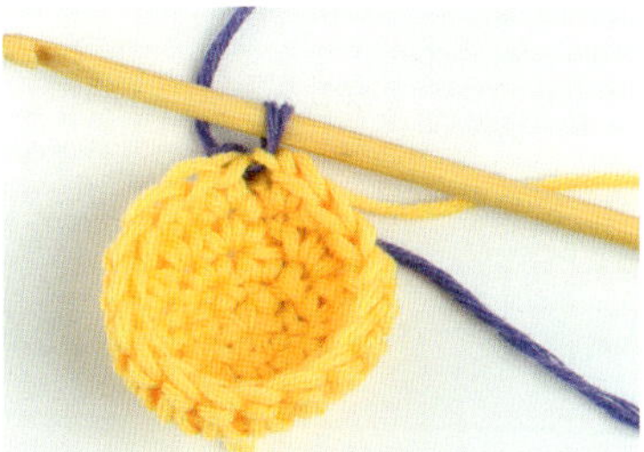

4 Using Colour B, yarn over and pull the yarn through. You have changed to a new colour but Colour A is still attached. Do not fasten it off.

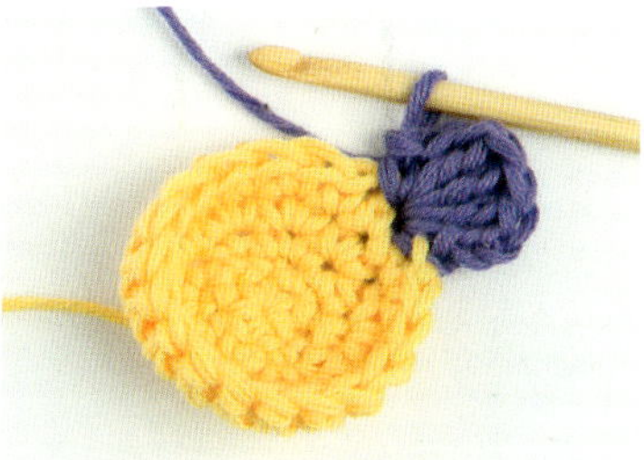

5 **Rnd 6:** Ch I, *[dc, ch 2, tr, dtr, tr, ch 2, dc] into the next dc, sl st into the next dc, then repeat from * eight more times to create nine petals.

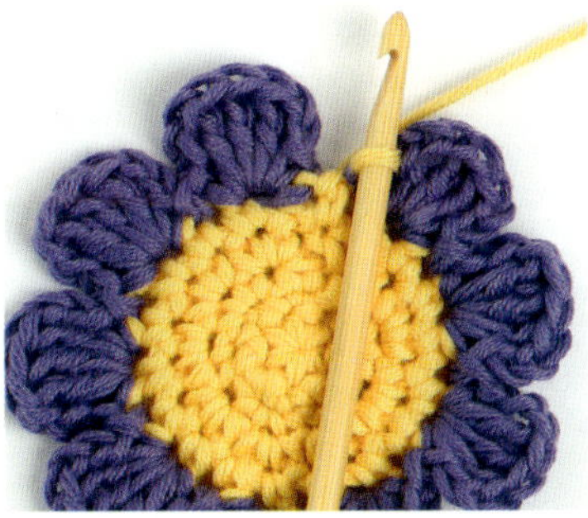

6 Fasten off Colour B and change back to Colour A.

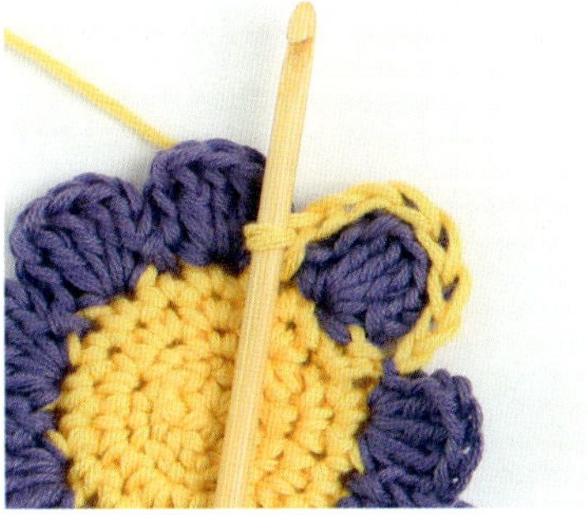

7 **Rnd 7:** *Ch 2, sl st into the next tr, sl st into the next dtr, sl st into the next tr, ch 2, dc into the sl st. Repeat from * eight more times.

8 Fasten off Colour A and weave in all ends to complete the flower.

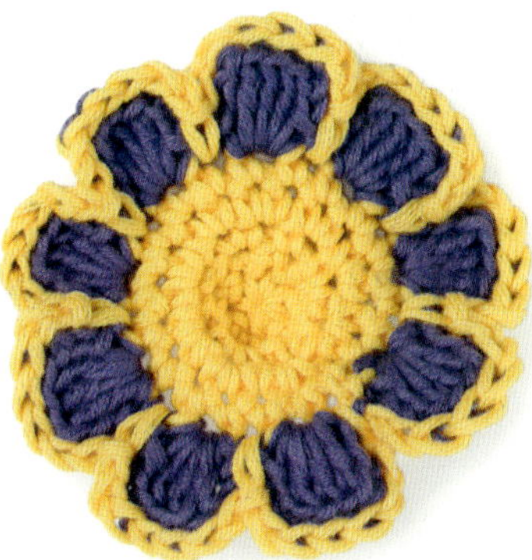

12 Mini Rose

Skill level:

This is another sweet and delicate flower to make. While crocheting this rose, you will learn some very simple new techniques for creating beautiful three-dimensional flowers.

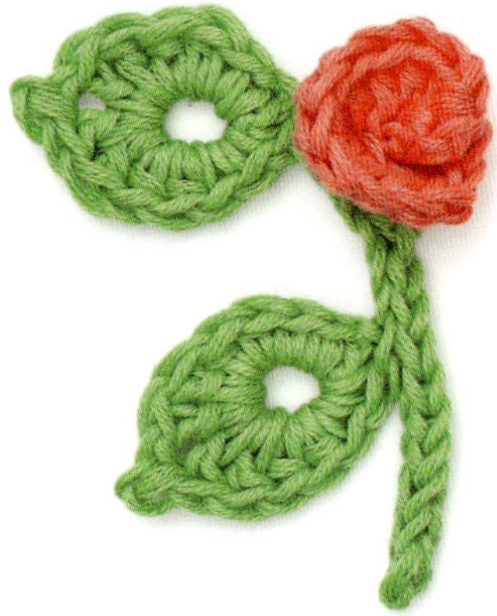

Diam. of finished flowers: small – 1.3 cm (½ in), large – 2 cm (¾ in)

Length of finished leaf: 2.5 cm (1 in)

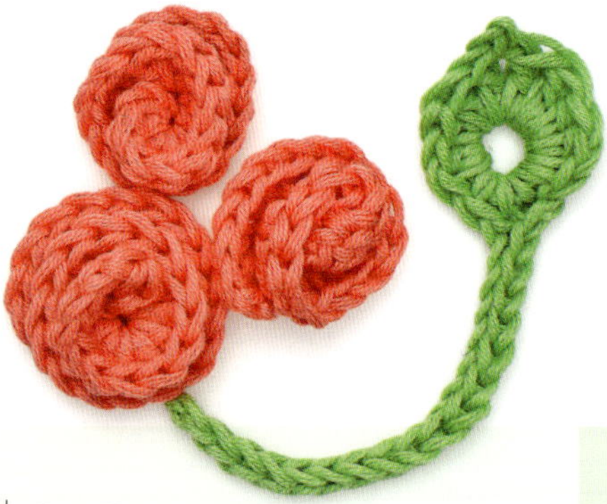

Materials:

4-ply yarn in 2 colours:

- Colour A: 1.75 m (2 yds) per flower
- Colour B: 2.25 m (2½ yds) per stem with 1 leaf

Tools:

Hook size: 3.25 mm (D-3)
Yarn needle
Scissors

Pattern

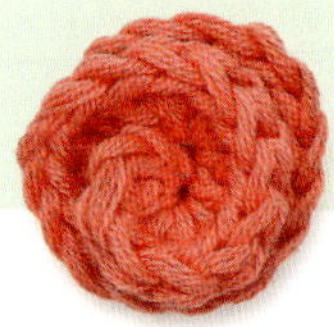

Small flower:

With Colour A, ch 7, 5 tr in 3rd ch from hook, 5 tr in each ch. Ch 2, sl st in same ch as last tr. Fasten off (**see Steps 1–2**).

Large flower:

With Colour A, ch 9, 5 tr in 3rd ch from hook, 5 tr in each ch. Ch 2, sl st in same ch as last tr. Fasten off.

Leaf:

With Colour B, ch 6. Join rnd with sl st in first ch.

Ch 1, [2 dc, 2 htr, 2 tr, 2 ch picot, 2 tr, 2 htr, 2 dc] in ch-6 loop. Join rnd with sl st.

Fasten off.

Stem with leaf:

With Colour B, ch 6. Join rnd with sl st in first ch.

Ch 1 [2 dc, 2 htr, 2 tr, 2 ch picot, 2 tr, 2 htr, 2 dc] in ch-6 loop, ch 20, starting from 2nd ch from hook, sl st in each ch, sl st in first dc of leaf. Fasten off.

Follow **Steps 3–8** to learn how to join extra leaves and flowers to a stem.

Small flower

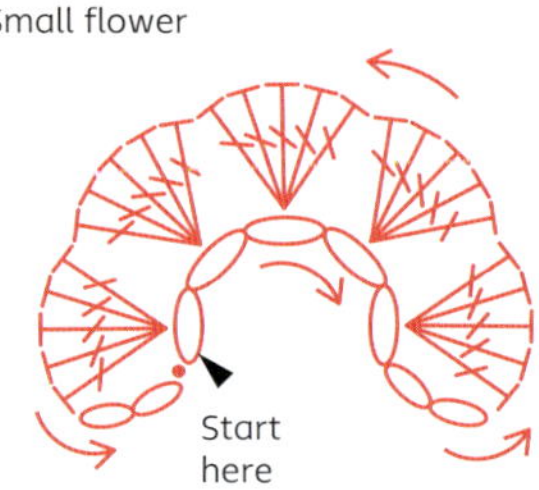

Chart key:

- Ch Chain
- Tr Treble crochet
- Sl st Slip stitch
- Htr Half treble crochet
- 2 ch picot (ch 2, sl st in 2nd ch from hook)

Leaf

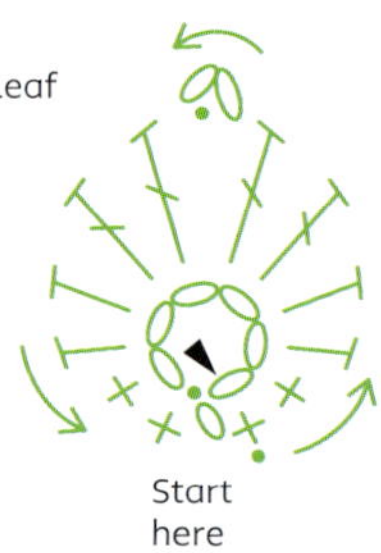

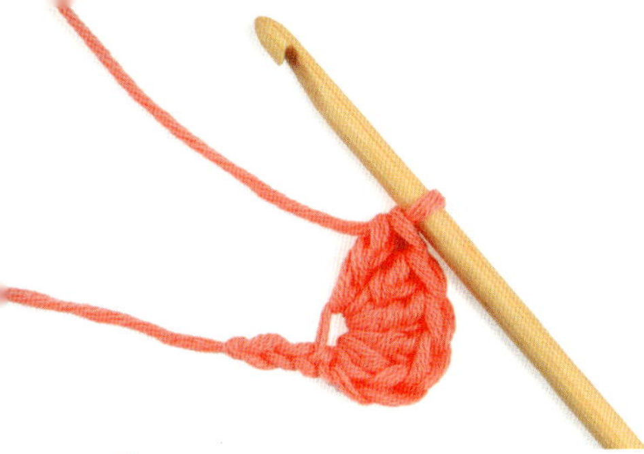

1 **To make a small flower:** Ch 7, work 5 tr into the 3rd ch from the hook, as shown here. Yarn over and pull the yarn through. To make a large flower, follow the written pattern.

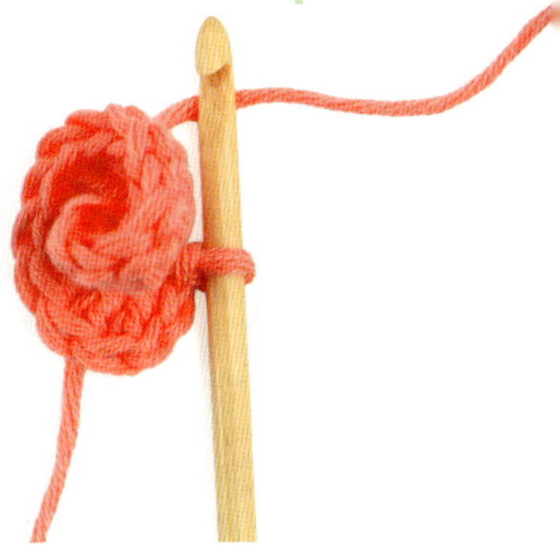

2 5 tr into each remaining ch. Ch 2, then sl st into the same st as the final tr. Fasten off and leave a long yarn end. The rose will fold itself into a bud. Make a few stitches with the yarn and needle to secure the shape of the rose.

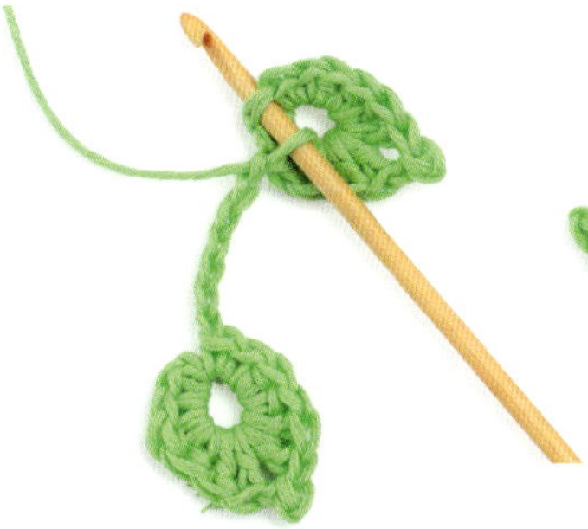

3 **To attach multiple leaves to the stem:** Follow the pattern for 'Stem with leaf' but ch 7 for the stem part, rather than ch 20. Insert the hook into a second leaf to attach. Yarn over, then pull the yarn through both loops on the hook.

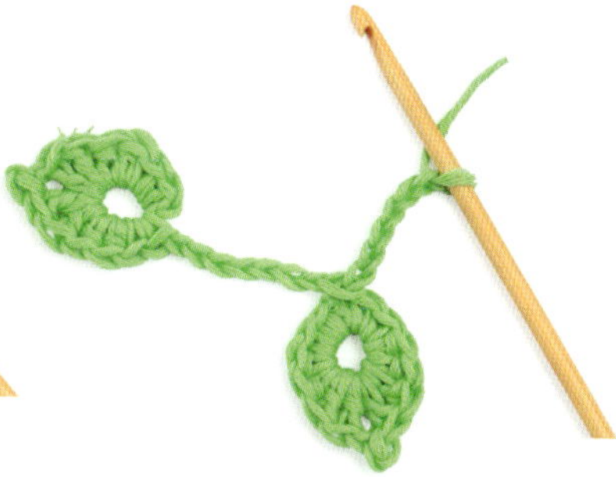

4 Continue making ch stitches for as long as you want to make the stem.

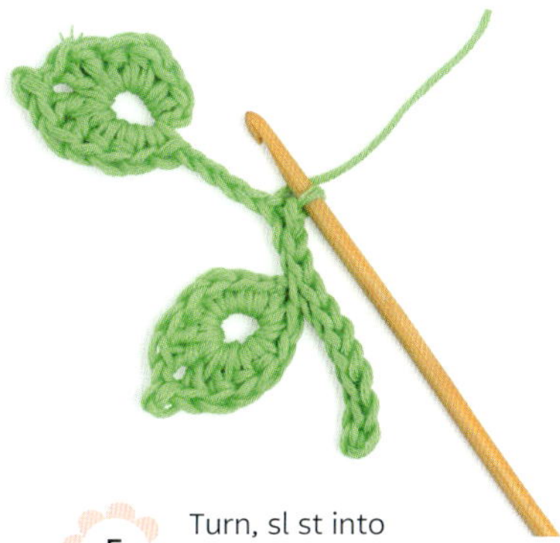

5 Turn, sl st into every ch.

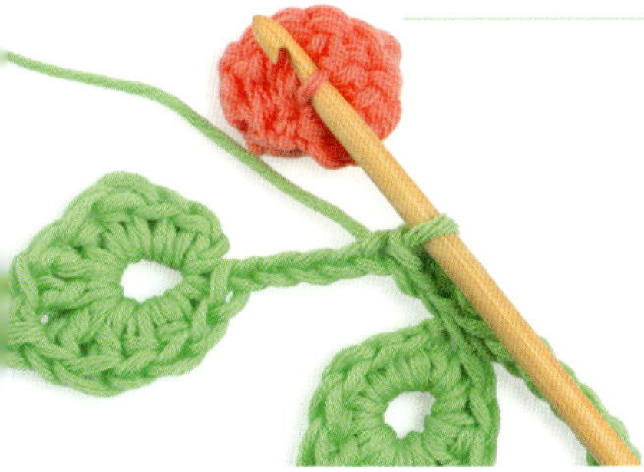

6 When you reach a place on the stem where you want to attach a rose, insert the hook into any loop at the wrong side of the rose. Yarn over, then pull the yarn through both loops on the hook to secure the rose.

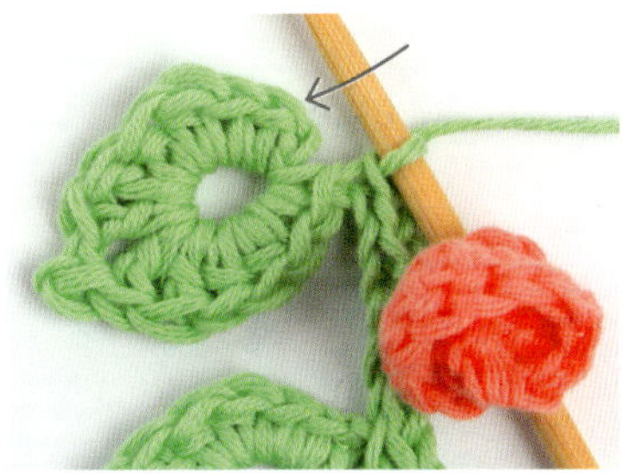

7 Continue making a sl st into every ch of the stem. Finish by making a sl st into the first dc of the leaf, indicated by the arrow.

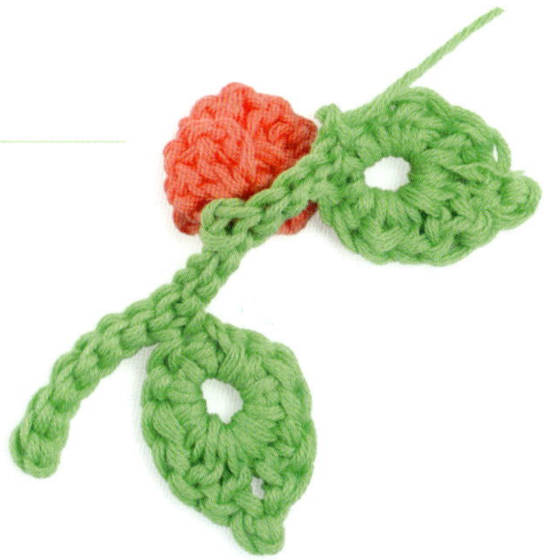

8 Fasten off and weave in all ends. As you can see, the leaf and the rose will be securely attached to the stem.

13 Purple Rose

Skill level:

This gorgeous flower can be made by crocheting in rows, instead of rounds. It will only require a few connecting stitches with a needle, but you will love the volume created by this technique.

Materials:

4-ply yarn in 1 colour:

20 m (22 yds)

Tools:

Hook size: 3.25 mm (D-3)
Yarn needle
Scissors

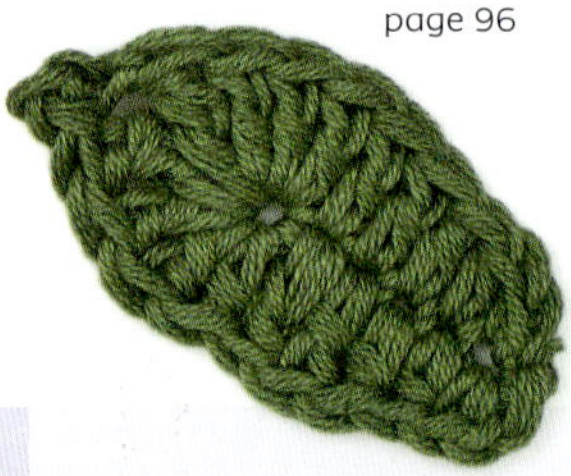

Simple Leaf, page 96

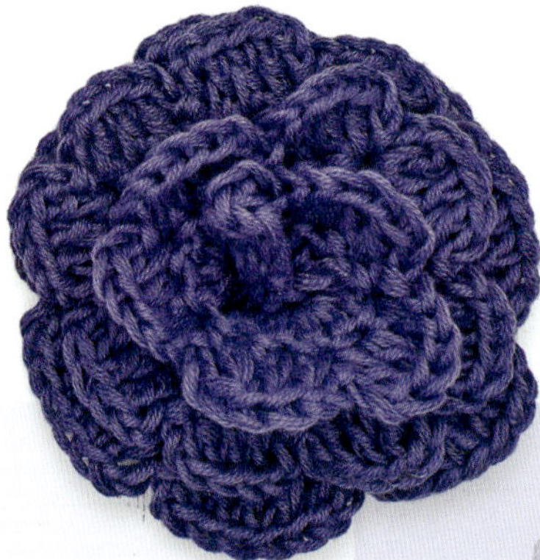

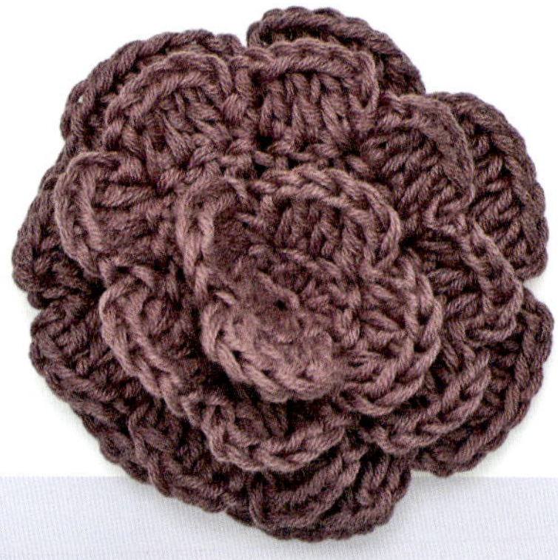

Pattern

Ch 48.

Row 1: 5 tr in 3rd ch from hook, [miss 2 ch, 5 tr in next ch] 15 times (**see Steps 1–2**).

Row 2: Turn work, [ch 2, tr in next 5 tr, ch 2, sl st in same st as last tr] eight times (**see Steps 3–5**).

[Ch 2, tr in next 3 tr, ch 2, sl st in same st as last tr, ch 2, tr in same st as last sl st, tr in next 2 tr, ch 2, sl st in same st as last tr] 16 times (**see Step 6**).

Fasten off, leaving a 30.5-cm (12-in) end for sewing.

Fold flower as shown in **Steps 7–8**. Using the long yarn end, sew the flower at the bottom to hold its shape.

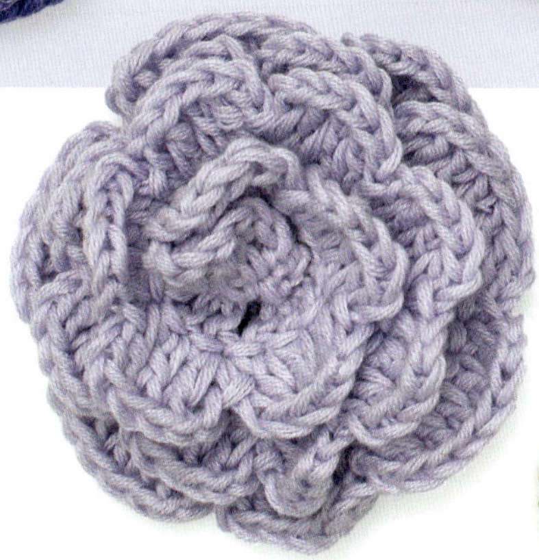

Diam. of finished flower: 6.5 cm (2½ in)

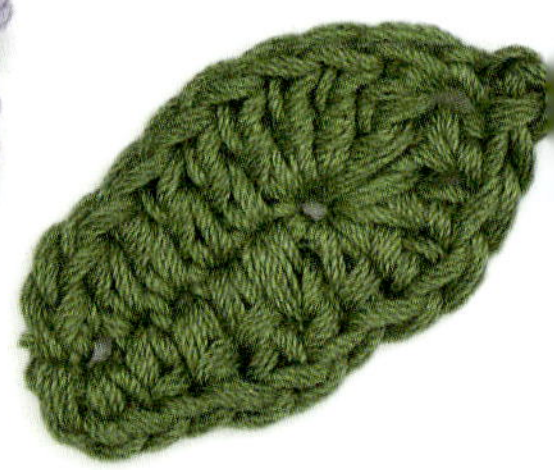

Chart key:

Ch Chain

Tr Treble crochet

Sl st Slip stitch

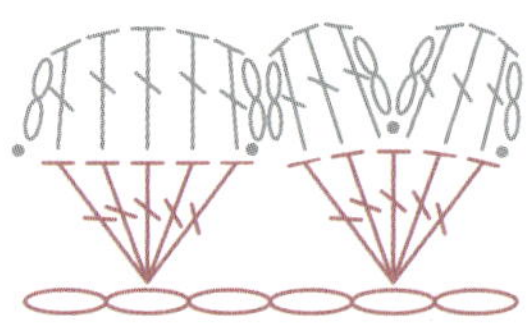

Enlarged view

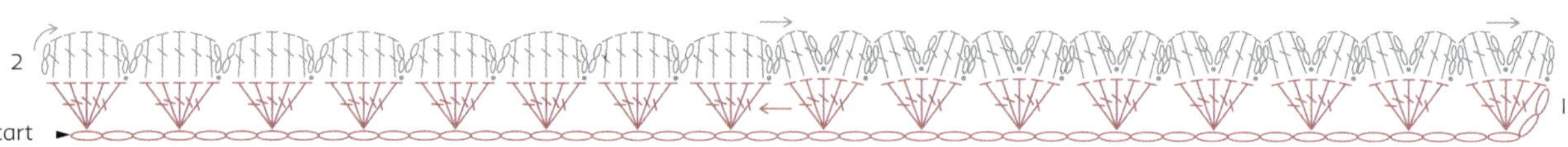

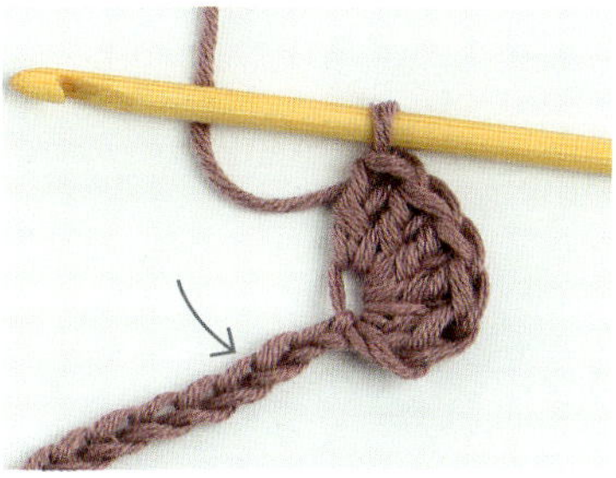

1 **Row I:** Work 5 tr into the 3rd ch from the hook. Miss 2 ch, then work 5 tr into the next ch (place five stitches in the chain indicated by the arrow).

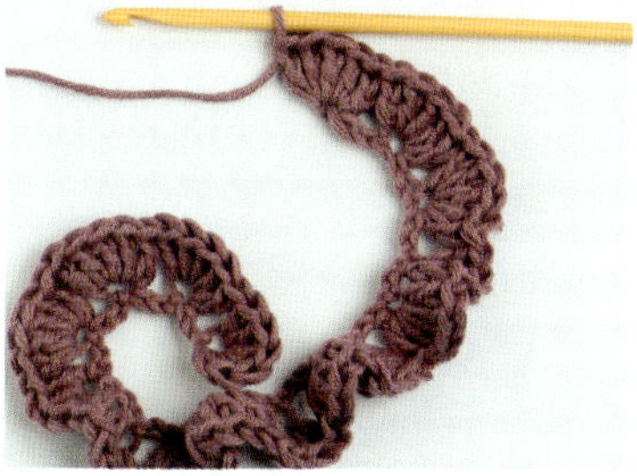

2 [Miss 2 ch, 5 tr into the next ch] I4 more times, until you reach the end of the chain.

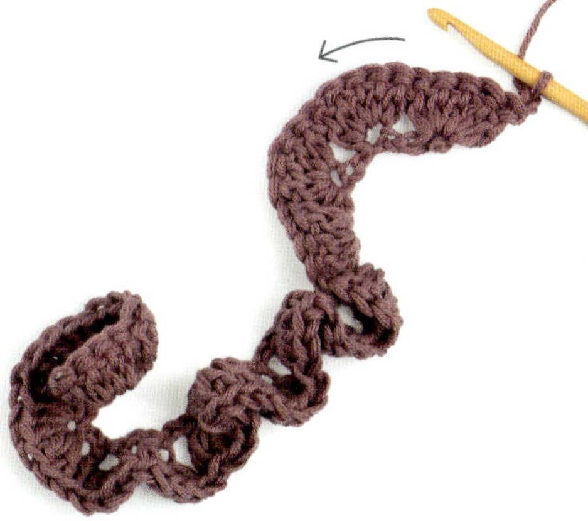

3 **Row 2:** Ch 2, turn your crocheted work to start crocheting in the opposite direction, as shown here.

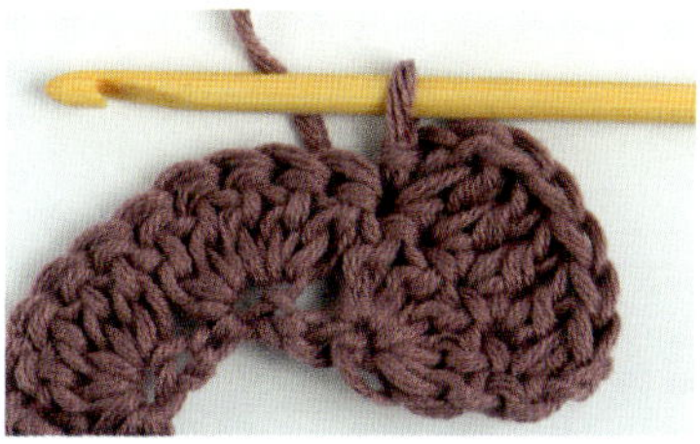

4 Tr into each of the next 5 tr, ch 2, then work a sl st into the same st as the last tr.

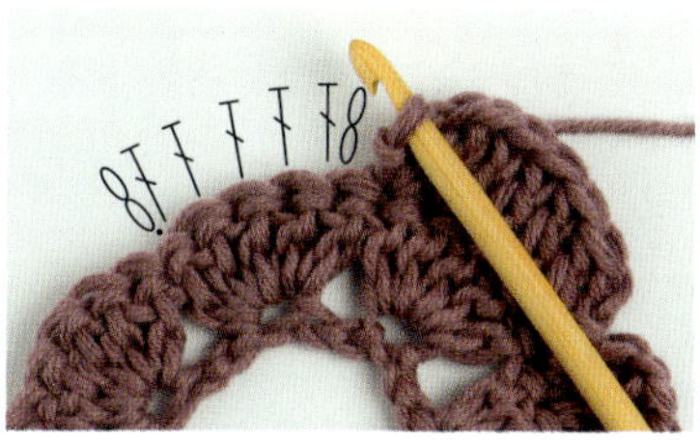

5 [Ch 2, tr into each of the next 5 tr, ch 2, sl st into the same st as the last tr] seven more times.

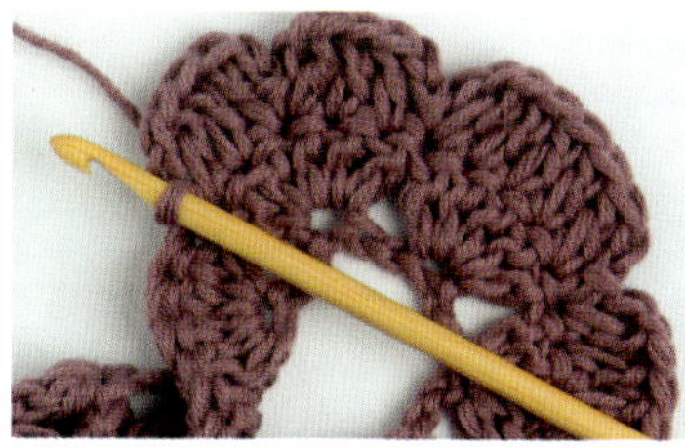

6 [Ch 2, tr into the next 3 tr, ch 2, sl st into the same st as the last tr, ch 2, tr into the same st as the last sl st, tr into the next 2 tr, ch 2, sl st into the same st as the last tr] I6 times.

7 Fasten off the yarn, leaving a long tail of 30.5 cm (I2 in) for sewing up the flower. The side of the flower with the smaller petals will be on the inside of the flower.

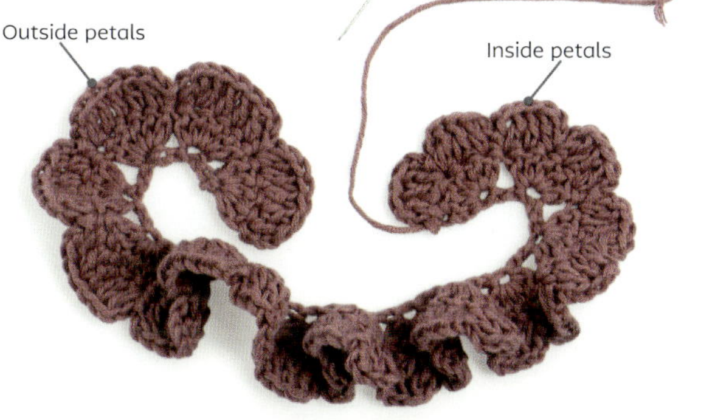

8 Starting from one end, fold the flower up in a spiral, with the smaller petals on the inside. Using the long yarn end, sew the flower at the base to secure. Fasten off and weave in all ends.

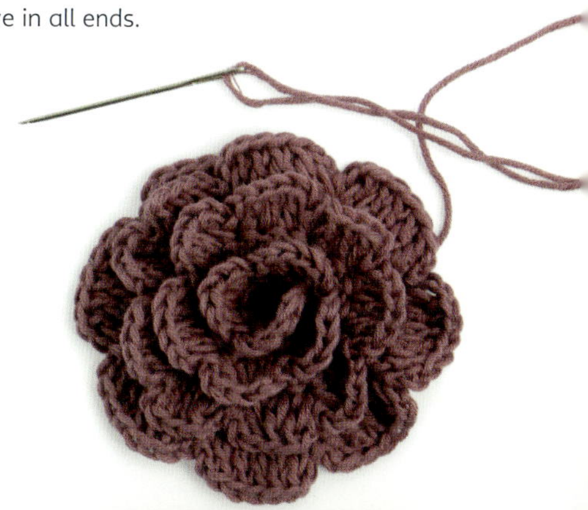

14 Harlequin

Skill level:

To create this colourful and striking harlequin flower, you will use familiar techniques, and learn one fun new technique for adding layers to your crochet flowers.

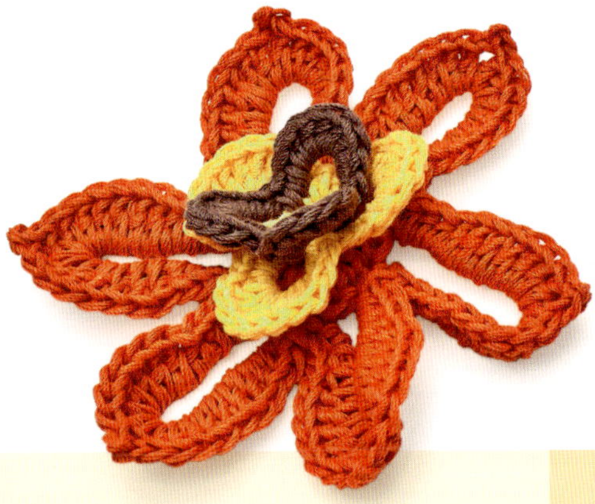

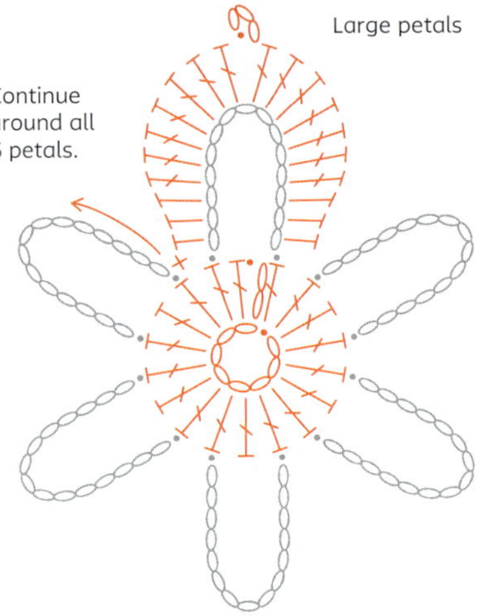

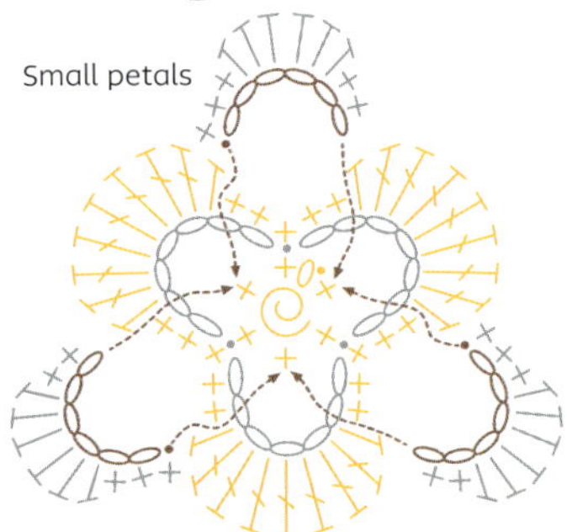

Materials:

4-ply yarn in 3 colours:

- Colour A: 10 m (11 yds)
- Colour B: 4.5 m (5 yds)
- Colour C: 2.75 m (3 yds)

Tools:

Hook size: 3.25 mm (D-3)
Yarn needle
Scissors

Chart key:

- Ch Chain
- Sl st Slip stitch
- Tr Treble crochet
- Htr Half treble crochet
- 3 ch picot (ch 3, sl st in 3rd ch from hook)
- Dc Double crochet
- Magic ring

Pattern

Large petals:

With Colour A, ch 8. Join rnd with sl st.

Rnd 1: Ch 2, 18 tr in rnd. Join rnd with sl st in first tr.

Rnd 2: [Ch 15, miss next tr, sl st in next 2 tr] six times (**see Step 1**).

Rnd 3: *[3 htr, 7 tr, 3 ch picot, 7 tr, 3 htr] in ch-15 loop, dc in 2nd sl st between petals (**see Step 2**).

Rep from * five more times (6 petals in total).

Fasten off Colour A.

Small petals:

With Colour B, make a magic ring (see page 12).

Rnd 1: Into magic ring, ch 1, 6 dc. Pull on short end to close middle. Join rnd with sl st.

Rnd 2: [Ch 7, miss next dc, sl st in next dc] three times.

Rnd 3: *[2 dc, htr, 7 tr, htr, 2 dc] in ch-7 loop, dc in sl st between petals (**see Step 3**).

Rep from * twice more.

Fasten off Colour B leaving a 30.5-cm (12-in) end for sewing.

Attach Colour C to any missed dc in Rnd 1 (**see Steps 4–5**).

Rnd 4: [Ch 6, sl st in next missed dc] three times (**see Steps 6–7**).

Rnd 5: *[2 dc, 6 htr, 2 dc] in ch-6 loop, dc in sl st between petals.

Rep from * twice more (**see Step 8**).

Fasten off Colour C.

Weave in ends. Use long yarn end in Colour B to sew flower together.

Diam. of finished flower: 11.5 cm (4½ in)

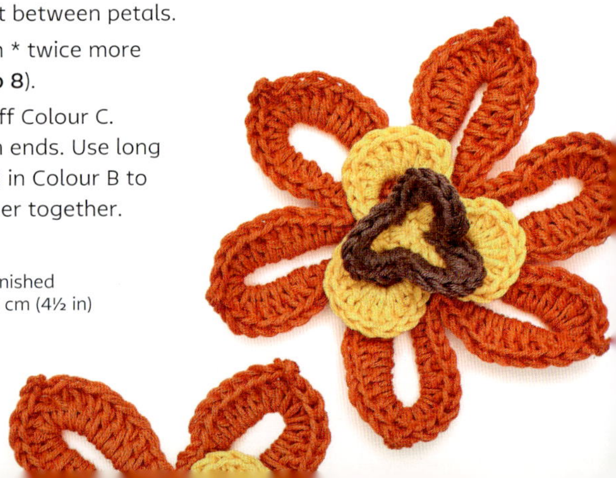

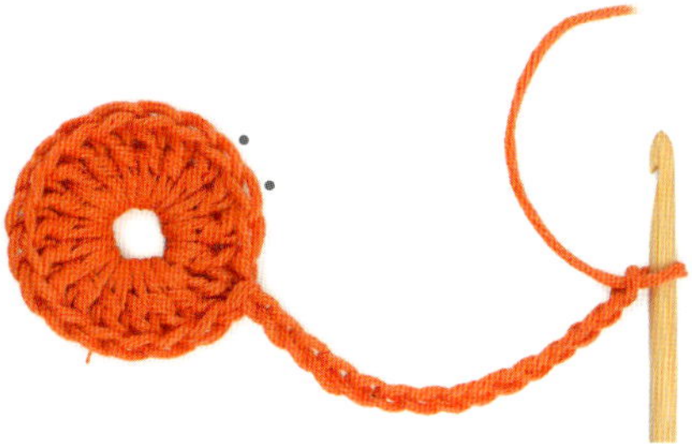

1 Follow the pattern to make Round I. On Round 2, you will be making long loops with chain stitches and joining them back to the centre of the flower to form petals. After you make a chain, miss one tr, then make a sl st into each of the next 2 tr, which are marked with sl st symbols on the above picture.

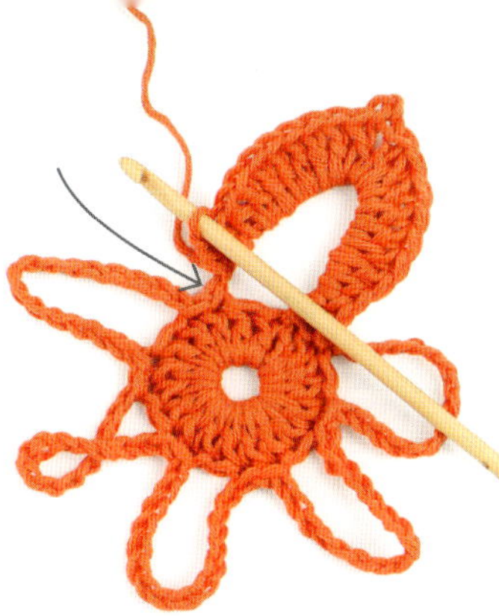

2 **Rnd 3:** Work [3 htr, 7 tr, 3 ch picot, 7 tr, 3 htr] evenly into the first ch-15 loop. Dc into the 2nd sl st between the petals (as indicated by the arrow above). Follow the pattern to repeat for all six petals, then fasten off Colour A.

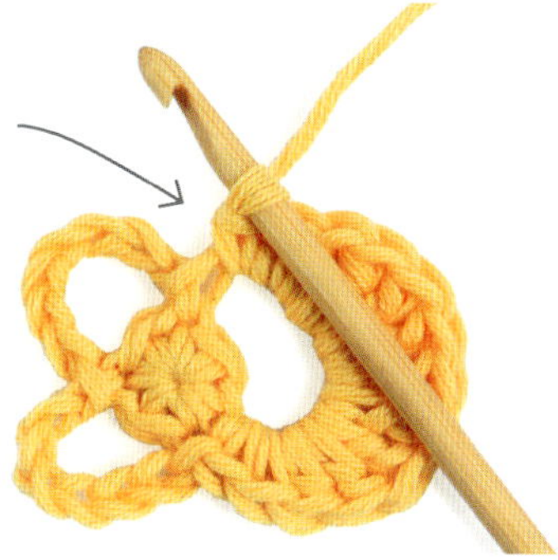

3 Follow the pattern to make the small petals. Use the arrow above as a guide for placing the sl sts between petals. The small petals part will only have three petals per layer. When you fasten off Colour B, remember to leave a 30.5-cm (12-in) end for sewing.

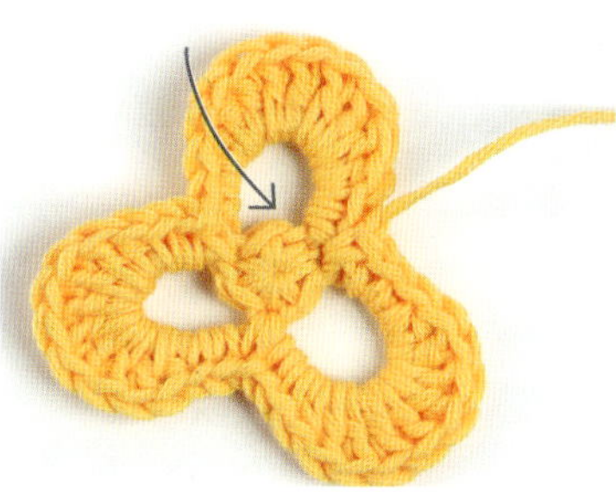

4 Attach Colour C to any missed dc in Round I of the small petals, as marked with an arrow.

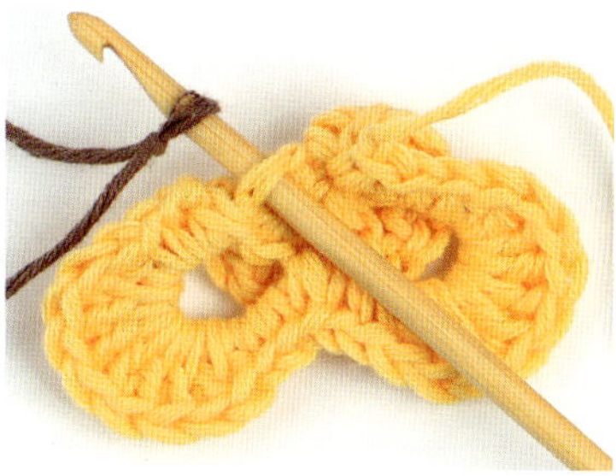

5 Fold the petals out of the way as you go. This will make adding another layer of petals easier.

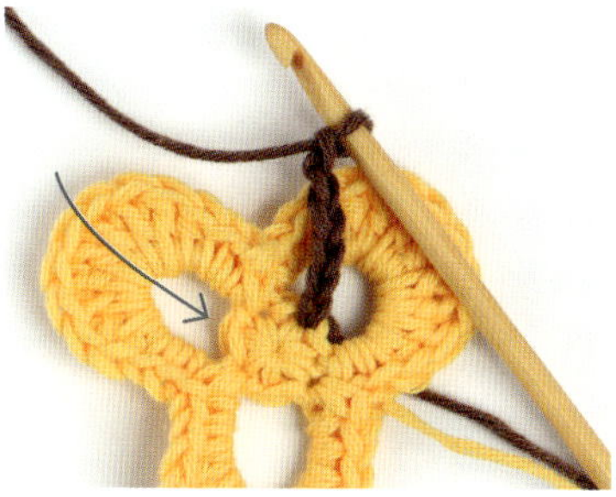

6 Create the second layer of small petals, following the pattern on the left. Place the next sl st into the next missed dc in Round I.

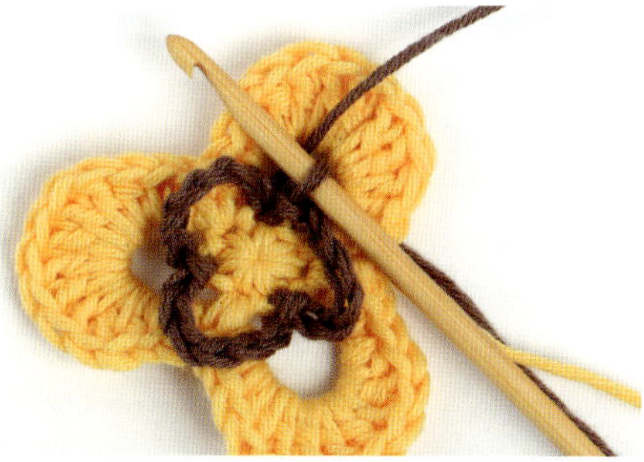

7 This is how this part of the flower will look once one round in Colour C has been crocheted over the small petals. Notice how they fall between the Colour B petals.

8 **Rnd 5**: Work *[2 dc, 6 htr, 2 dc] into a ch-6 loop, dc into the sl st between the petals. Repeat from * for the two remaining petals. Fasten off Colour C and weave in all ends. Sew the two parts of the flower together using the long yarn end of Colour B you left in Step 3.

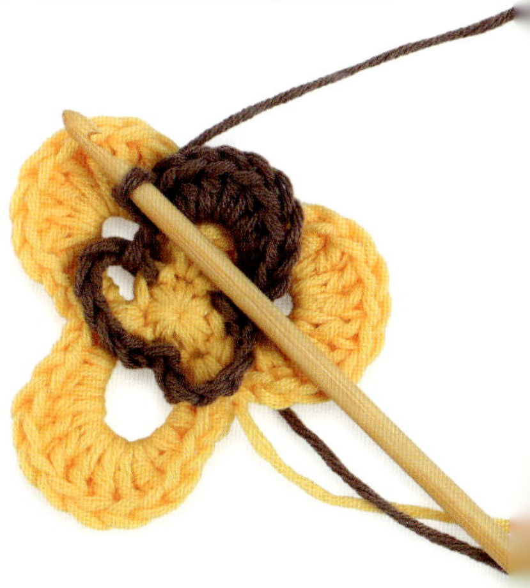

15 Purple Dahlia

Skill level:

This is a bright and colourful flower that uses only techniques you have used before in earlier patterns. This is the perfect pattern to practise making slip stitches without making them too tight.

Materials:

4-ply yarn in 4 colours:

- Colour A: 2.75 m (3 yds)
- Colour B: 10 m (11 yds)
- Colour C: 6.5 m (7 yds)
- Colour D: 10 m (11 yds)

Tools:

Hook size: 3.25 mm (D-3)
Yarn needle
Scissors

Chart key:

- Magic ring
- Ch Chain
- Dc Double crochet
- Sl st Slip stitch
- Htr Half treble crochet
- Tr Treble crochet
- 2 ch picot (ch 2, sl st in 2nd ch from hook)

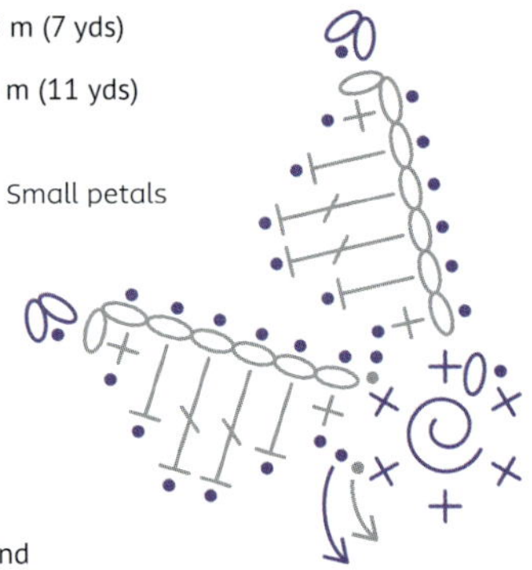

Pattern

Small petals:

With Colour A, make a magic ring (see page 12).

Rnd 1: Into magic ring, ch 1, 6 dc. Pull on short end to close middle. Join rnd with sl st.

Rnd 2: *Ch 7, dc in 2nd ch from hook, htr in next ch, tr in next 2 ch, htr in next ch, dc in next ch.

Sl st in next dc of Rnd 1.

Rep from * five more times (6 petals) (**see Steps 1–2**).

Fasten off Colour A.

Attach Colour B to base of petal (**see Step 3**).

*Sl st in each of 6 ch on one side of petal, 2 ch picot, sl st in back loop of 6 sts on other side of petal. Sl st in sl st between petals.

Rep from * five more times – around each petal (**see Steps 4–7**).

Medium petals:

With Colour C, make a magic ring.

Rnd 1: Into magic ring, ch 1, 6 dc. Pull on short end to close middle. Join rnd with sl st. (6 dc)

Rnd 2: Ch 1, 2 dc in each dc. Join rnd with sl st. (12 dc)

Rnd 3: *Ch 9, dc in 2nd ch from hook, htr in next ch, tr in next 3 ch, htr in next 2 ch, dc in next ch.

Sl st in next dc of Rnd 2.

Rep from * 11 more times (12 petals).

Fasten off Colour C.

Attach Colour B to base of petal (**see Step 3**).

*Sl st in each of 8 ch on one side of petal, 2 ch picot, sl st in back loop of 8 sts on other side of petal. Sl st in sl st between petals.

Rep from * 11 more times – around each petal.

Large petals:

With Colour D, make a magic ring.

Rnd 1: Into magic ring, ch 1, 6 dc. Pull on short end to close middle. Join rnd with sl st. (6 dc)

Rnd 2: Ch 1, 2 dc in each dc. Join rnd with sl st. (12 dc)

Rnd 3: Ch 1, [2 dc in next dc, dc in next dc] six times. Join rnd with sl st. (18 dc)

Rnd 4: *Ch 10, dc in 2nd ch from hook, htr in next ch, tr in next 3 ch, htr in next 2 ch, dc in next 2 ch.

Sl st in next dc of Rnd 3.

Rep from * 17 more times (18 petals).

Fasten off Colour D, leaving a long yarn end for sewing.

Attach Colour B to base of petal (**see Step 3**).

*Sl st in each of 9 ch on one side of petal, 2 ch picot, sl st in back loop of 9 sts on other side of petal. Sl st in sl st between petals.

Rep from * 17 more times – around each petal.

Join tiers of petals by sewing them together using long yarn end and yarn needle.

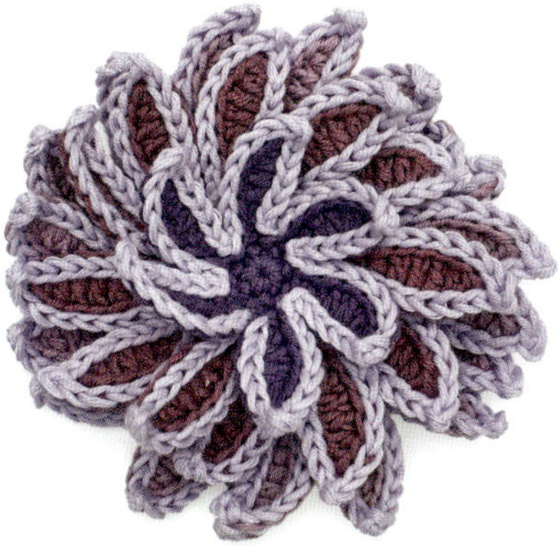

Diam. of finished flower: 10 cm (4 in)

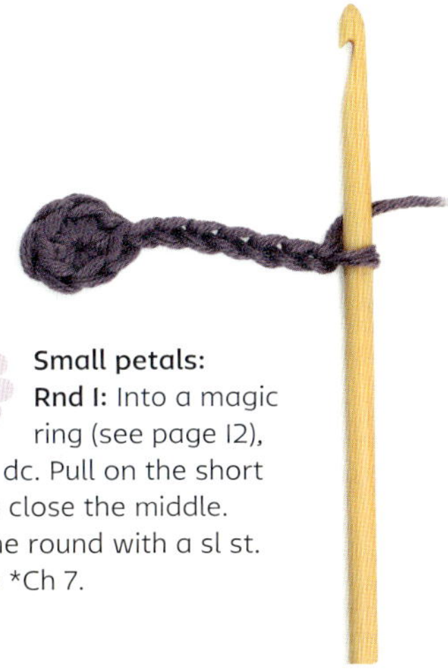

1 **Small petals:**
Rnd 1: Into a magic ring (see page 12), ch 1, 6 dc. Pull on the short end to close the middle. Join the round with a sl st.
Rnd 2: *Ch 7.

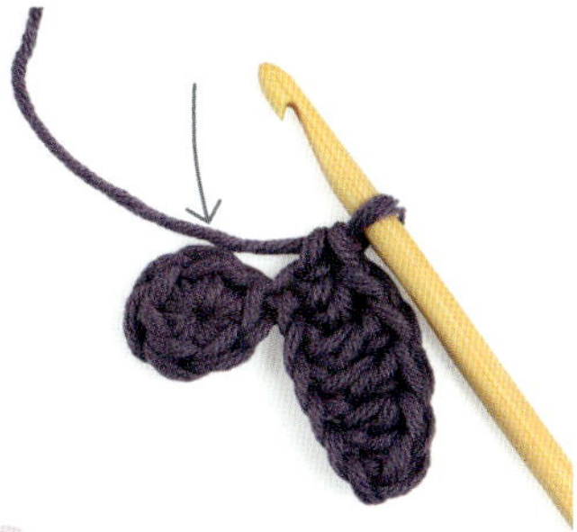

2 Dc into the 2nd ch from the hook, htr into the next ch, tr into the next 2 ch, htr into the next ch, dc into the next ch. Then work a sl st into the next dc of Round 1 (marked by the arrow).

3 Repeat Steps 1 and 2 five more times to create six petals in total. Fasten off Colour A and attach Colour B to the base of any petal, as marked by the arrow. Use this picture as a guide for placing the stitches in Steps 4–6.

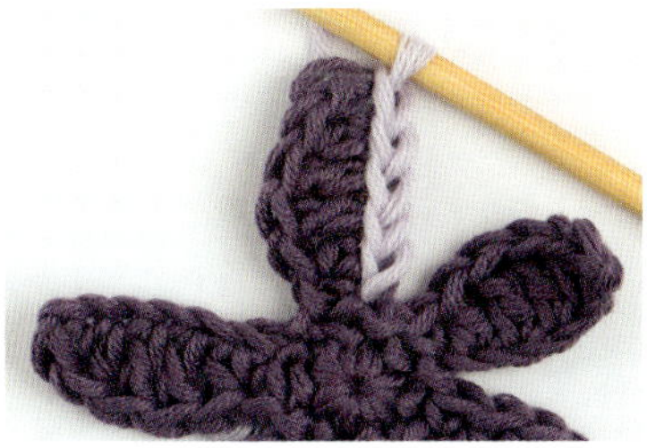

4 Sl st into each ch along one side of the petal. Do not tighten the yarn too much when you are making slip stitches. If you are finding that your slip stitches are too tight, try using a hook that is one size larger for this part of the pattern.

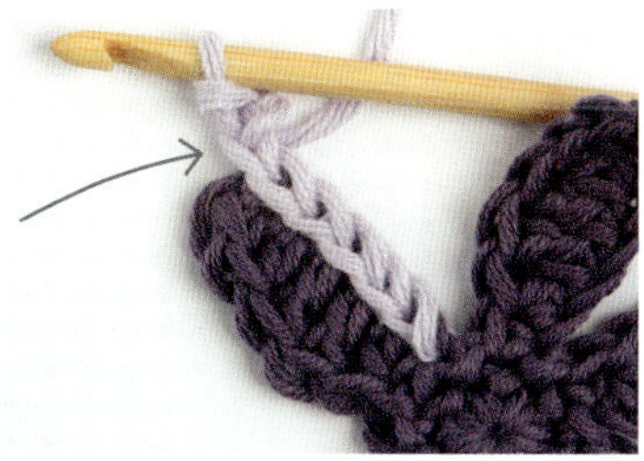

5 Work a 2 ch picot. To do this: ch 2, sl st into the second ch from the hook (marked by the arrow).

6 Sl st into the back loop of each of the 6 stitches along the other side of the petal. Sl st into the sl st between the petals.

7 Repeat Steps 4–6 five more times. Fasten off Colour B and weave in all ends.

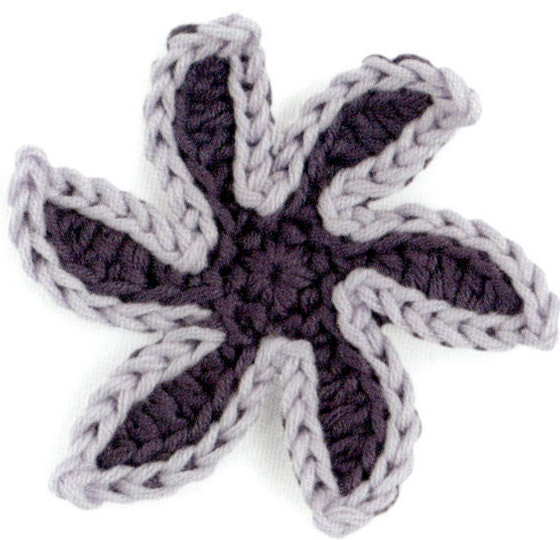

8 Make medium and large petals in the same way. Layer the petals with the largest at the bottom and sew the flower together.

16 Rain Lily

Skill level:

These are such delicate summer flowers, and so easy to make using soft shades of pink and a small amount of yellow yarn. Always use a stitch marker when you are working many rounds in double crochet stitches so you can easily find the beginning of each round.

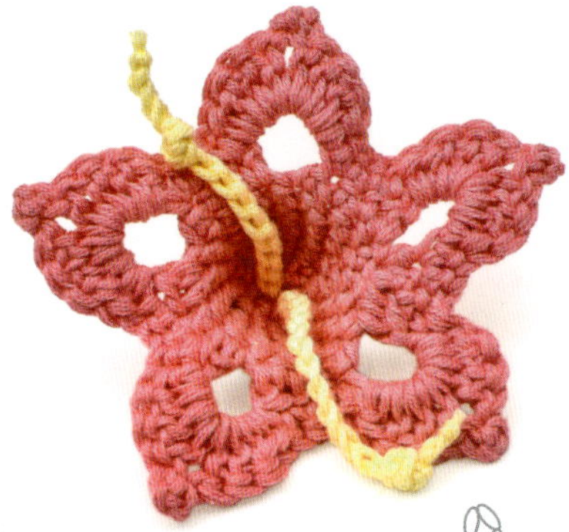

Diam. of finished flower: 7.5 cm (3 in)

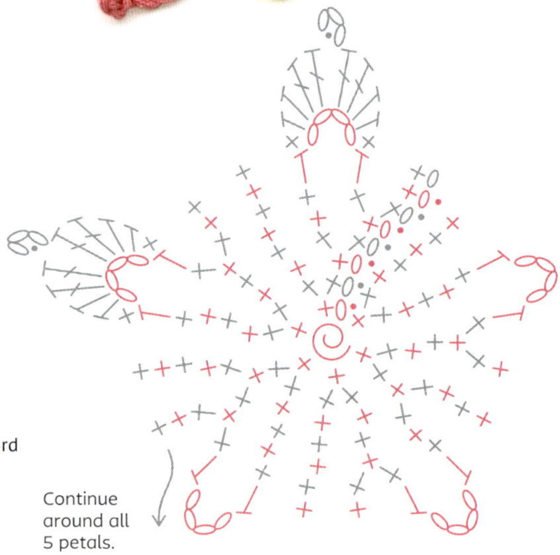

Continue around all 5 petals.

Materials:

4-ply yarn in 2 colours:

- Colour A: 9 m (10 yds)
- Colour B: 1 m (1 yd)

Tools:

Hook size: 3.25 mm (D-3)
Yarn needle
Scissors
Stitch marker

Chart key:

- Magic ring
- Ch Chain
- Dc Double crochet
- Sl st Slip stitch
- Htr Half treble crochet
- Tr Treble crochet
- 3 ch picot (ch 3, sl st in 3rd ch from hook)

Pattern

Petals:

With Colour A, make a magic ring (see page 12).

Rnd 1: Into magic ring, ch 1, 6 dc. Pull on short end to close middle. Join rnd with sl st. (6 dc)

Rnd 2: Ch 1, 2 dc in each dc. Join rnd with sl st. (12 dc)

Rnd 3: Ch 1, dc in each dc. Join rnd with sl st.

Rnd 4: Ch 1, [2 dc in next dc, dc in next 3 dc] three times. Join rnd with sl st. (15 dc)

Rnd 5: Ch 1, dc in each dc. Join rnd with sl st.

Rnd 6: Ch 1, [2 dc in next dc, dc in next 2 dc] five times. Join rnd with sl st (**see Step 1**). (20 dc)

Rnd 7: Ch 1, *dc in next dc, htr in next dc, ch 4, htr in next dc, dc in next dc.

Rep from * four more times. (5 petals)

Join rnd with sl st (**see Steps 2–4**).

Rnd 8: Ch 1, *dc in next 2 sts, [2 htr, 2 tr, 3 ch picot, 2 tr, 2 htr] in next ch-4 loop, dc in next 2 sts.

Rep from * four more times. Join rnd with sl st.

Fasten off and weave in ends (**see Step 5**).

Stamens:

With Colour B, ch 30.

Fasten off. Tighten knots on both ends of chain to prevent unravelling (**see Step 6**).

Thread yellow chain through middle of flower as pictured in **Step 7**. Tie knots at both ends of chain (**see Step 8**).

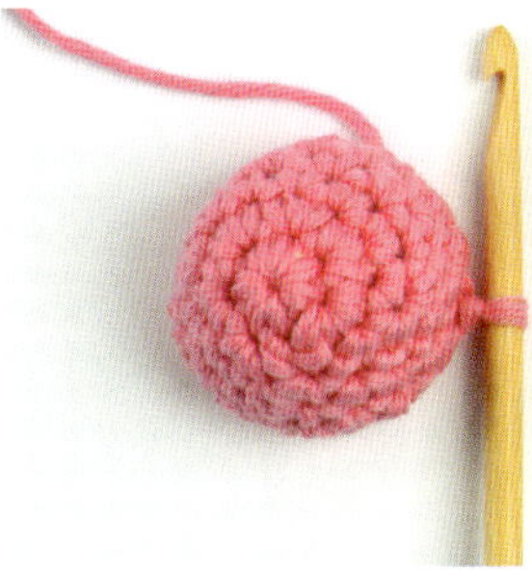

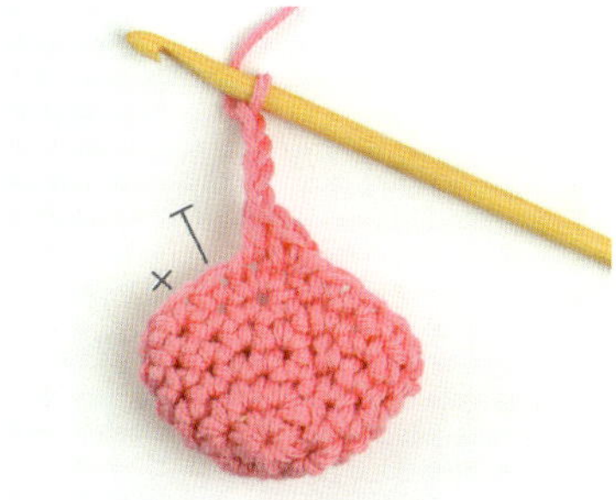

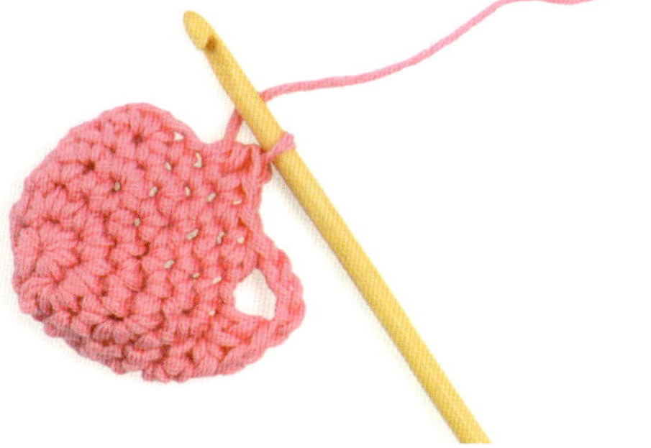

1 Follow the pattern to make Rounds 1–6. At the end of Round 6, your piece will look like this.

2 **Rnd 7:** Ch 1, dc into the next dc, htr into the next dc, ch 4, htr into the next dc, dc into the next dc (use the symbols above as a guide for placing the last two sts).

3 Work [dc into the next dc, htr into the next dc, ch 4, htr into the next dc, dc into the next dc] another four times.

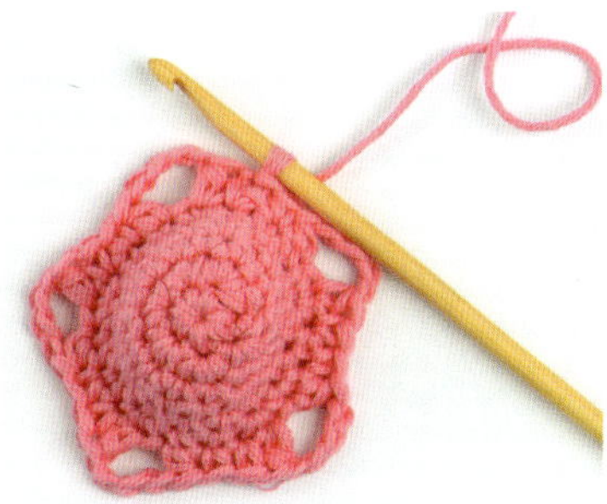

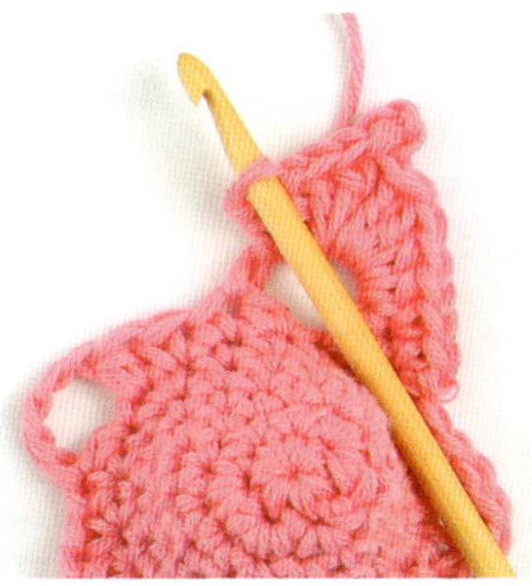

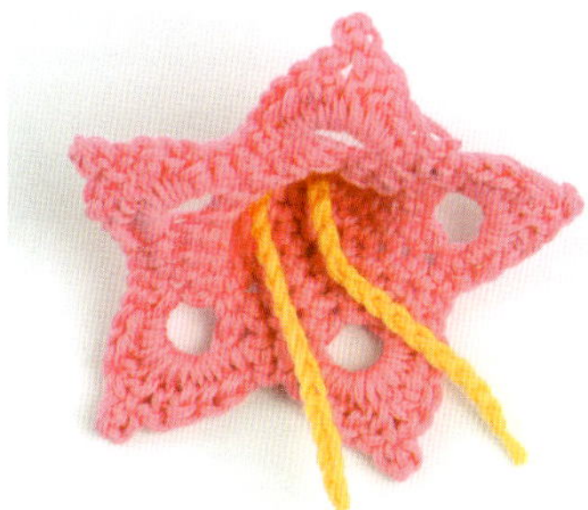

4 Join the round with a sl st. You will see five petals start to emerge.

5 **Rnd 8:** Ch 1, *dc into the next 2 sts, [2 htr, 2 tr, 3 ch picot, 2 tr, 2 htr] into the next ch-4 loop, dc into the next 2 sts. Repeat from * four more times. Join the round with a sl st. Fasten off and weave in ends.

6 **To make the stamens:** Ch 30 with Colour B. Fasten off and tighten the knots at either end of this chain.

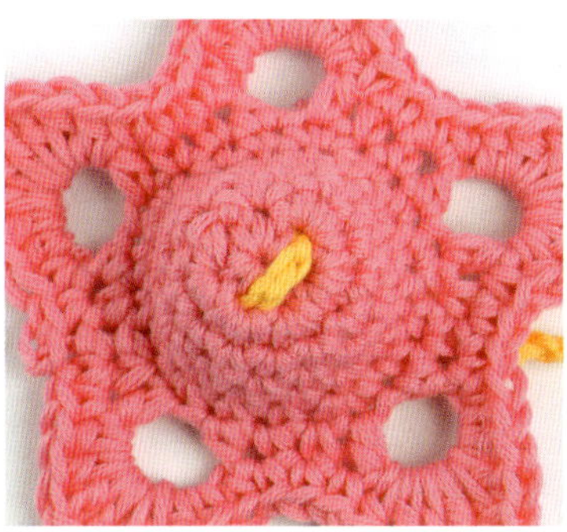

7 Thread the yellow chain through the middle of the pink flower. The back of the flower will look like this.

8 Tie knots at both ends of the yellow chain to finish.

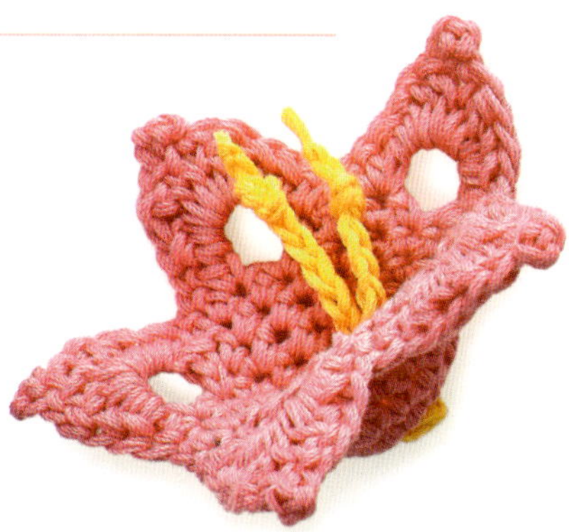

17 Yellow Poppy

Skill level:

This is a classic flower that has to be in everyone's collection. You can choose to only use two colours without the border for a simpler flower, or add a colourful border.

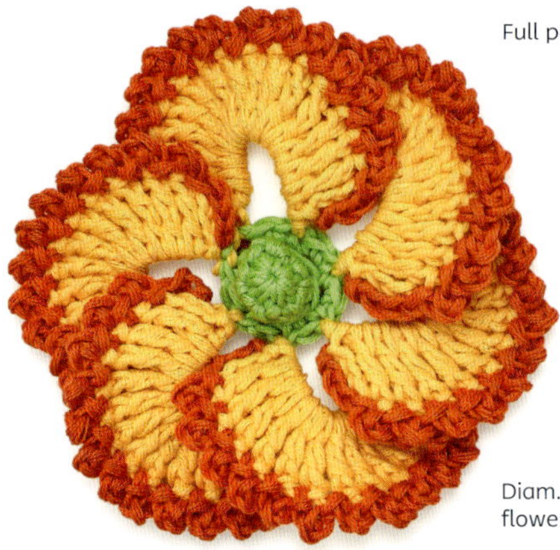

Full poppy

Diam. of finished flower: 9 cm (3½ in)

Materials:

4-ply yarn in 3 colours:

- Colour A: 1.75 m (2 yds)
- Colour B: 12 m (13 yds)
- Colour C: 4.5 m (5 yds)

Tools:

Hook size: 3.25 mm (D-3)
Yarn needle
Scissors

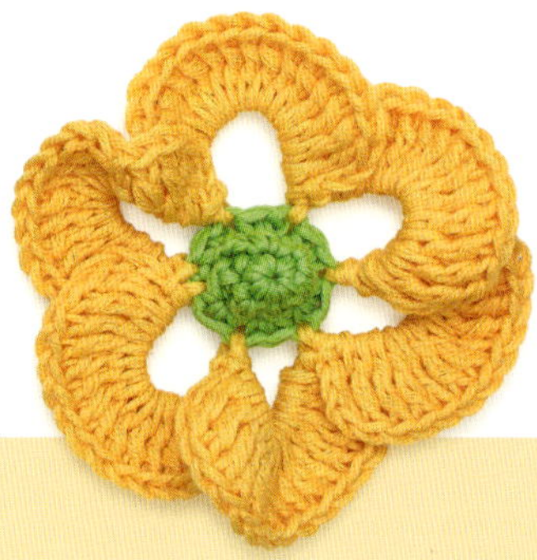

Simple poppy

Pattern

With Colour A, make a magic ring (see page 12).

Rnd 1: Into magic ring, ch 1, 6 dc. Pull on short end to close middle. Join rnd with sl st. (6 dc)

Rnd 2: Ch 3 (counts as first tr), miss first dc, tr in each dc. Join rnd with sl st. (6 tr)

Rnd 3: Ch 1, 2 dc in each tr. Join rnd with sl st. (12 dc)

Fasten off Colour A.

Attach Colour B to any dc of Rnd 3.

Rnd 4: [Ch 10, miss next dc, sl st in next dc] six times (**see Steps 1–2**). (6 ch-10 loops)

Rnd 5: *[Sl st, ch 3, 15 dtr, ch 3, sl st] in ch-10 loop.

Rep from * five more times (6 petals) (**see Steps 3–4** for a refresher on the double treble crochet stitch).

Fasten off Colour B.

Attach Colour C to sl st between any two petals (**see Step 7**).

Rnd 6: *Ch 3, sl st in first dtr, [ch 3, sl st in next dtr] 14 times. Ch 3, sl st in base of same petal.

Rep from * for each remaining petal.

Fasten off. Weave in all ends.

Chart key:

- Magic ring
- Ch Chain
- Dc Double crochet
- Sl st Slip stitch
- Tr Treble crochet
- Dtr Double treble crochet

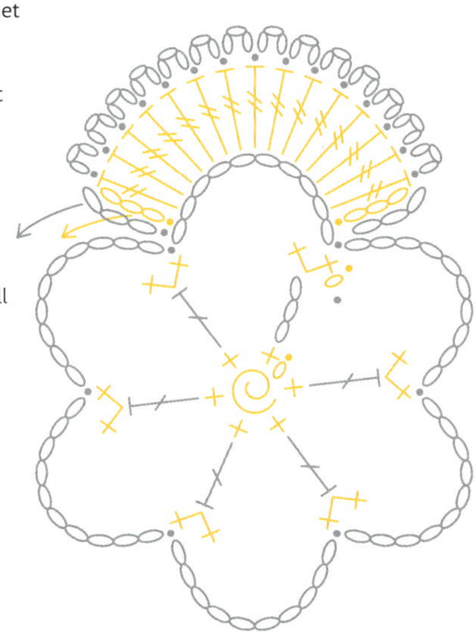

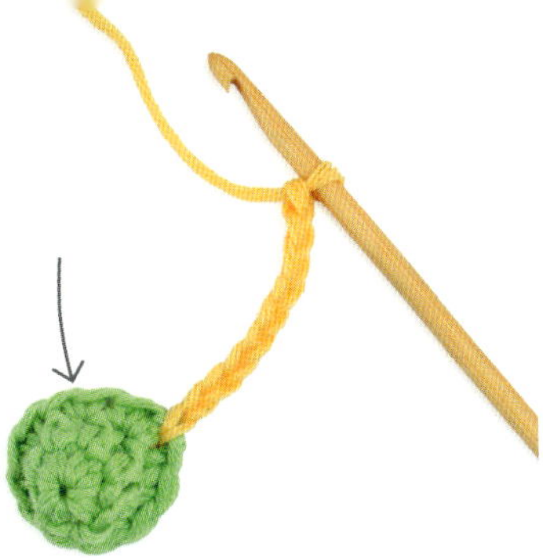

1 Follow the pattern instructions for Rounds 1–3. Attach Colour B to any dc of Round 3. **Rnd 4:** Ch 10, miss the next dc, then sl st into the next dc (use the arrow above as a guide).

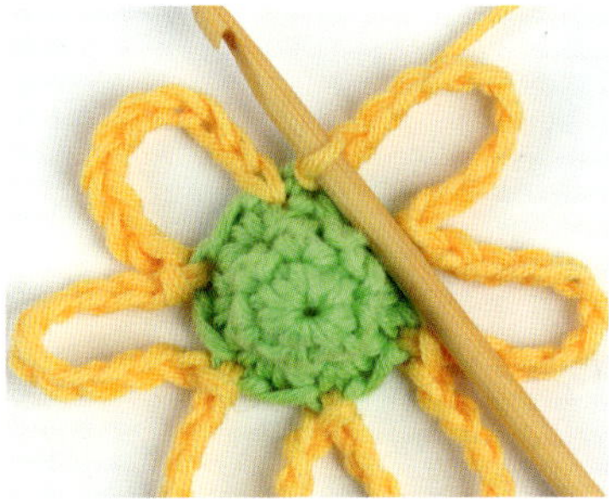

2 [Ch 10, miss the next dc, then sl st into the next dc] five more times to create six ch-10 loop petals in total.

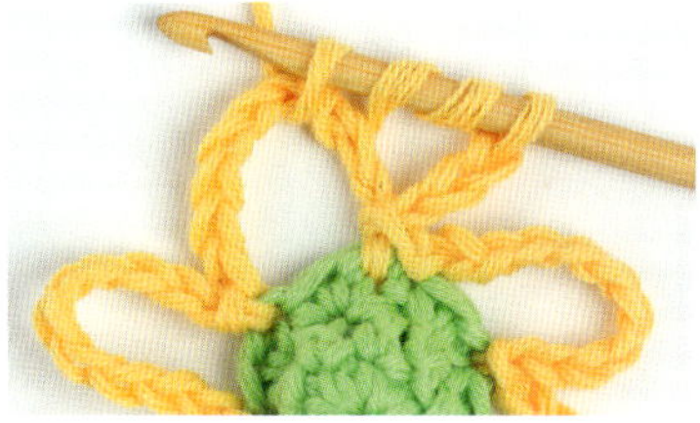

3 **Rnd 5:** Sl st into the next ch-10 loop. Ch 3, dtr into the same ch-10 loop. To make a double treble crochet, yarn over twice, then insert the hook into the chain loop, yarn over and pull the yarn through. You will have four loops on the hook, as shown.

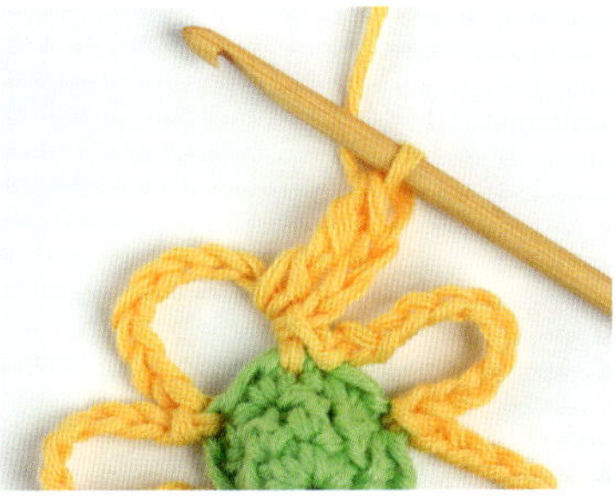

4 [Yarn over and pull the yarn through two loops] three times. You have completed one double treble crochet stitch.

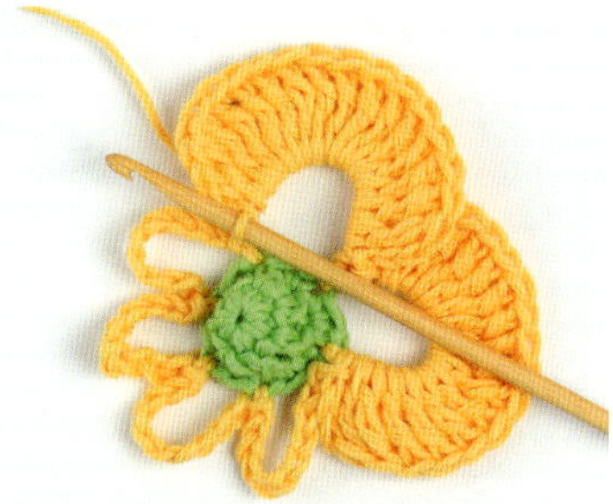

5 Work another 14 dtr into the ch-10 loop, ch 3, sl st into the same loop.

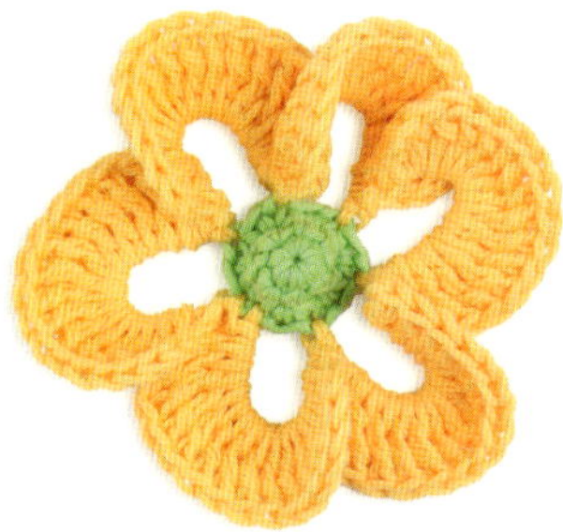

6 Repeat Steps 3–5 five more times to create six petals in total. Fasten off Colour B. Stop here for the Simple Poppy.

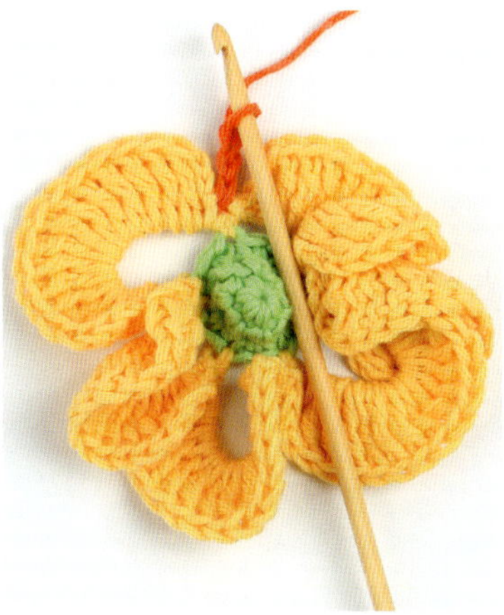

7 To continue to create the Full Poppy, attach Colour C to the sl st between any two of the petals. **Rnd 6:** Ch 3.

8 Sl st into the first dtr, [ch 3, sl st into the next dtr] 14 times. Ch 3, sl st into the base of the same petal. Repeat Steps 7–8 for each of the remaining five petals. Fasten off Colour C and weave in all ends.

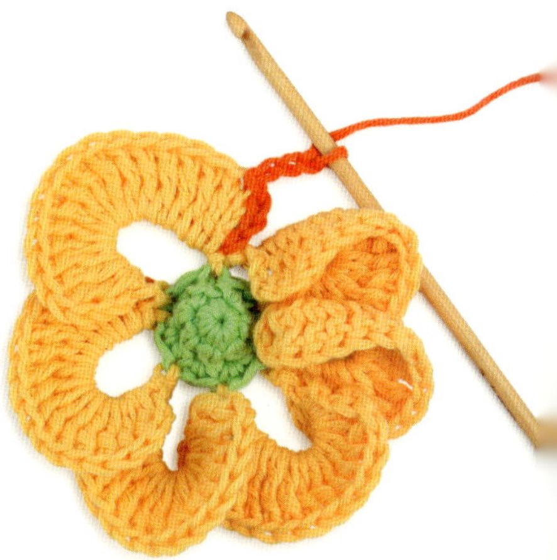

18 Cherry Blossom

Skill level: ✿✿

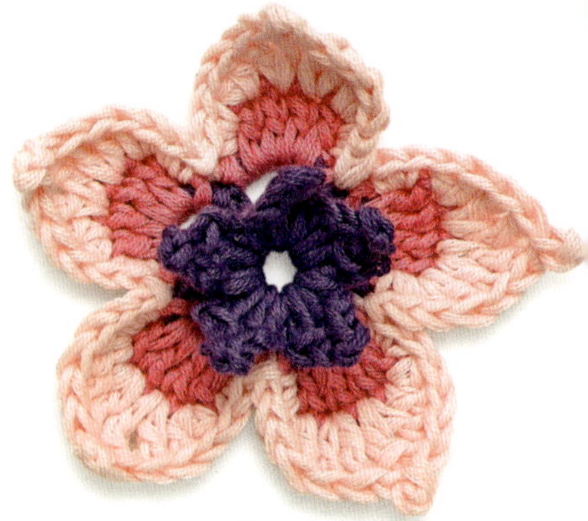

Many beautiful crochet flowers are created by combining layers of different colours and petal shapes. This delicate cherry blossom is a wonderful example of that. As some of these petals overlap, you will also learn a new way of reading crochet charts.

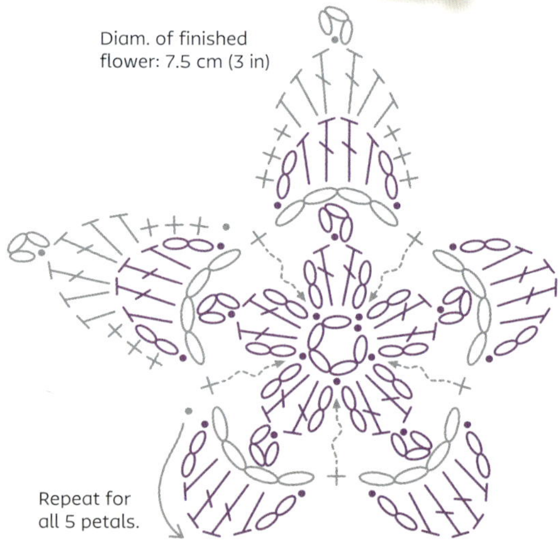

Materials:

4-ply yarn in 3 colours:

- Colour A: 2.75 m (3 yds)
- Colour B: 3.75 m (4 yds)
- Colour C: 5.5 m (6 yds)

Tools:

Hook size: 3.25 mm (D-3)
Yarn needle
Scissors

Chart key:

- Ch Chain
- Sl st Slip stitch
- Tr Treble crochet
- 3 ch picot (ch 3, sl st in 3rd ch from hook)
- Dc Double crochet
- Htr Half treble crochet

Pattern

With Colour A, ch 5, sl st in first ch to make a ring.

Rnd I: Into ring: [ch 2, tr, 3 ch picot, tr, ch 2, sl st] five times (**see Step I**). (5 petals)

Rnd 2: [Ch 4, dc in sl st between petals] five times, making sure ch-4 loops are behind petals (**see Steps 2–3**).

Fasten off Colour A.

Attach Colour B to any ch-4 loop (**see Step 4**).

Rnd 3: *[Sl st, ch 2, htr, 2 tr, htr, ch 2, sl st] in ch-4 loop.

Rep from * four more times (**see Step 5**).

Fasten off Colour B.

Attach Colour C to a 2nd sl st between petals (**see Step 6**).

Rnd 4: Work around next petal: *Dc in next 2 ch, [dc, htr] in next htr, [htr, tr] in next tr, 3 ch picot, [tr, htr] in next tr, [htr, dc] in next htr, dc in next 2 ch, sl st in 2nd sl st between petals (**see Step 7**).

Rep from * for each petal (**see Step 8**). Fasten off Colour C. Weave in ends.

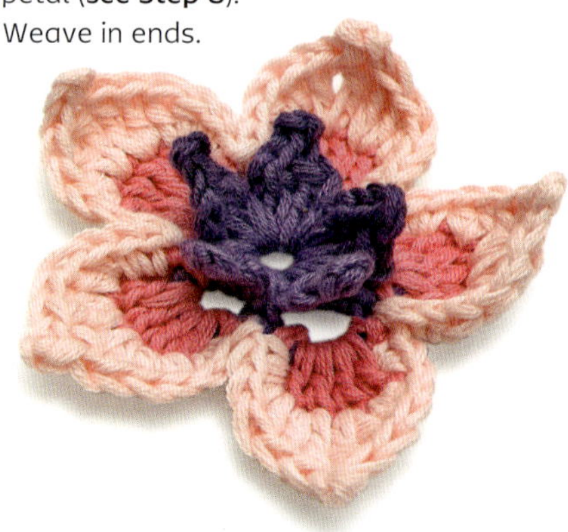

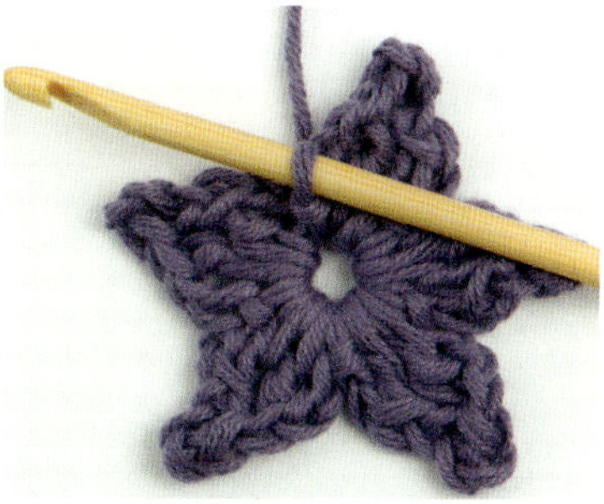

1 Following the pattern, crochet Round I using Colour A.

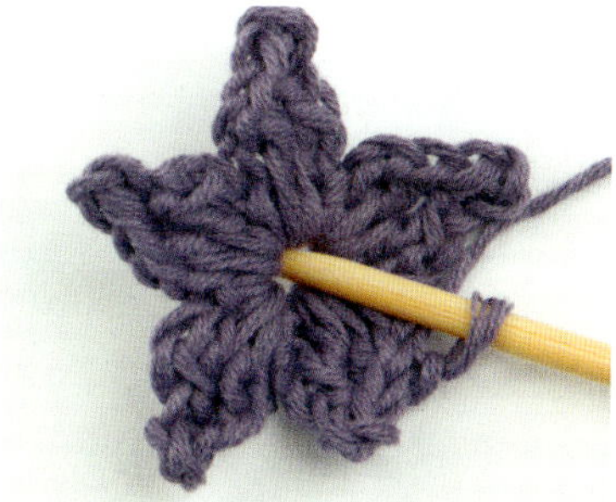

2 In Round 2, ch 4, then dc between two petals. To make a dc between petals, insert the hook into the centre of the flower, pull the yarn through then finish as a regular dc stitch. Continue following the instructions for Round 2 of the pattern.

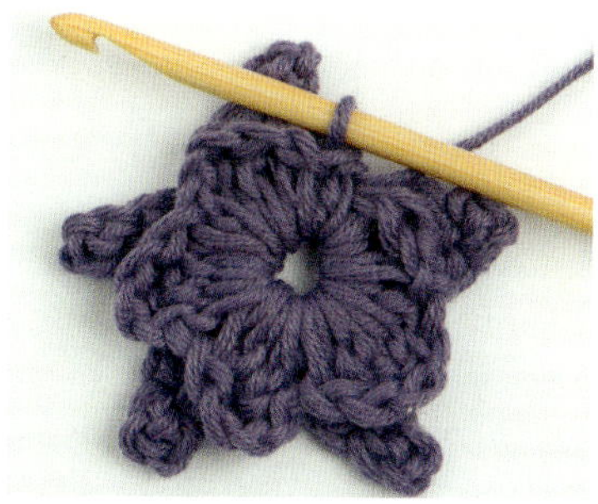

3 Make sure that you crochet the chain stitches behind the petals. This is the view from the wrong side.

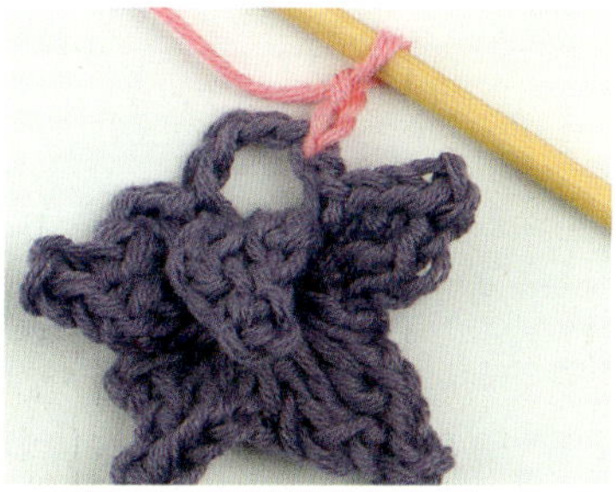

4 Attach Colour B to one of the ch-4 loops. You can fold each petal over to view the chain better when crocheting Round 3.

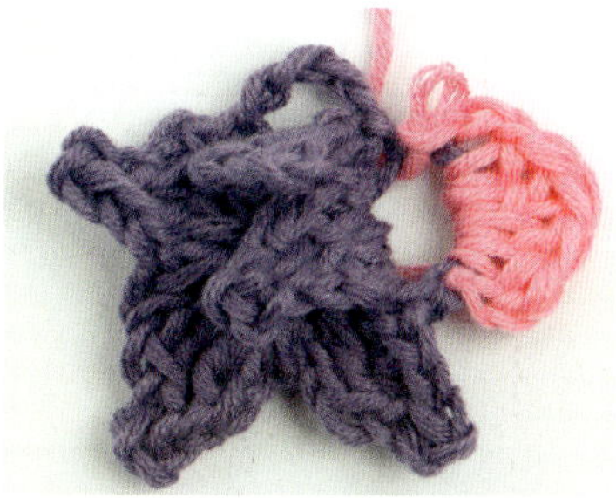

5 Continue working Round 3. Make each petal into a separate ch-4 loop of Round 2.

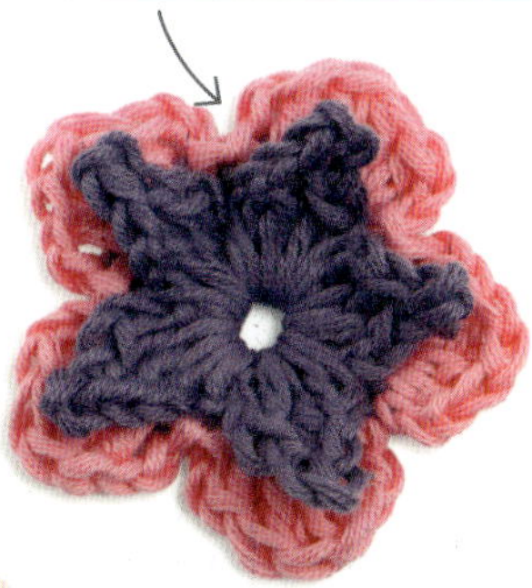

6 Complete Round 3 and fasten off Colour B. Attach Colour C into a second sl st between two petals, as indicated by the arrow above.

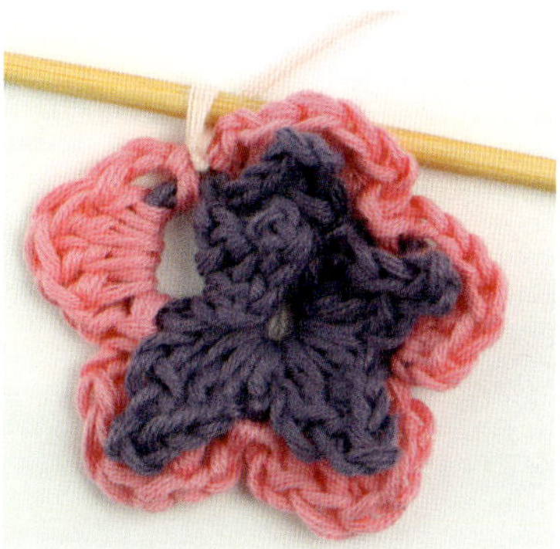

7 Begin crocheting Round 4 into the stitches of first petal.

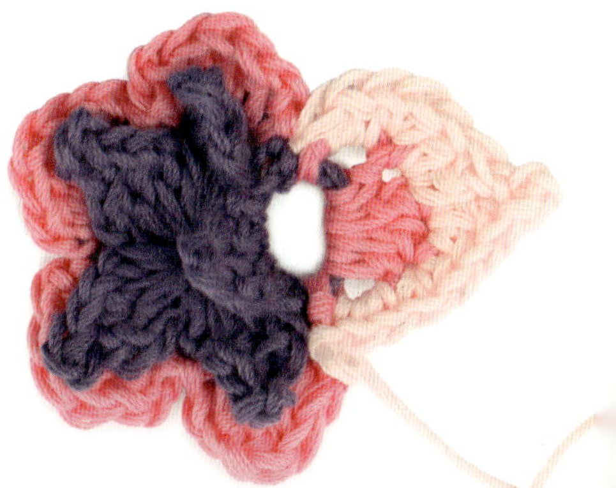

8 Continue working Round 4 into all five petals. Fasten off Colour C and weave in all ends.

19 Lacy Carnation

Skill level:

This flower pattern introduces a new technique for adding a second layer. You can stop after Round 5 for a beautiful flower, or continue and add Rounds 6 and 7 for something extra.

Materials:

4-ply yarn in 2 colours:

Colour A: 10 m (11 yds)

Colour B: 5.5 m (6 yds)

Tools:

Hook size: 3.25 mm (D-3)
Yarn needle
Scissors

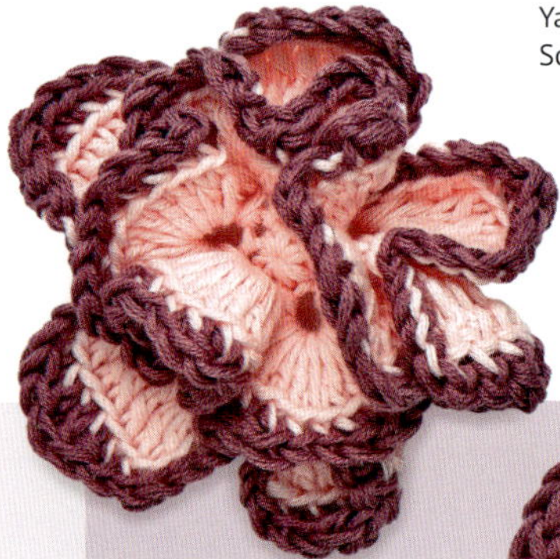

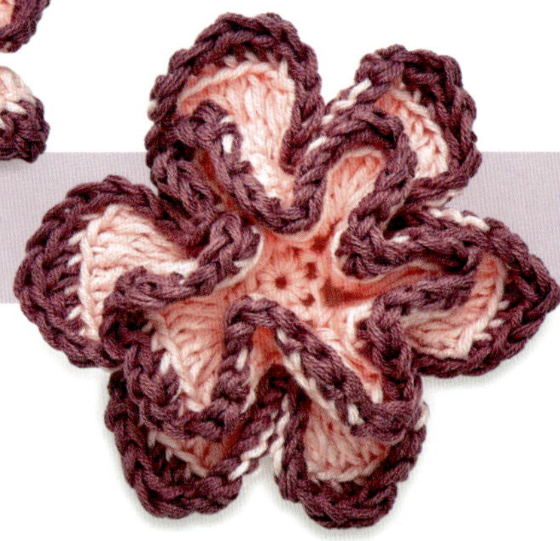

Diam. of finished flower: 9 cm (3½ in)

Pattern

With Colour A, make a magic ring (see page 12).

Rnd 1: Into magic ring, ch 1, 6 dc. Pull on short end to close middle. Join rnd with sl st. (6 dc)

Rnd 2: [Ch 4, sl st in next dc] six times.

Rnd 3: Ch 3, [12 tr in ch-4 loop] six times. Join with sl st in first tr.

Rnd 4: Ch 3, dc between petals of Rnd 3, [ch 5, dc between next two petals] five times, ch 5, sl st in first ch-5 loop of this rnd (**see Steps 1–3**).

Rnd 5: [Ch 4, 7 dtr in ch-5 loop, ch 4, sl st in same loop, sl st in next ch-5 loop] six times (**see Step 4**).

Fasten off Colour A.

Attach Colour B to a first tr of Rnd 3 (inner petals) (**see Step 5**).

Rnd 6: Ch 1, *dc in next tr, htr in next tr, dc in next tr, sl sl in next tr. Rep from * to end of rnd. Last sl st will be made in same st as first ch of rnd (**see Step 6**).

Rnd 7: Ch 3, sl st in st between large petals (outside layer). *Sl st in next 4 ch, dc in next 2 dtr, htr in next dtr, tr in next dtr, htr in next dtr, dc in next 2 dtr, sl st in next 4 ch (**see Steps 7–8**).

Rep from * around each petal.

Fasten off Colour B. Weave in ends.

Chart key:

- Magic ring
- Ch Chain
- Dc Double crochet
- Sl st Slip stitch
- Tr Treble crochet
- Dtr Double treble crochet
- Htr Half treble crochet

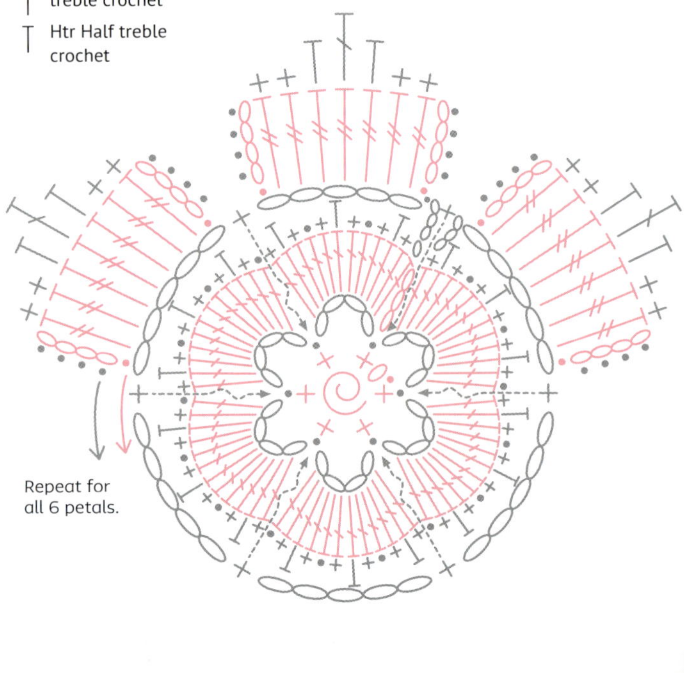

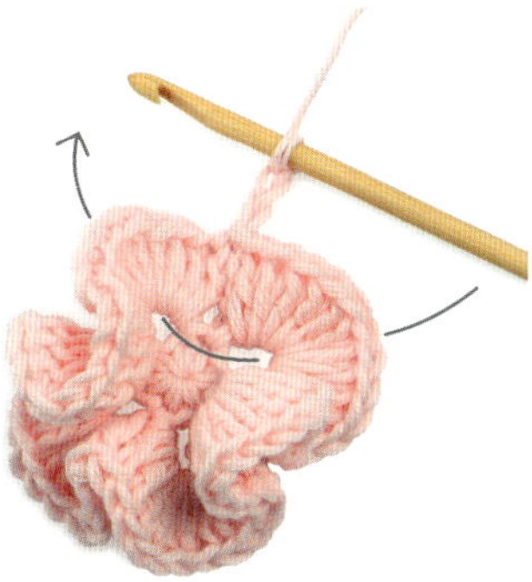

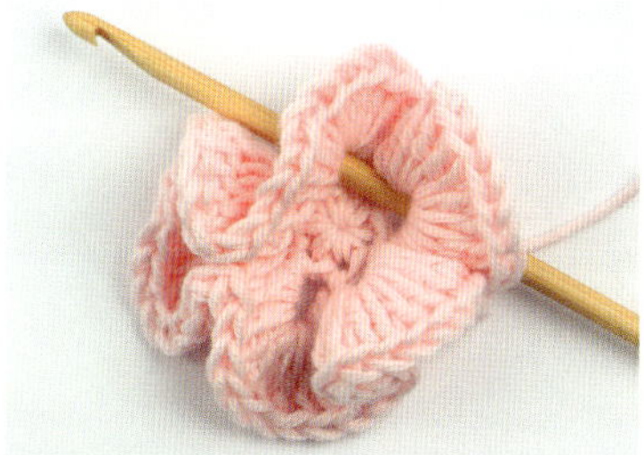

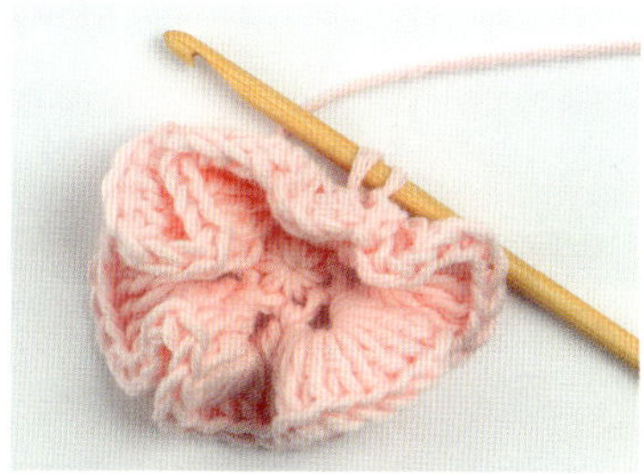

1 Follow the pattern for Rounds 1–4. When you come to Round 4, you will need to make one dc stitch between two petals. To do that, follow the arrow to insert the hook.

2 Yarn over, and then pull the yarn through.

3 Now you have two loops on the hook. Yarn over, pull the yarn through both loops on the hook. You have made one dc between two petals.

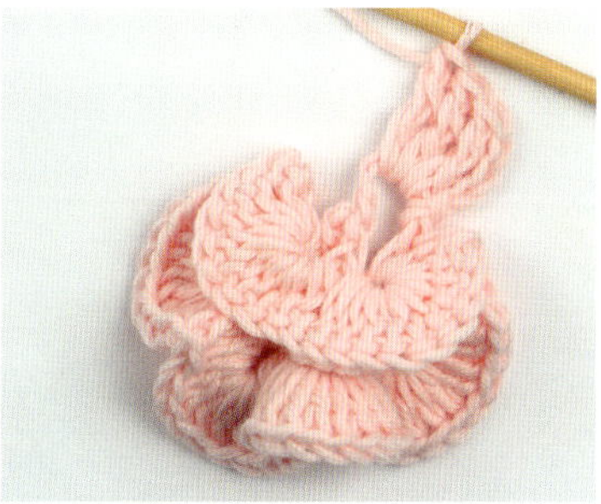

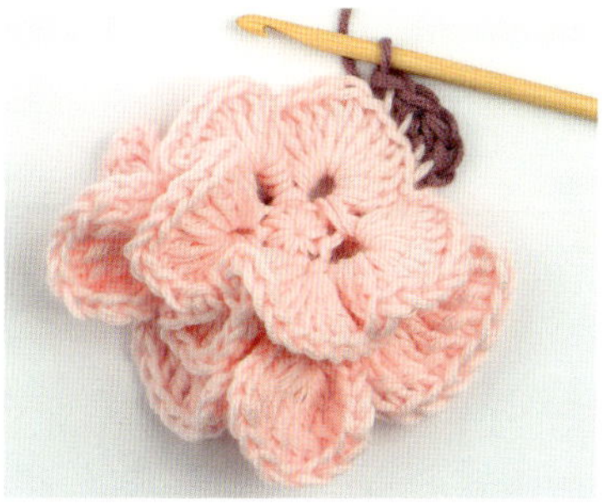

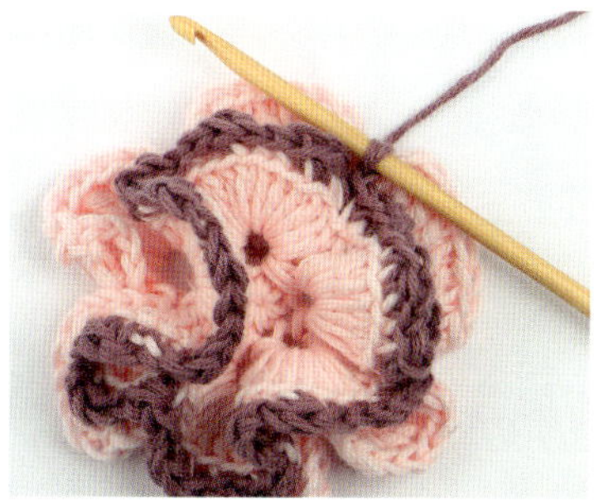

4 In Round 5, crochet into the ch-5 loops that you have created.

5 Attach Colour B to the inner petals by joining it to the first tr of one of the petals in Round 3, as pictured.

6 Following the pattern, complete Round 6.

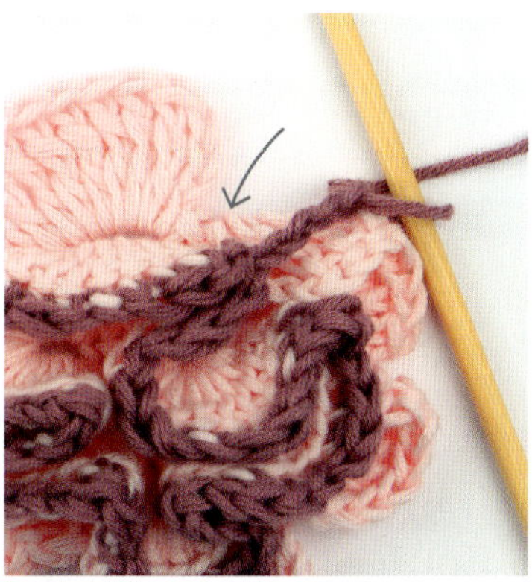

7 To start Round 7, make a sl st into the space between two of the large petals, as pointed out by the arrow.

8 Follow the pattern instructions for Round 7 to crochet around each petal. Fasten off Colour B and weave in ends.

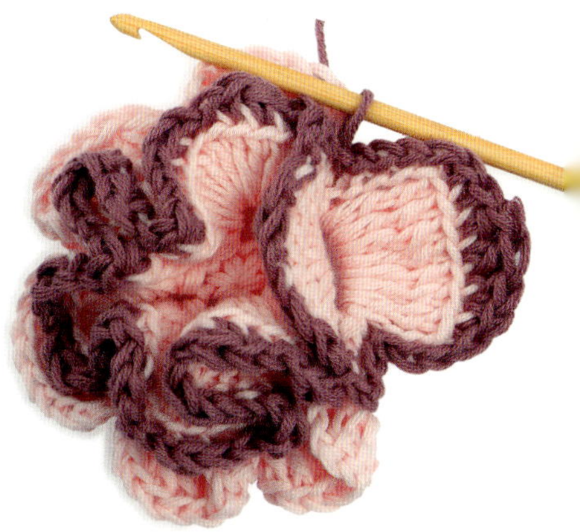

20 Cornflower

Skill level:

To make this beautiful field flower, you will need to crochet into back and front loops. This may be quite challenging when you try it for the first time, but you'll soon get the hang of it. Use stitch markers to help you with finding the right stitches.

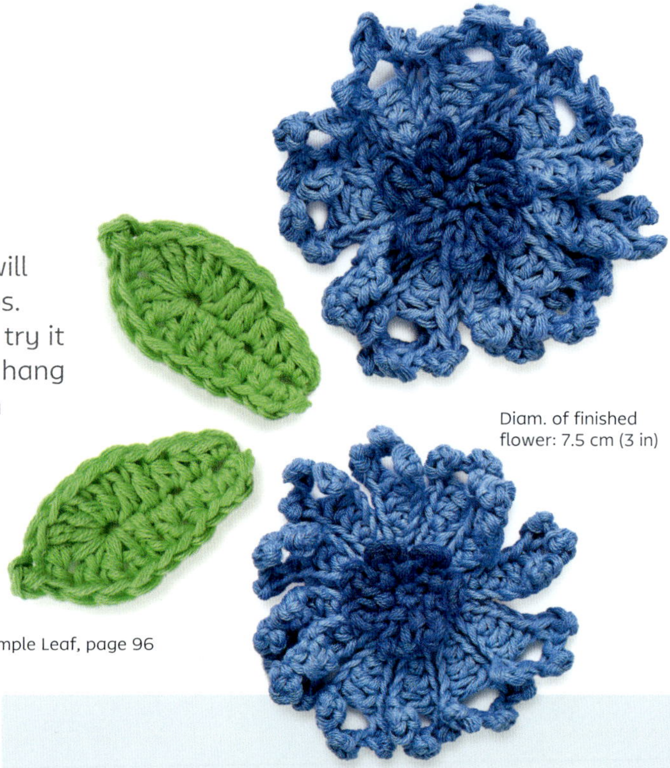

Diam. of finished flower: 7.5 cm (3 in)

Simple Leaf, page 96

Pattern

With Colour A, make a magic ring (see page 12).

Rnd 1: Into magic ring, ch 1, 7 dc. Pull on short end to close middle. Join rnd with sl st in a front loop only. (7 dc)

Rnd 2: Working in front loops of Rnd 1: [Ch 6, sl st in next st] seven times (**see Steps 1–3**).

Fasten off Colour A.

Attach Colour B to back loop of first dc of Rnd 1 (**see Steps 4–5**).

Rnd 3: *Ch 7, dc in 2nd and 3rd ch from hook, [ch 3, dc in 2nd and 3rd ch from hook] twice, tr in next 2 ch, htr in next ch, dc in next ch, sl st in same back loop of Rnd 1. Ch 7, dc in 2nd and 3rd ch from hook, [ch 3, dc in 2nd and 3rd ch from hook] twice, tr in next 2 ch, htr in next ch, dc in next ch, sl st in next back loop of Rnd 1 (**see Steps 6–8**).

Rep from * six more times (14 petals).

Fasten off Colour B. Weave in ends.

Materials:

4-ply yarn in 2 colours:

- Colour A: 2.75 m (3 yds)
- Colour B: 8.25 m (9 yds)

Tools:

Hook size: 3.25 mm (D-3)
Yarn needle
Scissors
Stitch marker

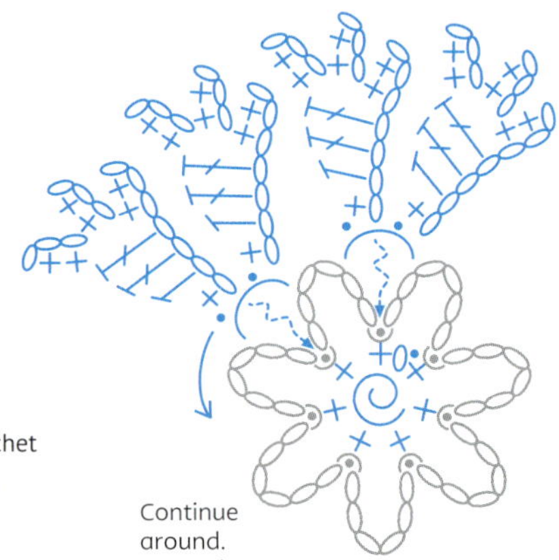

Continue around. 14 petals in total.

Chart key:

- Magic ring
- Ch Chain
- Dc Double crochet
- Sl st Slip stitch
- Front loop
- Back loop
- Tr Treble crochet
- Htr half treble crochet

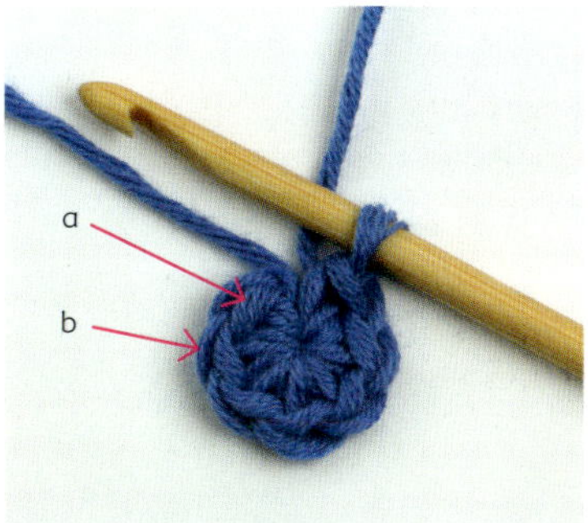

1 Notice that crochet stitches have two loops: a front loop and a back loop. The front loop is on the inside of your work (a), while the back loop is on the outer side of your work (b).

2 In Round 2, insert the hook into the front loops of the stitches only.

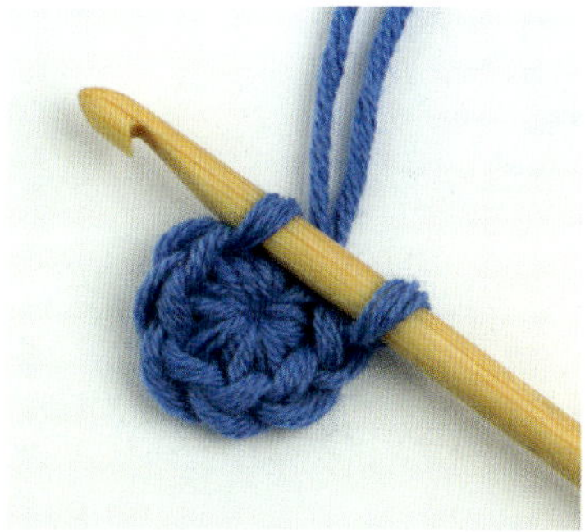

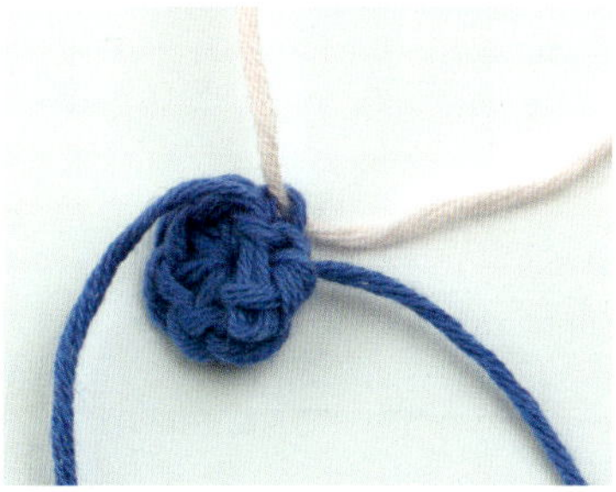

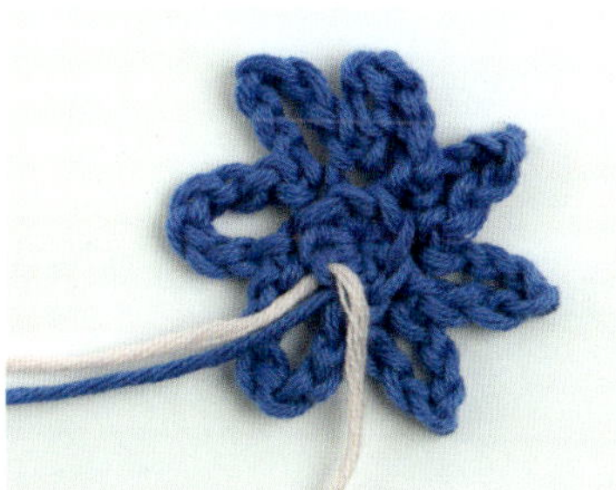

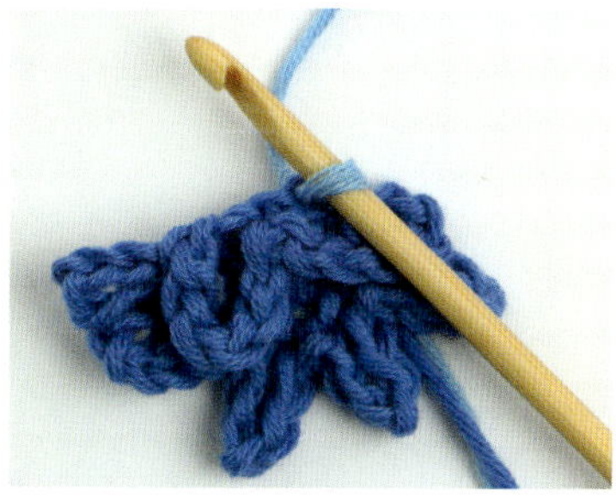

3 It's a good idea to mark the back loop of the first dc of Round 1 with a stitch marker or a piece of contrasting yarn.

4 When you come to attach Colour B to the back loop of the first dc of Round 1, use your stitch marker as a guide.

5 Fold the petals forwards and out of the way to make the crocheting of Round 3 easier.

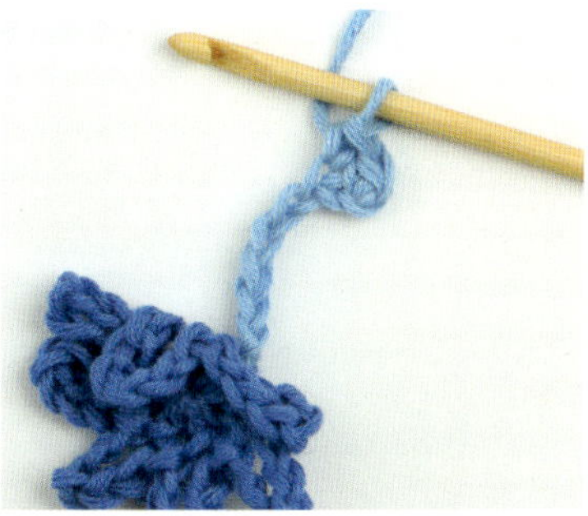

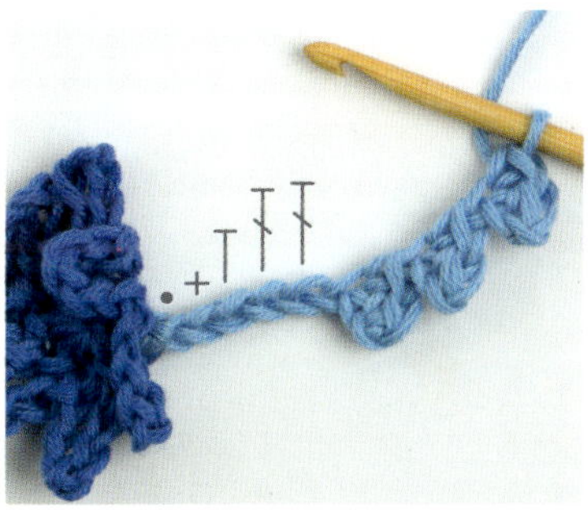

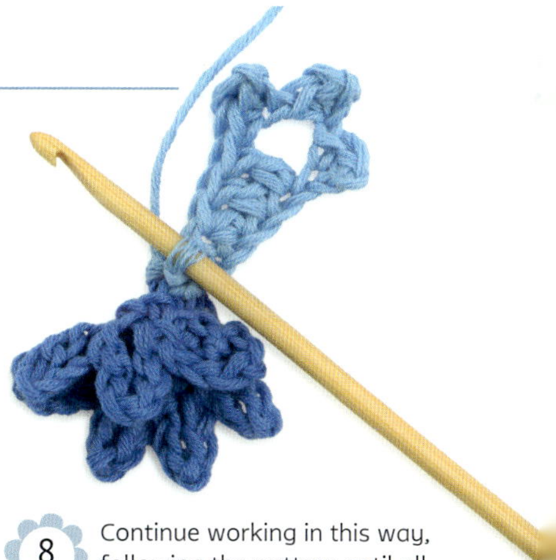

6 The next three pictures illustrate the creation of the outer petals. Follow the pattern for Round 3 and refer to the photographs for a visual guide.

7 Use the image above as a reference for the correct placement of the last few stitches of Round 3.

8 Continue working in this way, following the pattern until all 14 petals are complete. You will work two outer petals into each slip stitch in Round 2.

21 Tulip

Skill level:

Tulips are a symbol of spring and you can crochet a whole bouquet of them. This pattern has many turns, and some assembly is required, so follow the steps carefully, comparing your work to the pictures as you go.

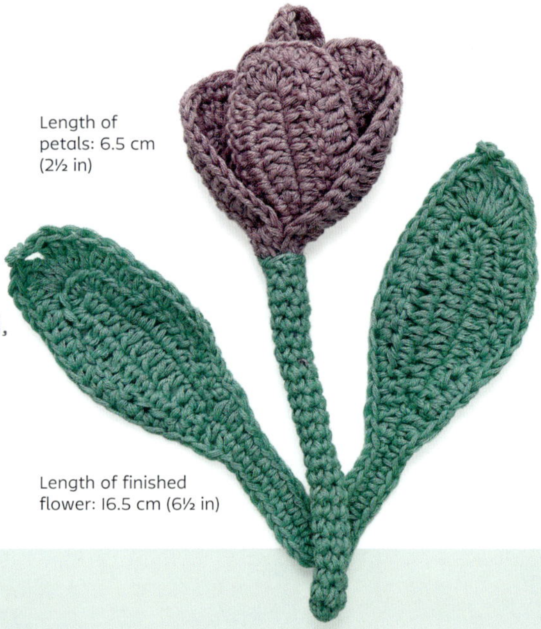

Length of petals: 6.5 cm (2½ in)

Length of finished flower: 16.5 cm (6½ in)

Pattern

Small petal (make 2)**:**

With Colour A, ch 12.

Row 1: Htr in 3rd ch from hook, tr in next 5 ch, htr in next 2 ch, dc in next 2 ch.

Row 2: Ch 2, turn, htr in next dc, tr in next 8 sts, 2 tr in next 4 sts, tr in next 8 ch, htr in next ch, ch 2, sl st in same ch as last htr (**see Steps 1–2**).

Fasten off Colour A.

Large petal (make 3)**:**

With Colour A, ch 12.

Row 1: Htr in 3rd ch from hook, tr in next 5 ch, htr in next 2 ch, dc in next 2 ch.

Row 2: Ch 2, turn, htr in next dc, tr in next 8 sts, 2 tr in next 4 sts, tr in next 8 ch, htr in next ch (**see Steps 3–4**).

Row 3: Ch 2, turn, htr in next htr, tr in next 9 tr, 3 htr in next tr, 2 htr in next tr, dc in next 2 tr, 2 htr in next tr, 3 htr in next tr, tr in next 9 tr, htr in next htr, ch 2, sl st in same st as last htr.

Fasten off Colour A.

One of the petals should have a long yarn end for sewing (**see Step 5**).

Stem:

With Colour B, make a magic ring (see page 12). Into magic ring, ch 1, 6 dc. Pull on short end to close middle. Join rnd with sl st (**see Step 6**).

Work in spiral, dc in each dc. Make sure right side is on the outside. Crochet until desired length reached. Sl st in next 2 sts (**see Steps 7–8**).

Fasten off Colour B, leaving a long yarn end for sewing.

Leaf:

With Colour B, ch 25.

Row 1: Starting from 3rd ch from hook, htr in next 3 ch, tr in next 5 ch, htr in next 2 ch, sl st in next ch.

Row 2: Ch 1, turn, dc in next 2 htr, htr in next 2 tr, tr in next 5 sts, 2 htr in next 4 sts, tr in next 5 ch, htr in next 2 ch, dc in next 2 ch (**see Steps 9–11**).

Row 3: Ch 1, turn, dc in next 4 sts, htr in next 7 sts, [htr, tr] in next htr, [tr, 2 dtr] in next htr, 3 ch picot, [2 dtr, tr] in next htr, [tr, htr] in next htr, htr in next 7 sts, dc in next 4 sts (**see Step 12**).

Continue working in ch without turning work: tr in first ch, htr in next ch, dc in next 9 ch, 3 dc in next ch (corner), dc in next 9 ch, htr in next ch, tr in next ch. Join with sl st in first dc of Row 3 (**see Steps 13–14**).

Fasten off Colour B.

See **Steps 15–17** for instructions on how to assemble your flower.

Materials:

4-ply yarn in 2 colours:

Colour A: 18.25 m (20 yds)

Colour B: 18.25 m (20 yds)

Tools:

Hook size: 3.25 mm (D-3)
Yarn needle
Scissors

Small petal

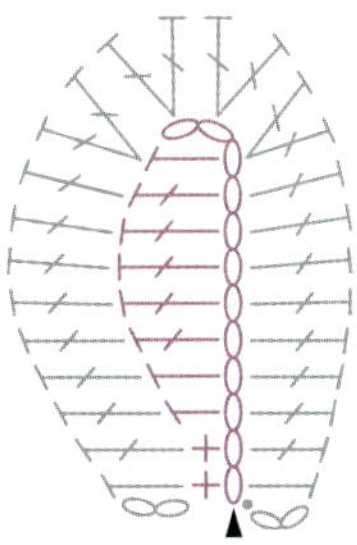

Start here

Large petal

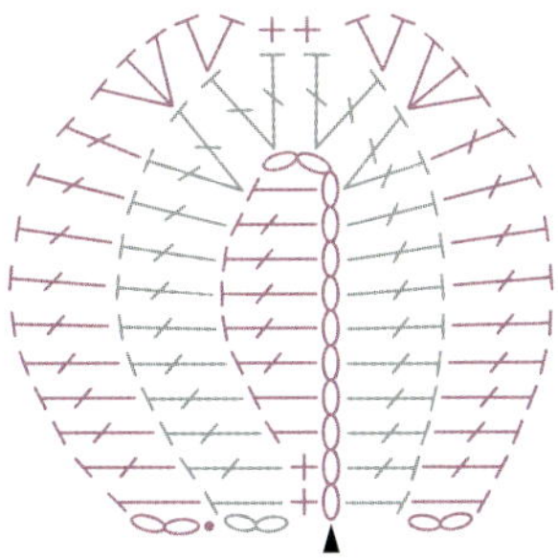

Start here

Leaf

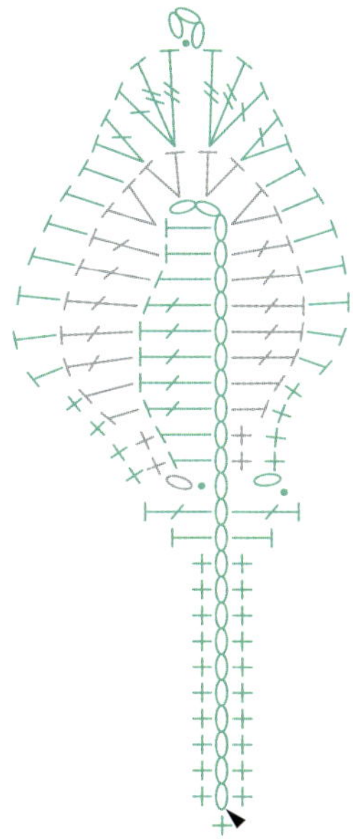

Start here

Chart key:

- Ch Chain
- Htr Half treble crochet
- Tr Treble crochet
- Dc Double crochet
- Sl st Slip stitch
- Dtr Double treble crochet
- 3 ch picot (ch 3, sl st in 3rd ch from hook)

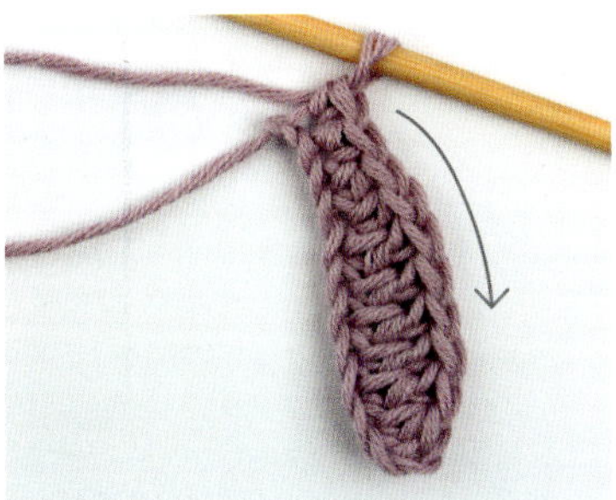

1 At the beginning of Row 2 of a small petal, turn your work around and start crocheting in the opposite direction.

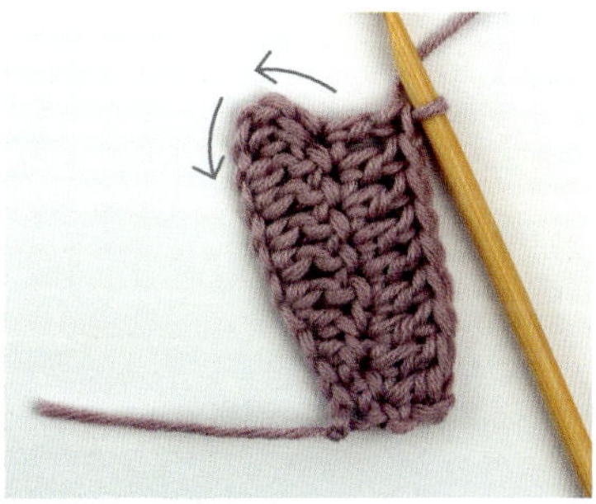

2 Once you reach the middle of Row 2, continue crocheting around the corner and down the other side of the petal (follow the arrows).

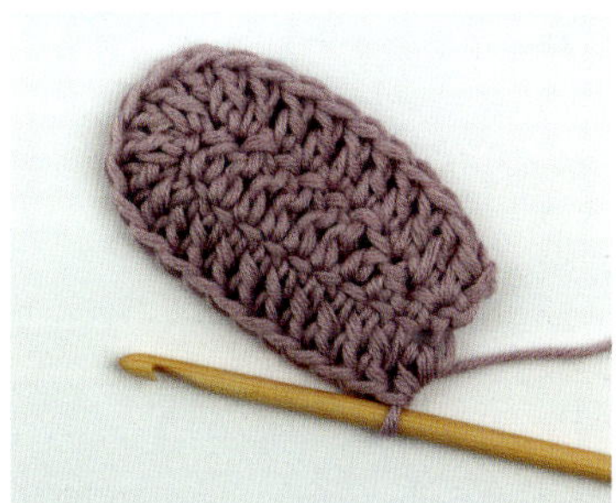

3 When making a large petal, you will turn your work again in Row 2, and crochet in the opposite direction to the previous row.

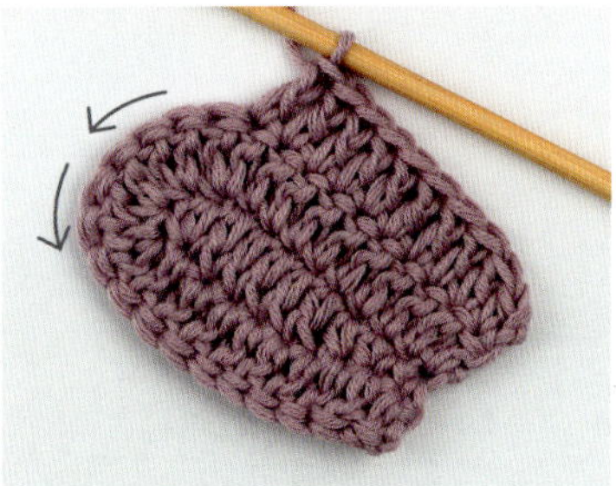

4 Follow the pattern to crochet around the whole of the large petal.

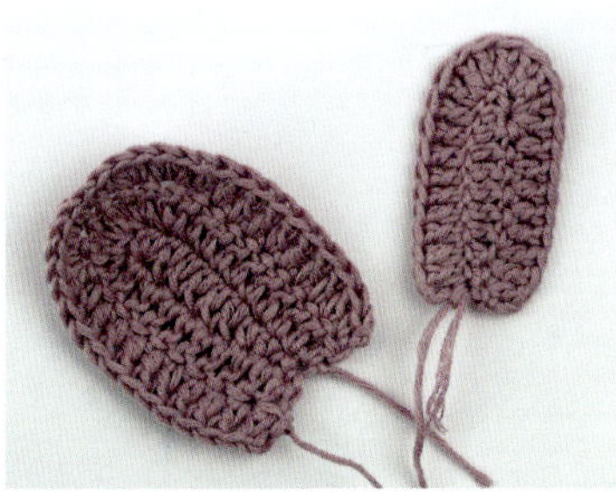

5 Make two small and three large petals. On one petal, leave a long yarn end for sewing the flower together.

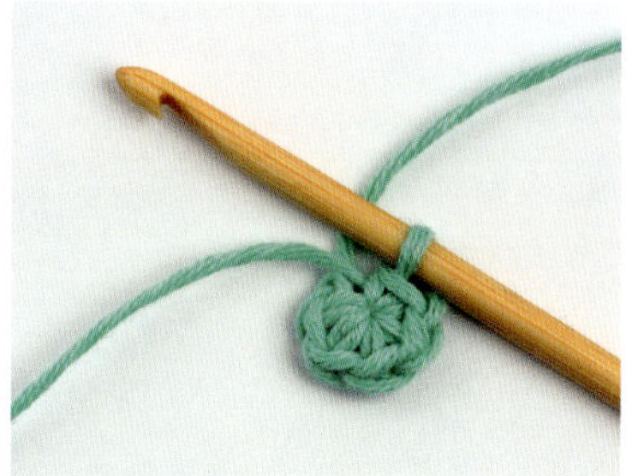

6 To make a stem, start by working 6 dc into a magic ring.

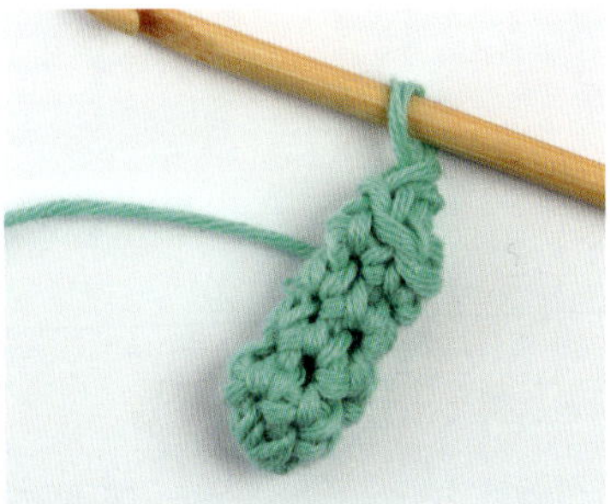

7 Make sure that the right side of the work is facing outwards.

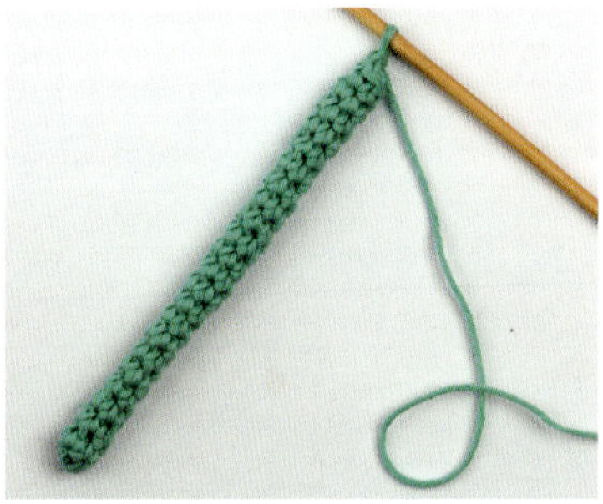

8 Crochet around in a spiral, working dc into each dc, and creating a long stem.

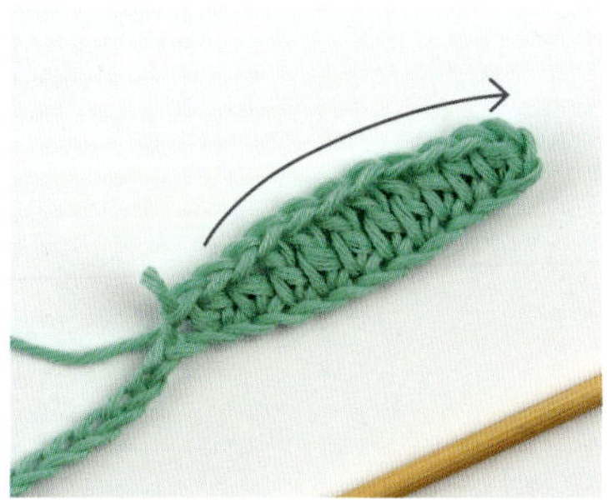

9 When making a leaf, you will turn at the start of Row 2, leaving a chain tail behind.

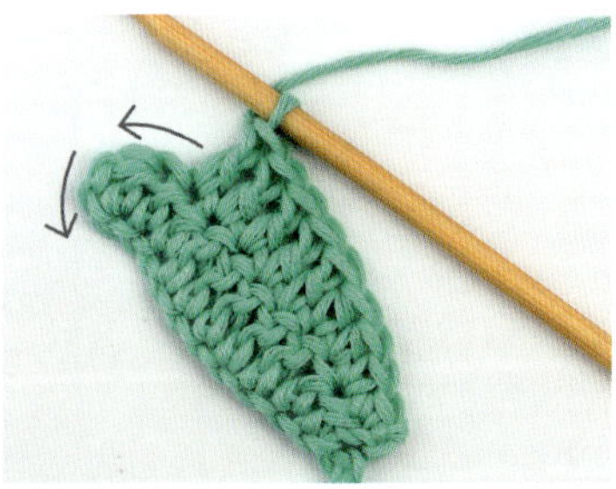

10 Crochet around the tip of the leaf and then along the opposite side.

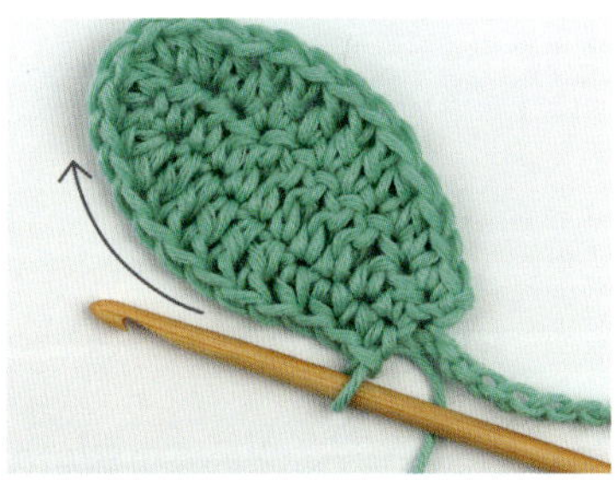

11 At the end of Row 2, turn the work once again and crochet back around the leaf.

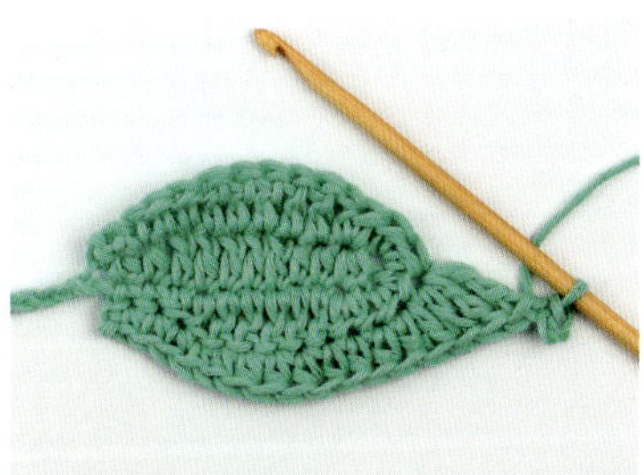

12 Crochet following the pattern until you reach the chain tail.

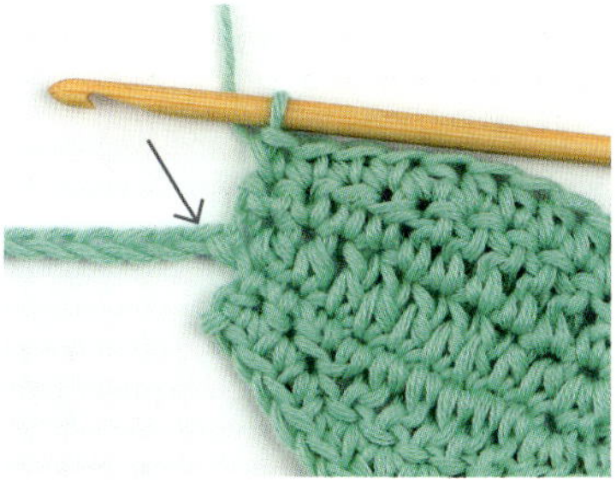

13 Follow the arrow for the placement of the first tr into the chain.

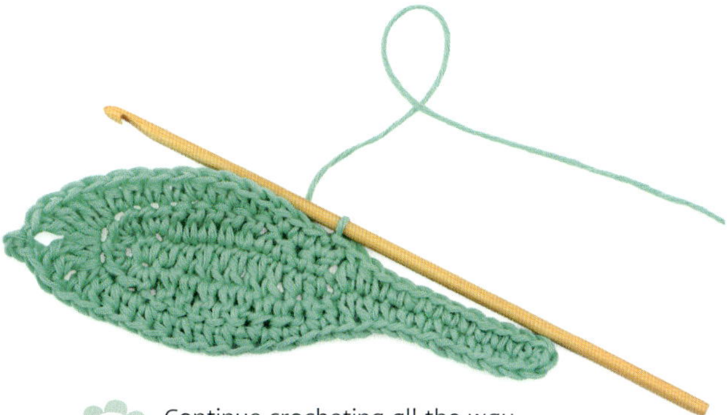

14 Continue crocheting all the way around the chain tail.

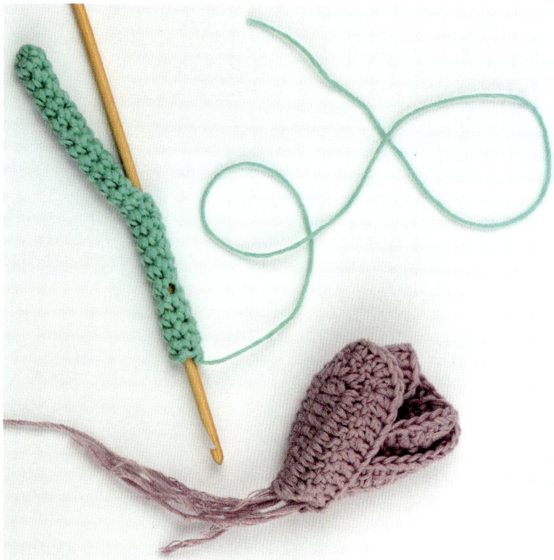

15 Using the long yarn end you left on one of them, sew the five petals together, with the large petals on the outside. To attach the stem to the petals, insert the hook into the stem as pictured, and pull the petal yarn ends into the stem.

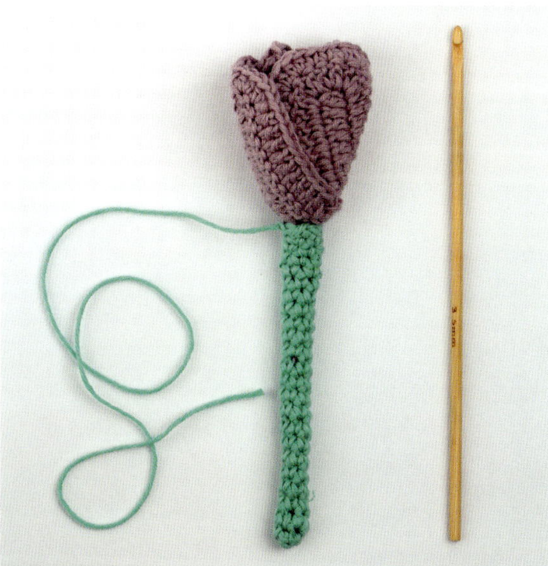

16 Finish by using the stem yarn end to sew the petals securely into the stem.

17 Make a few flowers and attach some leaves to create a beautiful crocheted bouquet of tulips.

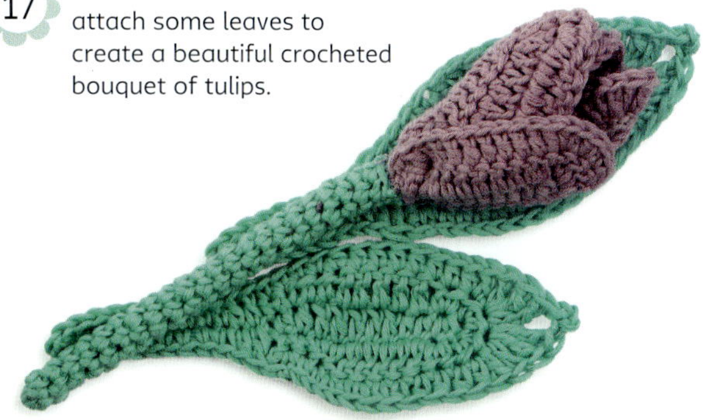

22 Hibiscus

Skill level:

Diam. of finished flower: 6.5 cm (2½ in)

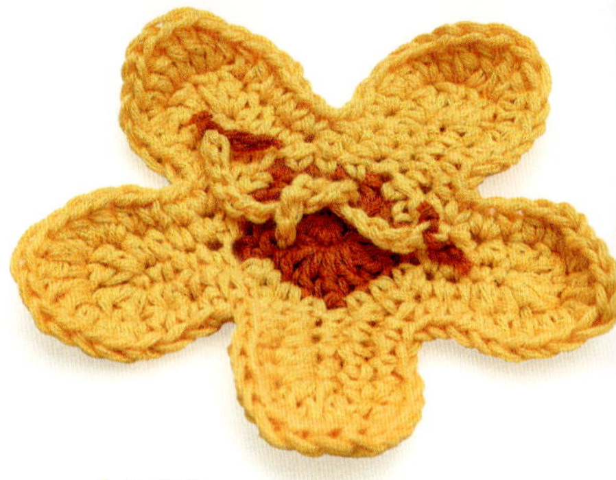

This familiar flower will make a beautiful decoration in any combination of colours. It holds its shape well, so is a good choice for using in projects. Be very careful with the stitch count in this flower.

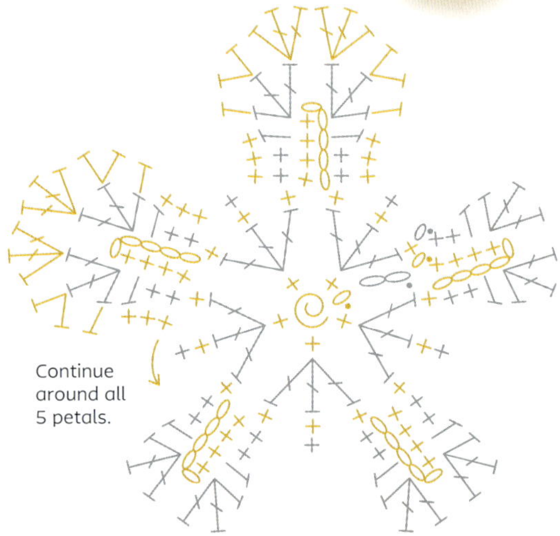

Materials:

4-ply yarn in 2 colours:

Colour A: 2.75 m (3 yds)

Colour B: 10 m (11 yds)

Tools:

Hook size: 3.25 mm (D-3)
Yarn needle
Scissors

Chart key:

- Magic ring
- Ch Chain
- Dc Double crochet
- Sl st Slip stitch
- Tr Treble crochet
- Htr Half treble crochet

Pattern

Flower:

With Colour A, make a magic ring (see page 12).

Rnd 1: Into magic ring, ch 1, 5 dc. Pull on short end to close middle. Join rnd with sl st. (5 dc)

Rnd 2: Ch 2, 3 tr in each dc. Join rnd with sl st (**see Step 1**). (15 tr)

Fasten off Colour A.

Attach Colour B.

Rnd 3: Ch 1, [dc in next 3 tr, ch 5, starting from 2nd ch from hook, dc in next 4 ch] five times. Join rnd with sl st in first dc (**see Step 2**).

Rnd 4: Ch 1, *miss next dc, dc in next dc, miss next dc, dc in next 2 ch, htr in next ch, [htr, 2 tr] in next ch, [2 tr, htr] in next dc, htr in next dc, dc in next 2 dc (**see Steps 3–5**).

Rep from * four more times.

Rnd 5: *Miss next dc, dc in next 3 sts, htr in next htr, 2 htr in next tr, [htr, 2 tr] in next tr, [2 tr, htr] in next tr, 2 htr in next tr, htr in next htr, dc in next 3 sts (**see Steps 6–7**).

Rep from * four more times. Join rnd with sl st.

Fasten off Colour B. Weave in ends.

Stamens:

With Colour B, ch 30. Fasten off.

With Colour A, ch 1, sl st in first ch of stamen, ch 1, fasten off.

Ch 1, sl st in last ch of stamen, ch 1, fasten off. Tighten both ends of yarn and snip with scissors 2–3 mm away from ch sts. (**see Step 8**).

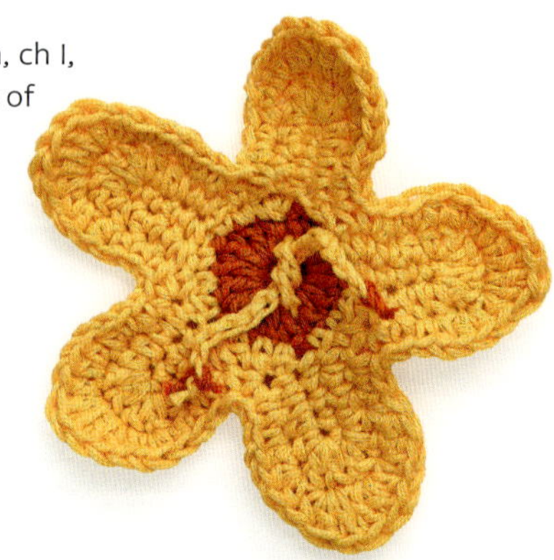

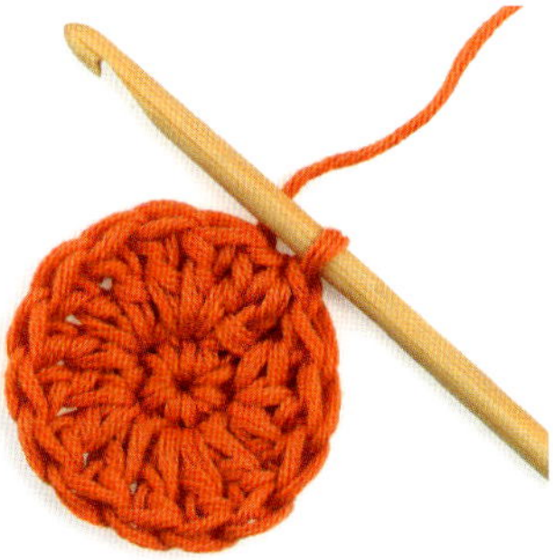

1 Follow the pattern for the first two rounds to create the centre of the flower in Colour A.

2 After crocheting Round 3 in Colour B, you will see the beginnings of five clearly defined petals.

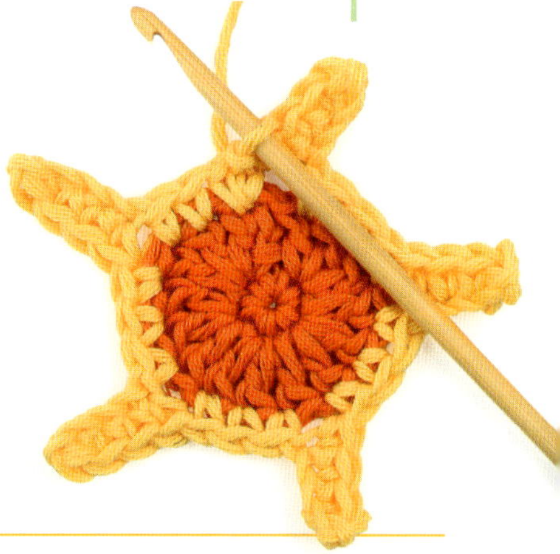

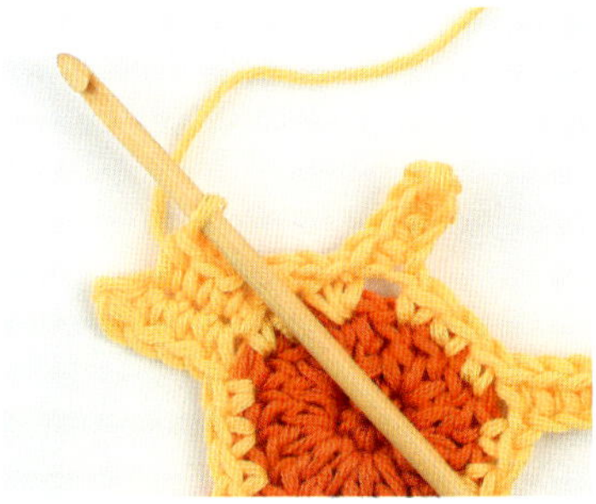

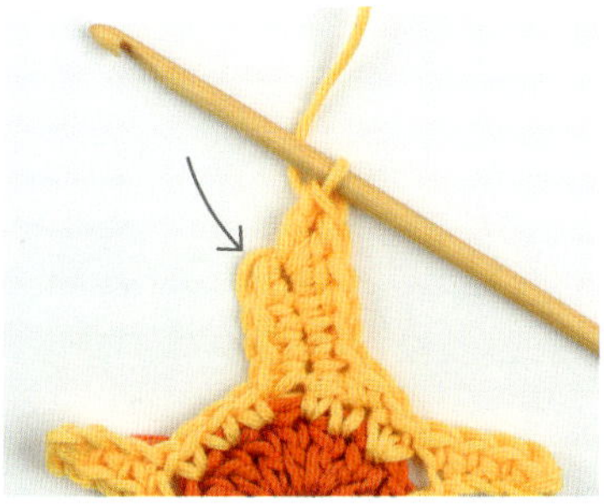

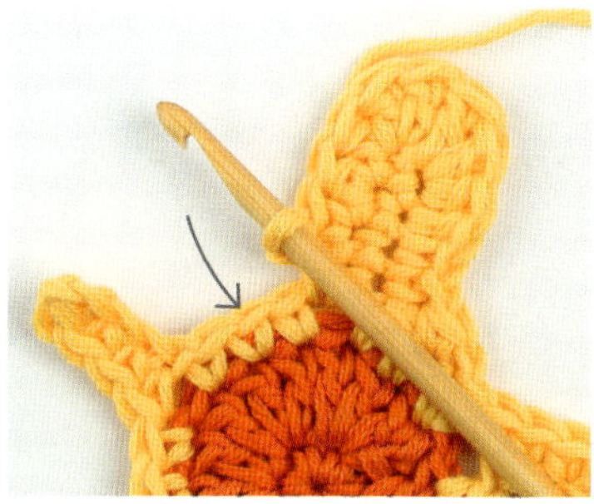

3 You will be crocheting all the way around the flower and its petals as shown.

4 In Round 4, after working [htr, 2 tr] into the next ch, your next stitch will be on the opposite side of the petal, as indicated here with an arrow.

5 Between each petal you can clearly see 3 dc. However, you miss the first and third of these, and crochet into the middle dc only.

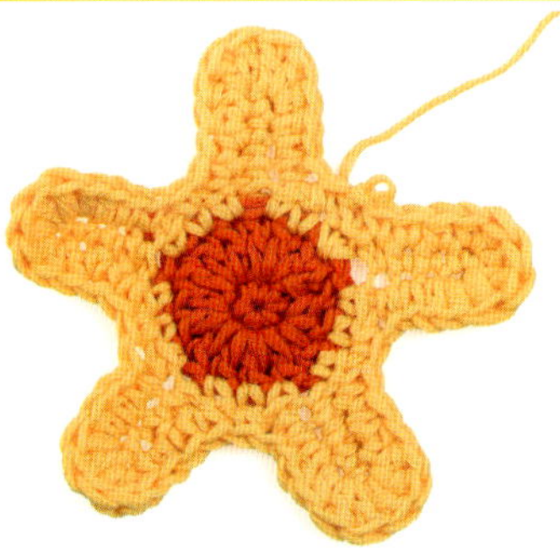

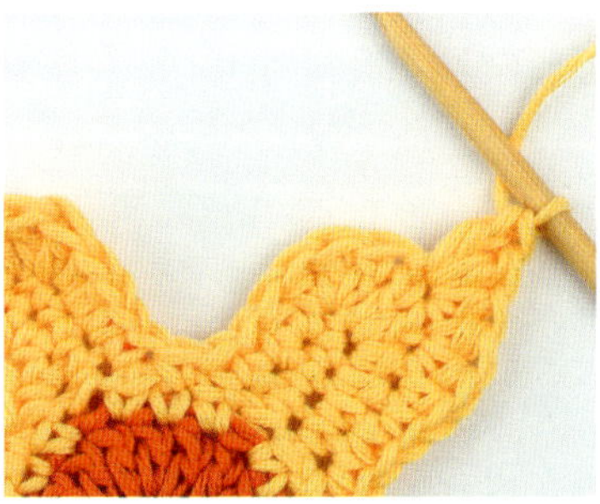

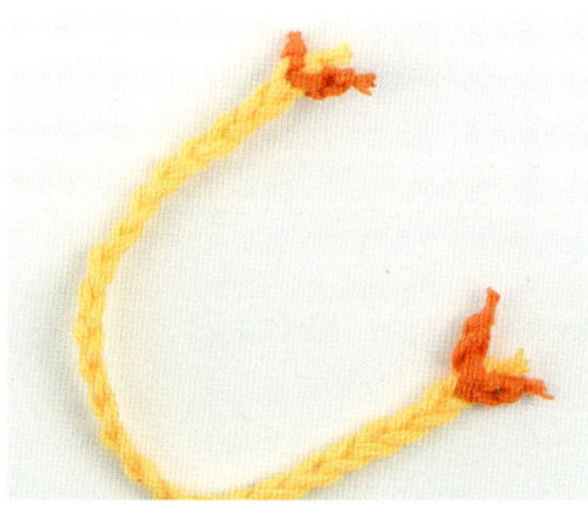

6 After Round 4, your flower will look like this. Start working Round 5 by crocheting into the next petal.

7 Each petal should be equal on both sides.

8 Following the pattern, create a long chain. Thread it through the centre of the flower and tie it to represent the stamens.

23 Blue Columbine

Skill level:

Create a striking flower using contrasting colours, and practise the techniques you have previously learnt. Count your stitches carefully and use stitch markers when working in the round.

Materials:

4-ply yarn in 3 colours:

- Colour A: 1.75 m (2 yds)
- Colour B: 4.5 m (5 yds)
- Colour C: 13.75 m (15 yds)

Tools:

Hook size: 3.25 mm (D-3)
Stitch markers
Yarn needle
Scissors

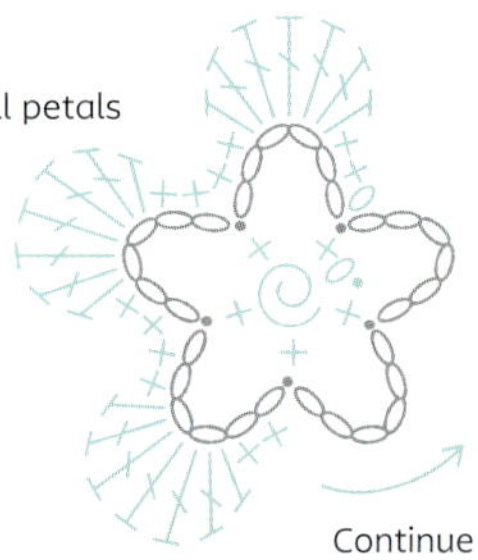

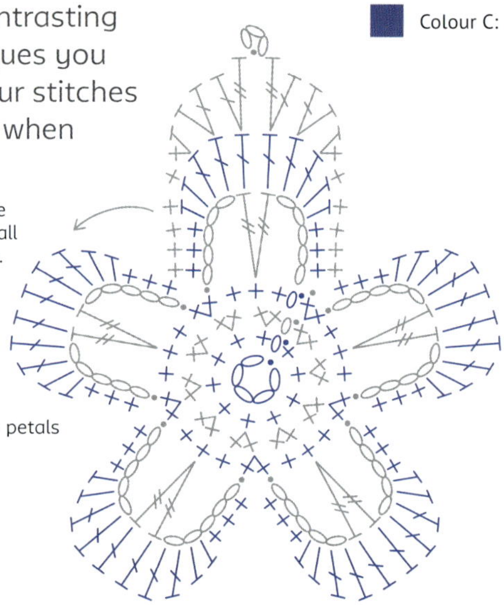

Chart key:

- Magic ring
- Ch Chain
- + Dc Double crochet
- • Sl st Slip stitch
- Htr Half treble crochet
- Tr Treble crochet
- Dtr Double treble crochet
- 3 ch picot (ch 3, sl st in 3rd ch from hook)

Pattern

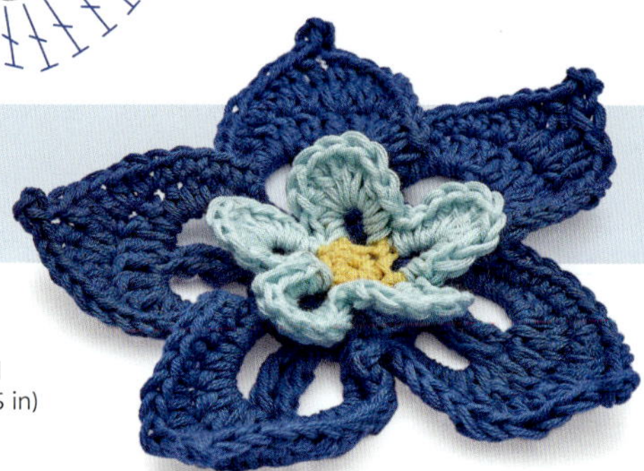

Diam. of finished flower: 12.5 cm (5 in)

Small petals:

With Colour A, make a magic ring (see page 12).

Rnd 1: Into magic ring, ch 1, 5 dc. Pull on short end to close middle. Join rnd with sl st. (5 dc)

Rnd 2: [Ch 6, sl st in next dc] five times (**see Step 1**).

Fasten off Colour A.

Attach Colour B to any ch-6 loop (petals).

Rnd 3: Ch 1, *[2 dc, htr, 5 tr, htr, 2 dc] in ch-6 loop. Rep from * four more times (**see Step 2**).

Finish with sl st in next ch-6 loop. Fasten off Colour B, leaving a long yarn end for sewing (**see Step 3**).

Large petals:

With Colour C, ch 5. Sl st in first ch to make a ring.

Rnd 1: Ch 1, 10 dc in ring. Join rnd with sl st. (10 dc)

Rnd 2: Ch 1, 2 dc in each dc. Join rnd with sl st. (20 dc)

Rnd 3: Ch 1, [dc in next 3 dc, 2 dc in next dc] five times. Join rnd with sl st. (25 sts)

Rnd 4: [Ch 5, miss next dc, 2 dtr in next dc, ch 5, miss next dc, sl st in next 2 dc] five times (**see Steps 4–5**).

Rnd 5: *[3 dc, 2 htr, 2 tr] in ch-5 loop, tr in next 2 dtr, [2 tr, 2 htr, 3 dc] in next ch-5 loop (**see Step 6**).

Rep from * four more times (5 petals).

Rnd 6: Working in each st of next petal: *Dc in next 5 sts, [dc, htr] in next tr, [htr, tr] in next tr, [tr, dtr] in next tr, 3 ch picot, [dtr, tr] in next tr, [tr, htr] in next tr, [htr, dc] in next tr, dc in next 5 sts.

Rep from * for each petal (**see Steps 7–8**).

Fasten off Colour C. Place the small petals on top of the large petals and sew the two layers together using the long yarn end left on the small petals.

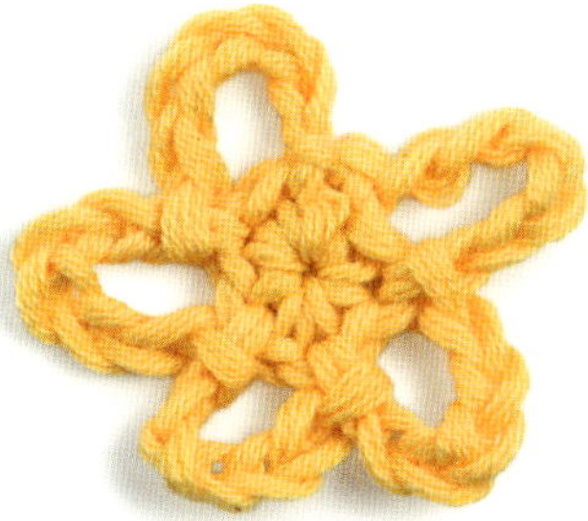

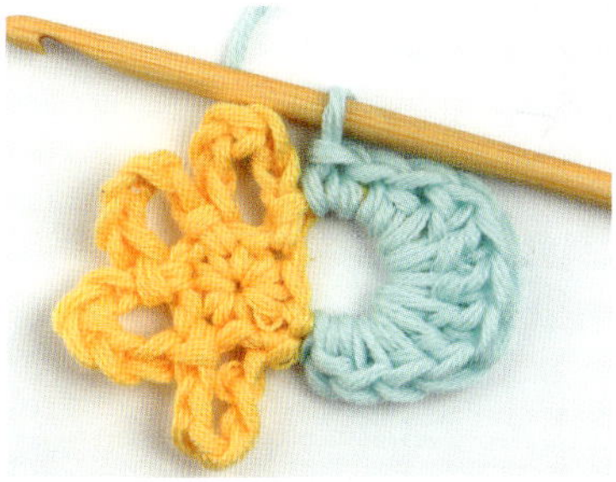

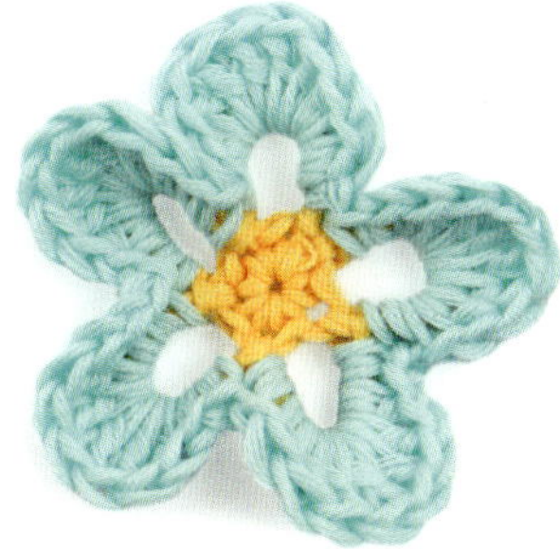

1 **Small petals:** Follow the pattern to begin making the small petals in Colour A. Fasten off Colour A after Round 2.

2 Attach Colour B to the beginning of any of the ch-6 loops. Crochet into the loop following the Round 3 instructions.

3 After you have completed the small petals, fasten off Colour B, leaving a long yarn end for sewing the flower together.

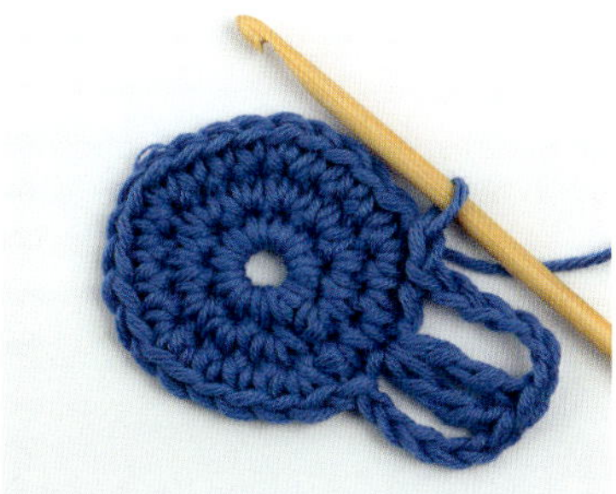

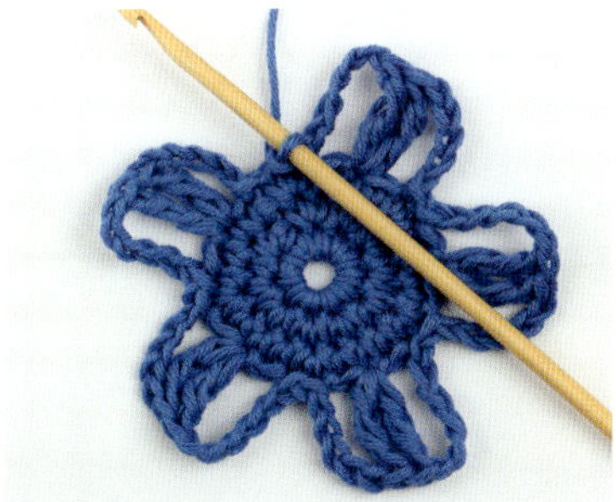

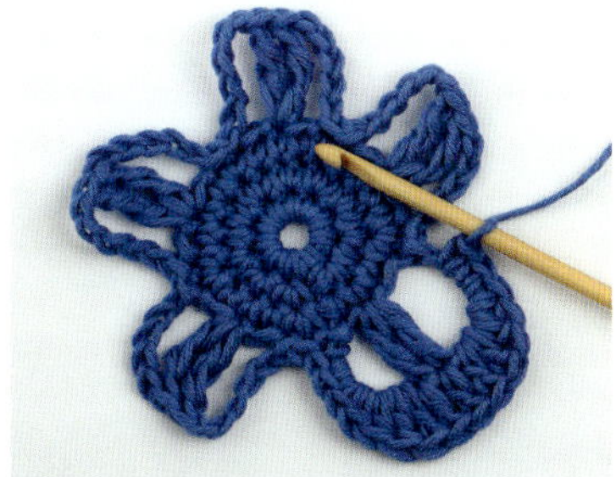

4 **Large petals:** Follow Rounds 1–3 of the pattern for the large petals. This image shows the first petal of Round 4, completed.

5 At the end of Round 4, you will have completed all five petals and the flower will look like this.

6 In Round 5, you will build up another layer, crocheting around each petal.

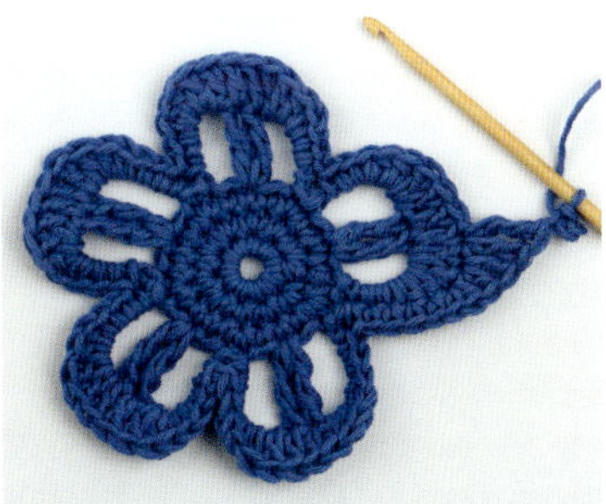

7 Follow the pattern for Round 6, placing the 3 ch picot directly in the middle of each petal. Make sure that you crochet into each stitch according to the pattern to create a symmetrical flower.

8 Once you complete the picot, continue following the pattern to crochet down the other side of the petal. Continue for the remaining four petals.

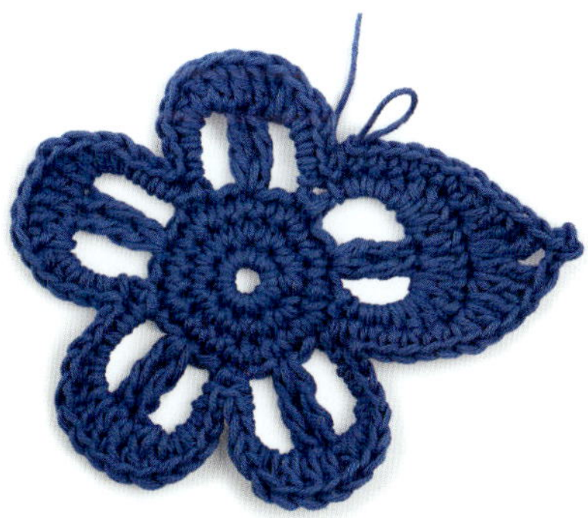

24 Chaenomeles Japonica

Skill level: ✿✿

These simple flowers are such a joy to make. In this pattern, you will be combining two skills: crocheting in the round and crocheting in rows.

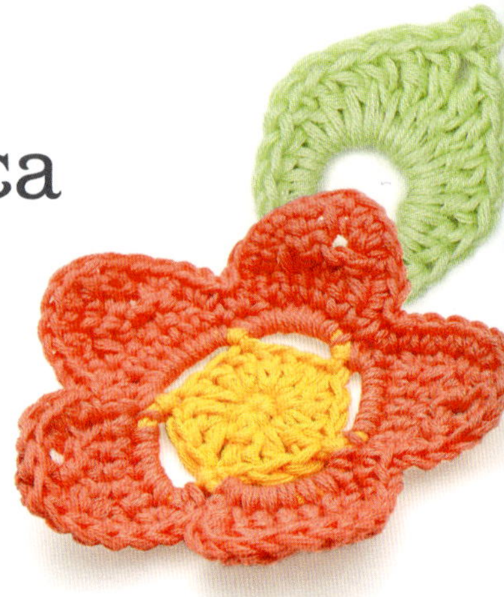

Diam. of finished flower: 9 cm (3½ in)

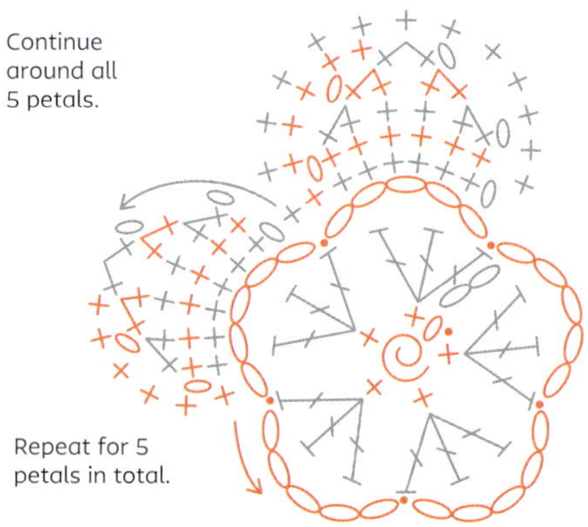

Chart key:

- Magic ring
- Ch Chain
- \+ Dc Double crochet
- • Sl st Slip stitch
- Tr Treble crochet
- Dc2tog Double crochet 2 together (see Step 3)

Materials:

4-ply yarn in 2 colours:

- Colour A: 3.75 m (4 yds)
- Colour B: 9 m (10 yds)

Tools:

Hook size: 3.25 mm (D-3)
Yarn needle
Scissors

Pattern

With Colour A, make a magic ring (see page 12).

Rnd 1: Into magic ring, ch 1, 5 dc. Pull on short end to close middle. Join rnd with sl st. (5 dc)

Rnd 2: Ch 2, 3 tr in each dc. (15 tr)

Rnd 3: [Ch 5, miss next 2 tr, sl st in next tr] five times (**see Step 1**).

Fasten off Colour A.

Attach Colour B to any ch-5 loop.

First petal (**see Step 2**):

Row 1: Ch 1, 6 dc in ch-5 loop. (6 dc)

Row 2: Ch 1, turn, dc in each dc.

Row 3: Ch 1, turn, dc2tog, dc in next 2 dc, dc2tog (**see Step 3**). (4 dc)

Row 4: Ch 1, turn, [dc2tog] twice. (2 dc)

Row 5: Ch 1, turn, dc2tog. (1 dc)

Do not turn. 6 dc along side of petal until you reach ch-5 loop. Last dc is made in ch-5 loop (**see Steps 4–5**).

Rep 'first petal' pattern four more times (5 petals) (**see Step 6**).

Once five petals complete, 13 dc evenly around each petal. (**see Steps 7–8**).

Fasten off Colour B. Weave in ends.

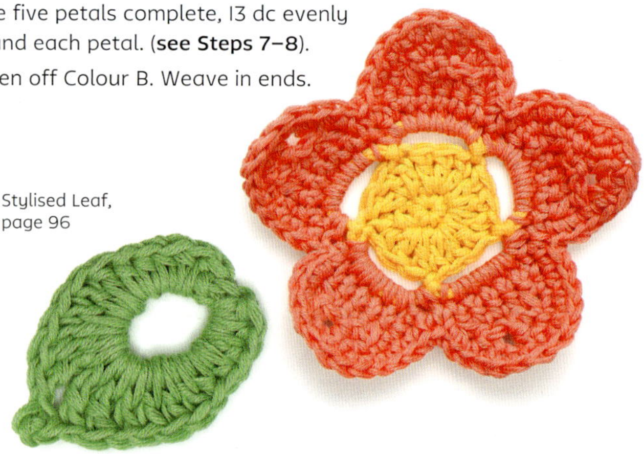

Stylised Leaf, page 96

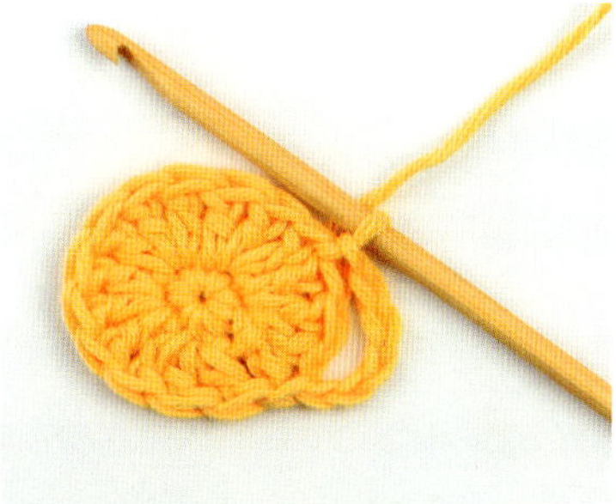

1 Follow the pattern for Rounds 1–3. In Round 3 you will create chain loops that will be used to attach Colour B, and build the flower's five petals.

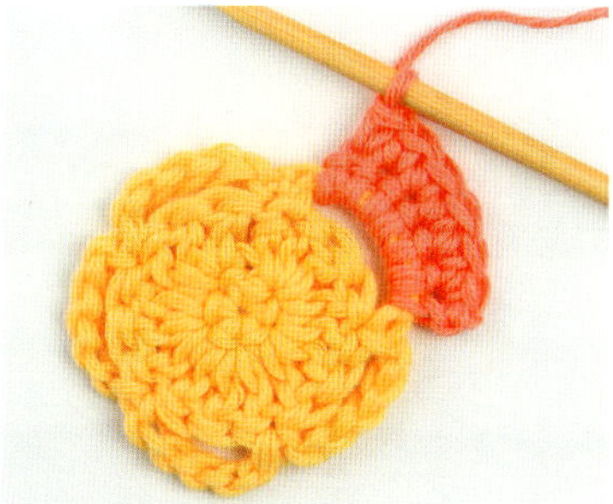

2 On this flower you create each petal separately, one at a time. Follow the 'first petal' pattern to begin making the first petal.

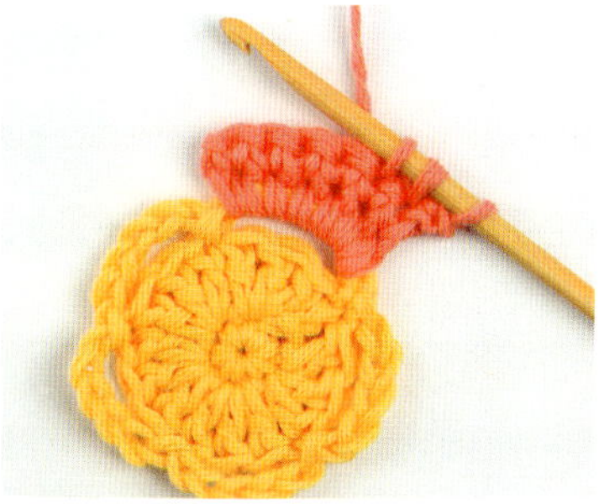

3 To make a dc2tog in Round 3: insert the hook into the next dc and pull out the yarn loop, insert the hook into the next st and pull out the yarn loop. Yarn over and pull the yarn through all loops on the hook.

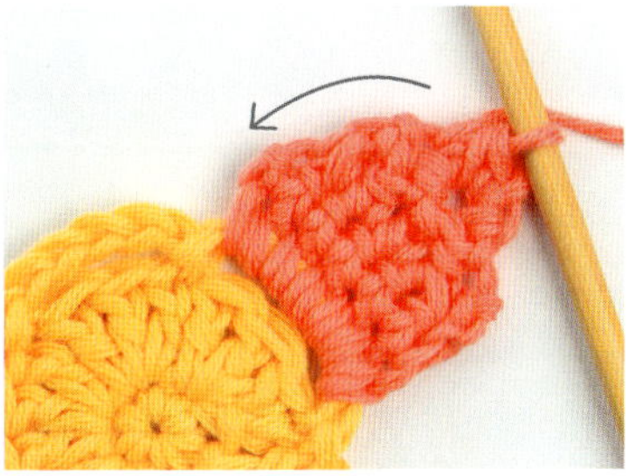

4 After Row 5, make 6 dc along the side of the petal towards the ch-5 loop.

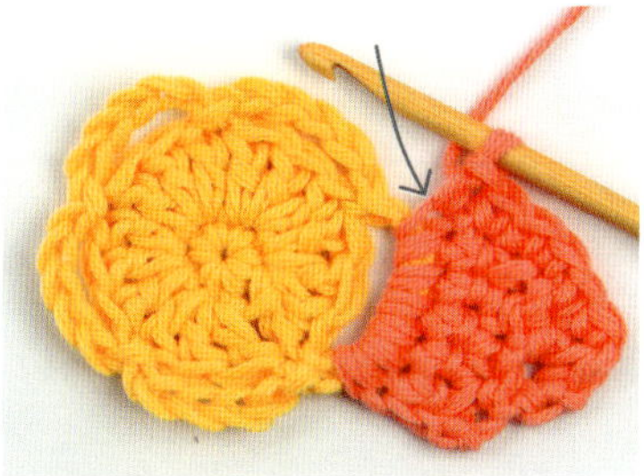

5 Make the last dc into the same ch-5 loop as you made the petal into.

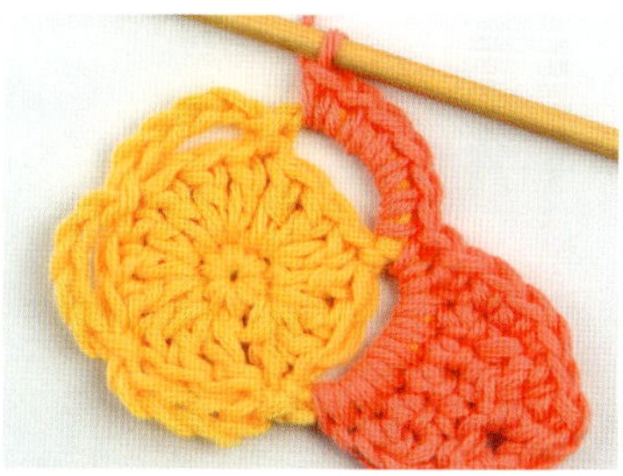

6 Follow the same instructions and repeat Steps 2–5 to make the second petal into the next ch-5 loop.

7

Once you have completed five petals, make 13 dc all the way around the next petal. Place dc sts equally along the petals – you will make 6 dc along each side of each petal and one at the top.

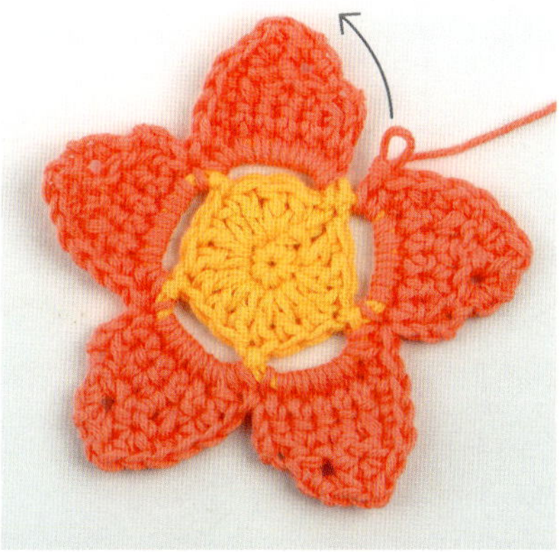

8

Continue making dc sts all the way around all five petals. Fasten off Colour B and weave in all ends.

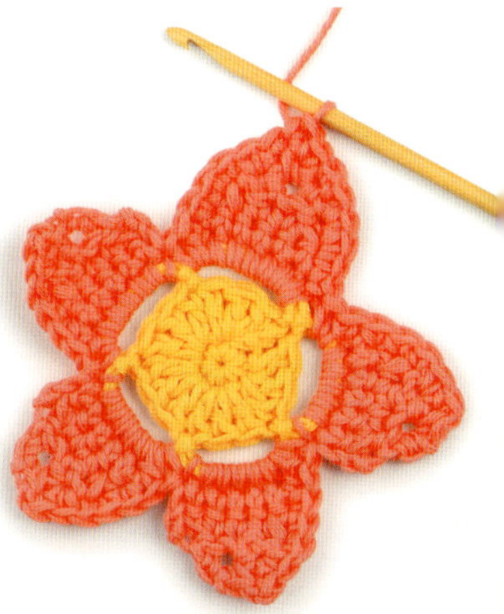

25 Esperanse Rose

Skill level:

Materials:

4-ply yarn in 2 colours:

Colour A: 11 m (12 yds)

Colour B: 13.75 m (15 yds)

Tools:

Hook size: 3.25 mm (D-3)

Stitch marker

Yarn needle

Scissors

By combining contrasting colours and layers of petals, you can create really elegant crochet flowers. Try crocheting just the first four or six rounds to make flowers in a variety of sizes.

Chart key:

- Magic ring
- Ch Chain
- Dc Double crochet
- Sl st Slip stitch
- Tr Treble crochet
- Front loop
- Back loop
- Htr Half treble crochet
- Dtr Double treble crochet

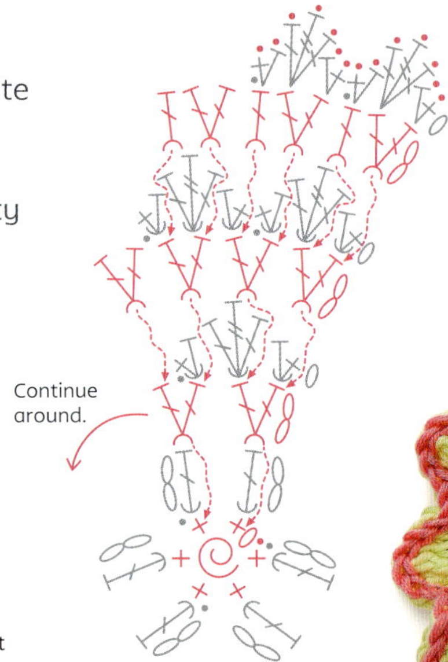

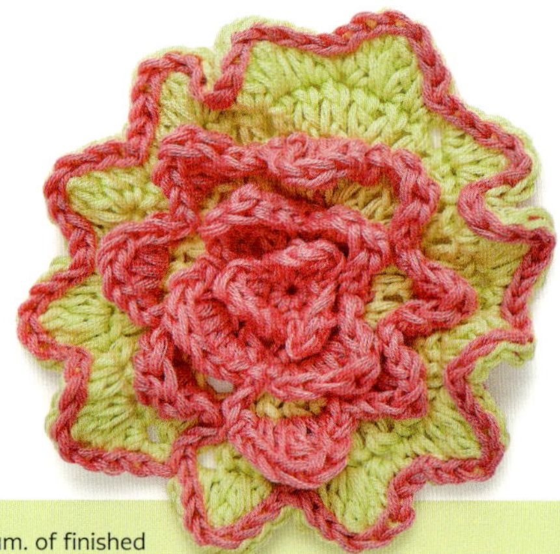

Diam. of finished flower: 10 cm (4 in)

Pattern

With Colour A, make a magic ring (see page 12).

Rnd 1: Into magic ring, ch 1, 6 dc. Pull on short end to close middle. Join rnd with sl st in front loop (**see Step 1**). (6 dc)

Rnd 2: Working in front loops only: *Ch 2, tr in same dc, [tr, ch 2, sl st] in next dc.

Rep from * twice more. Sl st in back loop of Rnd 1.

Rnd 3: Working in back loops of Rnd 1 only: Ch 2, 2 tr in each dc. Join rnd with sl st in front loop of first tr (**see Steps 2–3**). (12 tr)

Rnd 4: Working in front loops of Rnd 3 only: Ch 1, *[dc, htr] in next tr, [tr, dtr, tr] in next tr, [htr, dc, sl st] in next tr.

Rep from * three more times (4 petals).

Attach Colour B to back loop of first tr of Rnd 3. Do not fasten off Colour A.

Rnd 5: With Colour B, working in back loops of Rnd 3 only: Ch 2, 2 tr in each tr. Join with sl st in front loop of first tr (**see Step 4**). (24 tr)

Rnd 6: With Colour A, ch 3, sl st in first front loop of Rnd 5. Working in front loops only: Ch 1, *[dc, htr] in next st, [tr, dtr, tr] in next st, [htr, dc, sl st] in next st (**see Step 5**).

Rep from * seven more times (8 petals).

Rnd 7: With Colour B and working in back loops of Rnd 5, ch 2, [2 tr in next tr, tr in next tr] all around. Join with sl st in front loop of first tr (**see Step 6**). (36 tr)

Rnd 8: With Colour B and working through both loops of each st, ch 1, *[dc, htr] in next st, [tr, dtr, tr] in next st, [htr, dc, sl st] in next st (**see Step 7**).

Rep from * 11 more times (12 petals).

Rnd 9: With Colour A, ch 3, sl st in first dc of Rnd 8. Sl st in each st (**see Step 8**).

Fasten off both colours. Weave in ends.

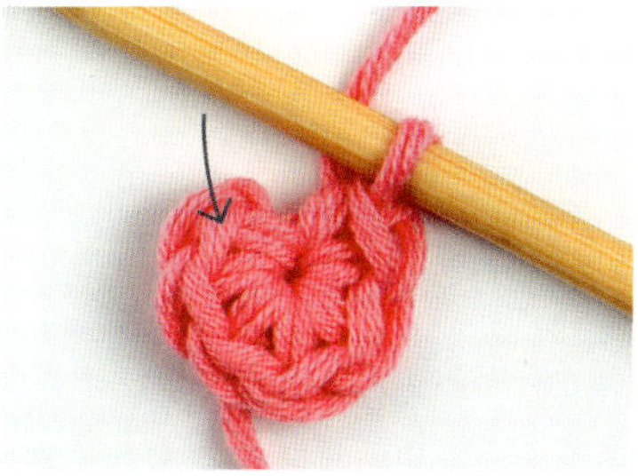

1 Follow the pattern for Round I. Join the round with a sl st into the front loop of the first dc (indicated by the arrow). Continue to follow the pattern for Round 2.

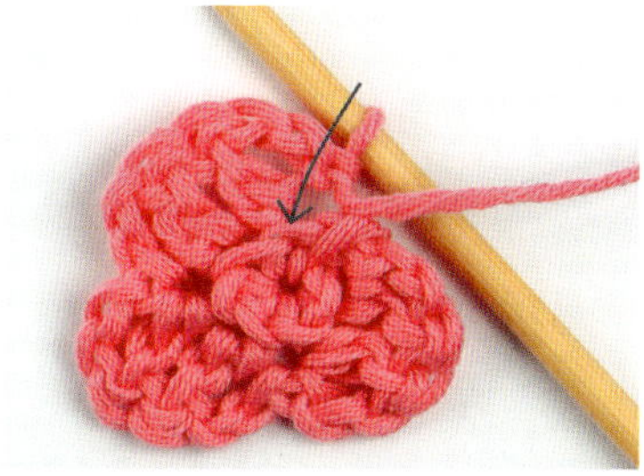

2 To locate the back loops for Round 3, turn your flower over so the wrong side is facing you, and notice the back loops arranged in a round.

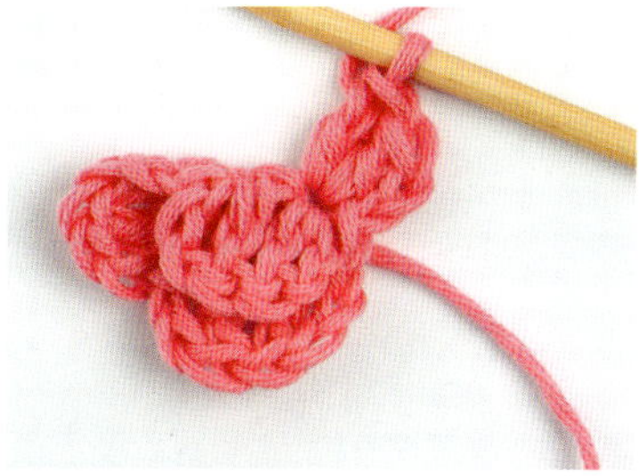

3 Follow the pattern, adding another layer by crocheting into the back loops of the stitches. Fold the petals forwards to see the stitch placement more easily.

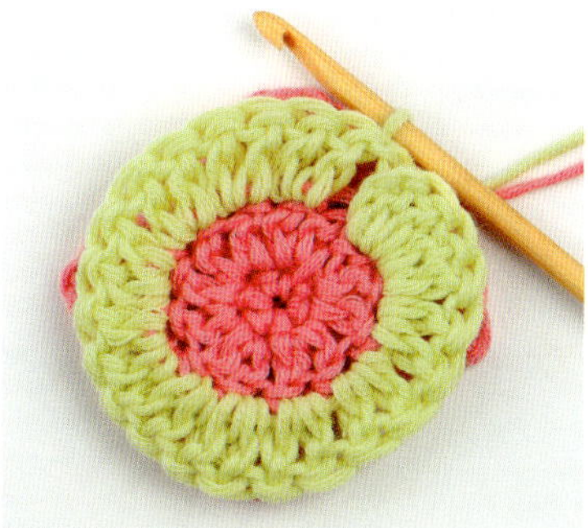

4 After completing Round 5, your flower will look like this from the wrong side.

5 As you crochet Round 6, leave the Colour B yarn attached, and be careful not to tangle it.

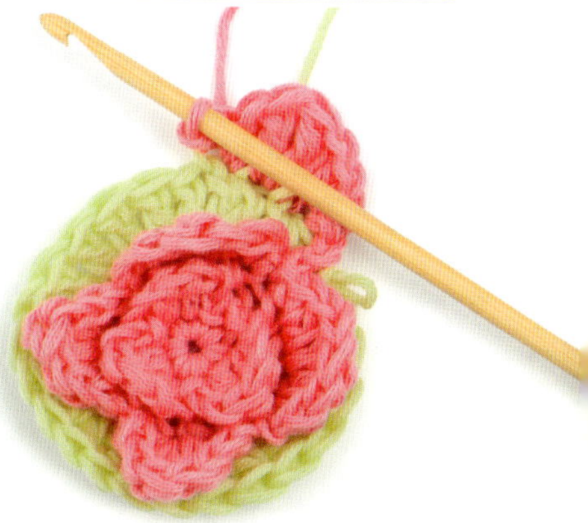

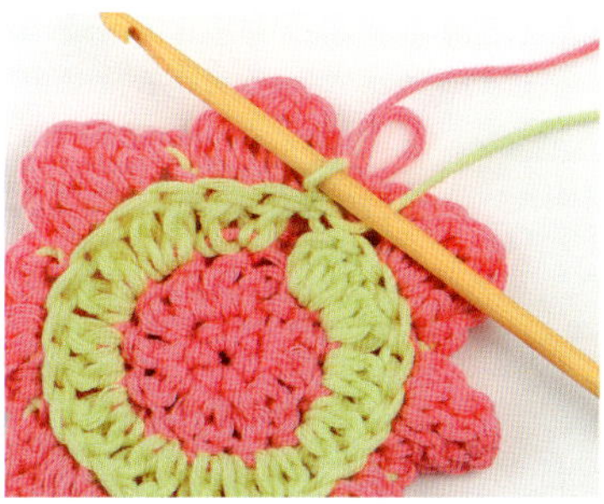

6 After Round 6, pick up Colour B, carefully setting aside Colour A. You can use a stitch marker, it will help you not to lose the loop.

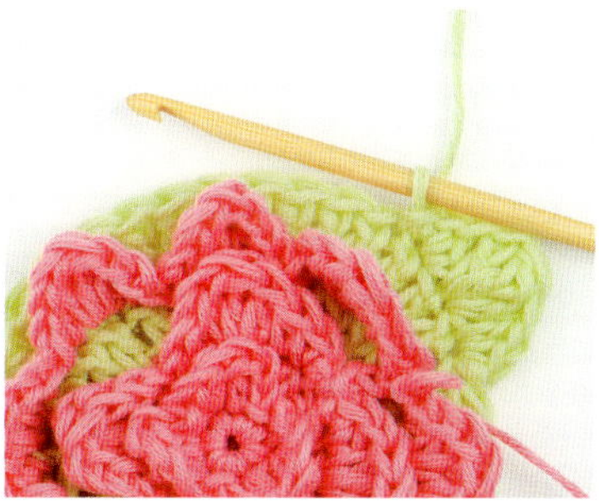

7 Notice that Round 8 is made into the front and back loops together.

8 Finish by crocheting slip stitches all the way around the last layer of petals in Colour A.

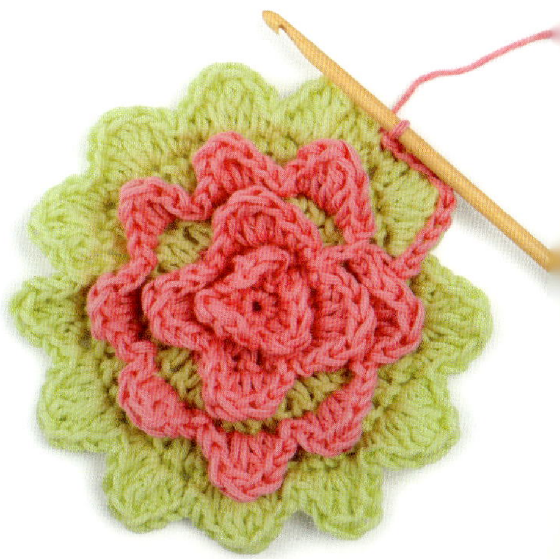

26 Ranunculus

Skill level: ✿ ✿

You will love making these exotic looking flowers. Once you get the concept of it, you can crochet them in many sizes and colours. Working the top yellow petals doesn't require much counting, so it's a perfect project to take along on a trip or long journey.

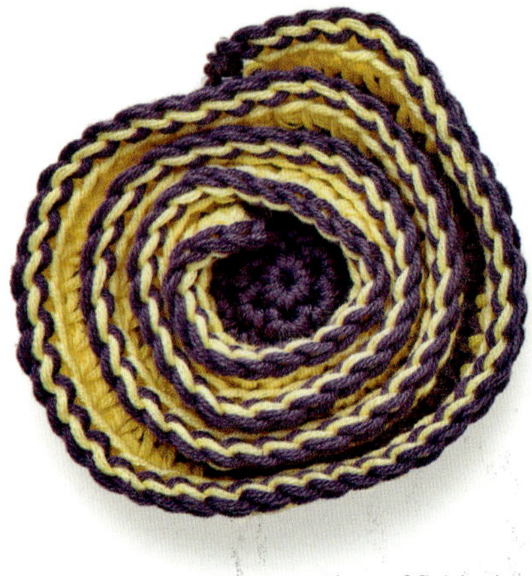

Diam. of finished flower: 6.5 cm (2½ in)

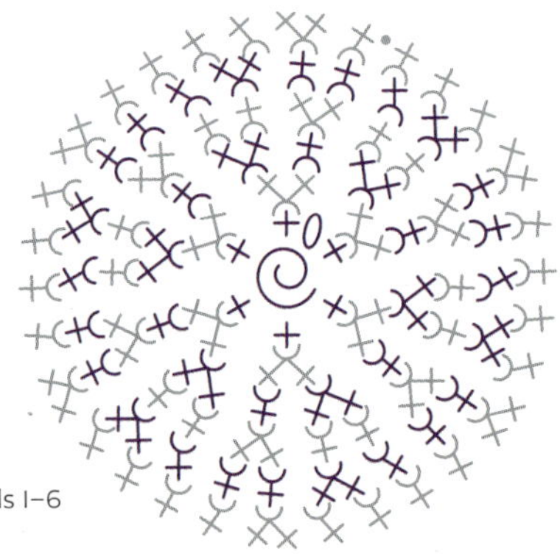

Rounds 1–6

Chart key:

- Magic ring
- ⬭ Ch Chain
- + Dc Double crochet
- ⌒ Back Loop
- • Sl st Slip stitch

Materials:

4-ply yarn in 2 colours:

- Colour A: 12 m (13 yds)
- Colour B: 12 m (13 yds)

Tools:

Hook size: 3.25 mm (D-3)
Stitch marker
Yarn needle
Scissors

Pattern

With Colour A, make a magic ring (see page 12).

Rnd 1: Into magic ring, ch 1, 6 dc. Pull on short end to close middle. Do not join rnd. Use stitch marker at end of each rnd. (6 dc)

Rnd 2: 2 dc in each dc (**see Step 1**). (12 dc)

From now on work in back loops only. Place stitch marker at front loop of first dc of Rnd 2 (**see Step 2**).

Rnd 3: [Dc in next dc, 2 dc in next dc] six times. (18 dc)

Rnd 4: [2 dc in next dc, dc in next 2 dc] six times. (24 dc)

Rnd 5: [Dc in next 2 dc, 2 dc in next dc, dc in next dc] six times. (30 dc)

Rnd 6: [Dc in next dc, 2 dc in next dc, dc in next 3 dc] six times. (36 dc)

Sl st in next st. Do not fasten off Colour A.

Attach Colour B to front loop of first dc of Rnd 2.

Rnd 7: With Colour B, ch 2 (**see Step 3**).

Tr in front loop of each dc until you reach last rnd (**see Steps 4–5**).

In final rnd, working into front loops only: [Tr in next dc, 2 tr in next dc] until you reach last dc (**see Step 6**).

Fasten off Colour B.

Rnd 8: With Colour A, ch 3, sl st in back loops of each tr around flower, working in a spiral.

Ch 3, sl st in first front loop of Rnd 2 (**see Steps 7–8**).

Fasten off Colour A.

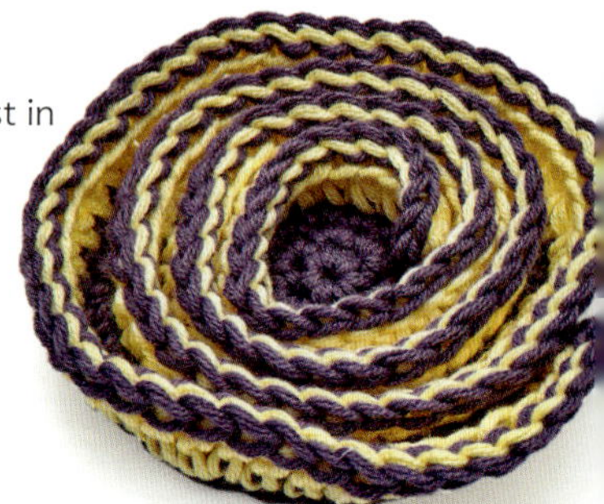

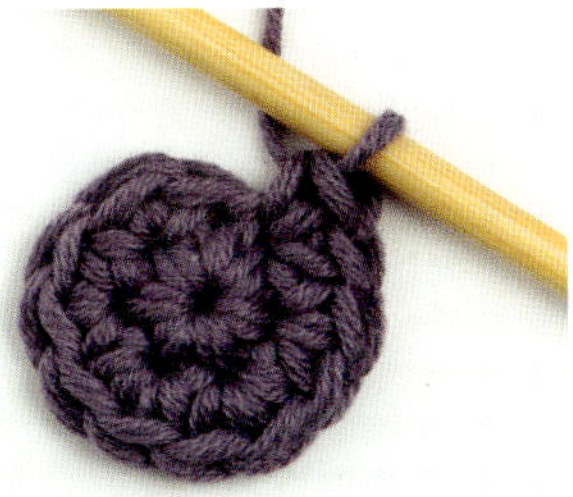

1 Follow the pattern to make Rounds 1–6.

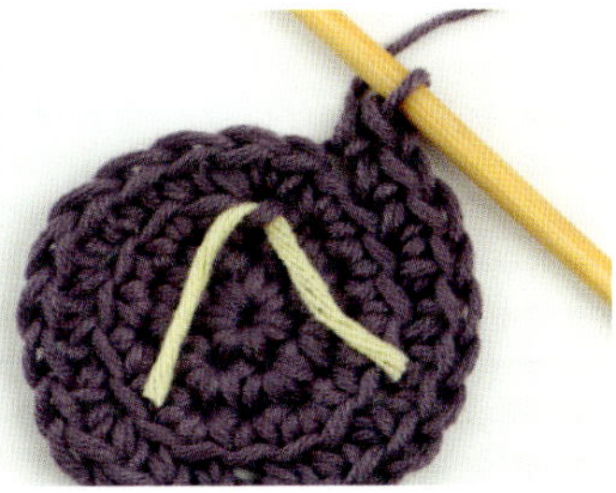

2 Mark the front loop of the first dc of Round 2 with a stitch marker.

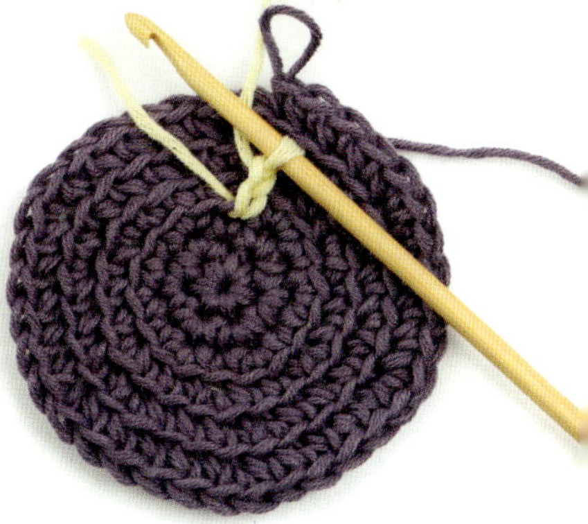

3 Once you have completed Rounds 1–6, attach Colour B to the front loop of the first dc of Round 2, where you placed the stitch marker. Ch 2.

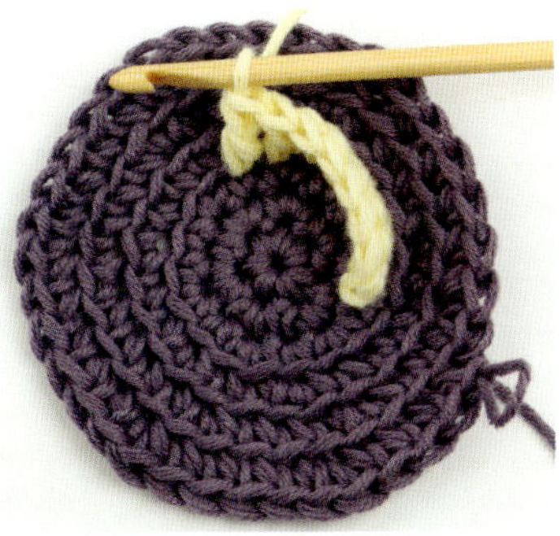

4 Work around the flower in a spiral, crocheting a tr into the front loop of every stitch.

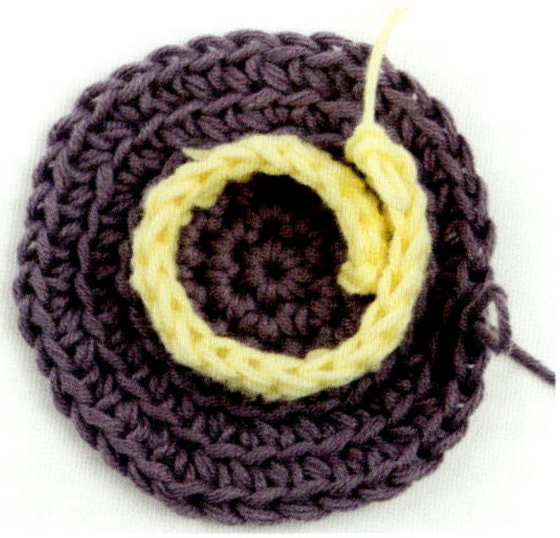

5 Once you reach the last round, as shown here, work [tr into the next 3 dc, 2 tr into the next dc] until you reach the last front loop.

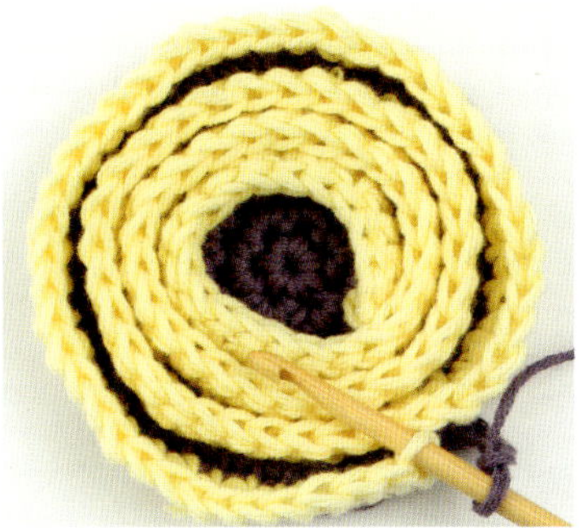

6 With Colour A, ch 3.

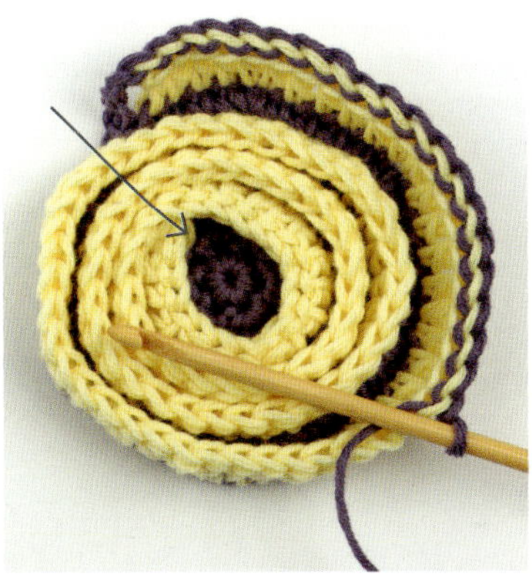

7 Starting from the last tr you made in Colour B, work a sl st into the back loop of each tr around the flower.

8 Continue to work in a spiral until you reach the first tr (shown here). Ch 3, sl st into the first front loop of Round 2 to finish.

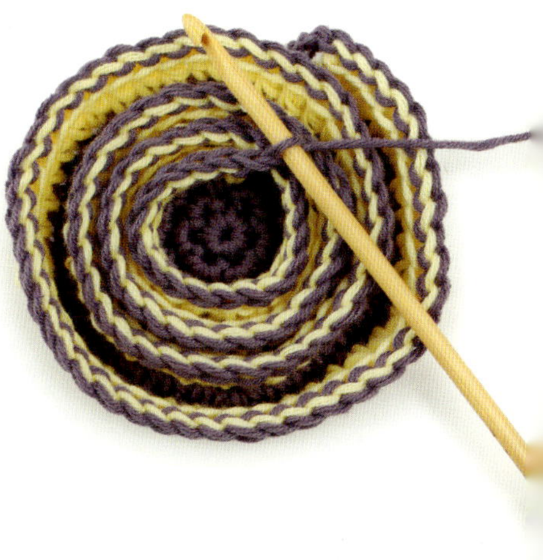

27 Passion Flower

Skill level:

Try using different combinations of contrasting colours to create this striking flower. Look at both the chart and the written instructions, particularly for tricky areas, such as the petals.

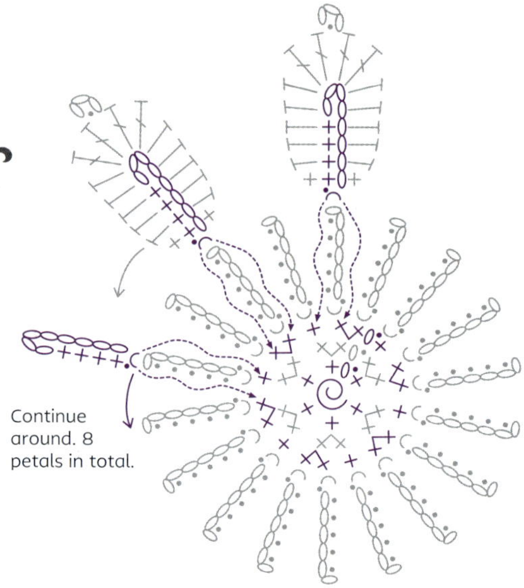

Materials:

4-ply yarn in 4 colours:

- Colour A: 3.75 m (4 yds)
- Colour B: 4.5 m (5 yds)
- Colour C: 10 m (11 yds)
- Colour D: 4.5 m (5 yds)

Tools:

Hook size: 3.25 mm (D-3)
Yarn needle
Scissors

Chart key:

- Magic ring
- Ch Chain
- Dc Double crochet
- Sl st Slip stitch
- Front loop
- Back loop
- Htr Half treble crochet
- Tr Treble crochet
- 3 ch picot (ch 3, sl st in 3rd ch from hook)

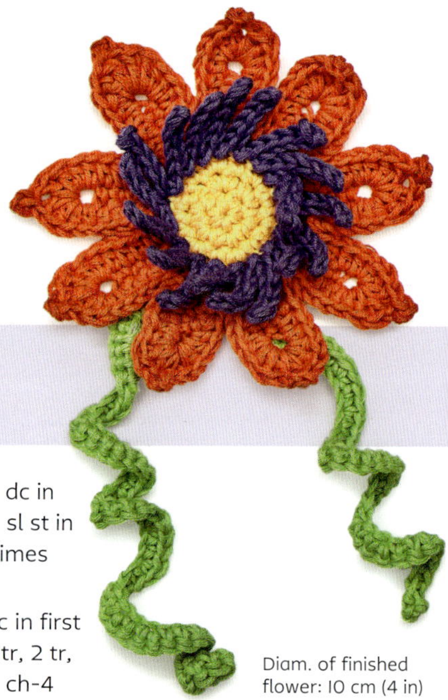

Diam. of finished flower: 10 cm (4 in)

Pattern

Flower:

With Colour A, make a magic ring (see page 12).

Rnd 1: Into magic ring, ch 1, 6 dc. Pull on short end to close middle. Join rnd with sl st. (6 dc)

Rnd 2: Ch 1, 2 dc in each dc. Join with sl st. (12 dc)

Rnd 3: Ch 1, [2 dc in next dc, dc in next dc] six times. Join with sl st (18 dc).

Fasten off Colour A.

Attach Colour B to front loop of Rnd 3 (**see Step 1**).

Rnd 4: Working in front loops only: [Ch 6, starting from 2nd ch from hook, sl st in each ch, sl st in front loop of next dc of Rnd 3] 18 times (**see Step 2**).

Fasten off Colour B.

Attach Colour C to back loop of Rnd 3 (**see Step 3**).

Rnd 5: Working in back loops only: [Ch 8, starting from 5th ch from hook, dc in next 4 ch, miss next dc, sl st in next dc of Rnd 3] nine times (**see Steps 4–5**).

Rnd 6: *In next petal: dc in first ch, htr in next 3 ch, [2 htr, 2 tr, 3 ch picot, 2 tr, 2 htr] in ch-4 loop, hdc in next 3 dc, dc in next dc (**see Step 6**).

Rep from * for each petal (9 petals).

Finish with sl st in first dc of Rnd 6.

Fasten off Colour C.

Swirl (make 2)**:**

With Colour D, ch 40 (ch 30 for shorter swirl).

Dc in 2nd ch from hook, [2 dc in next ch, dc in next ch] to end of ch (**see Steps 7–8**).

Fasten off. Sew swirls to back of flower.

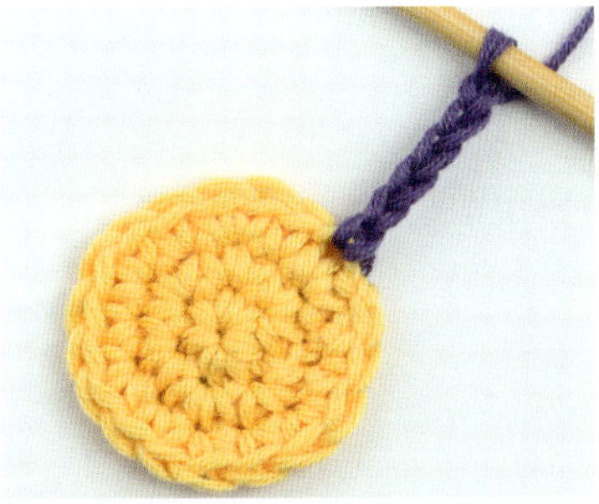

1 After you have created the centre of the flower in Colour A, fasten off and attach Colour B to the front loop of any dc of Round 3.

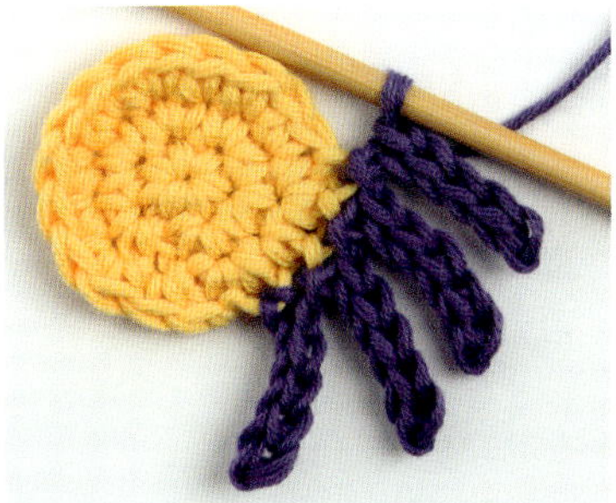

2 Follow the instructions for Round 4 to create 18 small petals around the centre. Fasten off Colour B.

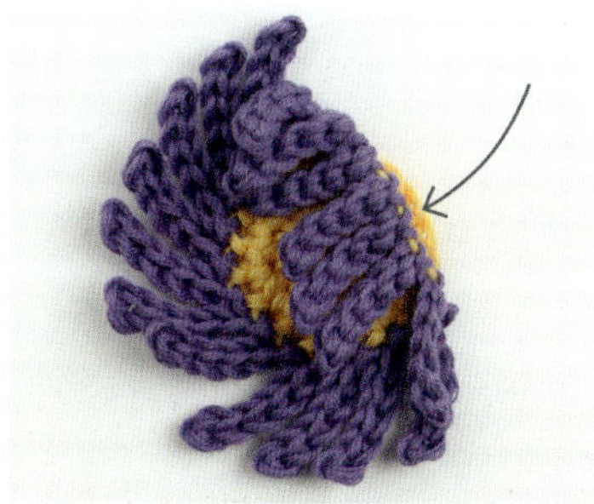

3 Fold the small petals forwards in order to locate the back loops of Round 3 (indicated by the arrow). Attach Colour C to one of these loops.

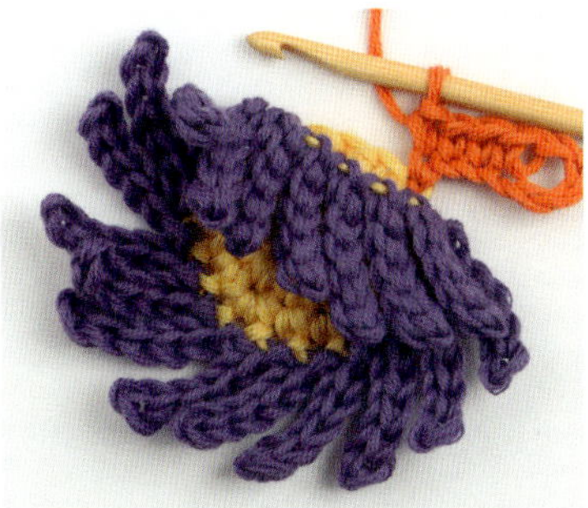

4 Follow the pattern to make nine large petals. Work in the back loops only and fold the small petals out of the way as you go.

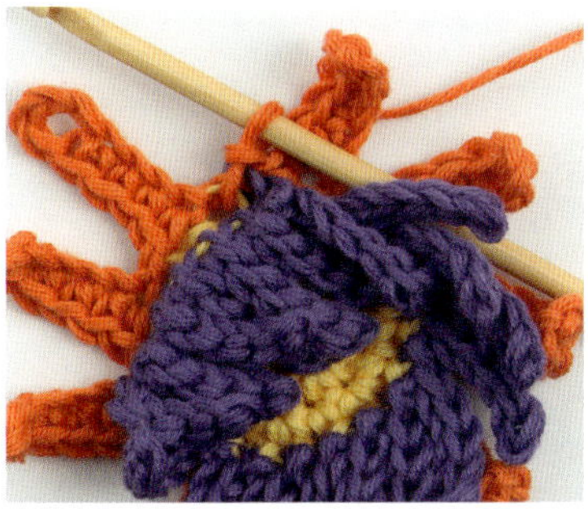

5 By the end of Round 5, you will see a three-dimensional shape emerging.

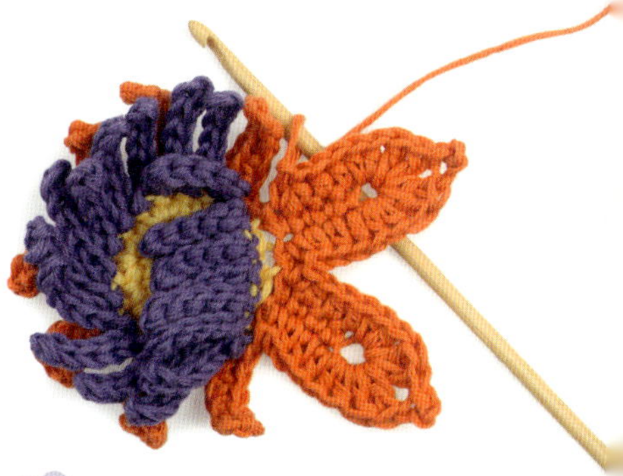

6 Follow the pattern and the chart for the correct placement of stitches around each large petal.

7 Start with a long chain of 30 or 40 chains to make a swirl.

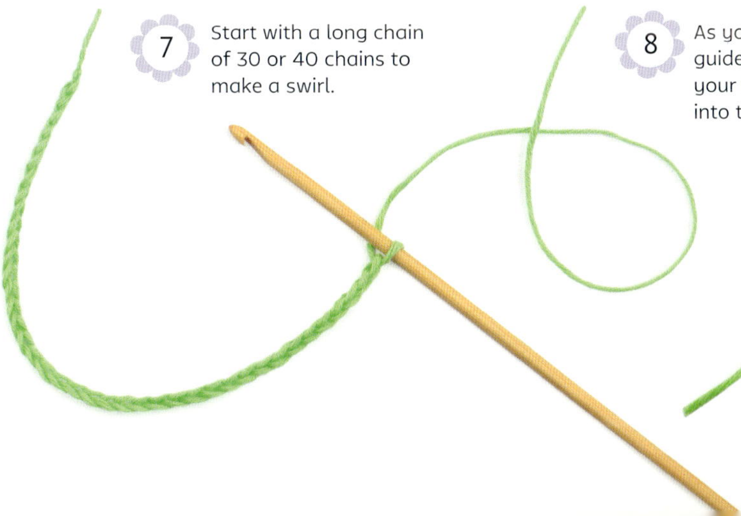

8 As you follow the pattern, guide the swirl around your finger to encourage it into the correct shape.

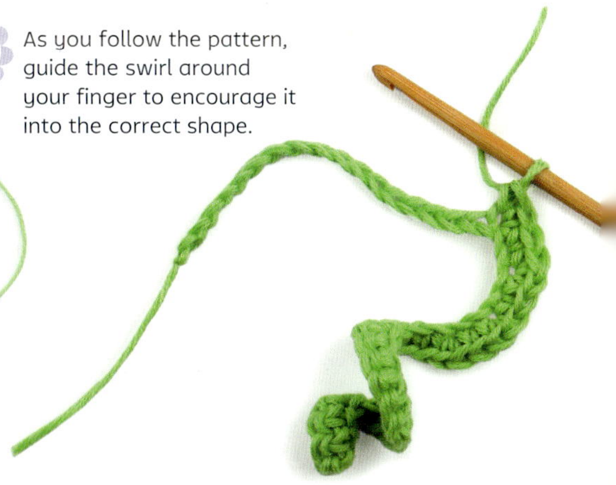

28 Tiger Lily

Skill level:

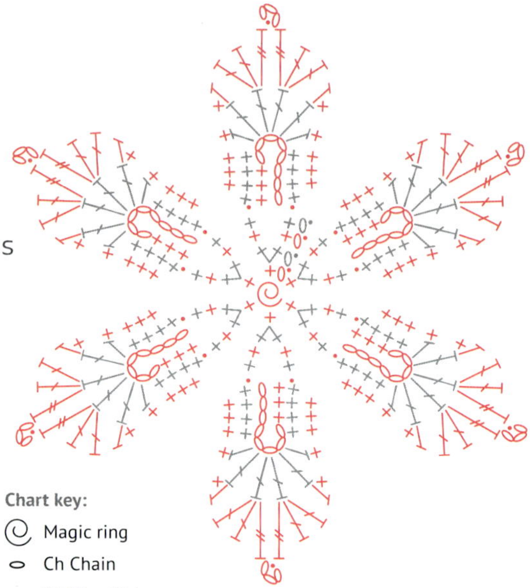

This flower is inspired by a tiger lily; the flower creates the impression of deep dimensions. Using a simple colour-changing technique, picot stitch and some shaping, this flower can be easily completed by a beginner based on previous tutorials in the book.

Materials:

4-ply yarn in 3 colours:

Colour A: 7.3 m (8 yds)

Colour B: 4.5 m (5 yds)

Colour C: 1.8 m (2 yds)

Tools:

Hook size: 3.25 mm (D-3)
Yarn needle
Scissors

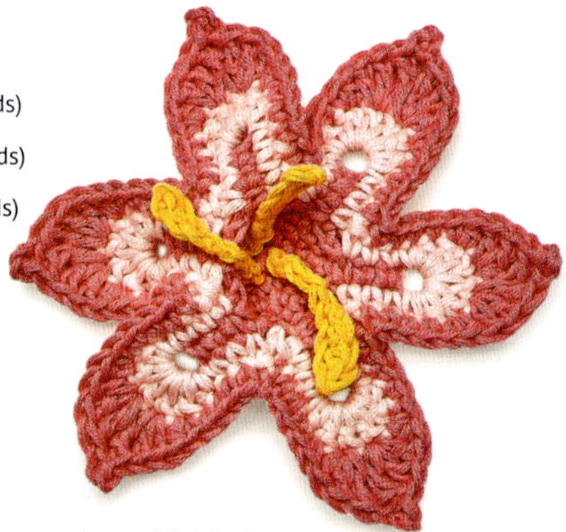

Diam. of finished flower: 10 cm (4 in)

Chart key:

- Magic ring
- Ch Chain
- Sl Slip stitch
- Dc Double crochet
- Htr Half treble crochet
- Tr Treble crochet
- Dtr Double treble crochet
- 3 ch picot (ch 3, sl st in 3rd ch from hook)

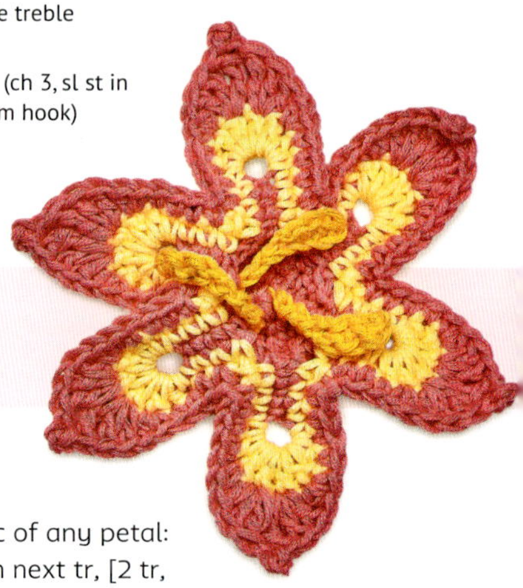

Pattern

With Colour A, make a magic ring (see page 12).

Rnd 1: Into magic ring, ch 1, 6 dc. Pull on short end to close middle. Join rnd with sl st. (6 dc)

Rnd 2: Ch 1, 2 dc in each dc. Join rnd with sl st. (12 dc)

Rnds 3–4: Ch 1, dc in each dc. Join rnd with sl st (**see Step 1**).

Rnd 5: [Ch 8, starting from 6th ch from hook, dc in next 3 ch, sl st in next 2 dc] six times (**see Steps 2–3**).

Fasten off Colour A.

Attach Colour B.

Rnd 6: Start this rnd by crocheting in first ch of Rnd 5. *Dc in first 3 ch, [dc, htr, 4 tr, htr, dc] in ch-5 loop, dc in next 3 dc.

Rep from * five more times (6 petals) (**see Steps 5–6**).

Fasten off Colour B.

Attach Colour A.

Rnd 7: Starting from 2nd dc of any petal: *dc in next 4 sts, [dc, htr] in next tr, [2 tr, dtr] in next tr, 3 ch picot, [dtr, 2 tr] in next tr, [htr, dc] in next tr, dc in next 4 sts.

Rep from * five more times (**see Step 7**).

Stamens (make 3):

With Colour C, ch 9, starting from 2nd ch from hook, dc in next 2 ch, sl st in next ch. Fasten off.

Thread stamens through the middle of the flower. With yarn needle, securely attach to flower and weave in all ends.

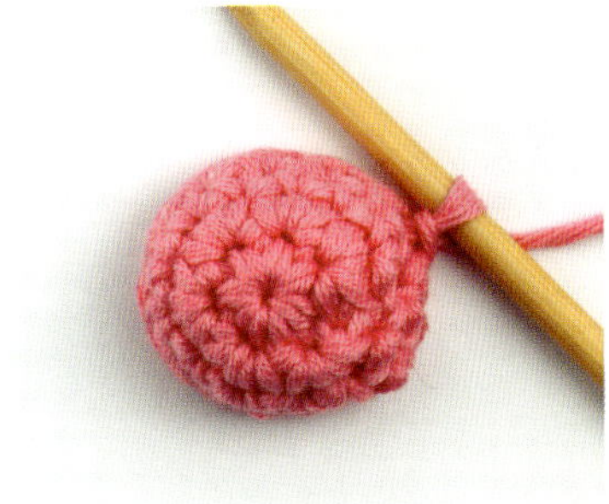

1 After Round 4 you will have a 3D shape of the flower centre.

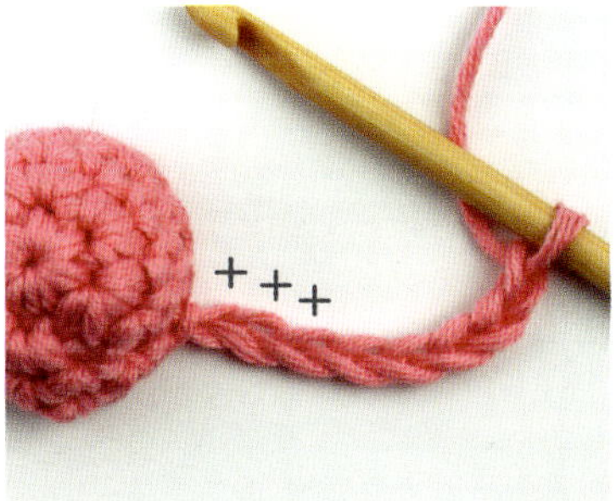

2 Ch 8, starting from the sixth ch from the hook, dc into the last 3 ch (use the picture above as a guide for correct stitch placement).

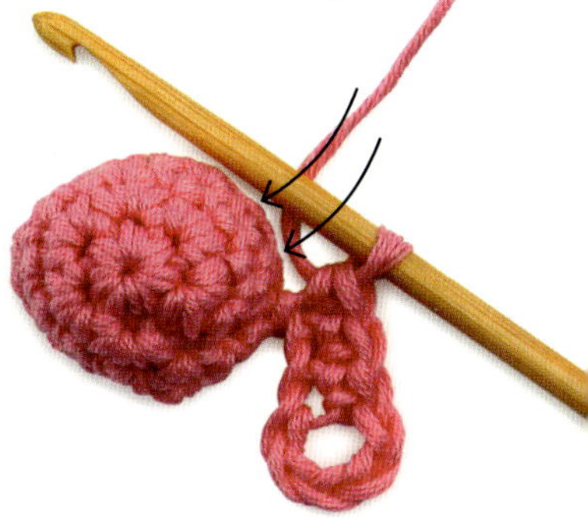

3 Then, work a sl st into each of the next 2 dc of Round 4.

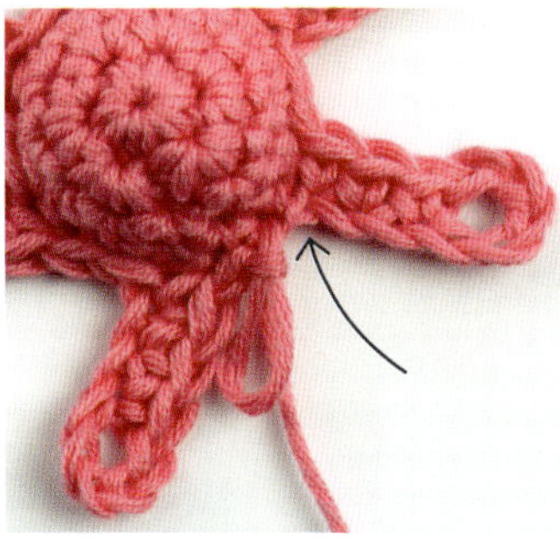

4 Continue making six small petals around the centre of your flower. Start the next round by crocheting into the first chain of Round 5, as shown by the arrow.

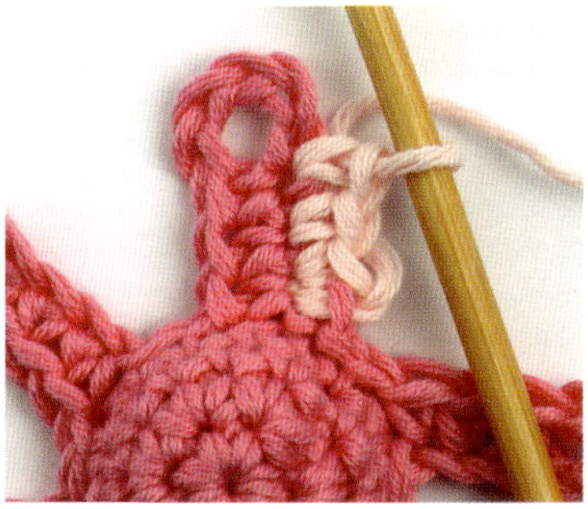

5 To begin Round 6, use the colour changing technique described on page 27.

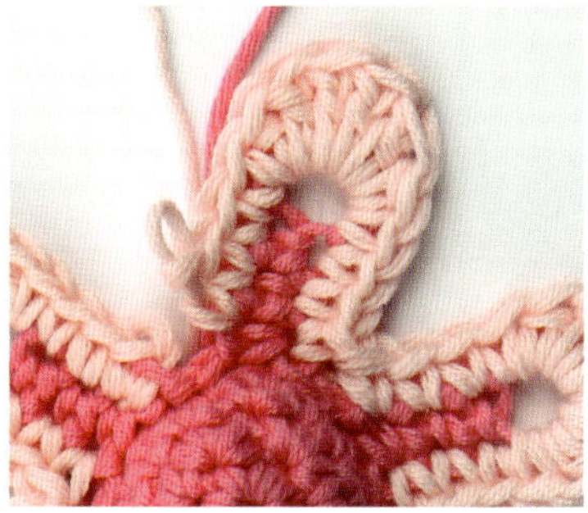

6 **Rnd 6:** Dc into the first 3 ch, [dc, htr, 4 tr, htr, dc] into the ch-5 loop, dc into the next 3 dc. Repeat this step for all six petals.

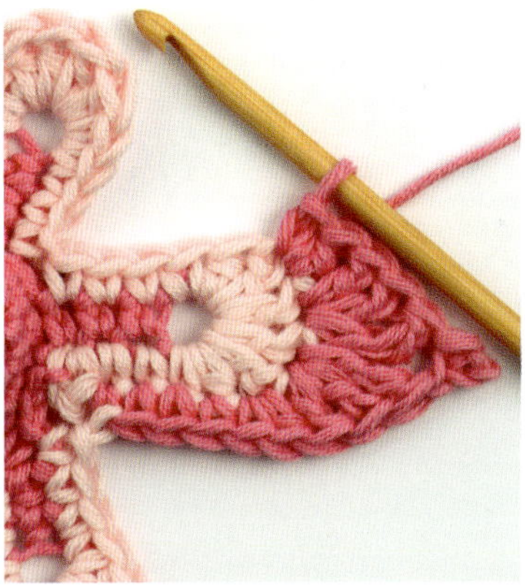

7 **Rnd 7:** Change back to Colour A and follow the pattern to crochet around each petal.

8 Make three stamens by following the pattern, making sure to leave long yarn ends. Using your yarn needle, thread the long yarn ends through the centre of the flower from front to back and secure by sewing to the back of the flower.

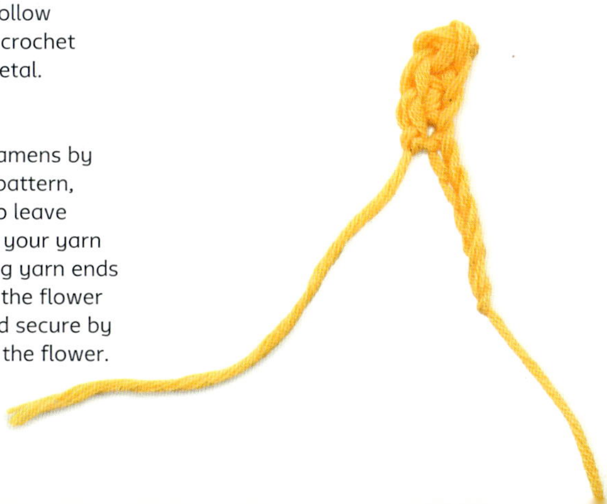

29 African Daisy

Skill level:

Follow the pattern here to create a yellow African daisy with a stem. Try using yellow and white to make a simple daisy with the same instructions.

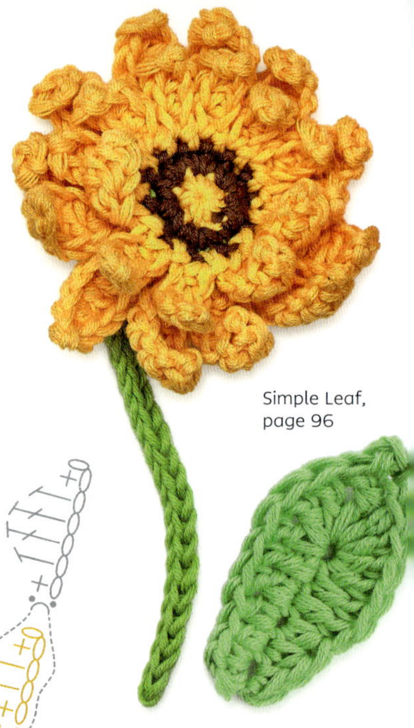

Materials:

4-ply yarn in 3 colours:

- Colour A: 7.3 m (8 yds)
- Colour B: 2.75 m (3 yds)
- Colour C: 6.5 m (7 yds)

Tools:

Hook size: 3.25 mm (D-3)
Yarn needle
Scissors

Chart key:

- Magic ring
- Ch Chain
- Dc Double crochet
- Sl st Slip stitch
- Back loop
- Htr Half treble crochet
- Front loop
- Tr Treble crochet

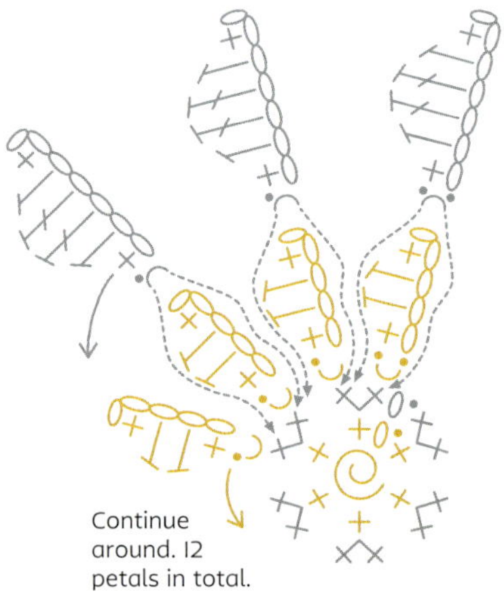

Diam. of finished flower: 6.5 cm (2½ in)

Length of finished stem: 9 cm (3½ in)

Pattern

Flower:

With Colour A, make a magic ring (see page 12).

Rnd 1: Into magic ring, ch 1, 6 dc. Pull on short end to close middle. Join rnd with sl st. (6 dc)

Attach Colour B to end of Rnd 1. Do not fasten off Colour A.

Rnd 2: With Colour B, ch 1, 2 dc in each st. Join rnd with sl st. (12 dc)

Fasten off Colour B.

Rnd 3: With Colour A, sl st in front loop of first dc of Rnd 2. Ch 5, dc in 2nd ch from hook, htr in next 2 ch, dc in next ch, sl st in front loop of same dc as last sl st (**see Step 1**).

*Ch 5, dc in 2nd ch from hook, htr in next 2 ch, dc in next ch, sl st in front loop of next dc.

Rep from * 10 more times (12 petals) (**see Step 2**).

Rnd 4: Sl st in back loop of first dc of Rnd 2. Ch 7, dc in 2nd ch from hook, htr in next ch, tr in next 2 ch, htr in next ch, dc in next ch, sl st in back loop of same dc as last sl st (**see Step 3**).

*Ch 7, dc in 2nd ch from hook, htr in next ch, tr in next 2 ch, htr in next ch, dc in next ch, sl st in back loop of next dc.

Rep from * 10 more times (12 petals) (**see Step 4**).

Fasten off Colour A.

Stem:

With Colour C, ch 12. Join with sl st in first ch. Be careful not to twist ch.

Rnd 1: Ch 1, dc in each ch. Join rnd with sl st. (12 dc)

Rnd 2: Ch 1, dc in each dc (**see Step 5**).

Rnd 3: Ch 1, [dc2tog] six times. Join rnd with sl st.

Rnd 4: Ch 2, [miss next dc, dc2tog] twice, sl st in dc2tog of Rnd 4 (**see Step 6**). (2 sts)

Ch 20, sl st in 2nd ch from hook, sl st until you reach bud. Fasten off Colour C (**see Step 7**).

Weave in all ends and sew stem to flower (**see Step 8**).

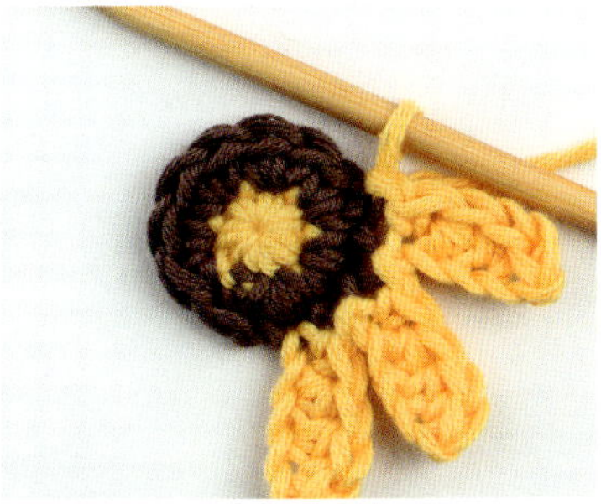

1 As you crochet the first three rounds, follow the steps on page 27 for invisible colour change instructions.

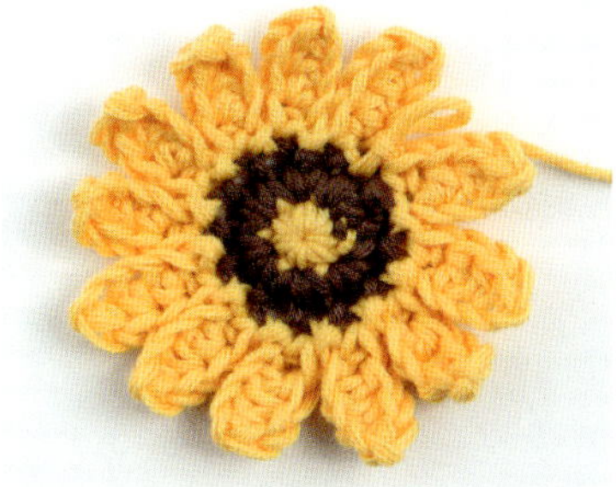

2 Once you have completed the first round of petals – worked into the front loops only – your daisy will look like this.

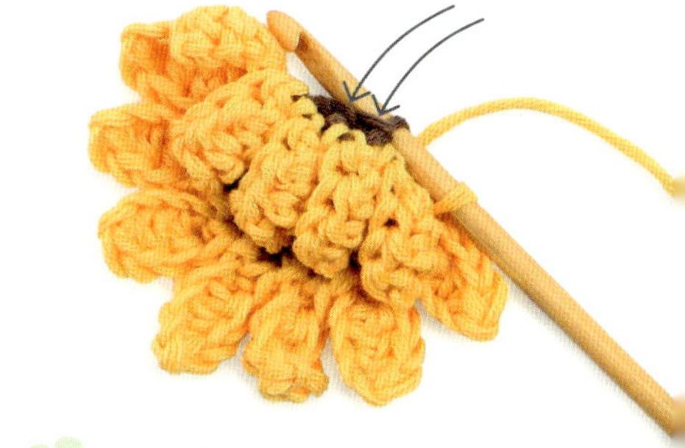

3 Fold the first round of petals forwards to find the back loops of Round 2.

4 When you have finished the second round of petals – worked into the back loops only – the flower will look like this. Fasten off.

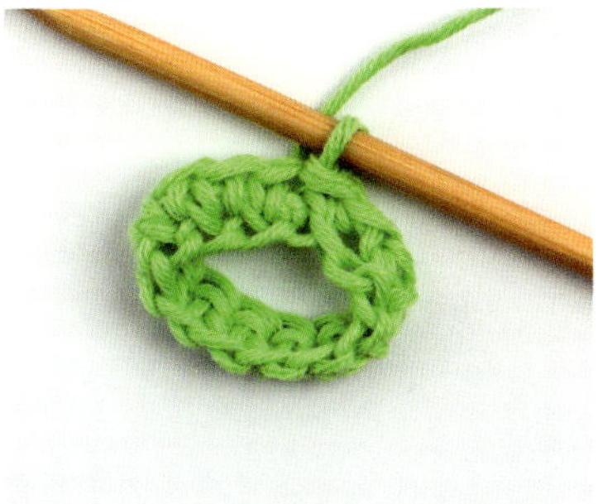

5 You will be crocheting the stem from top to bottom. After Round 2, it will look like this. Note the long yarn end, which you will need to sew the stem to the flower.

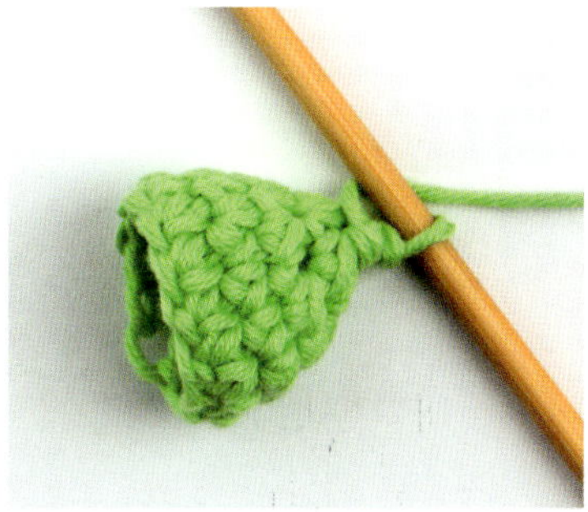

6 Crochet the bud and then continue to crochet 20 ch sts without fastening off to form the stem.

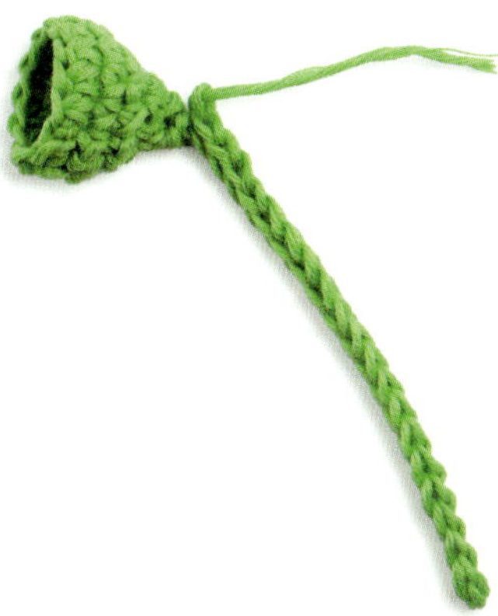

7 Weave in the loose yarn end inside the flower bud.

8 Sew the stem and the flower together.

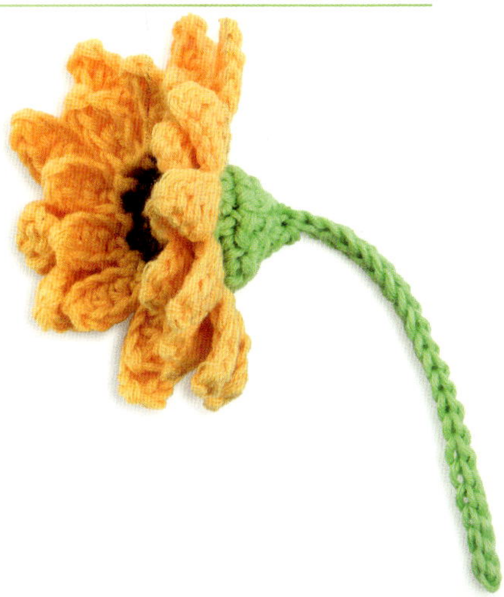

30 Fuchsia

Skill level:

These flowers would look so beautiful as a garland. Attach a little bit of string to the top of the flower, and you can decorate your home with these delicate flowers.

Materials:

4-ply yarn in 2 colours:

Colour A: 7.3 m (8 yds)

Colour B: 7.3 m (8 yds)

Tools:

Hook size: 3.25 mm (D-3)
Yarn needle
Scissors

Chart key:

- Magic ring
- Ch
- \+ Dc Double crochet
- • Sl st Slip stitch
- Htr Half treble crochet
- 3 ch picot (ch 3, sl st in 3rd ch from hook)
- Tr Treble crochet

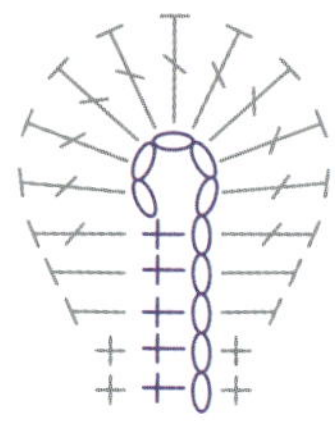

Outer petals (1 petal)

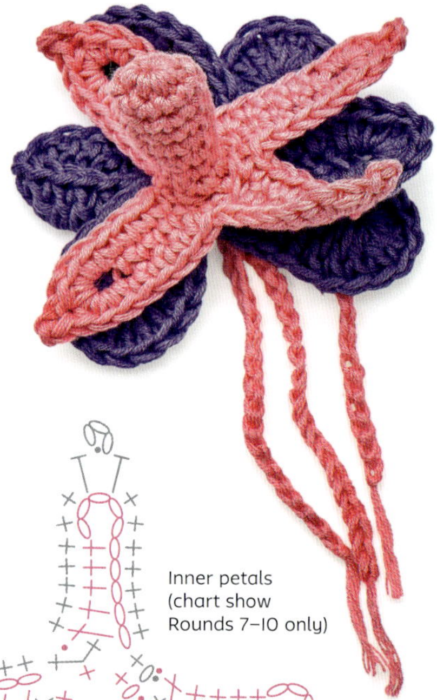

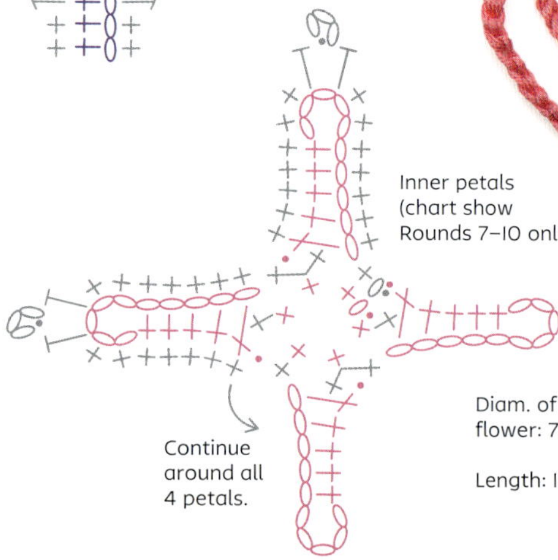

Inner petals (chart show Rounds 7–10 only)

Continue around all 4 petals.

Diam. of finished flower: 7.5 cm (3 in)

Length: 10 cm (4 in)

Pattern

Inner petals:

With Colour A, make a magic ring (see page 12).

Rnd 1: Into magic ring, ch 1, 8 dc. Pull on short end to close middle. Join rnd with sl st. (8 dc)

Rnds 2–5: Ch 1, dc in each dc. Join rnd with sl st.

Rnd 6: Ch 1, [dc2tog, dc in next 2 dc] twice. Join rnd with sl st. (6 dc)

Rnd 7: Ch 1, dc in each dc. Join rnd with sl st.

Rnd 8: Ch 1, dc in first dc, 2 dc in next dc, dc in next 2 sts, 2 dc in next dc, dc in next dc. Join rnd with sl st. (8 dc)

Rnd 9: *Ch 10, starting from 6th ch from hook, dc in next 5 ch, miss next dc, sl st in next dc.

Rep from * three more times (4 petals) (**see Step 1**).

Rnd 10: *Dc in 5 sts, [2 dc, htr, 3 ch picot, htr, 2 dc] in ch 10 loop, dc in next 5 sts, miss sl st at base of petal.

Rep from * three more times (4 petals).

Fasten off Colour A, leaving a long yarn end for sewing (**see Step 2**).

Outer petals:

Row 1: With Colour B, *ch 10, starting from 6th ch from hook, dc in next 5 ch (**see Step 3**).

Rep from * five more times (**see Step 4**).

Row 2: Ch 1, turn, *dc in next 2 dc, htr in next 2 dc, tr in next dc, 9 tr in ch-5 loop, tr in next ch, htr in next 2 ch, dc in next 2 ch.

Rep from * five more times (**see Step 5**).

Fasten off Colour B.

Stamens (make 5):

Attach Colour A to middle of first petal in Colour B (**see Step 6**).

Ch 22. Fasten off Colour A.

Fold petals with stamens in the middle as shown in **Step 7**. Sew the flower together. Fasten off and weave in ends (**see Step 8**).

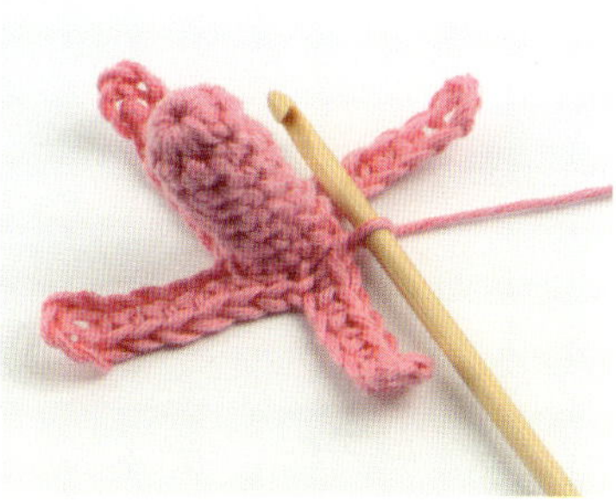

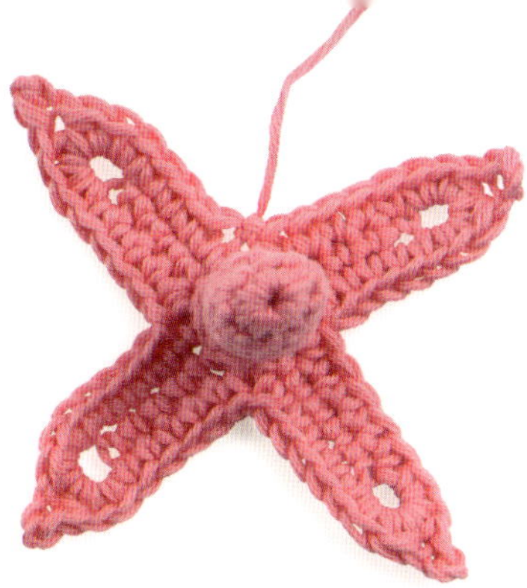

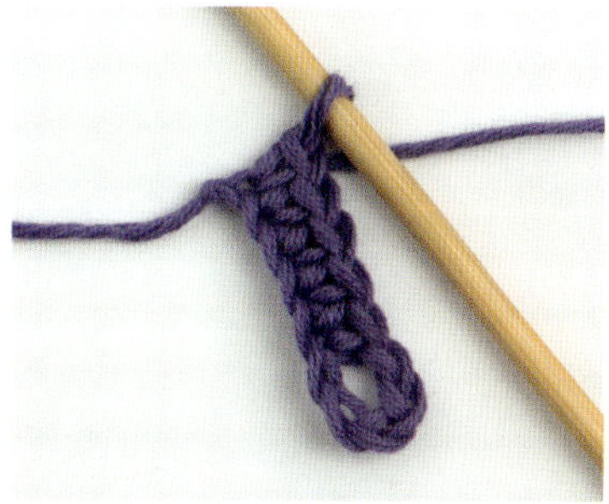

1 Follow the pattern for Rounds 1–9 to make the top part of the flower, with four petals.

2 Crochet around each petal, following the instructions for Round 10, and fasten off Colour A.

3 The outer petals are crocheted separately. To create one: ch 10, starting from the 6th ch from the hook, dc into each of the next 5 ch.

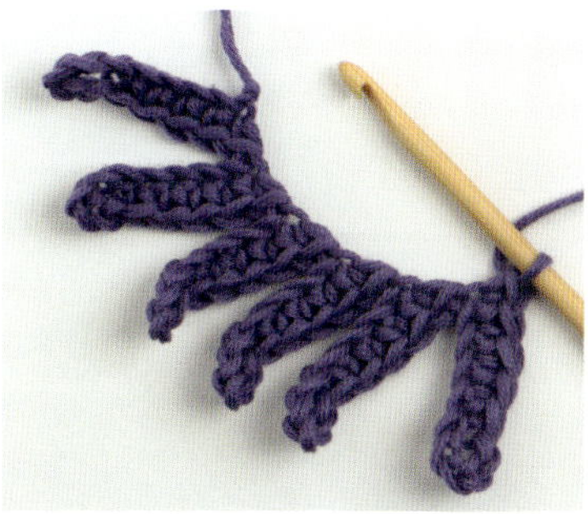

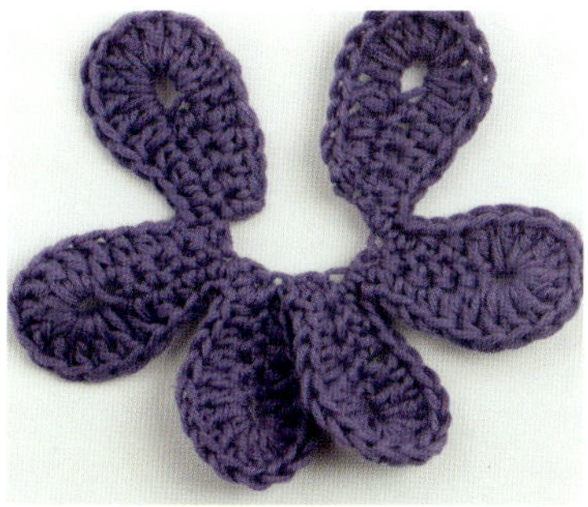

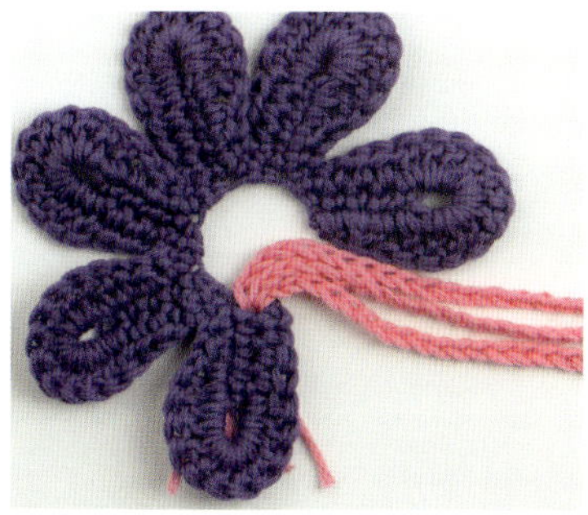

4 Repeat Step 3 five more times to create six short rows that will become the petals.

5 Crochet around each of the petals following the pattern for Row 2.

6 Attach Colour A to the bottom-centre of the first petal and ch 22. Fasten off and then create four more stamens in the same way.

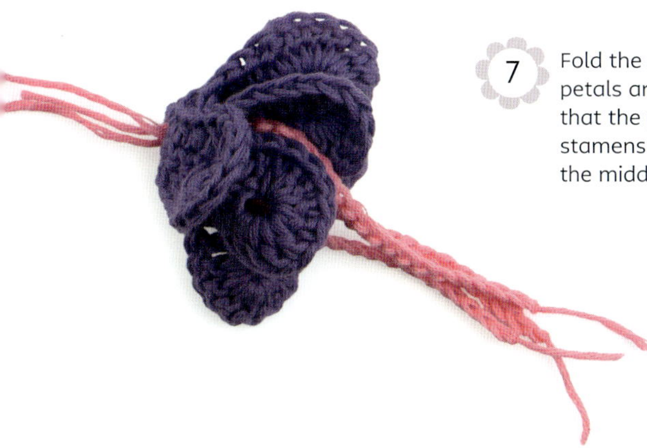

7 Fold the strip of outer petals around itself so that the petal with the stamens attached is in the middle.

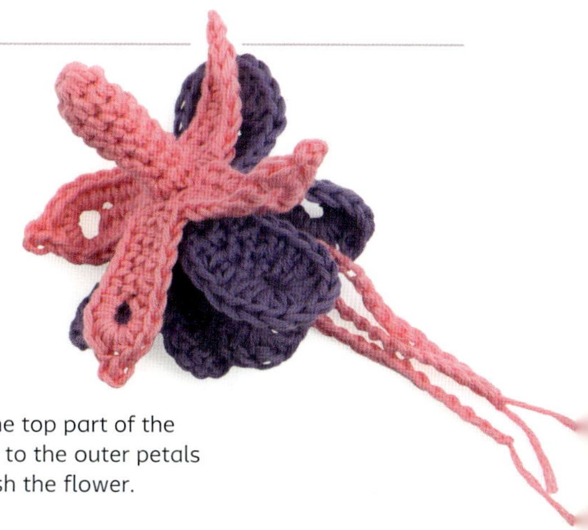

8 Sew the top part of the flower to the outer petals to finish the flower.

31 Gerbera

Skill level:

This is a soft and delicate flower that will be a beautiful addition to your crochet garden. A combination of very simple techniques creates this stunning effect when used together.

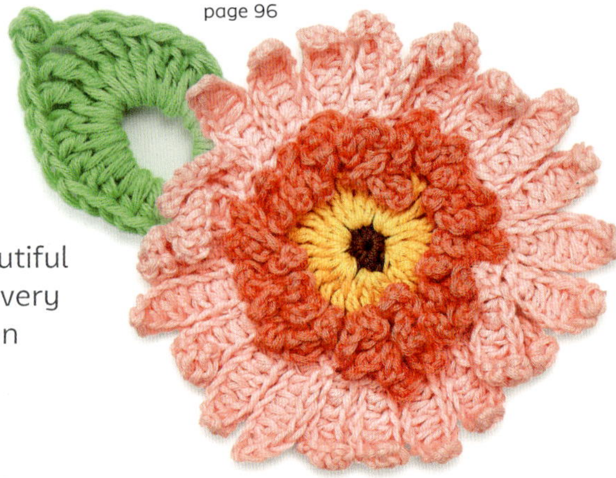

Stylised Leaf, page 96

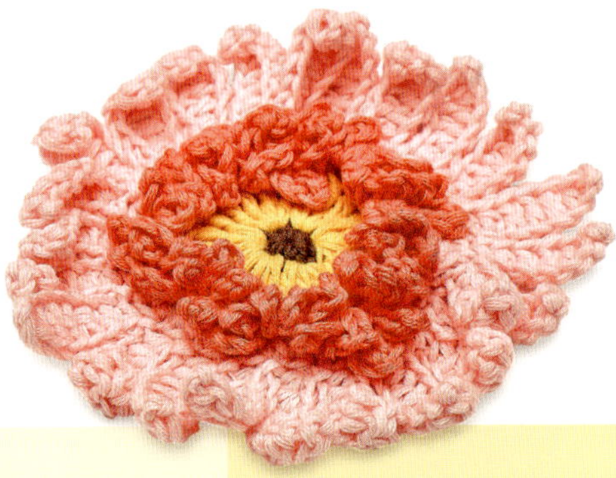

Diam. of finished flower: 11.5 cm (4½ in)

Materials:

4-ply yarn in 4 colours:

- Colour A: 1 m (1 yd)
- Colour B: 3.75 m (4 yds)
- Colour C: 4.5 m (5 yds)
- Colour D: 10 m (11 yds)

Tools:

Hook size: 3.25 mm (D-3)
Yarn needle
Scissors

Pattern

With Colour A, make a magic ring (see page 12).

Rnd 1: Into magic ring, ch 1, 6 dc. Pull on short end to close middle. Fasten off Colour A and weave in ends (**see Step 1**). (6 dc)

Attach Colour B to first dc of Rnd 1.

Rnd 2: Ch 3, 4 dtr in each dc. Join rnd with sl st (**see Steps 2–3**) (24 dtr).

Fasten off Colour B.

Attach Colour C to front loop of first dtr of Rnd 2.

Rnd 3: Working in front loops only: [ch 6, sl st in next dtr, ch 6, sl st in same dtr] 24 times, until end of rnd (**see Steps 4–5**).

Fasten off Colour C.

Attach Colour D to any back loop of Rnd 2.

Rnd 4: Working in back loops only: ch 2, 2 htr in each dtr. Join rnd with sl st (**see Steps 6–7**). (48 htr)

Rnd 5: *Ch 6, dc in 2nd ch from hook, htr in next ch, tr in next 2 ch, htr in last ch, miss next dc, sl st in next dc (**see Step 8**).

Rep from * 23 more times. Join rnd with sl st.

Fasten off and weave in all ends.

Chart key:

- Magic ring
- Ch
- + Dc Double crochet
- • Sl st Slip stitch
- Dtr Double treble crochet
- Back loop
- Front loop
- Htr Half treble crochet
- Tr Treble crochet

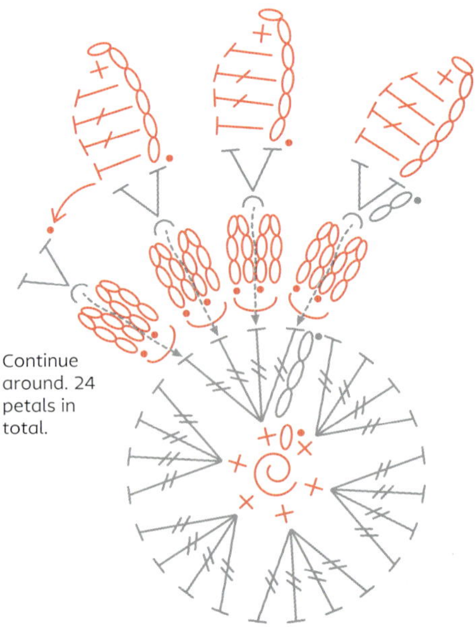

Continue around. 24 petals in total.

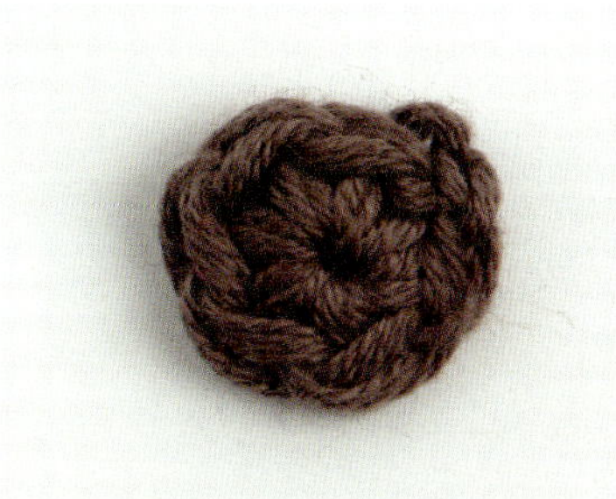

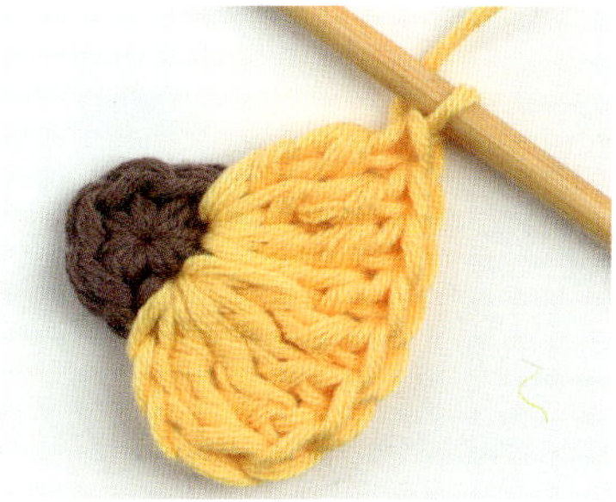

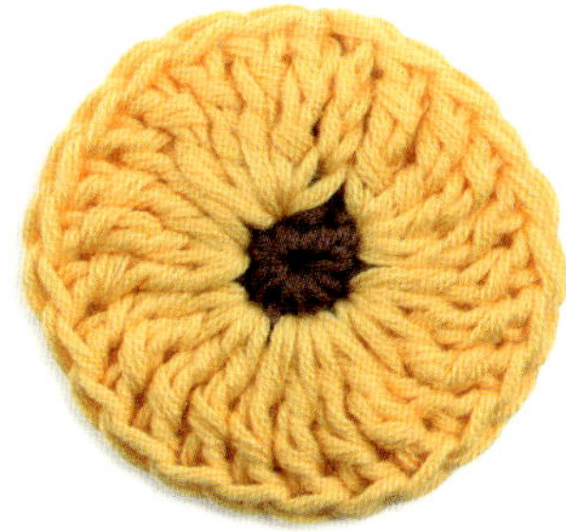

1 When you work Round I, be sure not to make your dc stitches too tight.

2 With Colour B, work 4 dtr into each dc. You should be able to easily place 4 dtr into each dc as long as you haven't crocheted the dc stitches in Round I too tightly.

3 You will make 24 dtr stitches in total around the centre of your flower. Join Round 2 with a sl st into the first dtr.

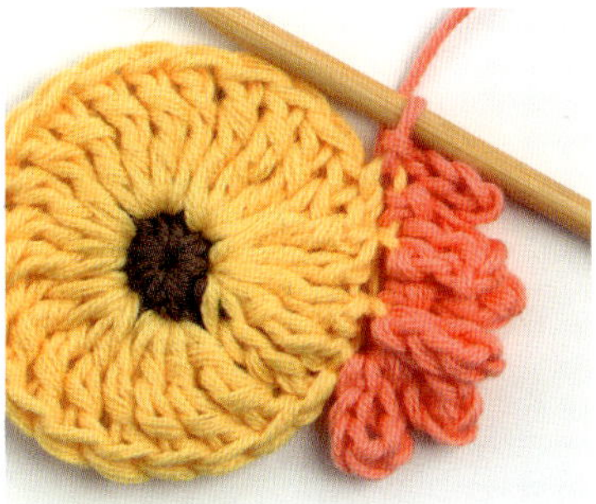

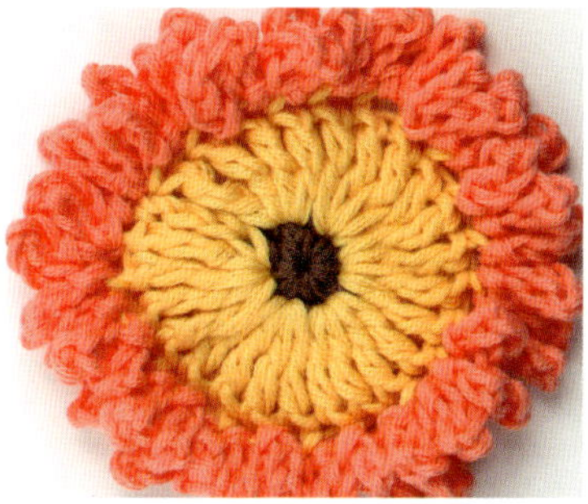

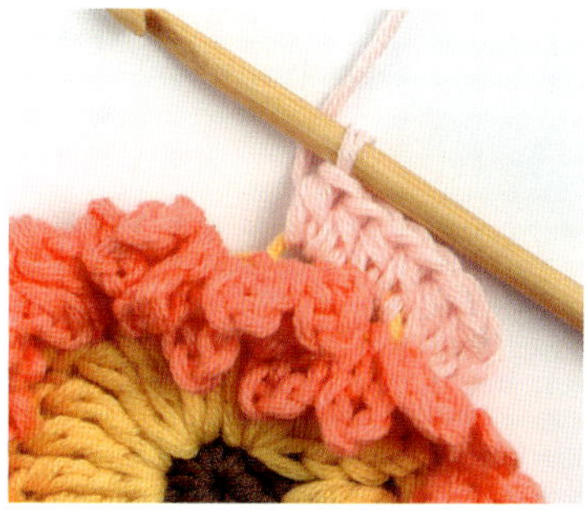

4 Attach Colour C to the front loops of Round 2 only. Ch 6, sl st into the next dtr, ch 6, then sl st into the same dtr as you worked the previous sl st.

5 As you finish Round 3, you will notice that behind the completed petals, you still have back loops of Round 2 free to crochet into.

6 Attach Colour D to the back loops of Round 2 and follow the instructions for Round 4 to create another layer of petals.

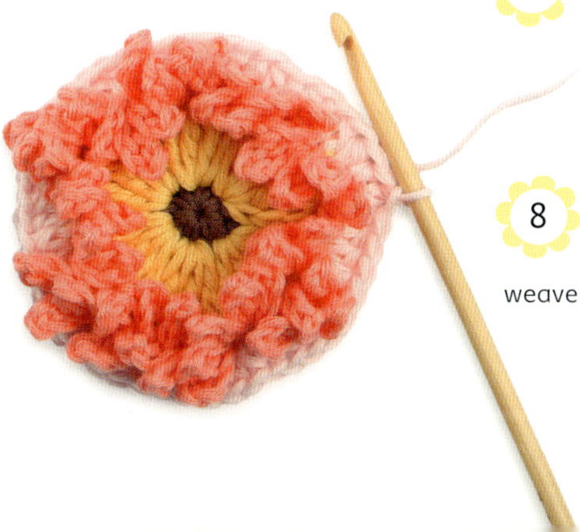

7 As you crochet Round 4, the small petals in Round 3 will acquire a more three-dimensional look.

8 Follow the pattern for Round 5, making 24 petals in total. Fasten off Colour D and weave in all yarn ends.

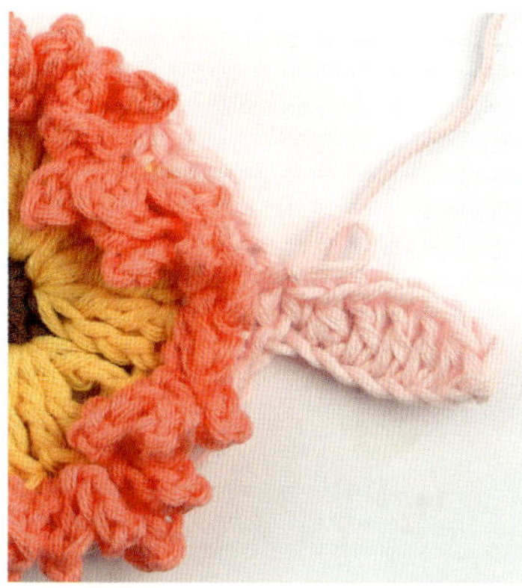

32 Peacock Flower

Skill level: ✿✿✿

This bright and colourful flower could be used to decorate a summer outfit, or maybe a hat? Weave in the yarn ends as you go, and you will not be left with too many to deal with at the end.

Chart key:

- Magic ring
- Ch Chain
- Dc Double crochet
- Sl st Slip stitch
- Htr Half treble crochet
- Tr Treble crochet
- Dtr Double treble crochet
- Trtr Triple treble crochet
- 3 ch picot (ch 3, sl st in 3rd ch from hook)

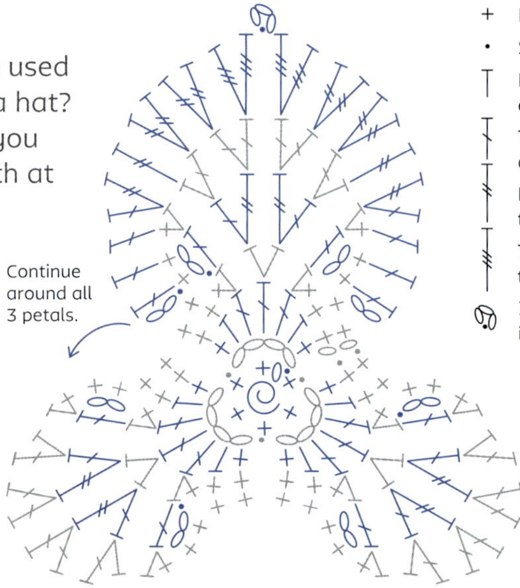

Materials:

4-ply yarn in 4 colours:

- Colour A: 3.75 m (4 yds)
- Colour B: 5.5 m (6 yds)
- Colour C: 4.5 m (5 yds)
- Colour D: 10 m (11 yds)

Tools:

Hook size: 3.25 mm (D-3)
Yarn needle
Scissors

Pattern

With Colour A, make a magic ring (see page 12).

Rnd 1: Into magic ring, ch 1, 6 dc. Pull on short end to close middle. Join rnd with sl st. (6 dc)

Rnd 2: [Ch 4, miss next dc, sl st in next dc] three times.

Rnd 3: [(Dc, htr, 3 tr, htr, dc) in next ch loop] three times.

Fasten off Colour A (**see Step 1**).

Attach Colour B (**see Step 2**).

Rnd 4: Ch 1, *dc in next 2 sts, [dc, htr] in next tr, 2 htr in next tr, [htr, dc] in next tr, dc in next 2 sts.

Rep from * twice more. Join rnd with sl st.

Do not fasten off Colour B.

*Attach Colour C to first htr of any petal (**see Step 3**).

Rnd 5: Ch 2, tr in htr, [tr, dtr] in next st, [dtr, tr] in next st, [tr, ch 2, sl st] in next st.
Fasten off Colour C.

Rep from * for each petal (**see Step 4**).

Pick up Colour B.

Rnd 6: Ch 1, *dc in 2 dc of Rnd 4, miss next dc, 2 dc in ch-2 loop of Rnd 5, [dc, htr] in next tr, [htr, tr] in next tr, 2 tr in next 2 dtr, [tr, htr] in next tr, [htr, dc] in next tr, 2 dc in ch-2 loop, miss next dc, dc in next 2 dc of Rnd 4 (**see Step 5**).

Rep from * twice more. Join rnd with sl st.

Fasten off Colour B (**see Step 6**).

Attach Colour D to first dc of first petal (3rd dc of Rnd 6).

Rnd 7: *Ch 2, tr in next 3 dc, [tr, dtr] in next htr, dtr in next htr, 2 dtr in next 2 tr, 2 trtr in next tr, 3 ch picot, 2 trtr in next tr, 2 dtr in next 2 tr, dtr in next htr, [dtr, tr] in next htr, tr in next 3 dc, ch 2, sl st in same dc as last tr (**see Step 7** to learn how to create the triple treble crochet stitch).

Miss next 4 dc, sl st in next dc (first dc of next petal).

Rep from * twice more (**see Step 8**).

Fasten off Colour D. Weave in ends.

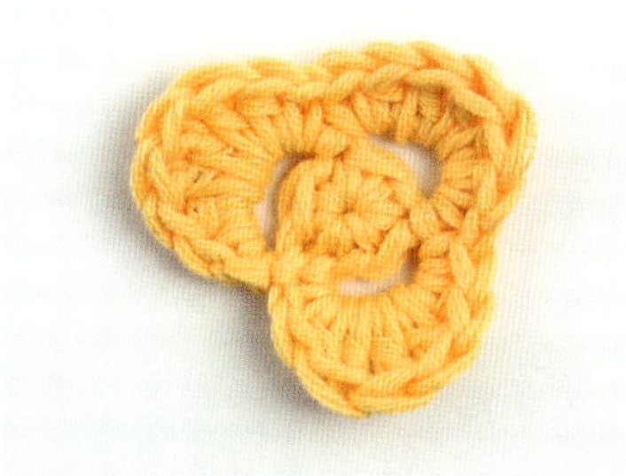

1 The flower has three petals, and the pattern repeats for each petal.

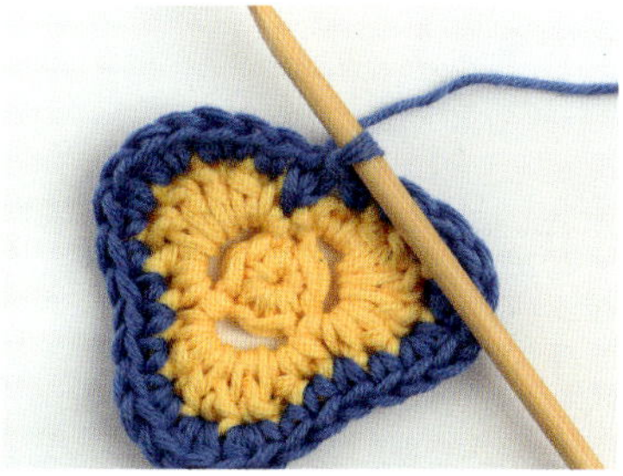

2 Choose a Colour B that contrasts with Colour A for a striking look.

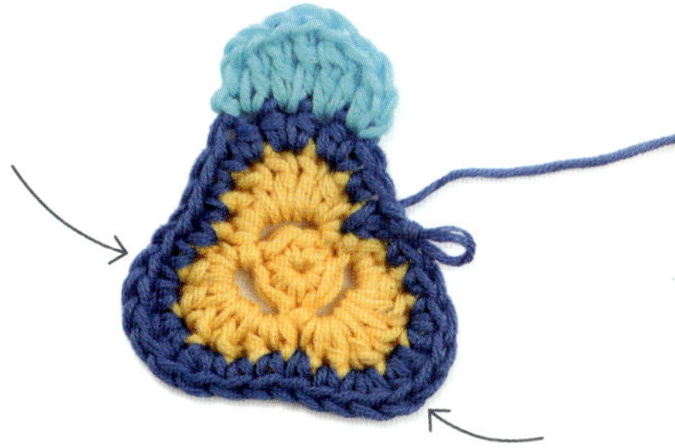

3 Attach Colour C to the first htr of any petal (shown by the arrows). Notice how Colour B is still attached.

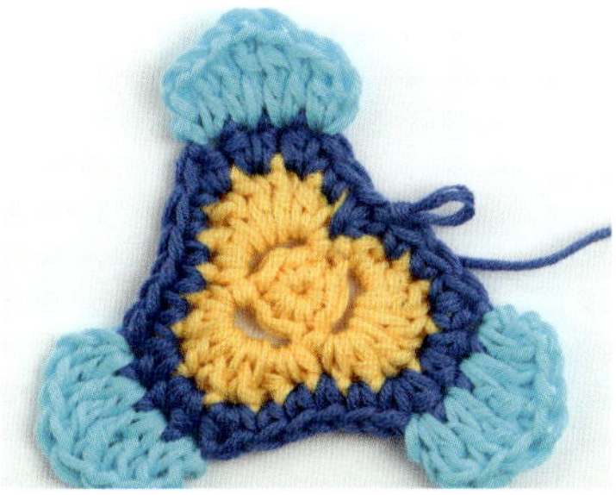

4 Follow the pattern for Round 5 for each pattern. Fasten off Colour C after each petal.

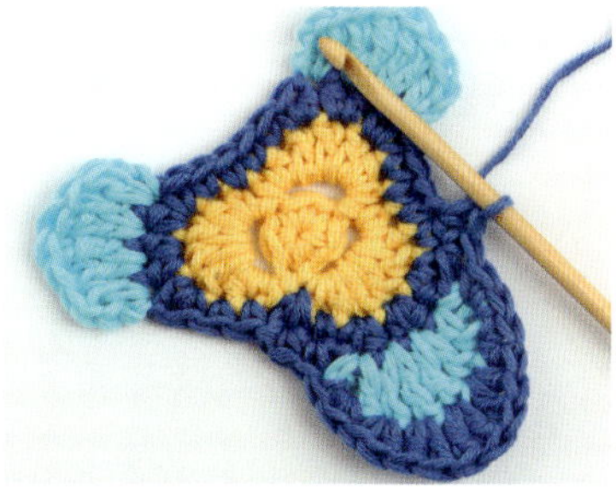

5 Pick up Colour B again and, following the pattern and chart, crochet around the whole flower, encasing Colour C.

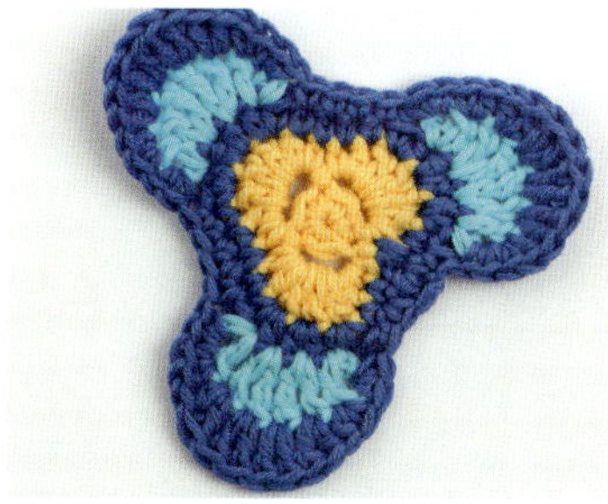

6 Fasten off Colour B. To save time at the end, weave in your ends as you go.

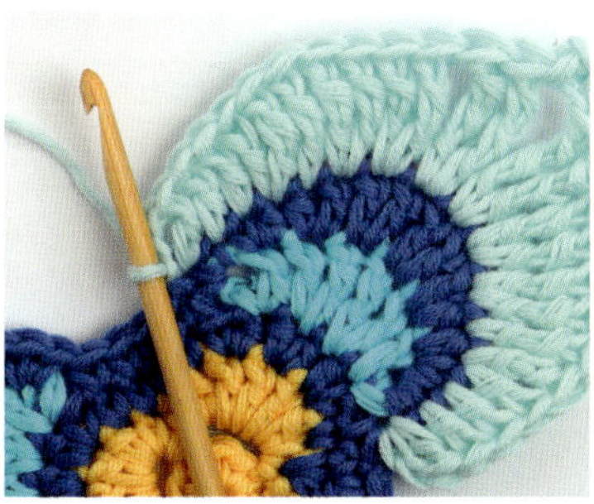

7 To create the triple treble crochet stitch (trtr) in Round 7, wrap the yarn around the hook three times, insert the hook into the next stitch and finish as you would a tr or a dtr stitch.

8 Once you complete Round 7, you will notice that the petals have been pulled together and the flower has become three-dimensional.

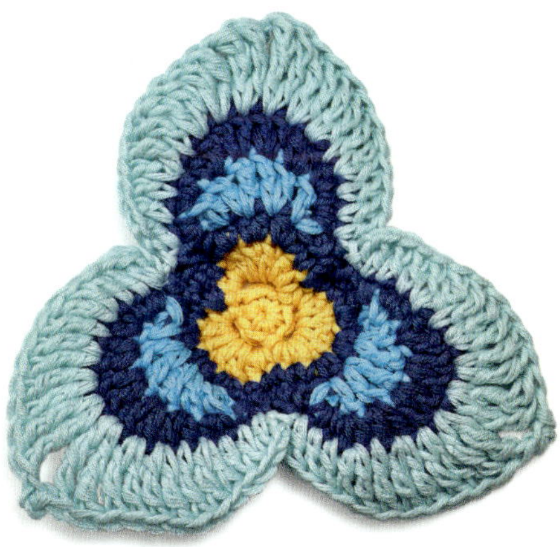

Diam. of finished flower: 10 cm (4 in)

33 Dandelion

Skill level:

When I see these bright flowers blooming, I know that spring is here! You can make a whole dandelion family using these patterns.

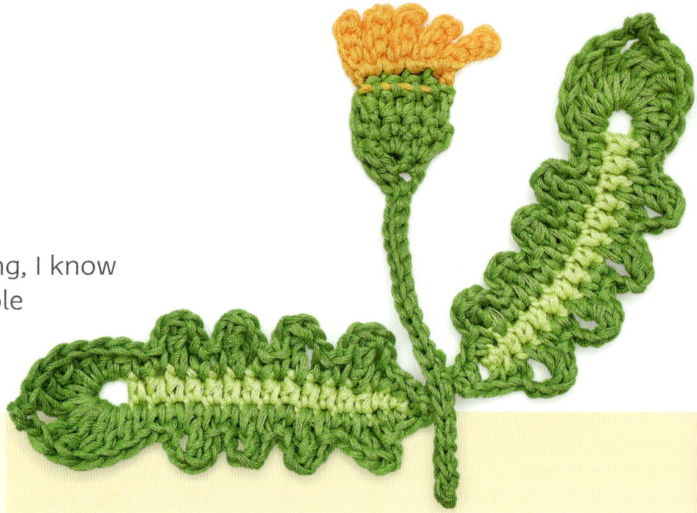

Pattern

Small flower:

With Colour A, make a magic ring (see page 12).

Rnd 1: Into magic ring, ch 1, 6 dc. Pull on short end to close middle. Join rnd with sl st in front loop of first dc (**see Step 1**). (6 dc)

Rnd 2: Working in front loops only: [ch 3, starting from 2nd ch from hook, sl st in each ch, sl st in next dc] six times (**see Step 2**).

Rnd 3: Working in back loops only of Rnd 1: ch 1, 2 dc in each dc. Join with sl st in front loop of first dc (**see Step 3**). (12 sts)

Rnd 4: Working in front loops only of Rnd 3: [ch 4, starting from 2nd ch from hook, sl st in each ch, sl st in next dc] 12 times (**see Step 4**).

Fasten off Colour A.

Large flower (**see Step 5**):

With Colour A, make a magic ring.

Rnds 1–4: Follow pattern and chart for Rnds 1–4 of 'Small flower'.

Rnd 5: Working in back loops only of Rnd 3: ch 1, [2 dc in next dc, dc in next dc] six times. Join Rnd with sl st in front loop of first dc. (18 sts)

Rnd 6: Working in front loops only of Rnd 5: [ch 4, starting from 2nd ch from hook, sl st in each ch, sl st in next dc] 18 times.

Fasten off Colour A.

Seed head:

In Colour D, [ch 6, starting from 2nd ch from hook, sl st in each ch] six times, sl st in first ch to create circle (**see Steps 8–9**).

Fasten off Colour D. Weave in ends.

Attach Colour E to last sl st.

Ch 12, sl st in 5th ch from hook.

Fasten off Colour E. Weave in ends (**see Steps 10–11**).

Leaf:

Row 1: In Colour B, ch 20, starting with 6th ch from hook, htr in next 13 ch, dc in next 2 ch.

Fasten off Colour B.

Attach Colour C.

Row 2: Ch 2, dc in first 2 dc of Row 1, [ch 2, dtr in next htr, ch 2, dc in next 2 htr] four times, htr in next htr, [2 tr, 3 dtr, 3 ch picot, 3 dtr, 2 tr] in ch-5 loop, htr in next ch, dc in next 2 ch, [ch 2, dtr in next ch, ch 2, dc in next 2 ch] four times, htr in next ch, dc in next ch (**see Steps 12–15**).

Fasten off Colour C. Weave in all ends.

Stem and bud:

In Colour C, ch 22.

Row 1: 2 dc in 2nd ch from hook. (2 dc)

Row 2: Ch 1, turn. 2 dc in each dc. (4 dc)

Rows 3–5: Ch 1, turn, dc in each dc, dc along edge of flower, sl st in each ch.

Fasten off Colour C at bottom of stem (**see Step 16**).

Attach Colour A to first dc of Row 5.

Ch 4, starting from 2nd ch from hook, sl st in each st, sl st in same dc, [ch 4, starting from 2nd ch from hook, sl st in each st, sl st in next dc] three times, ch 4, starting from 2nd ch from hook, sl st in each st, sl st in same dc.

Fasten off Colour A (**see Step 17**).

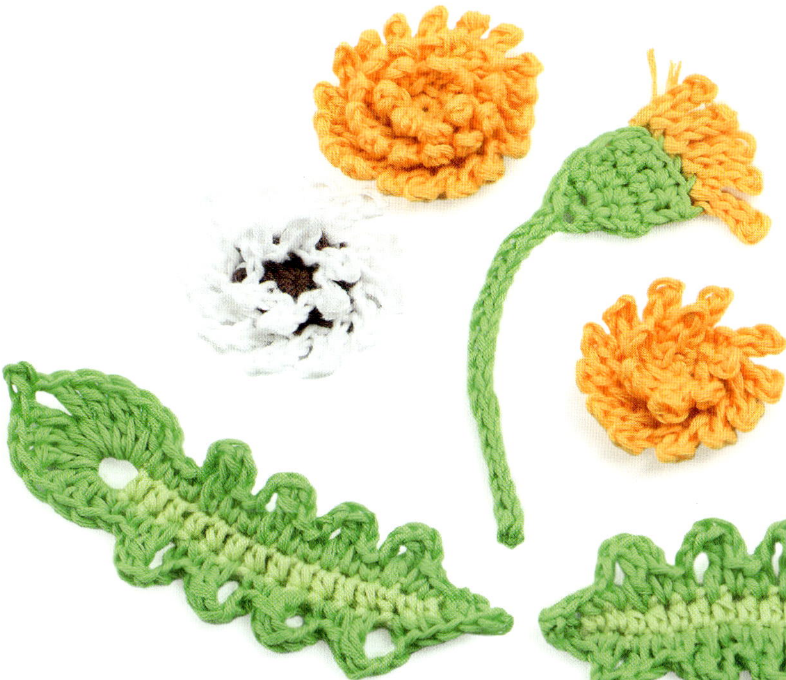

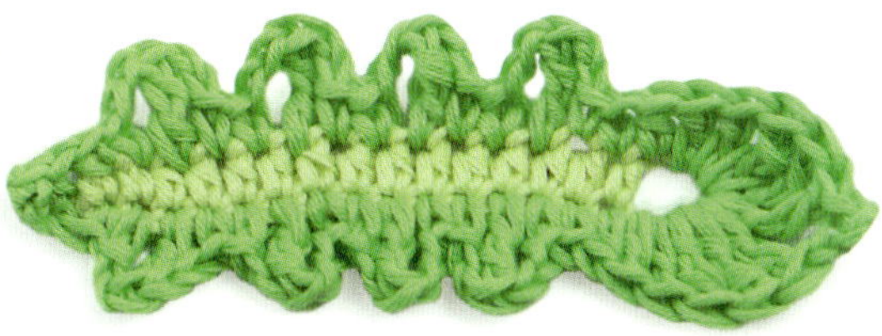

Diam. of finished flower: 5 cm (2 in)

Length of finished leaf: 10 cm (4 in)

Chart key:

- Magic ring
- Ch Chain
- Dc Double crochet
- Sl st Slip stitch
- Back loop
- Front loop
- Htr Half treble crochet
- Tr Treble crochet
- Dtr Double treble crochet
- 3 ch picot (ch 3, sl st in 3rd ch from hook)

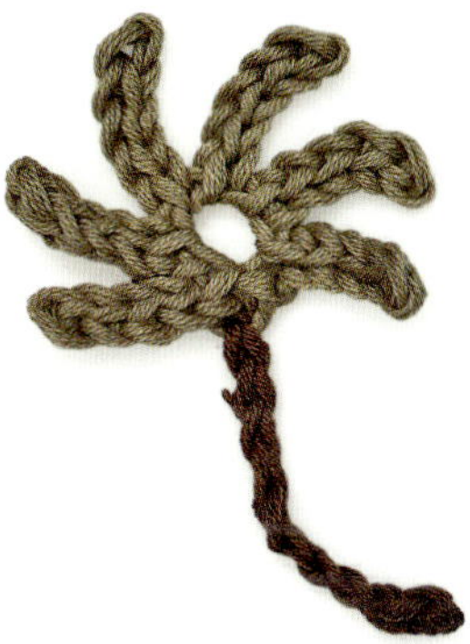

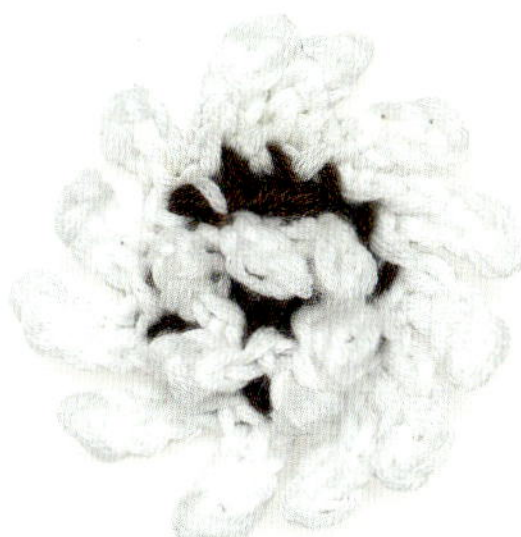

Small flower/seed head

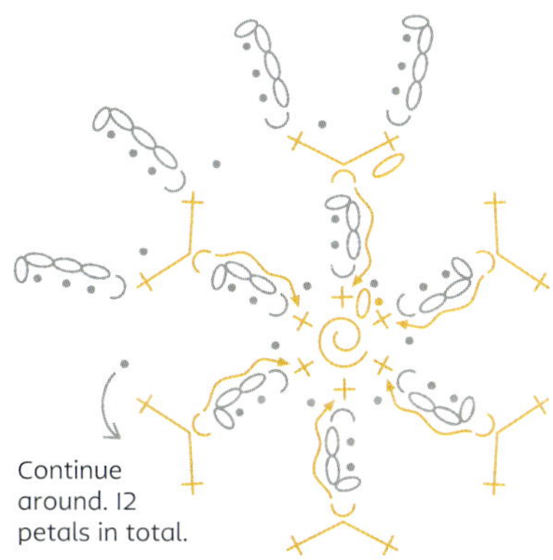

Materials:

4-ply yarn in 6 colours:

- Colour A: 7.3 m (8 yds)
- Colour B: 2.75 m (3 yds)
- Colour C: 7.3 m (8 yds)
- Colour D: 1 m (1 yd)
- Colour E: 1.8 m (2 yds)
- Colour F: 2.75 m (3 yds)

Tools:

Hook size: 3.25 mm (D-3)
Yarn needle
Scissors

Leaf

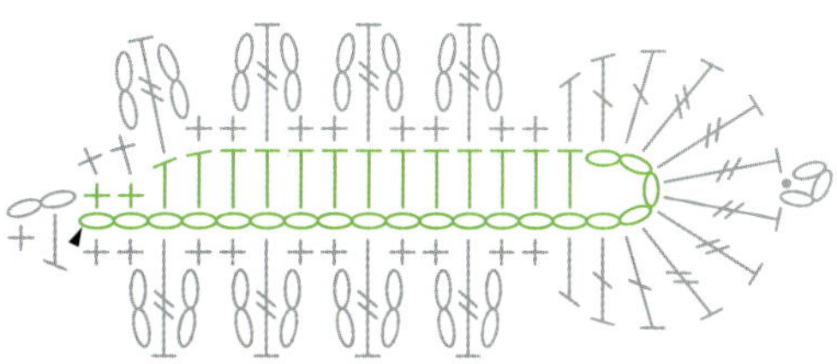

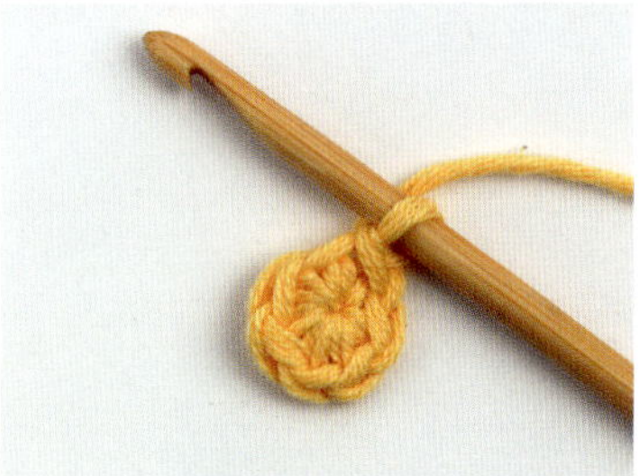

1 **Flower:** Make a dandelion flower by working 6 dc into a magic ring.

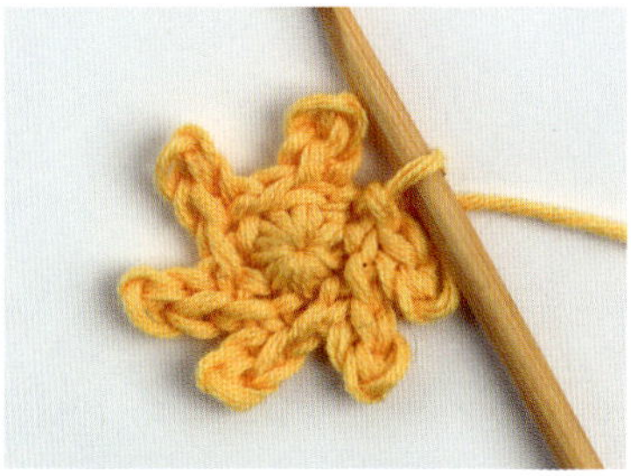

2 Working into the front loops only: ch 3, sl st into each ch starting with the 2nd ch from the hook, sl st into the next dc. Repeat this five times to make the first layer of six petals.

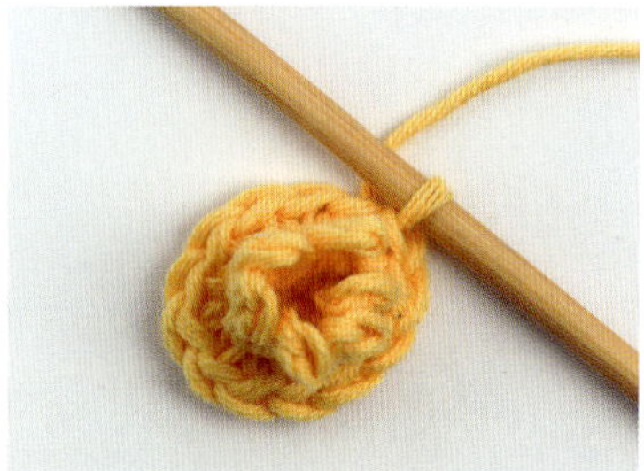

3 Fold the first layer of petals forwards, as pictured in order to crochet into the back loops of Round I.

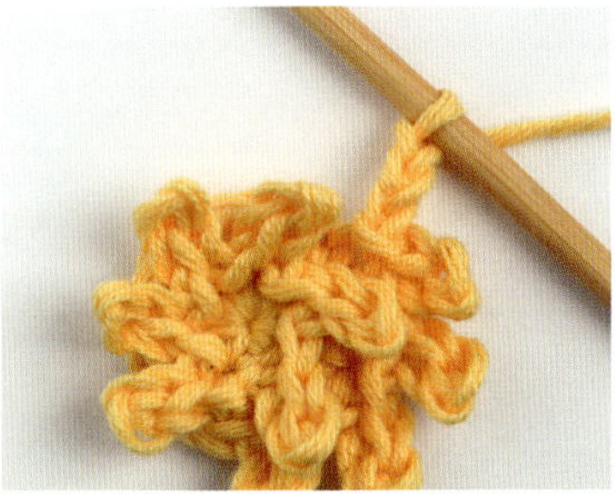

4 Make a second layer of petals by crocheting into the front loops only of Round 3.

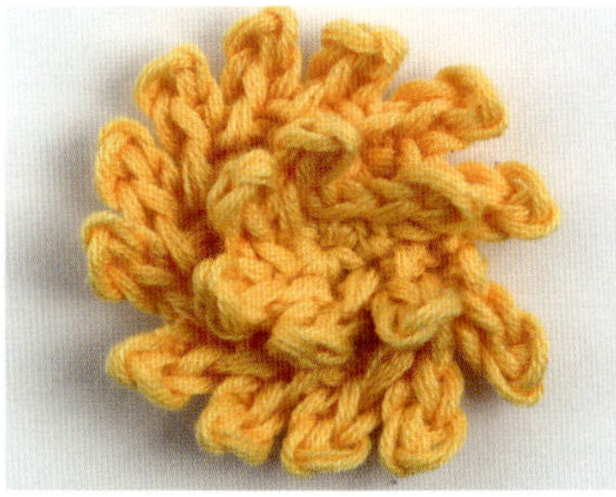

5 Fasten off Colour A at this point for a small flower or follow the pattern for the large flower, by adding two more rounds.

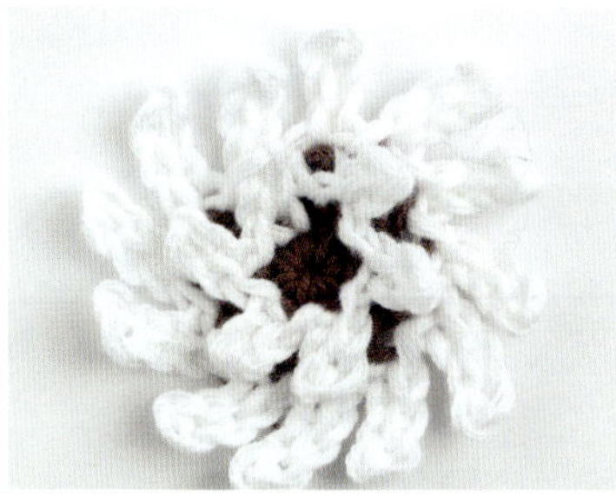

6 You can make a 3D seed head by replacing the yellow yarn of the flower with brown yarn in Rounds I and 3 and white yarn in Rounds 2 and 4.

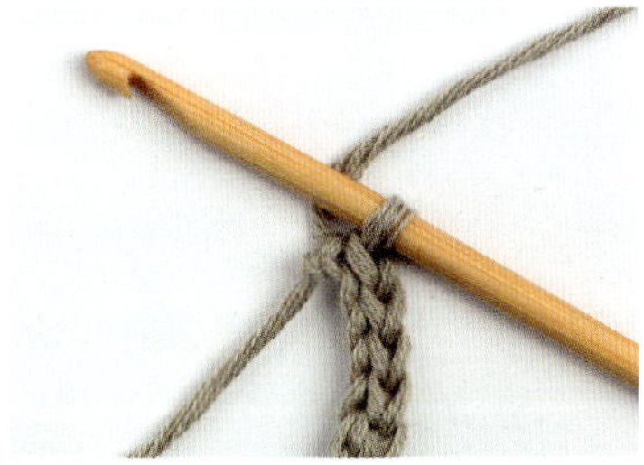

7 **Seed head:** You can also make flat seed heads separately, which work well for appliqué. In Colour D, ch 6 then sl st in each chain starting from the 2nd chain from the hook.

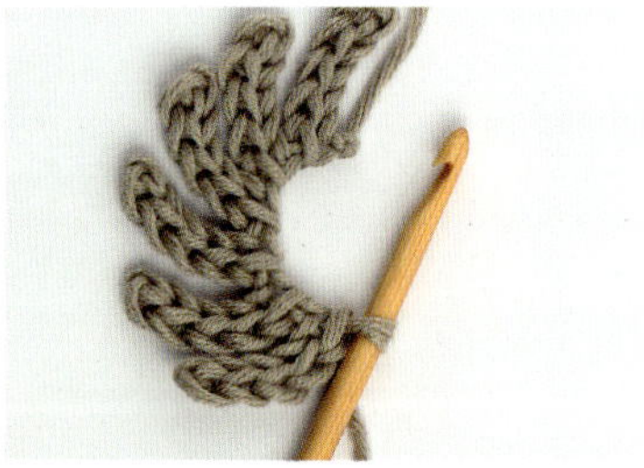

8 Repeat Step 7 five times then sl st into the first ch to form the seed head into a circle. You could also use white instead of grey for this part.

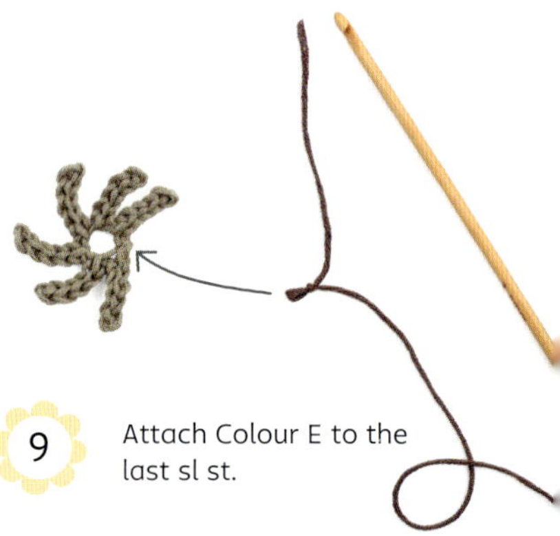

9 Attach Colour E to the last sl st.

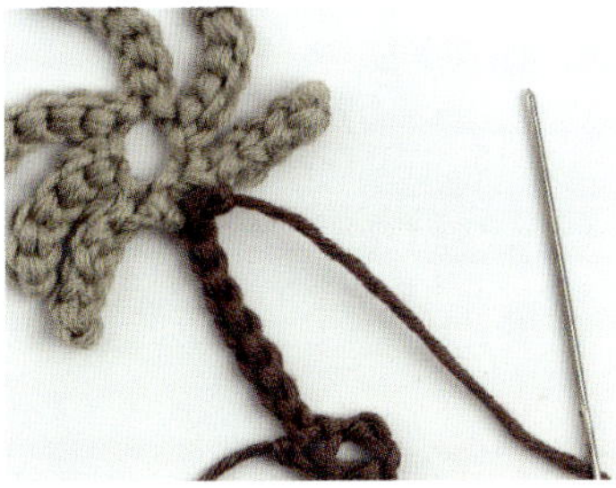

10 Ch 12, then sl st into the 5th ch from the hook. You are now ready to weave in the ends using a yarn needle.

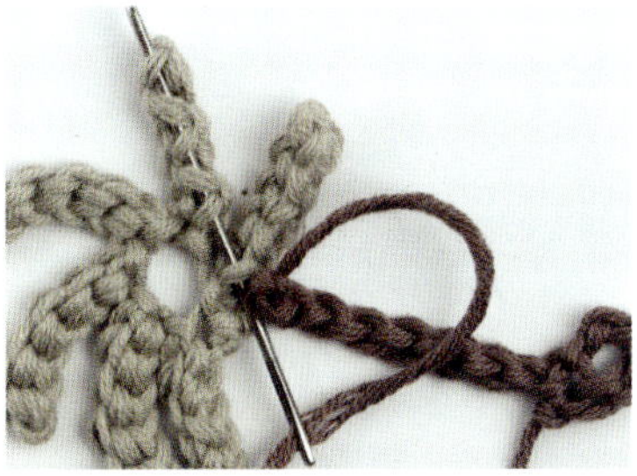

11 Weave the needle carefully through the wrong side of the seed head, as shown. Pull through to hide the yarn, then cut the ends.

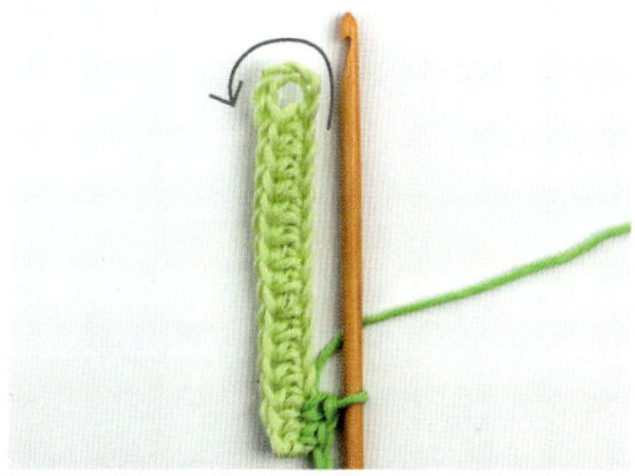

12 **Leaf:** Follow the pattern to crochet the first row for the leaf in Colour B, and then crochet around in Colour C.

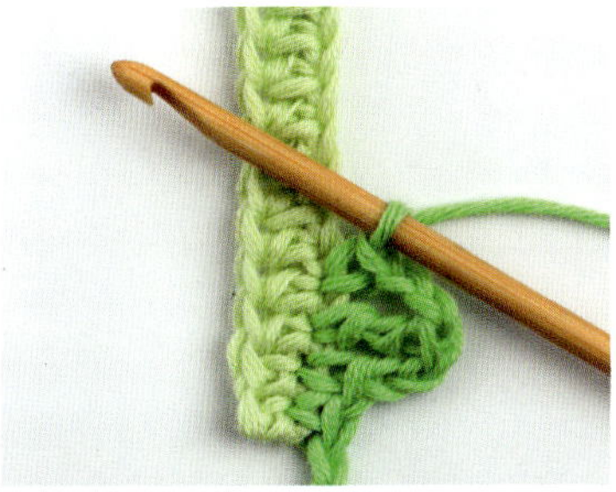

13 As you work Row 2, you will be crocheting small ridges along the leaf.

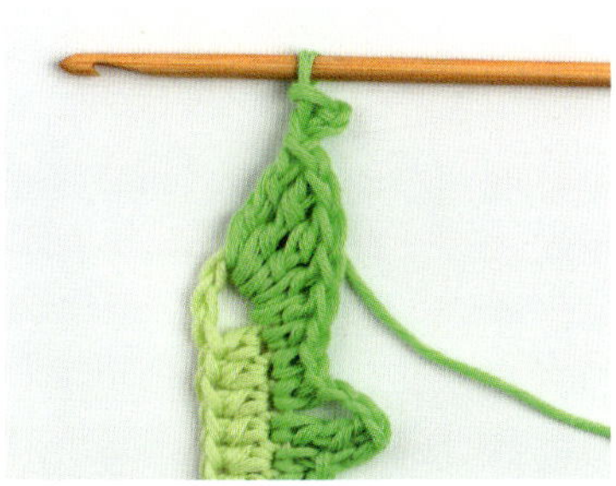

14 The 3 ch picot is located at the very tip of the leaf.

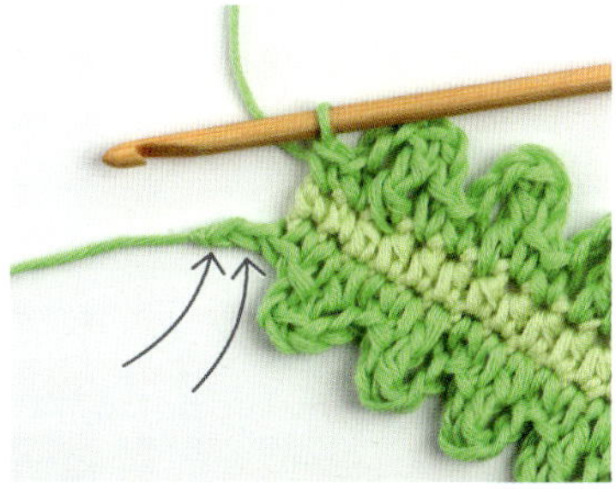

15 Continue to crochet around the leaf, finishing with a htr and dc into the last 2 chain stitches.

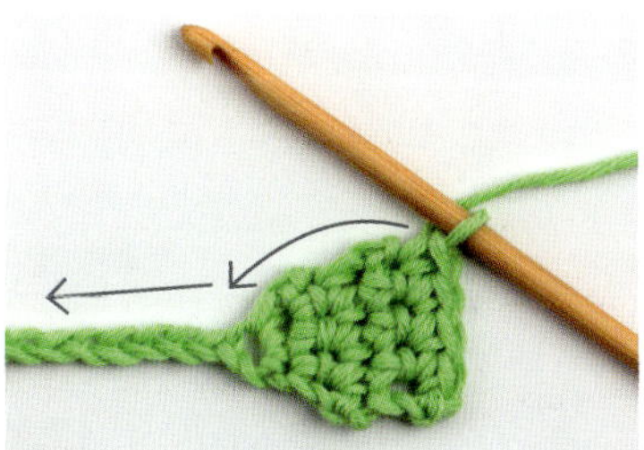

16 **Bud and stem:** As you make the stem, dc along the bud part (indicated by the arrow) and then sl st all the way down the stem.

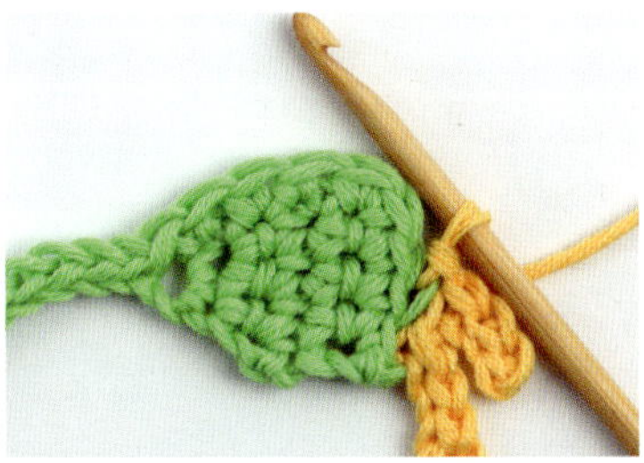

17 Attach Colour A to the first dc of the previous row and follow the pattern to crochet the small petals of the bud.

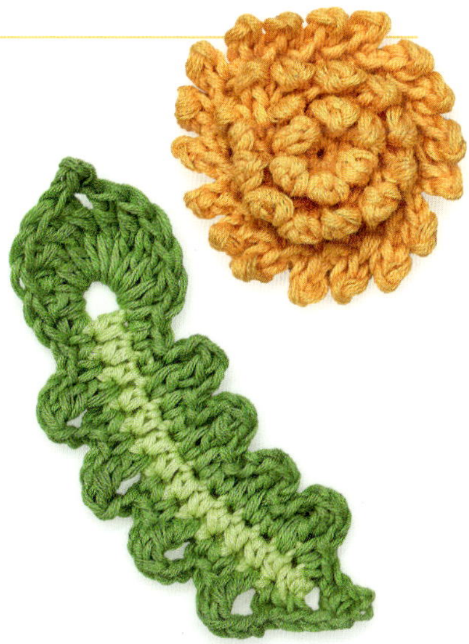

34 Day Lily

Skill level:

This is a unique variety of lily, with frilly petals and beautiful contrasting colours. It is a bigger flower that will hold its shape nicely as a decoration for any accessory.

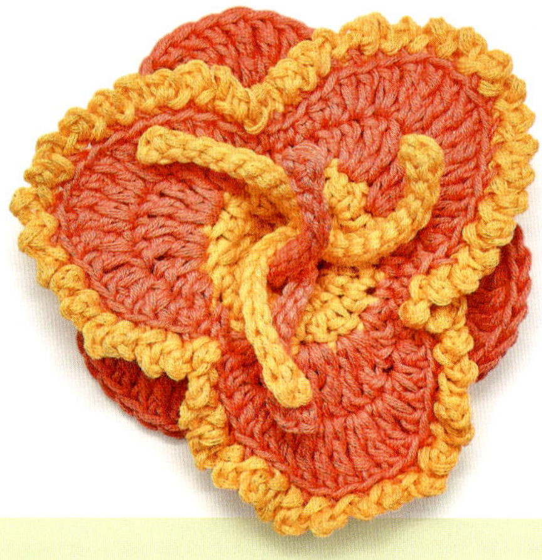

Pattern

With Colour A, make a magic ring (see page 12).

Rnd 1: Into magic ring, ch 2, 12 tr. Pull on short end to close middle. Join rnd with sl st (**see Step 1**). (12 tr)

Rnd 2: Ch 2, [tr in next 3 tr, 2 tr in next tr] three times. Join rnd with sl st (**see Step 2**). (15 tr)

Rnd 3: Ch 1, [dc in next tr, htr in next tr, 2 tr in next tr, htr in next tr, dc in next tr] three times. Join rnd with sl st (**see Step 3**). (18 sts)

Fasten off Colour A.

Attach Colour B to first dc of Rnd 3.

Rnd 4: Ch 1, *dc in first dc, [htr, tr] in next htr, [tr, 2 dtr] in next tr, [2 dtr, tr] in next tr, [tr, htr] in next htr, dc in next dc (**see Step 4**).

Rep from * twice more. Join rnd with sl st (**see Steps 5–6**). (36 sts)

Rnd 5: Ch 1, *dc in first dc, htr in next htr, [htr, tr] in next tr, 2 tr in next tr, [tr, dtr] in next dtr, 2 dtr in next 2 dtr, [dtr, tr] in next dtr, 2 tr in next tr, [tr, htr] in next tr, htr in next htr, dc in next dc.

Rep from * twice more. Join rnd with sl st. (60 sts)

Fasten off Colour B (**see Step 7**).

Attach Colour B to the wrong side of the first petal, as shown in **Step 8**.

Rnd 6: [Ch 10, sl st behind next petal] three times (**see Steps 9–10**).

Rnd 7: Ch 2, [10 tr in ch 10 loop] three times. Join rnd with sl st (**see Steps 11–12**). (30 sts)

Rnd 8: Ch 1, *dc in next 2 tr, htr in next tr, 2 tr in next tr, tr in next 2 tr, 2 tr in next tr, htr in next tr, dc in next 2 tr (**see Step 13**).

Rep from * twice more. Join rnd with sl st. (36 sts)

Rnd 9: Ch 1, *dc in next 2 dc, htr in next 2 sts, 2 tr in next tr, [tr, dtr] in next tr, [dtr, tr] in next tr, 2 tr in next tr, htr in next 2 sts, dc in next 2 dc (**see Step 14**).

Rep from * twice more. Join rnd with sl st. (48 sts)

Fasten off Colour B (**see Step 15**).

Attach Colour A to the last round of the top layer of petals.

[Ch 3, sl st in next st] all around (**see Step 16**). Fasten off Colour A and weave in all ends.

Stamens:

In Colour A, [ch 12, dc in 2nd ch from hook, sl st in next 10 ch] three times.

Fasten off Colour A.

Attach Colour B to last sl st.

[Ch 12, dc in 2nd ch from hook, sl st in next 10 ch] twice.

Fasten off Colour B (**see Step 17**).

Attach stamens to the middle of the flower.

Weave in all ends.

Materials:

4-ply yarn in 2 colours:

Colour A: 7.3 m (8 yds)

Colour B: 13.75 m (15 yds)

Tools:

Hook size: 3.25 mm (D-3)
Yarn needle
Scissors
Stitch marker

Diam. of finished flower:
10 cm (4 in)

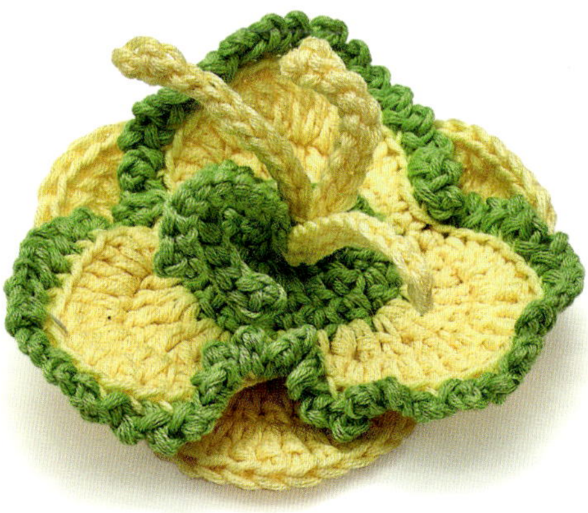

Chart key:

- Magic ring
- Ch Chain
- Tr Treble crochet
- Sl st Slip stitch
- Htr Half treble crochet
- Dc Double crochet
- Dtr Double treble crochet

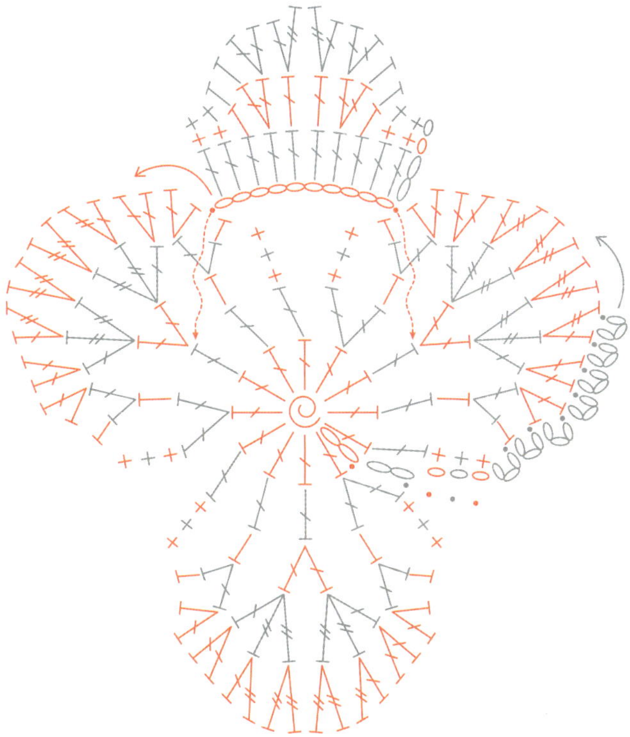

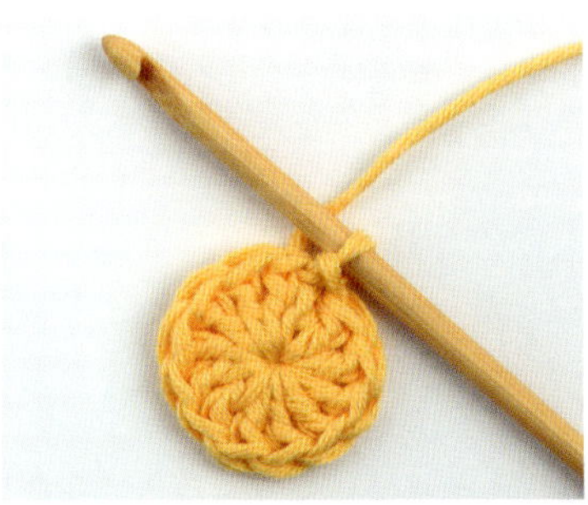

1 To begin your flower, follow the pattern for Round I.

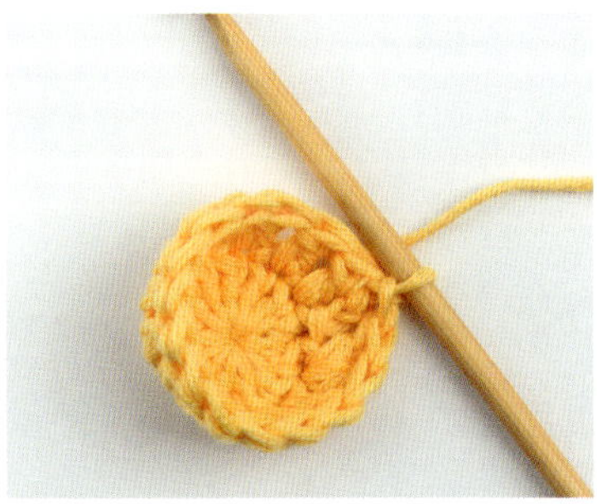

2 As you work Round 2, the flower will start taking on a three-dimensional shape.

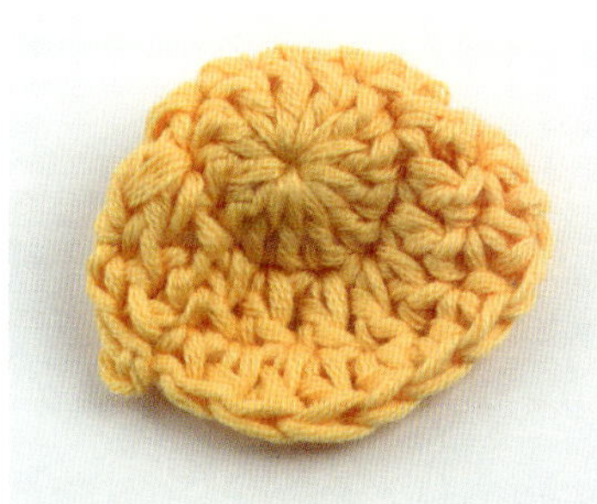

3 After Round 3, the flower will look like this. Notice that three slight petals are just beginning to emerge.

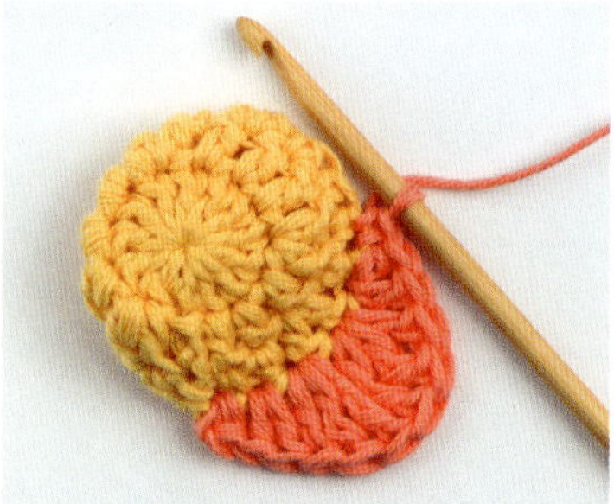

4 Change to Colour B and follow the pattern for Round 4, establishing the petal shape, as shown.

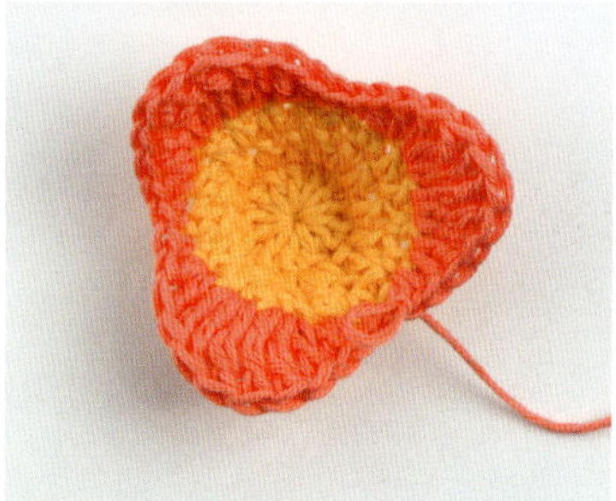

5 The pattern repeats three times – once for each petal.

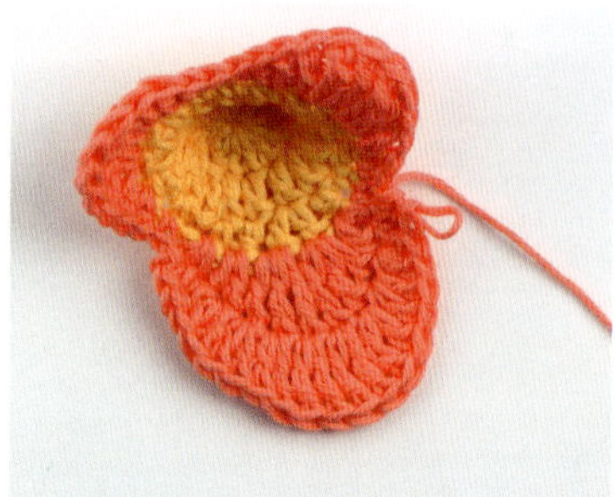

6 Use a stitch marker to help you identify the first stitch of the round. It is very important to keep a good stitch count.

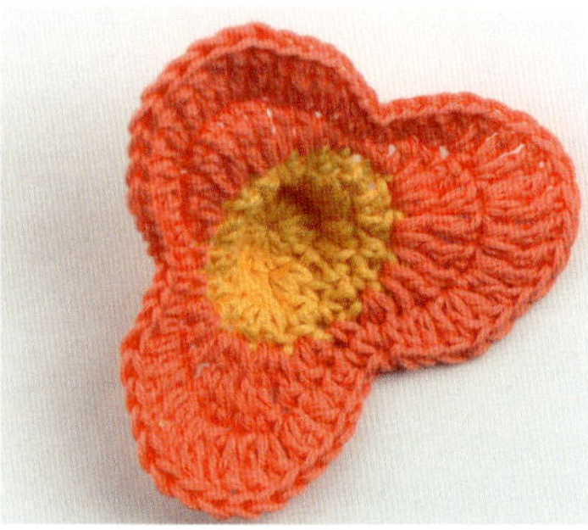

7 After Round 5, fasten off Colour B. The flower will look like this.

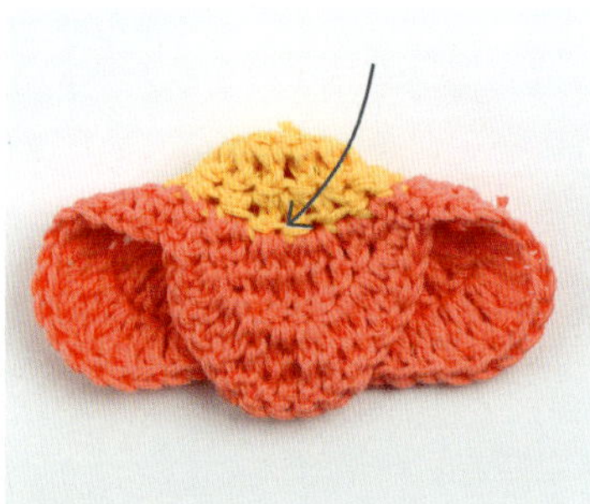

8 The arrow indicates where you should attach Colour B to begin Round 6.

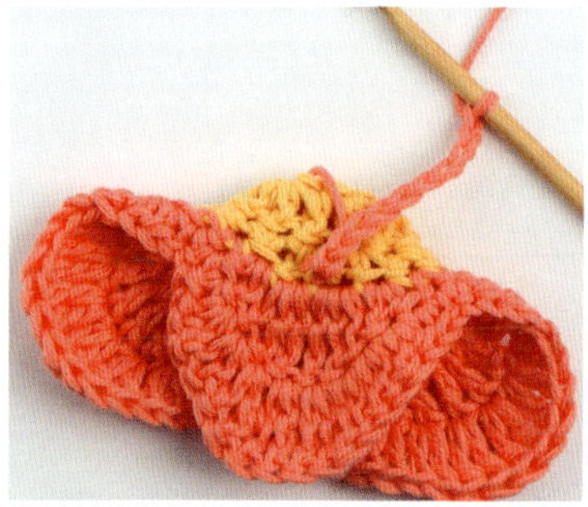

9 From here, ch 10.

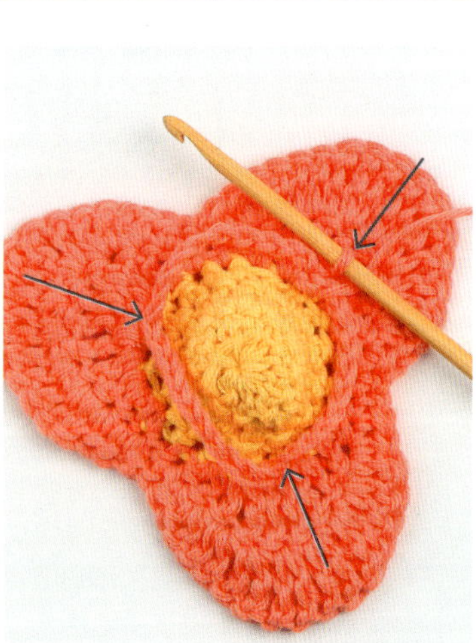

10 The arrows show where the sl sts are made at the end of each ch-10 loop in Round 6.

11 Round 7 is then crocheted into the ch-10 loops created in Steps 9–10, as shown.

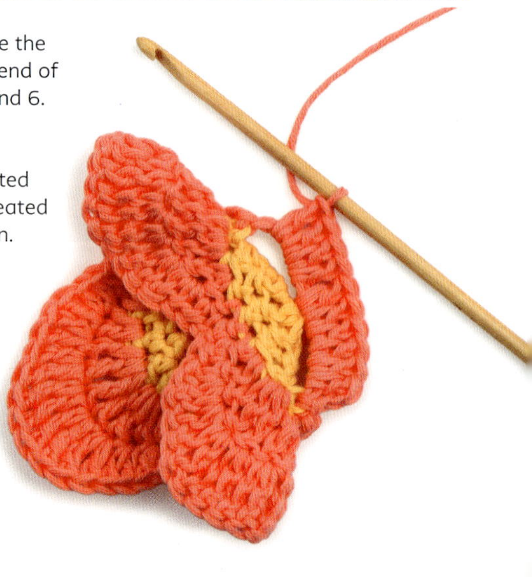

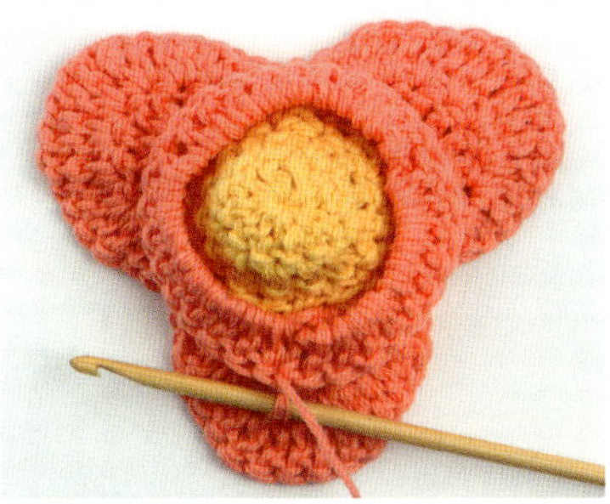

12 After Round 7, the flower will look like this from the back.

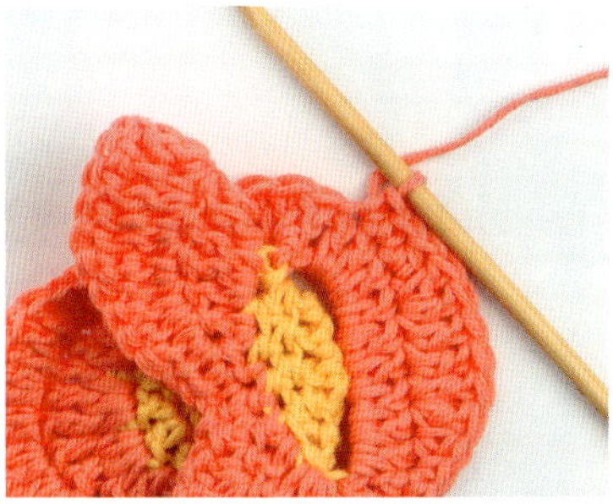

13 Follow the pattern for Rounds 8 and 9, using the photographs and chart for reference.

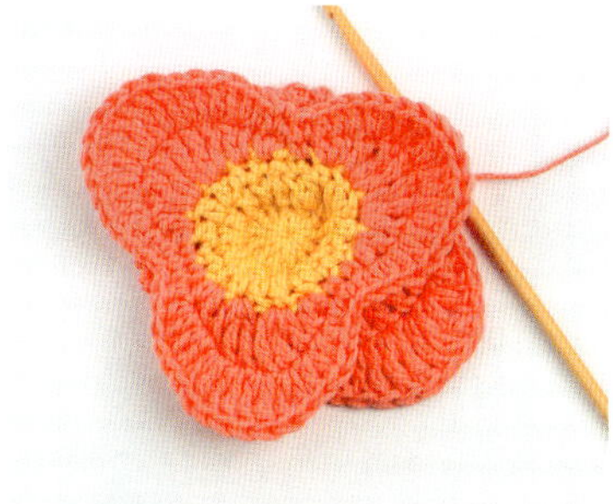

14 The second layer of petals will be aligned perfectly to peek out from behind the top layer of petals.

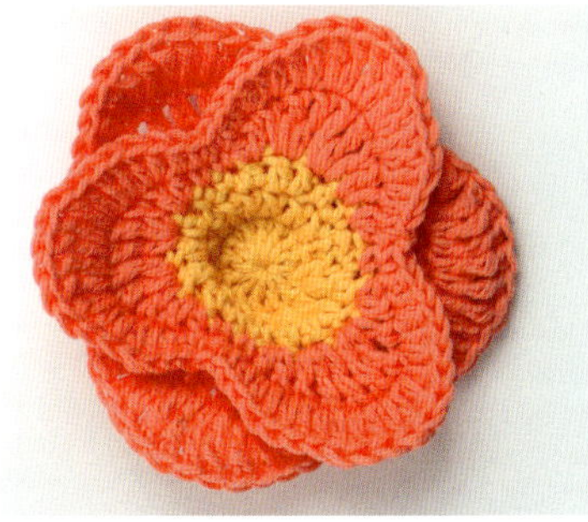

15 Fasten off Colour B as you complete Round 9.

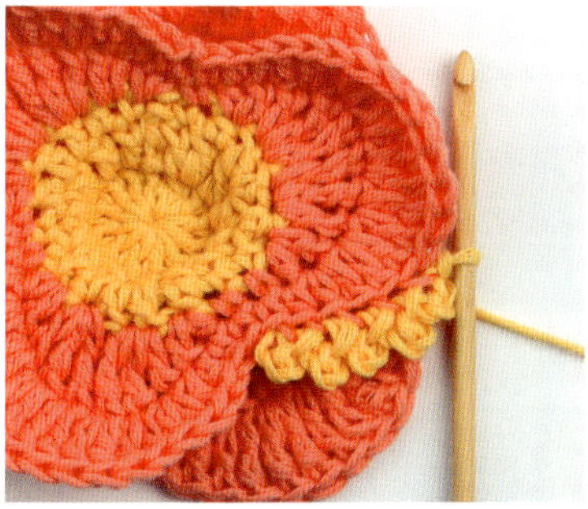

16 Attach Colour A to the top layer of petals, as shown, and work [ch 3, sl st in next st] all the way around to make a fringe.

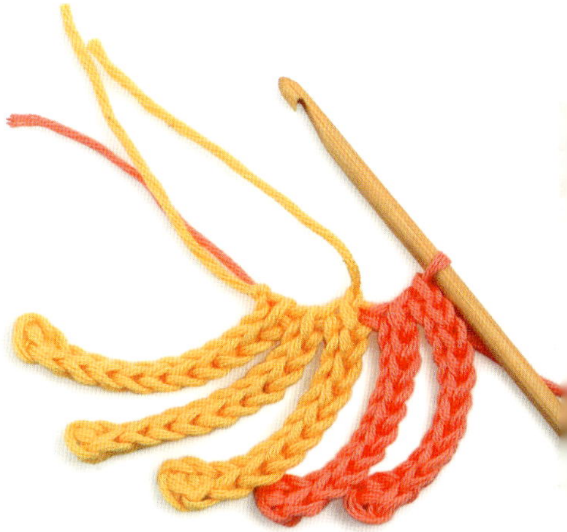

17 Follow the pattern to make stamens in both colours and sew to the centre of the flower to complete.

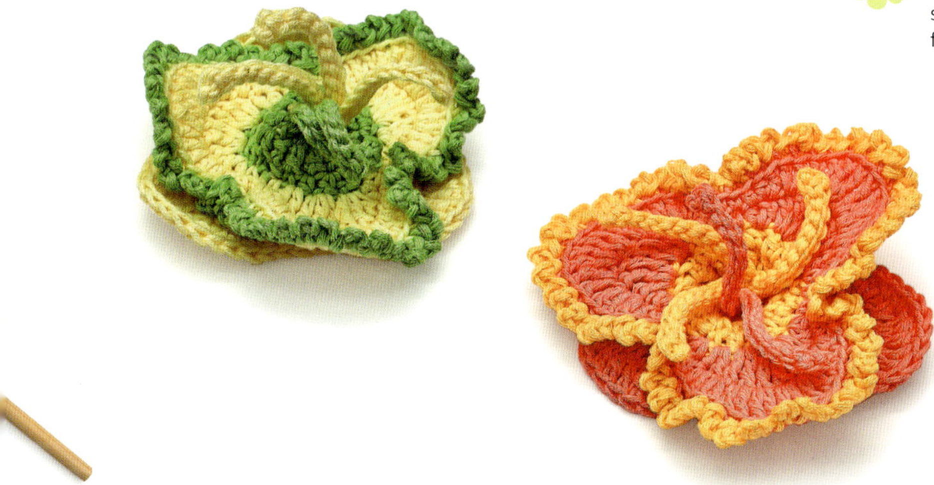

35 Pansy

Skill level: ✿✿✿

These flowers are a staple in any flower bed. They are so bright and colourful, so you can't go wrong with the colour choice. Use your imagination.

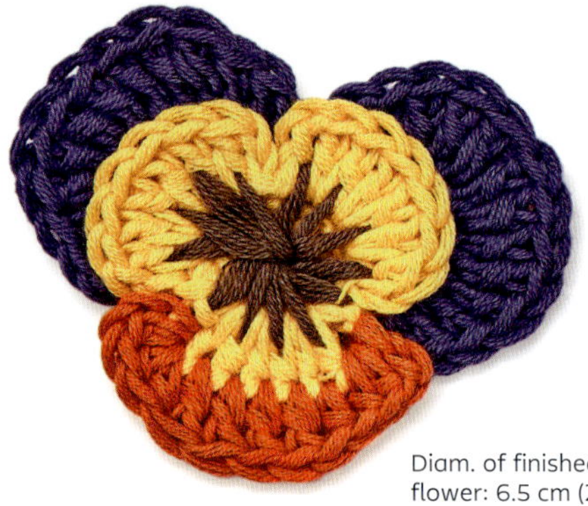

Diam. of finished flower: 6.5 cm (2½ in)

Materials:

4-ply yarn in 4 colours:

- Colour A: 2.75 m (3 yds)
- Colour B: 2.75 m (3 yds)
- Colour C: 3.75 m (4 yds)
- Colour B: 1.8 m (2 yds)

Tools:

Hook size: 3.25 mm (D-3)
Yarn needle
Scissors

Chart key:

- Magic ring
- Ch Chain
- Dc Double crochet
- Sl st Slip stitch
- Tr Treble crochet
- Htr Half treble crochet
- Dtr Double treble crochet

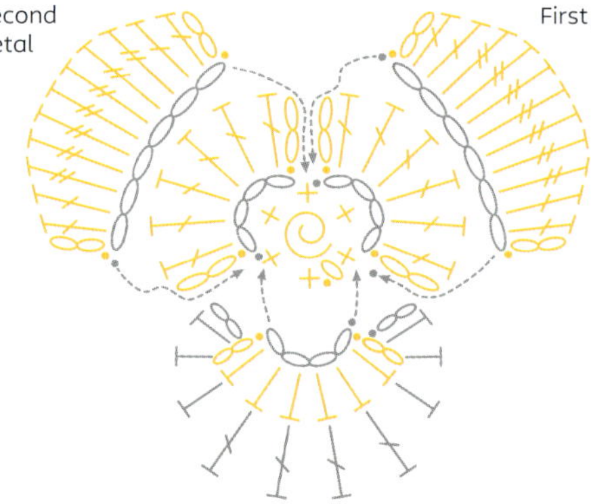

Pattern

With Colour A, make a magic ring (see page 12).

Rnd 1: Into magic ring, ch 1, 6 dc. Pull on short end to close middle. Join rnd with sl st. (6 dc)

Rnd 2: [Ch 4, miss next dc, sl st in next dc] three times (**see Step 1**).

Rnd 3: *[Sl st, ch 2, 6 tr, ch 2, sl st] in ch-4 loop.

Rep from * in 2nd ch-4 loop.

[Sl st, ch 2, 6 htr, ch 2, sl st] in 3rd ch-4 loop (**see Step 2**).

Rnd 4: Ch 6, sl st between first and 2nd petals, ch 6, sl st between 2nd and 3rd petals (**see Step 3**).

Fasten off Colour A (**see Step 4**).

Attach Colour B to ch-2 loop of 3rd petal.

Ch 2, 2 htr in ch-2 loop, htr in next htr, tr in next 4 htr, htr in next htr, [2 htr, ch 2, sl st] in ch-2 loop (**see Step 5**).

Fasten off Colour B.

Attach Colour C to ch-6 loop behind first petal (**see Step 6**).

Rnd 5: *Ch 2, [2 tr, 7 dtr, 2 tr, ch 2, sl st] in ch-6 loop.

Rep from * in next ch-6 loop (**see Step 7**).

Follow **Step 8** to embroider the stamens to the flower in Colour D.

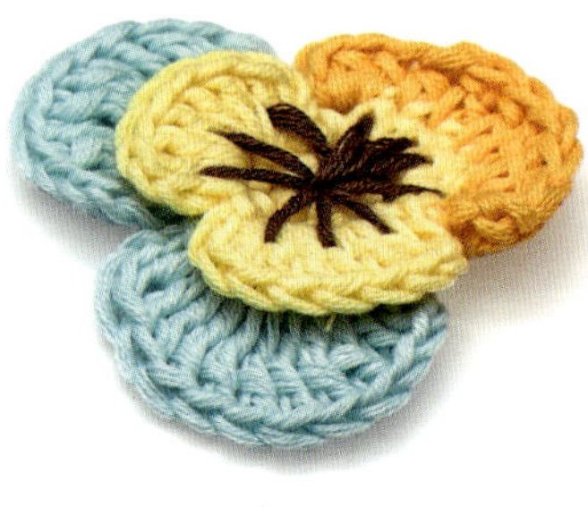

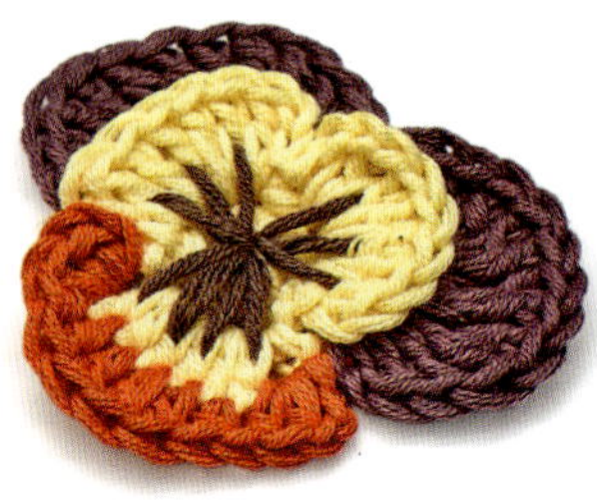

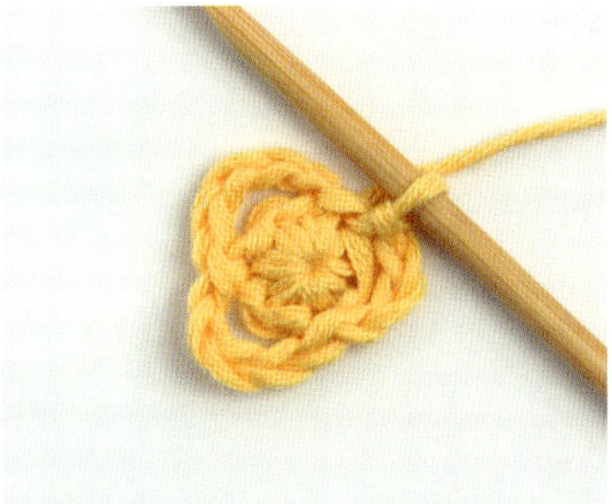

1 The ch-4 loops created in Round 2 are what the petals are built onto.

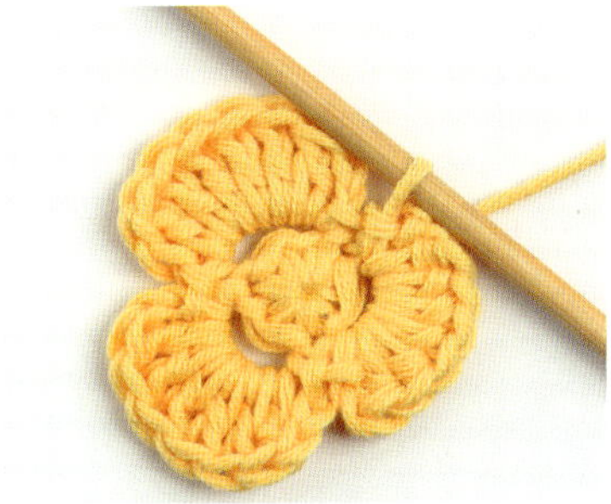

2 At the end of Round 3, you will notice that you have made two larger and one smaller petal.

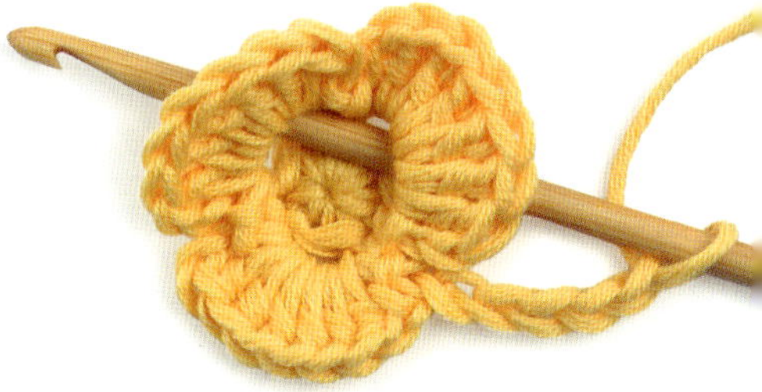

3 Insert the hook between the petals as pictured to make the sl sts between petals in Round 4.

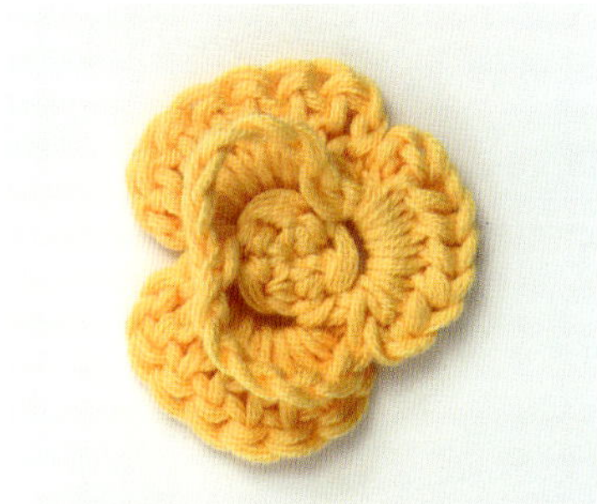

4 After Round 4 this is what the loops will look like from the back of the flower.

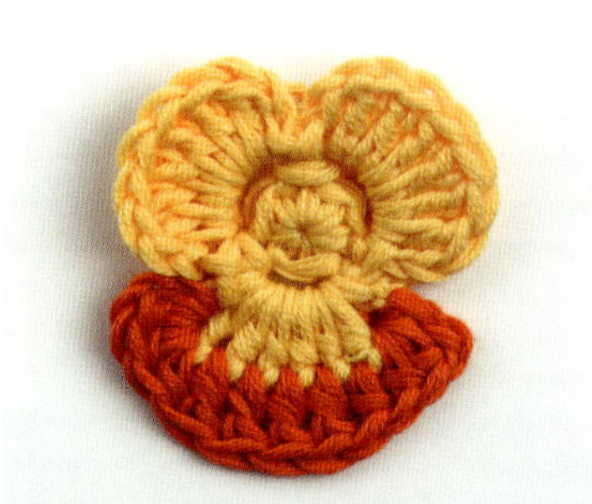

5 Follow the pattern to crochet around the smaller petal in a contrasting colour.

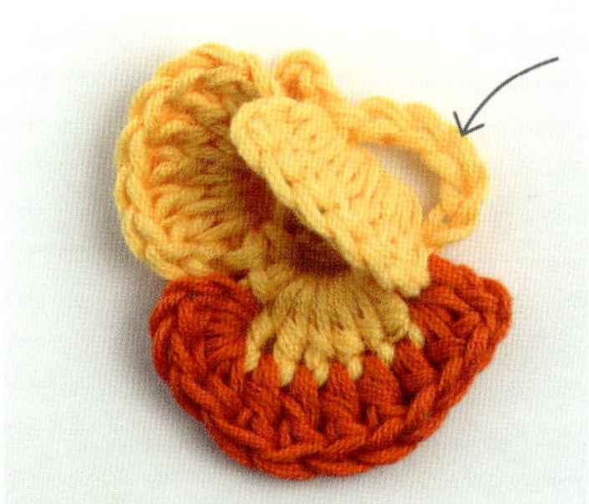

6 Fold the first petal forwards to find the ch-6 loop behind it, as indicated with an arrow. Attach Colour C here.

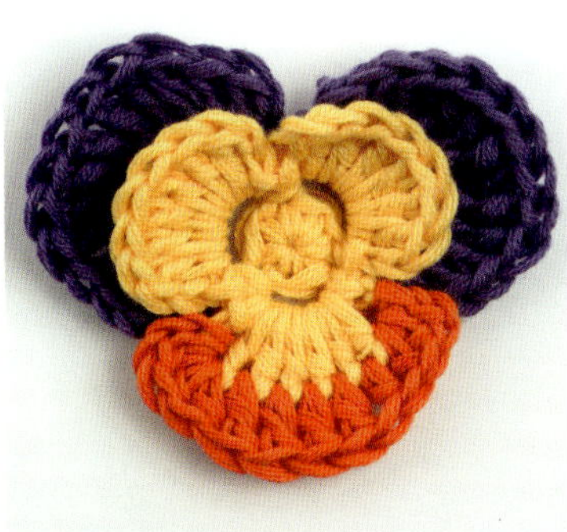

7 The two larger petals are created in Round 5, in Colour C.

8 Using the Colour D yarn and a yarn needle, embroider the stamens to finish. Work short stitches from the centre out, fanning around in a circle, as pictured.

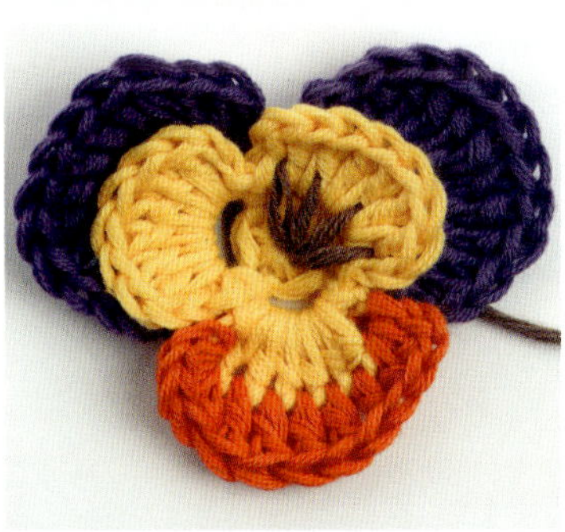

Leaves

Skill level:

Once you've created a bouquet of pretty crochet flowers, why not try one of these simple but effective leaf patterns to add a little something extra to your designs.

Tools for all leaves:

Hook size: 3.25 mm (D-3)
Yarn needle
Scissors

Chart key:

- Ch Chain
- Dc Double crochet
- Sl st Slip stitch
- Htr Half treble crochet
- Tr Treble crochet
- Dtr Double treble crochet
- 3 ch picot
- 4 ch picot

Simple Leaf

Materials:

4-ply yarn: 4.5 m (5 yds)

Pattern:

Ch 7, dc in 2nd ch from hook, htr in next 2 ch, tr in next 2 ch, [3 tr, dtr, 3 ch picot, dtr, 3 tr] in next ch, tr in next 2 ch, htr in next 2 ch, dc in next ch, ch I, sl st in last ch.

Fasten off. Weave in ends.

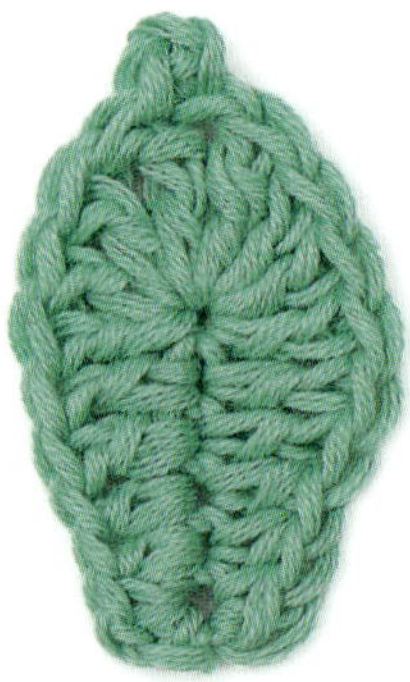

Leaf shown at actual size

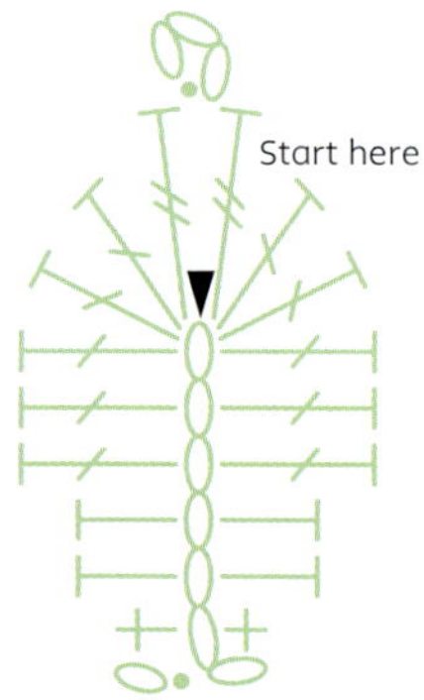

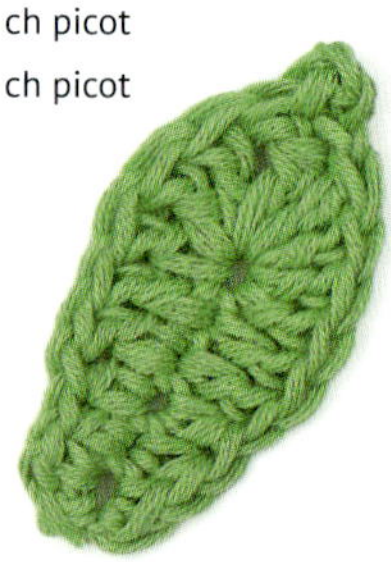

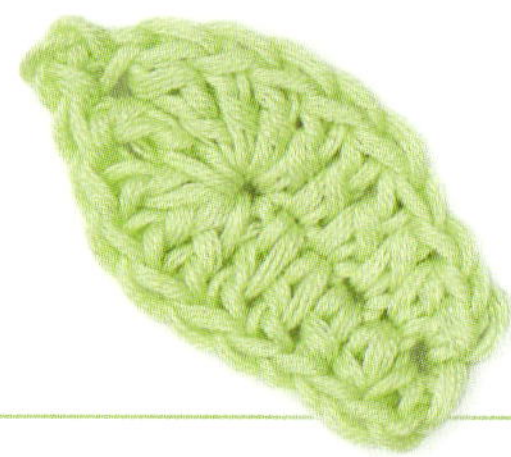

Stylised Leaf

Materials:

4-ply yarn: 4.5 m (5 yds)

Pattern:

Ch I2, sl st in first ch to make a ring.

[Ch 2, 5 htr, 4 tr, 2 dtr, 3 ch picot, 2 dtr, 4 tr, 5 htr] in ring.

Join rnd with sl st in first htr.

Fasten off. Weave in ends.

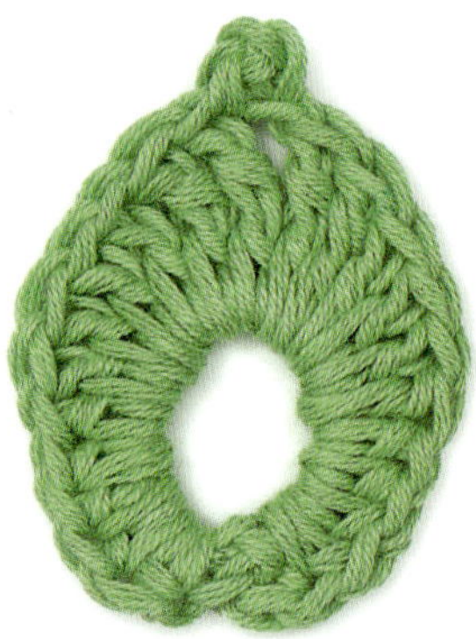

Leaf shown at actual size

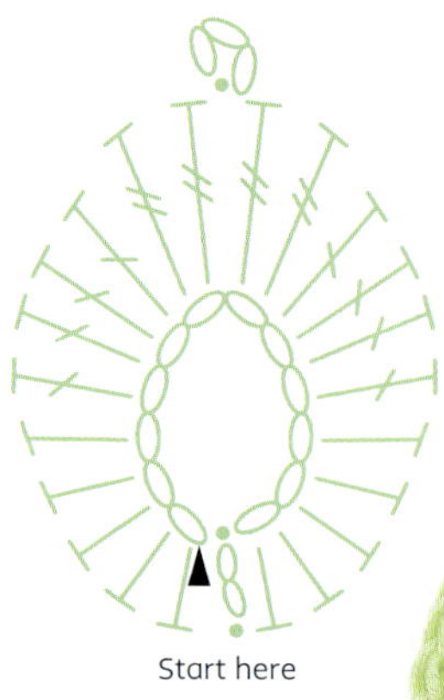

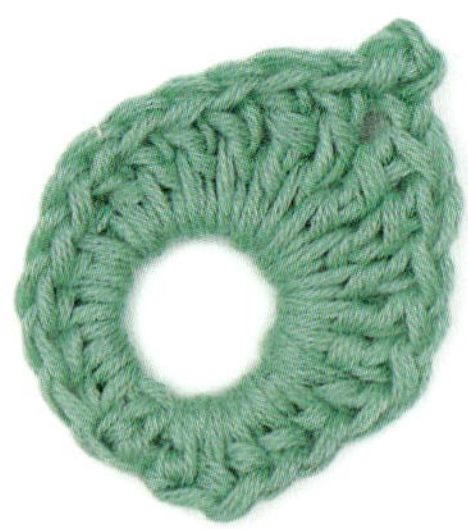

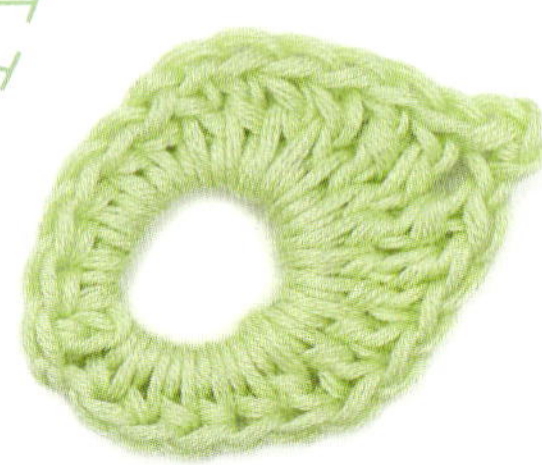

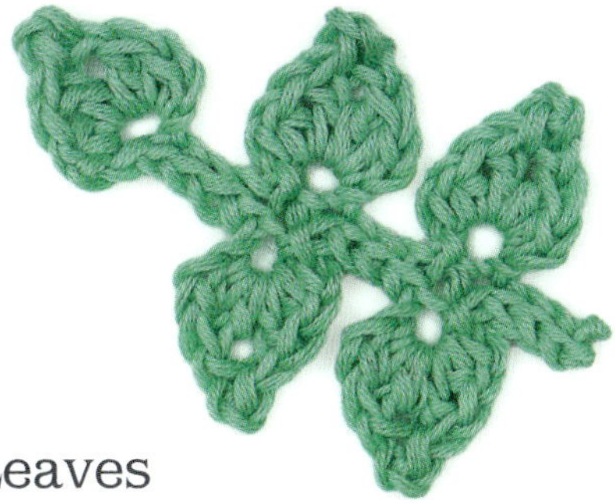

Little Leaves

Materials:

4-ply yarn: 6.4 m (7 yds)

Pattern:

*Ch 7, [htr, tr, 3 ch picot, tr, htr, ch 2, sl st] in 3rd ch from hook.

Rep from * twice more.

*Sl st in next 4 ch, ch 3, [htr, tr, 3 ch picot, tr, htr, ch 2, sl st] in 3rd ch from hook.

Rep from * once more.

Sl st in next 4 ch.

Fasten off. Weave in ends.

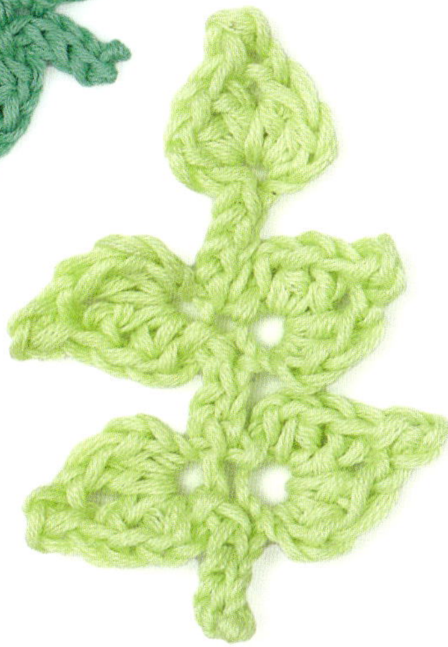

Leaf shown at actual size

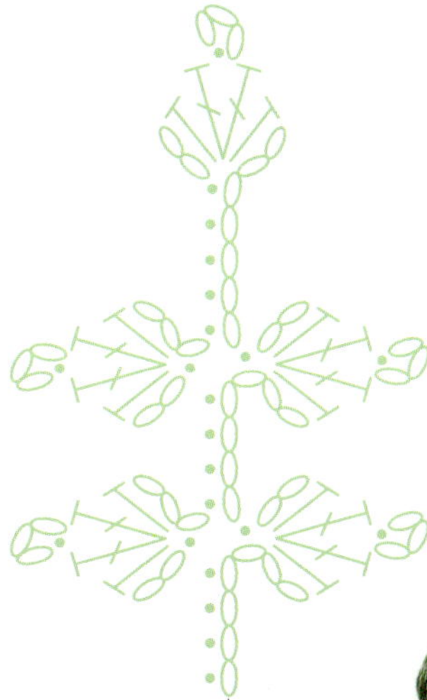

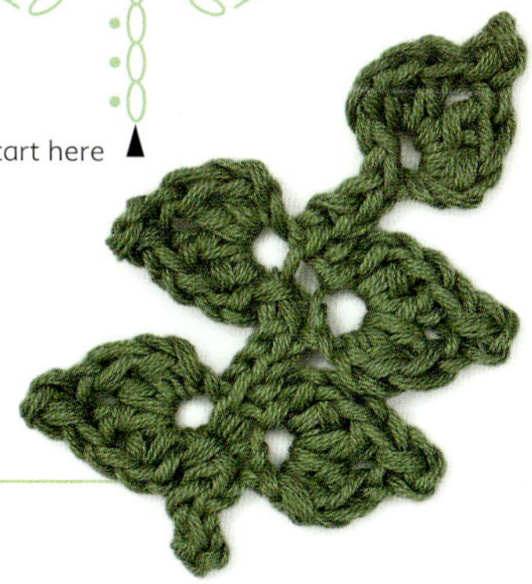

Lacy Leaf

Materials:

4-ply yarn: 6.4 m (7 yds)

Pattern:

Ch 7, sl st in first ch to make a ring.

Rnd 1: [Ch 2, htr, ch 2, tr, ch 2, (dtr, ch 2) four times, tr, ch 2, 2 htr] in ring.

Rnd 2: Ch 2, turn, htr in next htr, 3 htr in next 3 ch-2 loops, [2 htr, 4 ch picot, 2 htr] in next ch-2 loop, 3 htr in next 3 ch-2 loops, htr in next htr, ch 2, sl st in ch-2 of Rnd 1.

Fasten off. Weave in ends.

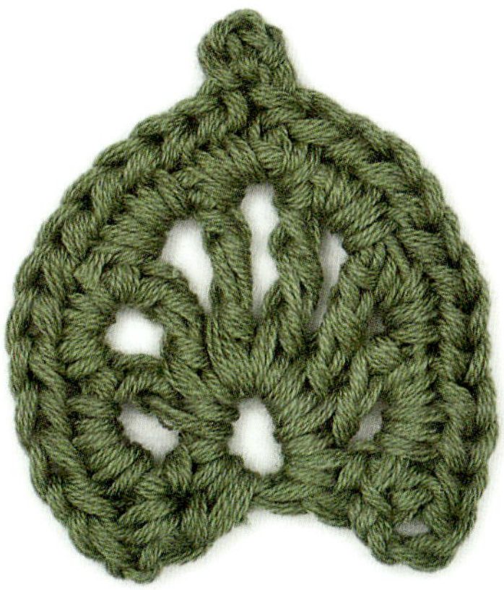

Leaf shown at actual size

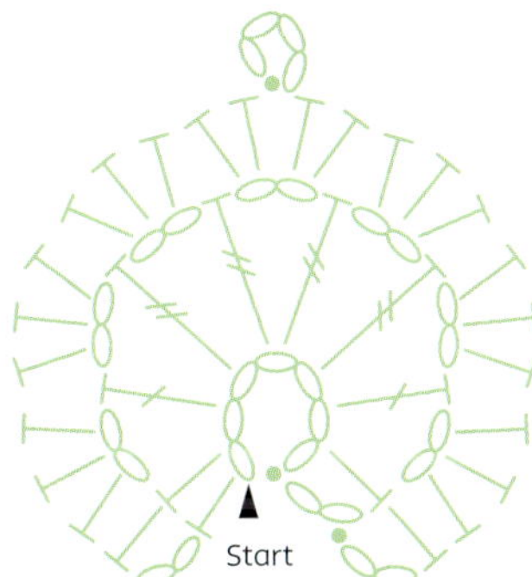

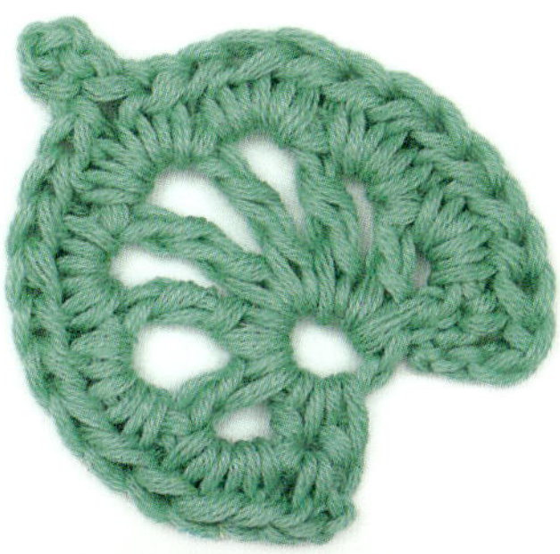

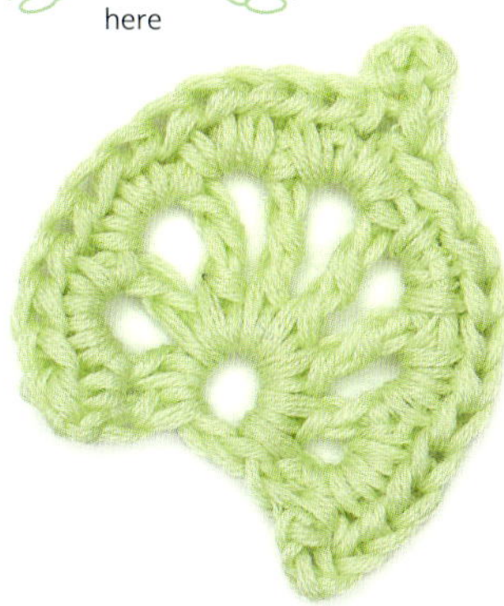

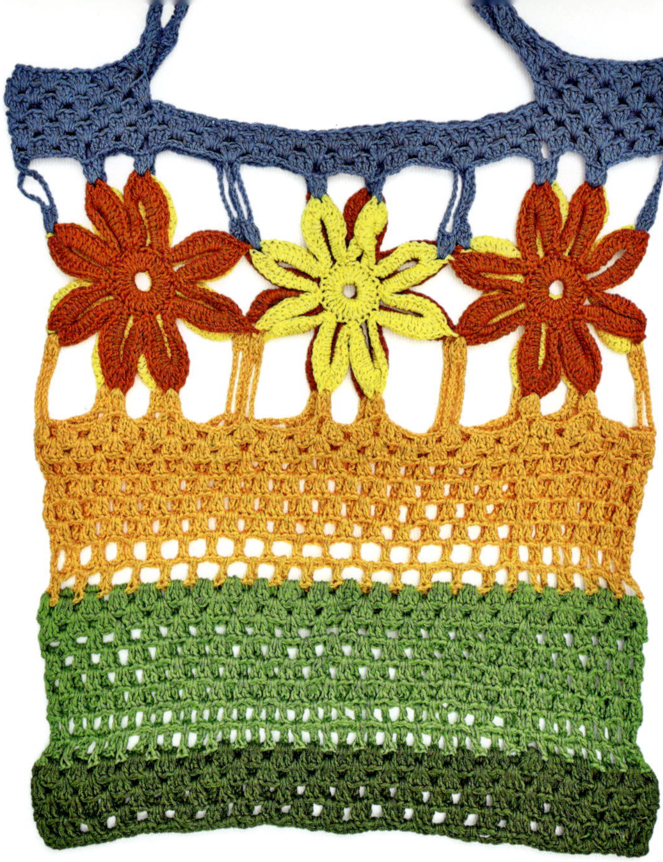

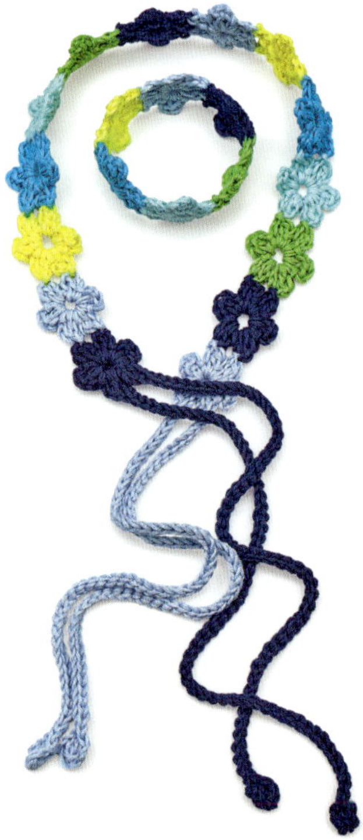

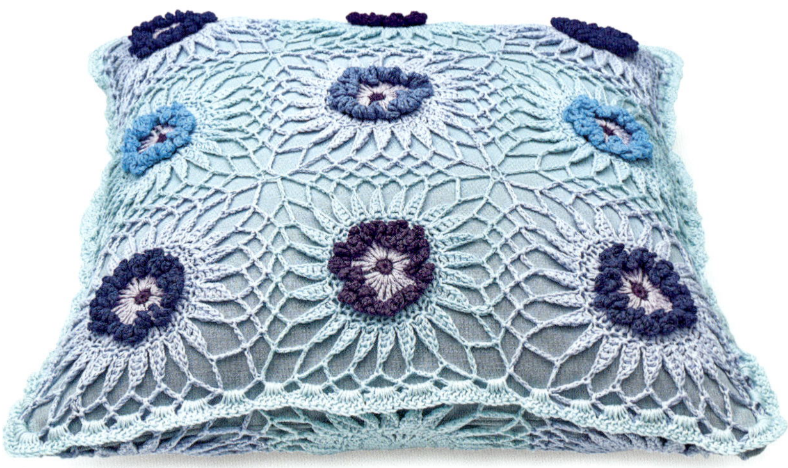

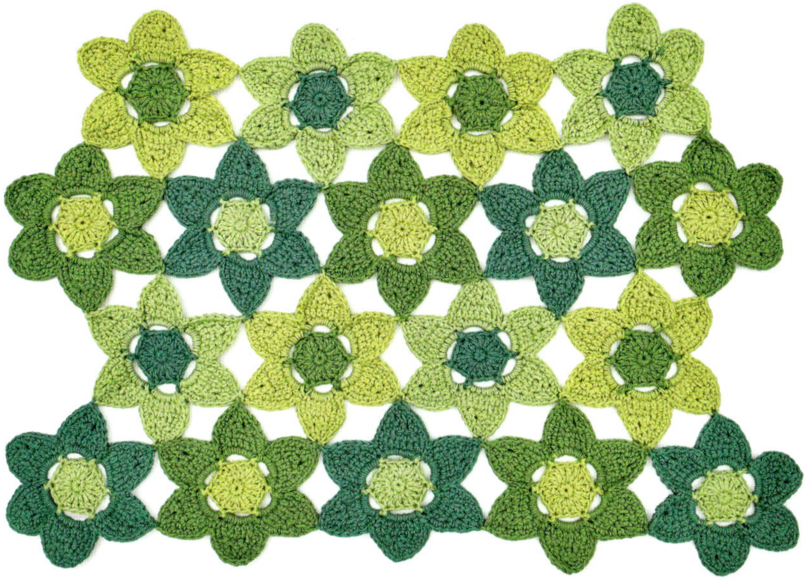

Projects

Now you've created some beautiful crochet flowers, here you'll find great ideas for how to use them in practical and unique projects. Use these ideas as inspiration and use your favourite flowers from throughout the book to create lovely, personalised creations.

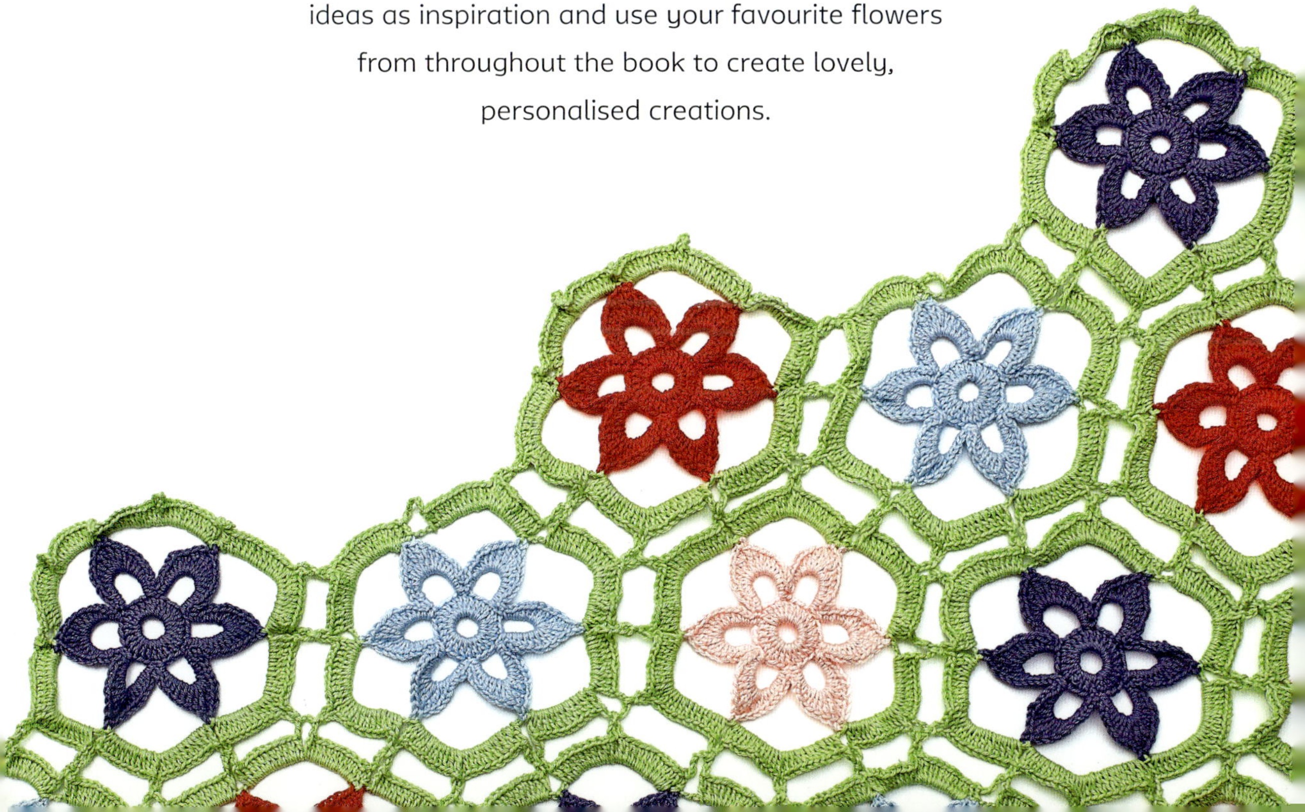

PROJECT 1

Forget-Me-Not Bracelet and Headband

Skill level: ✿

This simple project is very easy to make and follow: ideal for your first crochet project. By joining small, individually made flowers, you will create a string of flowers that can be made into a bracelet or a headband. The headband is one-size-fits-all – you can adjust the length using the ties. Why not experiment with the flowers and yarn to create different accessories?

Pattern:

Bracelet

First flower:

Ch 6. Sl st in first ch to make a ring.

[Ch 2, tr in ring, ch 2, sl st in ring] six times. (Six petals) Fasten off.

Second flower:

Ch 6. Sl st in first ch to make a ring.

[Ch 2, tr in ring, sl st in tr of first flower, ch 2, sl st in ring] twice.

[Ch 2, tr in ring, ch 2, sl st in ring] four times. (Six petals) Fasten off.

Add three more flowers following the 'Second flower' instructions.

Sixth flower:

Ch 6. Sl st in first ch to make a ring.

[Ch 2, tr in ring, sl st in tr of fifth flower, ch 2, sl st in ring] twice.

Ch 2, tr in ring, ch 2, sl st in ring.

[Ch 2, tr in ring, sl st in tr of first flower, ch 2, sl st in ring] twice.

Ch 2, tr in ring, ch 2, sl st in ring. Six petals in total.

Fasten off.

Headband

First flower:

Ch 6. Sl st in first ch to make a ring.

Ch 2, tr in ring, ch 60, [2 tr, ch 2, sl st] in 3rd ch from hook, sl st in each ch until you reach petal, sl st in tr, ch 2, sl st in ring.

[Ch 2, tr in ring, ch 2, sl st in ring] four times.

Ch 2, tr in ring, ch 60, [2 tr, ch 2, sl st] in 3rd ch from hook, sl st in each ch until you reach petal, sl st in tr, ch 2, sl st in ring. Six petals in total, and two long ties. Fasten off.

Second flower:

Ch 6. Sl st in first ch to make a ring.

[Ch 2, tr in ring, sl st in tr of previous flower, ch 2, sl st in ring] twice.

[Ch 2, tr in ring, ch 2, sl st in ring] four times. Six petals in total. Fasten off.

Add 11 more flowers following the 'Second flower' instructions.

Fourteenth flower:

Ch 6. Sl st in first ch to make a ring.

Ch 2, tr in ring, ch 60, [2 tr, ch 2, sl st] in 3rd ch from hook, sl st in each ch until you reach petal, sl st in tr, ch 2, sl st in ring.

Ch 2, tr in ring, ch 2, sl st in ring.

[Ch 2, tr in ring, sl st in tr of thirteenth flower, ch 2, sl st in ring] twice.

Ch 2, tr in ring, ch 2, sl st in ring.

Ch 2, tr in ring, ch 60, [2 tr, ch 2, sl st] in 3rd ch from hook, sl st in each ch until you reach petal, sl st in dc, ch 2, sl st in ring. Six petals in total, and two long ties.

Fasten off. Weave in all ends.

Materials:

4-ply yarn in 6 colours:

- Colour A: 22 m (24 yds)
- Colour B: 22 m (24 yds)
- Colour C: 11 m (12 yds)
- Colour D: 11 m (12 yds)
- Colour E: 11 m (12 yds)
- Colour F: 11 m (12 yds)

Tools:

Hook size: 3.25 mm (D-3)
Yarn needle
Scissors

Size:

98 cm (38½ in): headband incl. ties
18 cm (7 in): bracelet

Chart key:

- Ch Chain
- Sl st Slip stitch
- Tr Treble crochet

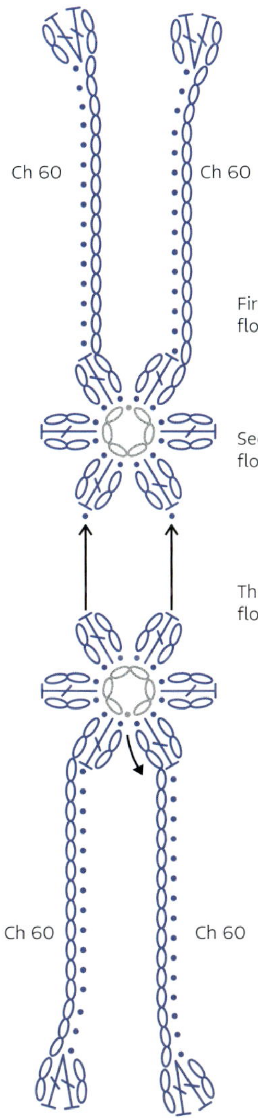

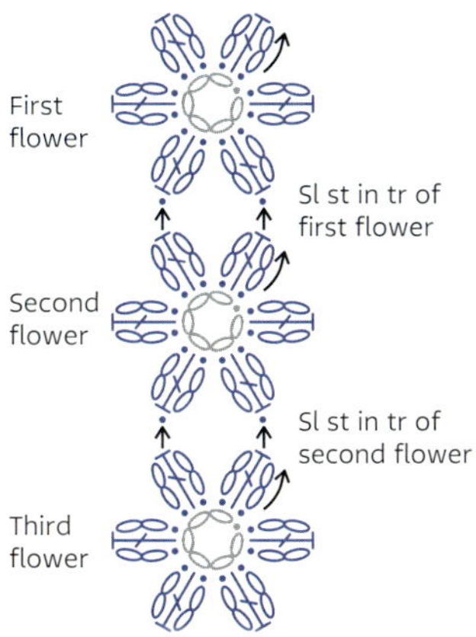

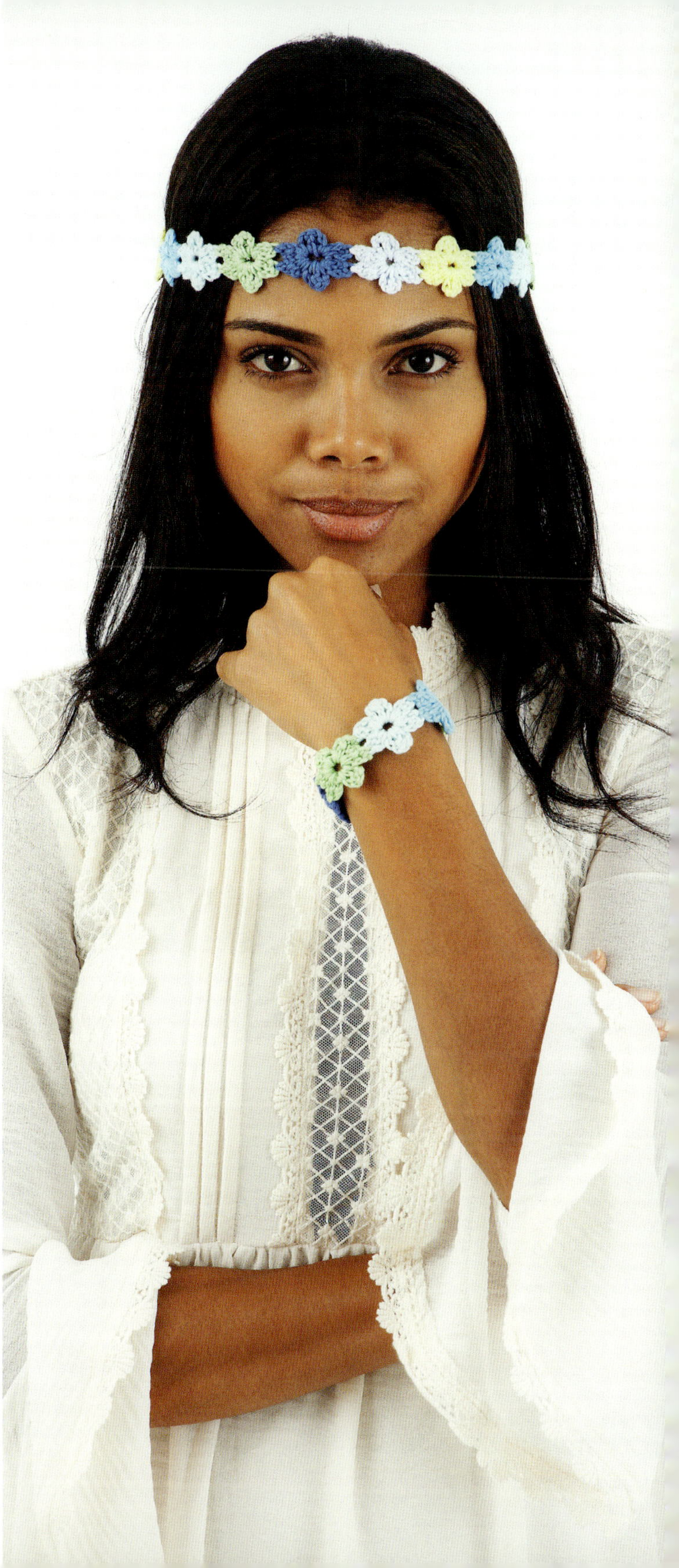

PROJECT 2

Floral Placemat

Skill level:

Add a splash of colour to your kitchen! Using the Chaenomeles Japonica flower pattern (see pages 68–69), combine your favourite colours to create a beautiful placemat. You can stick to the suggested size or change the number of flowers to make a coaster or add more flowers for a stunning table runner.

Materials:

4-ply yarn in 4 colours:

- Colour A: 60.3 m (66 yds)
- Colour B: 60.3 m (66 yds)
- Colour C: 60.3 m (66 yds)
- Colour D: 60.3 m (66 yds)

Tools:

Hook size: 3.25 mm (D-3)
Yarn needle
Scissors

Size:

30.5 × 45.5 cm (12 × 18 in): 18 flowers

Chart key:

- Magic ring
- Ch Chain
- Dc Double crochet
- Sl st Slip stitch
- Tr Treble crochet
- Dc2tog Double crochet two together

Pattern:

With Colour A, make a magic ring (see page 12).

Rnd 1: Into magic ring, ch 1, 6 dc. Pull on short end to close middle. Join rnd with sl st. (6 dc)

Rnd 2: Ch 2, 3 tr in each dc. (18 tr)

Rnd 3: [Ch 5, miss 2 tr, sl st in next tr] six times.

Fasten off Colour A.

Attach Colour B to one of the ch-5 loops.

Petal 1:

Row 1: Ch 1, 6 dc in ch-5 loop. (6 dc)

Row 2: Ch 1, turn, dc in each dc.

Row 3: Ch 1, turn, dc2tog, dc in next 2 dc, dc2tog. (4 dc)

Row 4: Ch 1, turn, [dc2tog] twice. (2 dc)

Row 5: Ch 1, turn, dc2tog. (1 dc)

Do not turn. 6 dc around the side of the petal until you reach ch loop.

Make petals 2–6 in the same way as petal 1.

12 dc evenly along edges of each petal.

Fasten off Colour B.

For the second flower and each subsequent flower, you will be connecting to the previous flower as you go. When you dc around each petal, stop at the top of the petal, make a sl st into the middle of the petal of the connecting flower, then continue crocheting around the petals. Connect the next petal the same way with a sl st. Continue connecting each subsequent flower as you go in the same way, following the diagrams at right.

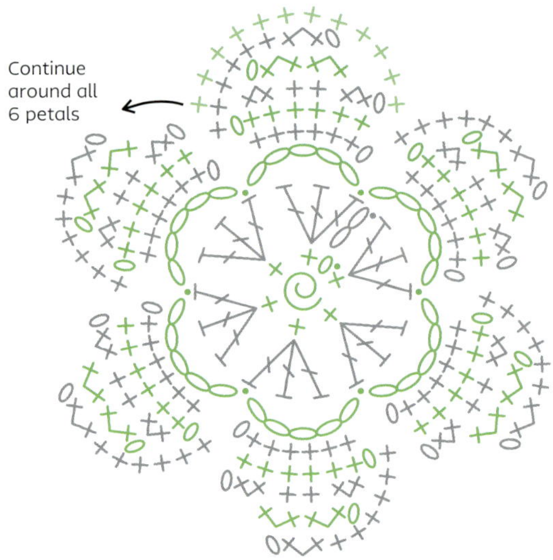

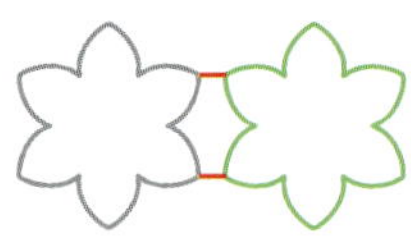

Connecting flower 2

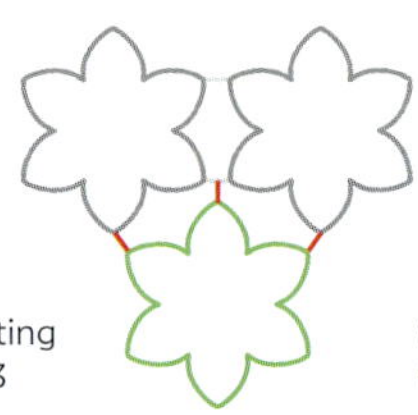

Connecting flower 3

Connecting flower 4

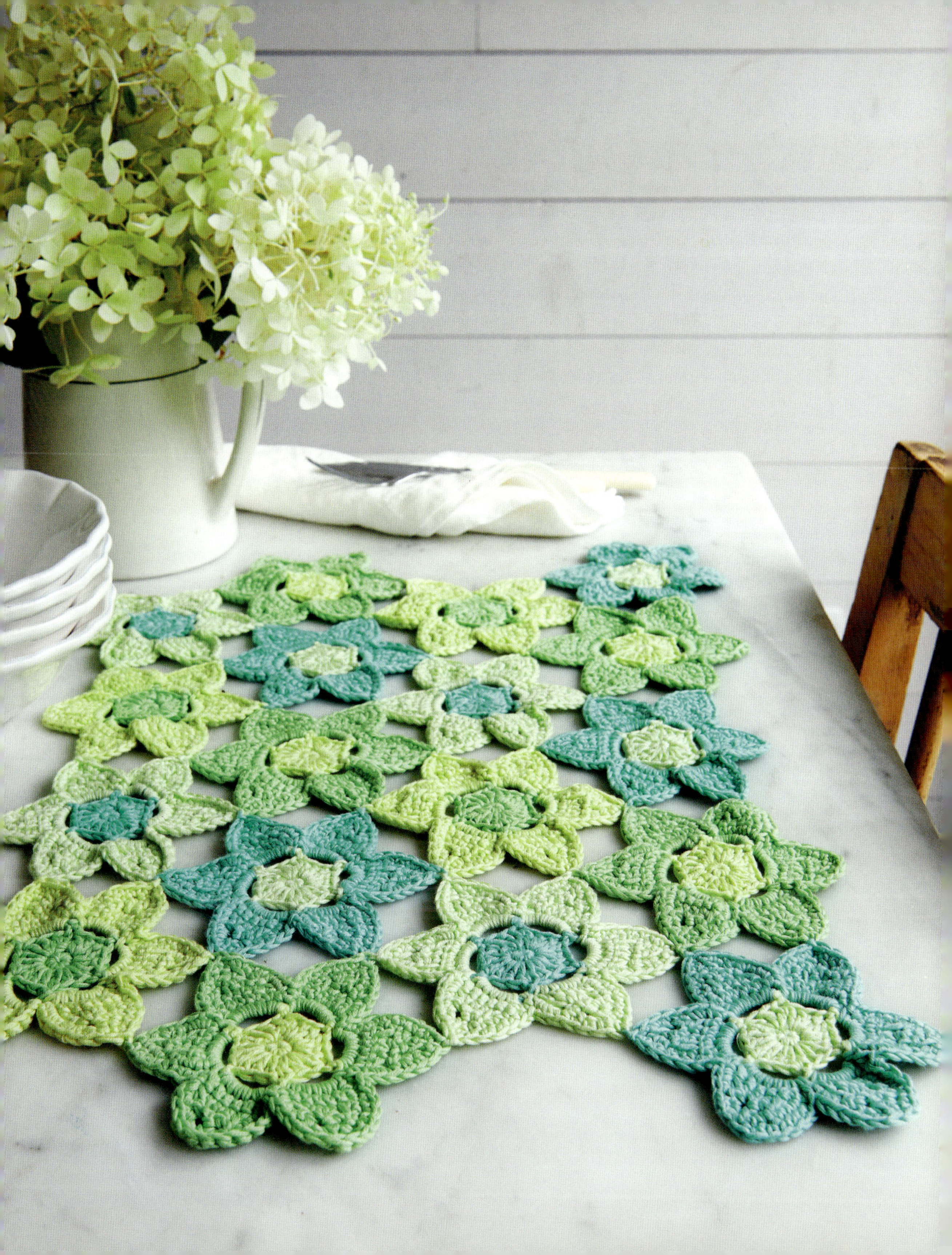

PROJECT 3

Gerbera Garden Pillowcase

Skill level:

Fully crochet a cushion cover that has flowers front and back, creating a perfect focal piece to decorate your living room couch or bedroom. This is a great 'take along' project, you can take a few colours with you at a time, and crochet on the go.

Pattern:

Front flowers (make 9): Follow the exact pattern for Gerbera flower on pages 82–83.

Back flowers (make 12): Follow the pattern for Gerbera flower on pages 82–83 but miss Round 3, and make the whole flower in one colour.

Do not fasten off yarn.

To connect flowers:

Flower 1:

Rnd 1: Sl st in top of petal, *[ch 5, sl st in top of next petal] four times, [ch 8, sl st in next petal] twice.

Rep from * three more times.

Rnd 2: Sl st to middle of loop, [ch 5, sl st in next loop] four times, ch 8, sl st in next loop.

*[Ch 5, sl st in next loop] five times, ch 8, sl st in next loop.

Rep from * twice more. Ch 5, sl st in first sl st. Fasten off.

Flowers 2–9:

The second flower will be attached to the first one as you go.

Rnd 1: As Rnd 1 above.

Rnd 2: Non-connecting side(s): Sl st in middle of loop, [ch 5, sl st in next loop] four times.

Connecting side(s): Ch 4, sl st in ch-8 loop of connecting flower, ch 4, sl st in next loop. [Ch 2, sl st in next loop of connecting flower, ch 2, sl st in next loop] five times. Ch 4, sl st in ch-8 loop of connecting flower, ch 4, sl st in next loop.

*[Ch 5, sl st in next loop] five times, ch 8, sl st in next loop.

Rep from * once more. Ch 5, sl st in first sl st. Fasten off.

Order of work:

1. Make nine front flowers and connect in a 3 × 3 grid.
2. Make 12 back flowers and connect in two 2 × 3 grids.
3. Place the front and back of the pillowcase with right sides facing. The two back pieces will overlap in the middle to form a flap. Tr all around to join all panels.

Follow the diagram below for the connecting tr count. Ensure that you are holding all necessary panels together securely for connecting.

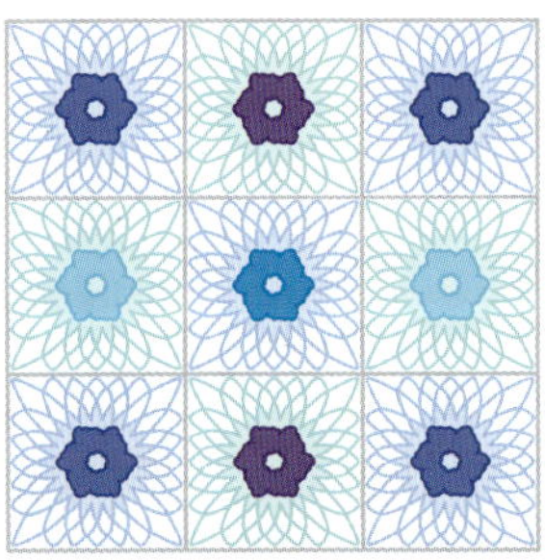

Front piece

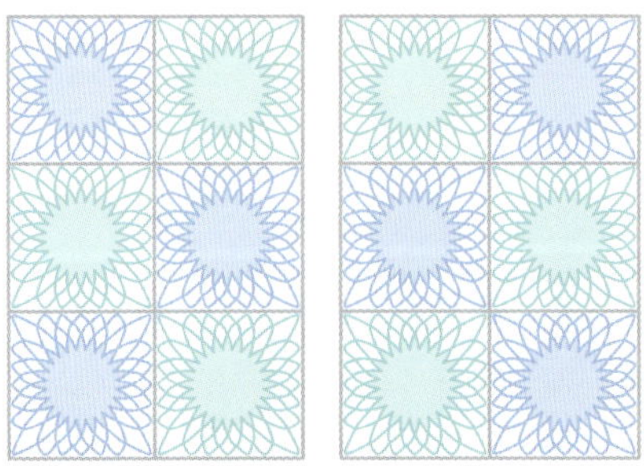

2 back pieces

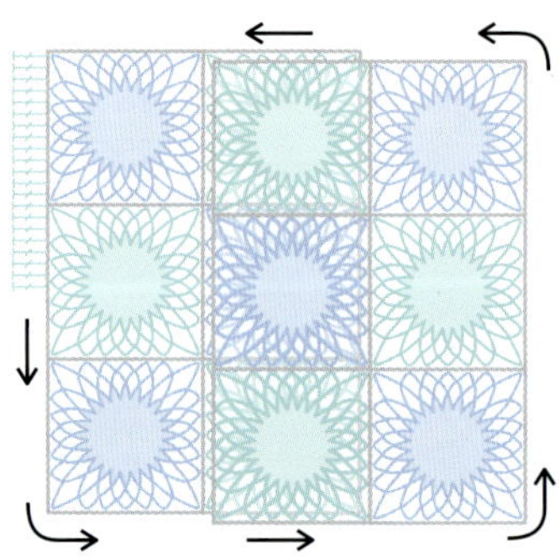

Overlapping back pieces

Materials:

4-ply yarn in 2 colours:

Colour A: 183 m (200 yds)

Colour B: 183 m (200 yds)

Tools:

Hook size: 3.25 mm (D-3)
Yarn needle
Scissors

Size:

40.5 × 40.5 cm (16 × 16 in)

Chart key:

Ch Chain

Sl st Slip stitch

Tr Treble crochet

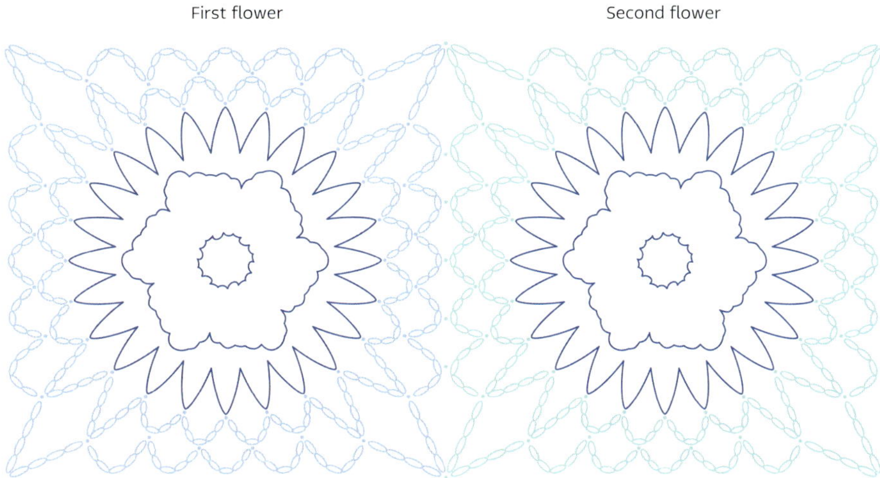

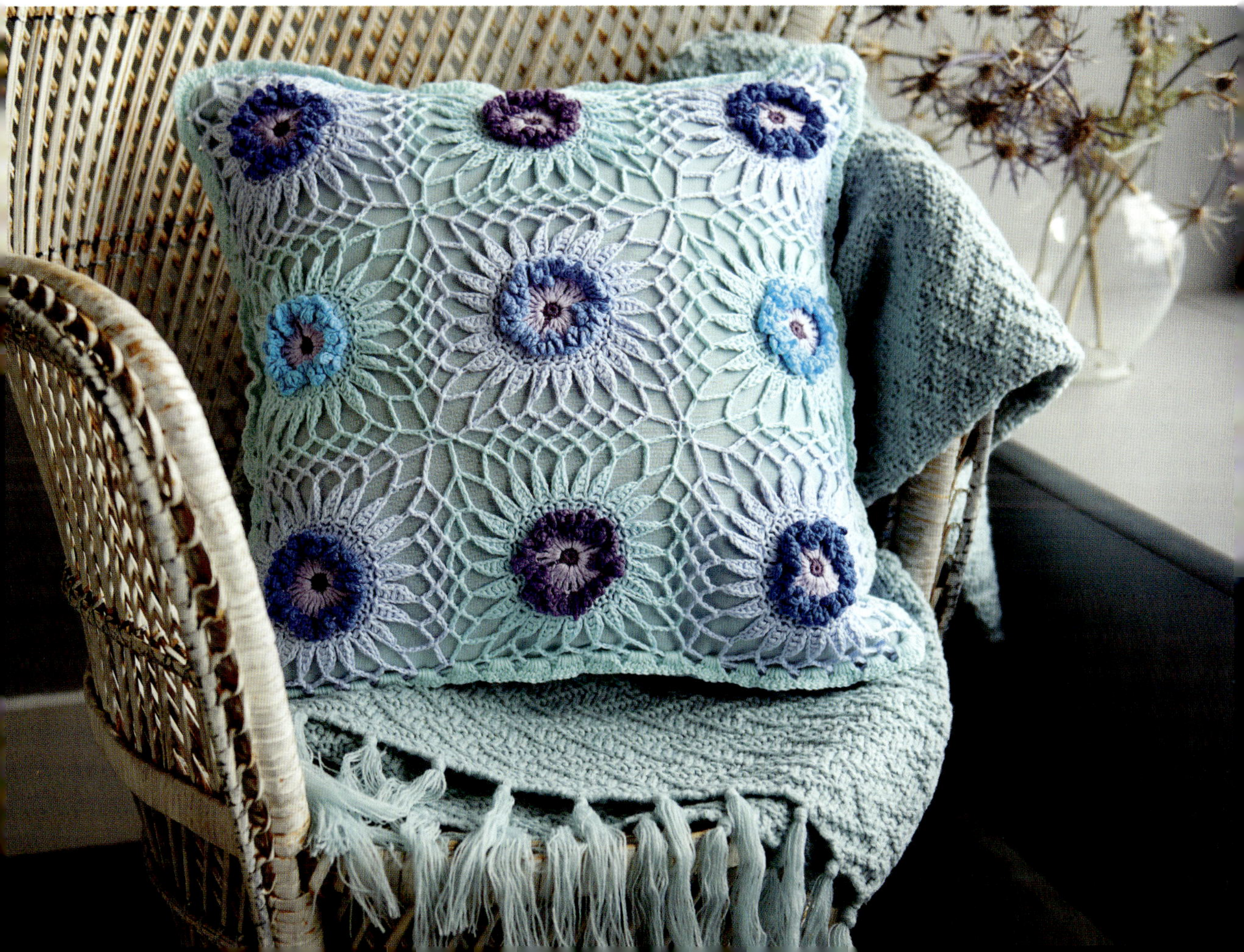

PROJECT 4

Landscape Market Bag

Skill level:

Materials:

4-ply yarn in 6 colours:

- Colour A: 183 m (200 yds)
- Colour B: 183 m (200 yds)
- Colour C: 183 m (200 yds)
- Colour D: 183 m (200 yds)
- Colour E: 91.5 m (100 yds)
- Colour F: 91.5 m (100 yds)

This is a bigger project, but don't be afraid to tackle it. A good rule to follow to avoid getting overwhelmed about a pattern, is to take it one step at a time, without trying to understand the whole concept at once. Soon you will see it unfolding nicely in your hands.

Pattern:

Flowers (Part 1):

The flowers in this pattern are based on the Harlequin pattern (see pages 46–47), with a few changes.

Ch 10. Sl st in first ch to make a ring.

Rnd 1: Ch 2, 24 tr in ring. Join rnd with sl st in first tr of rnd. (24 tr)

Rnd 2: [Ch 15, miss next tr, sl st in next 2 tr] seven times, ch 15, miss next tr, sl st in next tr.

Rnd 3: *[3 htr, 7 tr, ch 2, 7 tr, 3 htr] in 15-ch loop, dc in sl st between petals.

Rep from * seven more times (8 petals).

Fasten off Colour A.

Follow the pattern above to make six flowers, three in Colour A and three in Colour B. Connect them with sl sts into the tips of the flower petals: follow the diagram for connecting sl st placement.

Bag (Part 2):

Lay the flowers flat. Work as below, starting from the top right-hand petal of any flower.

Attach Colour C to top of the petal.

Rnd 1: Ch 2, *3 tr in ch-2 loop at top of petal, ch 9, 3 tr in top of next petal, ch 21, 3 tr in connection between flowers, ch 9, sl st in 9th ch from top of last 3 tr, ch 12.

Rep from * five more times. Join with sl st in first tr of rnd.

Rnd 2: Ch 3, *miss 3 tr, tr in next 3 ch, miss 3 ch, tr in next 3 ch, [miss 3 tr, tr in next 3 ch] twice, miss 3 ch, 3 tr in sl st, [miss 3 ch, tr in next 3 ch] twice.

Rep from * five more times. Join with sl st in first tr of rnd.

Rnd 3: Ch 3, *miss 3 tr, 3 tr in space before next tr. Rep from * around. Join with sl st in first tr of rnd.

Rnd 4: Ch 3, *miss 3 tr, 2 tr in space before next tr, ch 2.

Rep from * around. Join with sl st in first tr.

Rnds 5–7: Ch 3, *2 tr in next ch-2 loop, ch 2.

Rep from * around. Join with sl st in first tr.

Rnd 8: Ch 3, *tr in next ch-2 loop, ch 3.

Rep from * around. Join with sl st in first tr.

Rnd 9: Ch 3, *tr in next ch-3 loop, ch 3.

Rep from * around. Join with sl st in first tr.

Fasten off Colour C.

Attach Colour D and rep Rnds 2–9.

Fasten off Colour D.

Attach Colour E and rep Rnds 2–5.

Fold bag to make sure flowers are aligned. Dc along the bottom of the bag, through both sides, to close the bottom of the bag. Fasten off Colour E.

Handle (Part 3):

Rotate bag 180 degrees and attach Colour F to the top-right petal of the right-hand flower on the opposite side. Repeat Rnds 1–3 above.

Rnd 4: Follow instructions for Rnd 3, until you reach the top-left petal of the right-hand flower. Ch 93. Miss all sts until the top-right petal of the left-hand flower. Use the diagram on the right as a guide. Continue Rnd 3 to end. Join with sl st in first tr.

Rnd 5: Ch 3, *miss 3 tr, 3 tr in space before next tr. Rep from * to ch.

*[Tr in next 3 ch, miss 3 ch] to last 3 ch, tr in next 3 ch.

Rep from * once more. [Miss 3 tr, 3 tr in space before next tr] to end of rnd. Join with sl st.

Rnd 6: Ch 3, *miss 3 tr, 3 tr in space before next tr. Rep from * around. Join with sl st in first tr.

Fasten off Colour F and weave in all ends.

Tools:

Hook size: 3.25 mm (D-3)
Yarn needle
Scissors

Size:

45.5 × 38 cm (18 × 15 in)

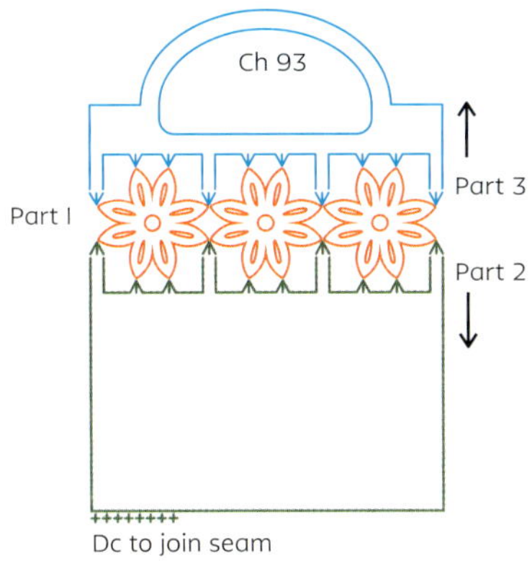

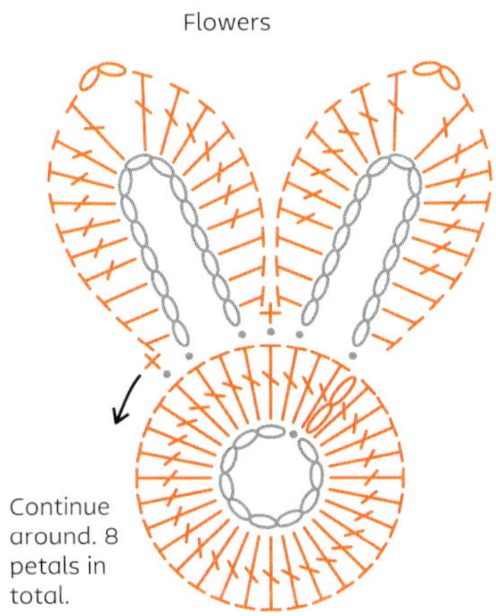

Chart key:

- Ch Chain
- Sl st Slip stitch
- Tr Treble crochet
- Htr Half treble crochet
- Dc Double crochet

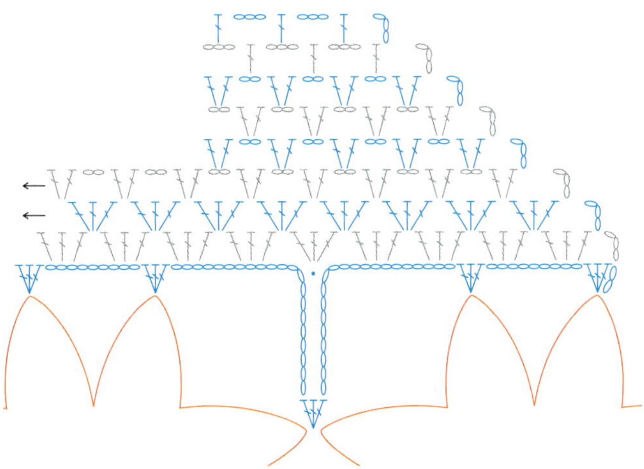

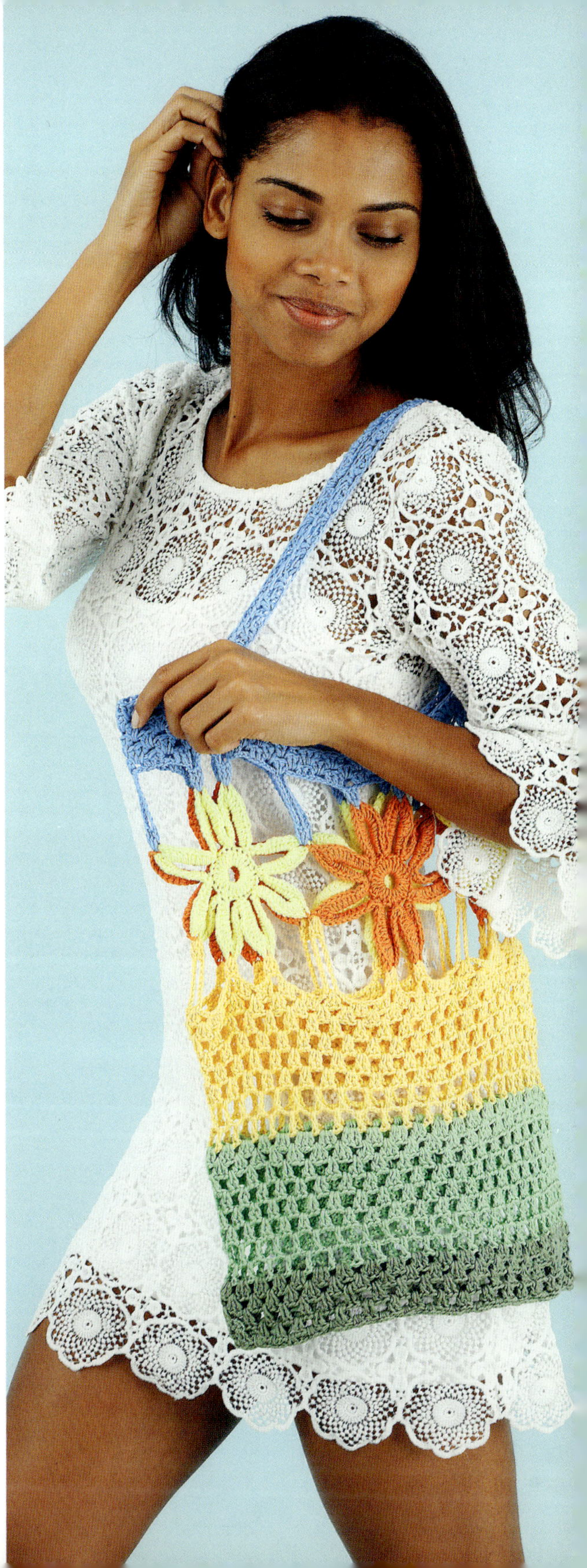

PROJECT 5

Patterned Floral Shawl

Skill level:

This beautiful and feminine shawl uses simple stitches and easy joining techniques to create a stunning and colourful accessory. All flowers are made separately, and then joined with green ribbon-like connecting strips.

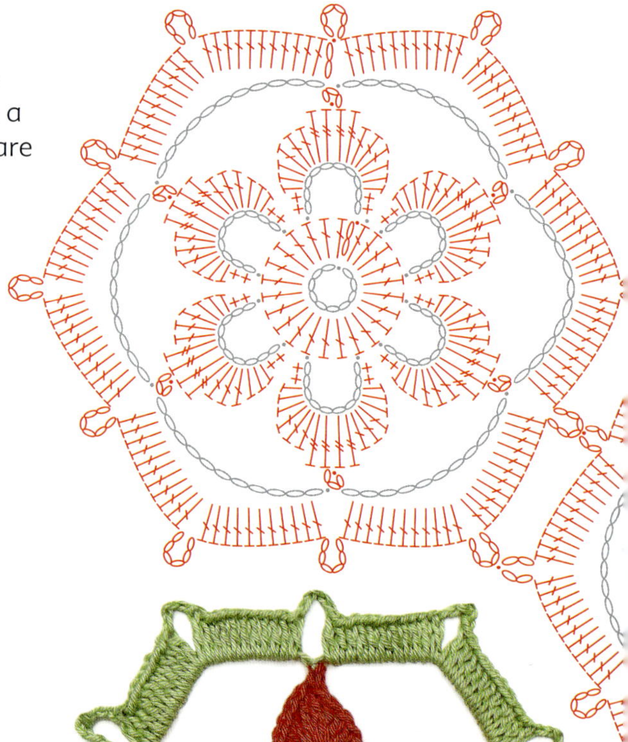

Pattern:

Flowers:

Ch 10, sl st in first ch to make ring.

Rnd 1: Ch 2, 24 tr in ring. Join rnd with sl st. (24 tr)

Rnd 2: [Ch 10, miss 2 tr, sl st in next 2 tr] six times.

Rnd 3: [2 dc, 3 htr, 3 tr, 2 dtr, 3 ch picot, 2 dtr, 3 tr, 3 htr, 2 dc] in each ch-10 loop. Fasten off.

Make seven flowers in each of Colours A, B, C and D.

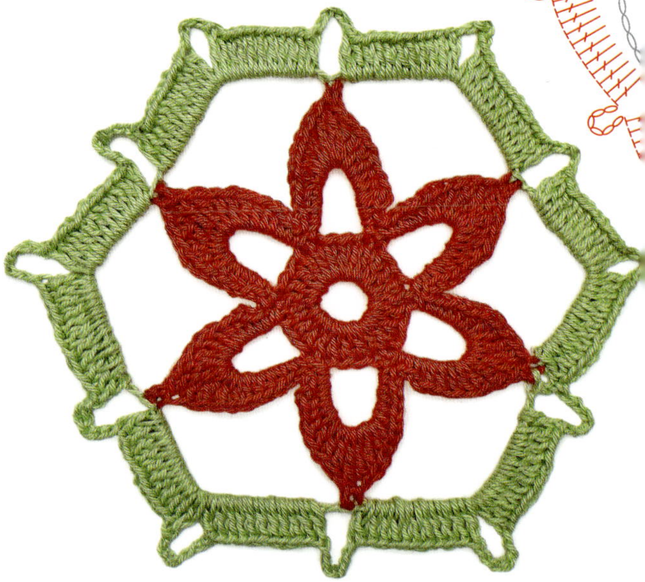

To join flowers:

Arrange flowers into desired pattern.

Starting from tip of a flower petal, attach Colour E.

[Ch 11, sl st in next 3 ch picot] six times. Join rnd with sl st.

Ch 2, [11 tr in next ch-11 loop, ch 6, 11 tr in same ch-11 loop, ch 6] six times. Join rnd with sl st.

Fasten off for first flower.

For next flower, repeat from start. At each joining point (refer to chart on the right) ch 2, sl st in ch-6 loop, ch 2.

Continue connecting flowers together.

Weave in all ends.

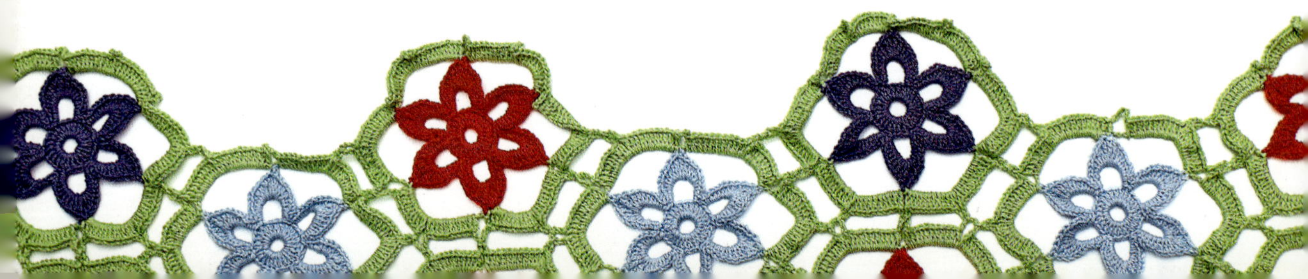

Materials:

Aran weight yarn in 5 colours:

- Colour A: 183 m (200 yds)
- Colour B: 183 m (200 yds)
- Colour C: 183 m (200 yds)
- Colour D: 183 m (200 yds)
- Colour E: 549 m (600 yds)

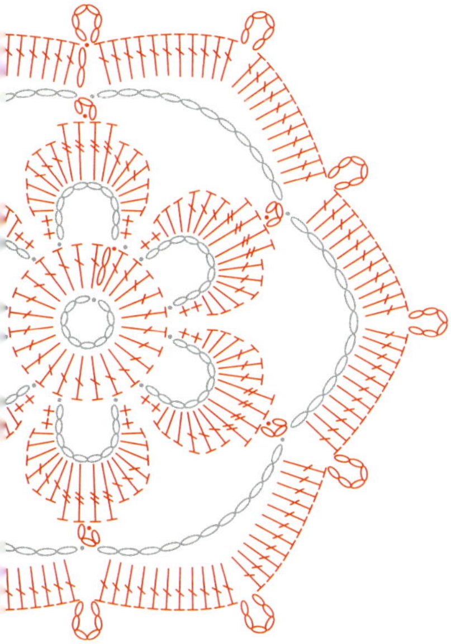

Chart key:

- Ch Chain
- Sl Slip stitch
- Dc Double crochet
- Htr Half treble crochet
- Tr Treble crochet
- Dtr Double treble crochet
- 3 ch picot (ch 3, sl st in 3rd ch from hook)

Tools:

Hook size: 3.25 mm (D-3)
Yarn needle
Scissors

Size:

17× 13 cm (6¾ × 5¼ in): each flower

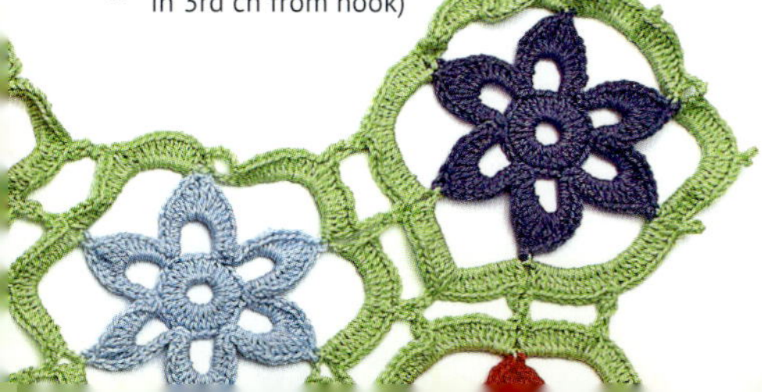

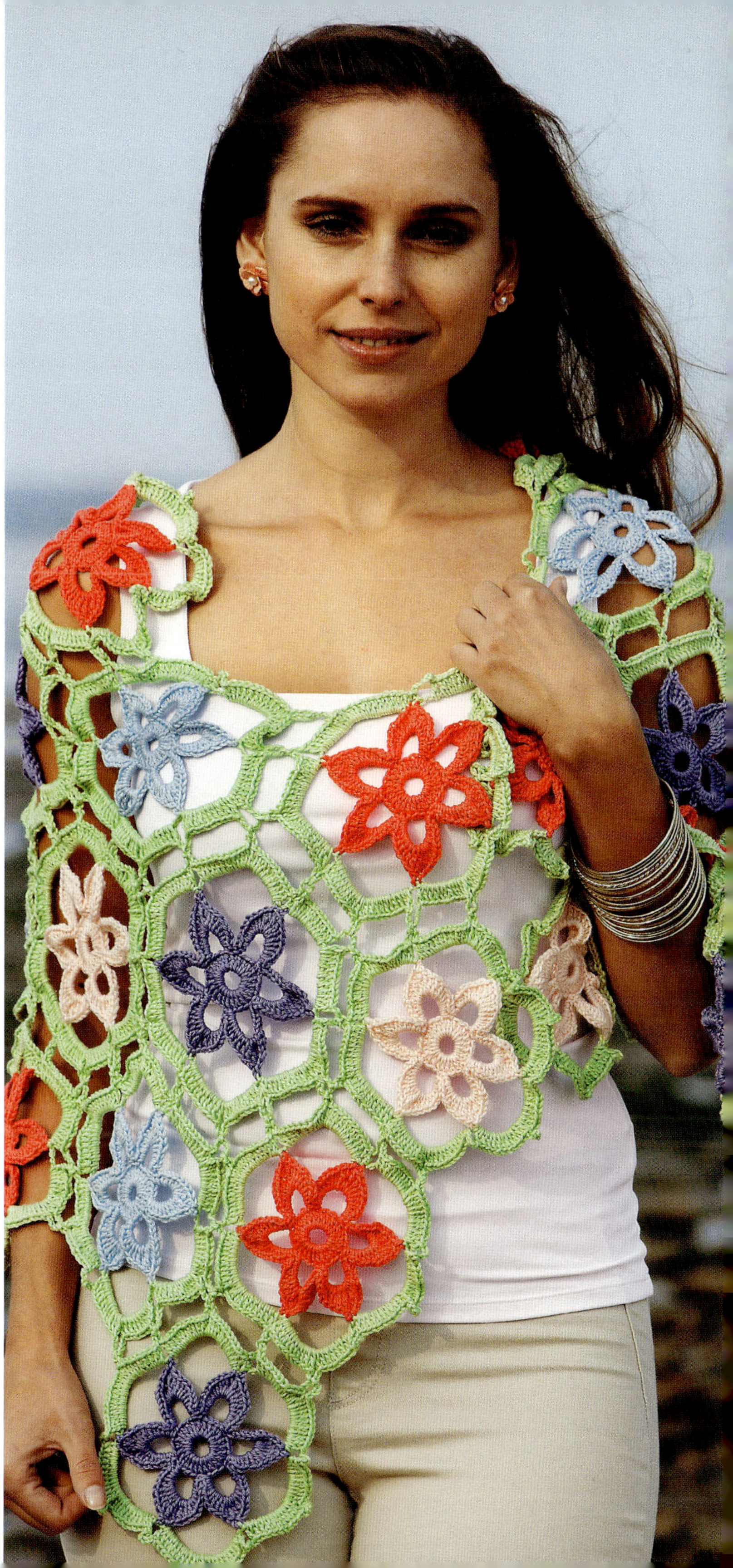

Symbols and Abbreviations

These are the abbreviations and symbols used in this book. There is no worldwide standard so, in other publications, you may find different abbreviations and symbols.

Stitch	Abbreviation	Symbol
Magic ring		
Chain	ch	
Slip stitch	sl st	•
Double crochet	dc	+
Half treble crochet	htr	
Treble crochet	tr	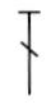
Double treble crochet	dtr	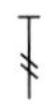
Triple treble crochet	trtr	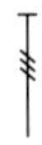
2 ch picot		
3 ch picot		
4 ch picot		
Single crochet 2 sts together	sc2tog	
Stitch worked into front loop only		
Stitch worked into back loop only		
Direction of working		
Start here		
Connecting points		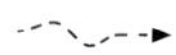

English/American Terms

English crochet terms are used throughout the book. Some American terms differ from the English system, as shown below. Patterns you encounter that are published using American terms can be very confusing unless you understand the difference.

Symbol	English	American	English abbreviation
+	Double crochet	Single crochet	sc
	Half treble crochet	Half double crochet	hdc
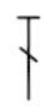	Treble crochet	Double crochet	dc
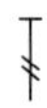	Double treble crochet	Treble crochet	tr

Remember that a chart represents how a stitch pattern is construted, and may not bear much resemblance to the actual appearance of the finished piece. Always read the written instructions together with the chart.

Index

Resources

The Craft Yarn Council: www.craftyarncouncil.com
The Crochet Guild of America: www.crochet.org

SELECTED SUPPLIERS
www.byclaire.eu/en/
www.coatscrafts.co.uk
www.colourway.co.uk
www.designeryarns.uk.com
www.dmccreative.co.uk
www.hantex.co.uk
www.hook-n-needle.com
www.kangaroo.uk.com
www.knitrowan.com
www.knittingfever.com
www.knitpicks.com
www.knitwellwools.co.uk
www.lionbrand.com
www.loveknitting.com
www.maggiescrochet.com
www.mcadirect.com
www.scaapi.nl
www.patternworks.com
www.patonsyarns.com
www.personalthreads.com
www.sirdar.co.uk
www.theknittinggarden.com
www.upcountry.co.uk
www.vinniscolours.co.za
www.yarn.com
www.yarnexpressions.com
www.yarnplaza.com

Author Acknowledgements
I would like to thank Michaela Gawlyta, Sasha Fernandes and Sandeep Aujla for constantly encouraging me and being so supportive at different stages of my work.